PENS OF MANY COLOURS

A CANADIAN READER

PENS OF MANY COLOURS

A CANADIAN READER

Eva C. Karpinski
Seneca College

Ian Lea
Seneca College

HBJ

Harcourt Brace Jovanovich Canada Inc.

Toronto Montreal Orlando Fort Worth San Diego
Philadelphia London Sydney Tokyo

Requests for permission to make copies of any part of the work should be
mailed to: Permissions, College Division, Harcourt Brace Jovanovich, Canada
Inc., 55 Horner Avenue, Toronto, Ontario, M8Z 4X6.

Every reasonable effort has been made to acquire permission for copyright
material used in this text, and to acknowledge all such indebtedness accurately.
Any errors and omissions called to the publisher's attention will be corrected
in future printings.

Canadian Cataloguing in Publication Data
   Karpinski, Eva C.
      Pens of many colours : a Canadian reader

   Includes bibliographical references and index.
   ISBN 0–7747–3146–X

   1. Multiculturalism - Canada.*   2. Readers -
   Multiculturalism - Canada.*   3. College readers.
   4. Readers (Secondary).   I. Lea, Ian.   II. Title.

   FC104.P4 1993   306.4'46'0971   C92–095149–X
   F1035.A1P4 1993

Publisher: Heather McWhinney
Editor and Marketing Manager: Michael Young
Developmental Editor: Nancy S. Ennis
Editorial Assistant: Lisa Stamp
Editorial Manager: Marcel Chiera
Production Editor: Theresa Fitzgerald
Production Manager: Sue-Ann Becker
Manufacturing Co-ordinator: Denise Wake
Copy Editor: Cy Strom
Cover and Interior Design: The Brookview Group Inc.
Typesetting: Debbie Fleming
Assembly: Louisa Schulz
Printing and Binding: Best Gagné Book Manufacturers

Cover Art: Bob Boyer, *I'm a Happy Hippy Hopi from Oraibi*. Collection:
Galerie Dresdnere, Toronto. Photography: Helena Wilson, Toronto.
Reproduced by permission of the artist.

PREFACE

In putting together this collection, we recognized a growing need among the reading audience to explore the areas outside of what used to be called the literary mainstream. The 1980s and 1990s have seriously put into question the centrality of culture that has been mostly white, European based and male dominated. The so-far marginalized or silenced groups of women, minority, Native, or ethnic writers have become visible and active participants in a dialogue for a pluralistic society. Of primary importance in the process of revising cultural assumptions and traditional literary canons is the increasingly multi-ethnic and multicultural make-up of Canadian society. To reflect this changing reality, which is also the reality of our classrooms, we have to be prepared to respect our differences as well as to be able to learn from them. It is hard to imagine a better first step than exposure to a mosaic of texts that privilege no one particular voice over any other!

Thus the major goal of our multicultural reader is to give a realistic account of the presence of women and men of Native and immigrant stock in our society and to celebrate their contributions to Canadian life and letters. They speak for themselves, in their own voices, which for most of them means speaking and writing in English. We have sought, within the widest compass, representative voices of Canadians, new and old, hyphenated or assimilated, that articulate hopes, resentments, fears, and joys of being here. We have tried to show those men and women in a variety of roles and situations, including non-conventional ones, so as to give the reader an insider's view of a distinctly individual lifestyle and history, which might help to awaken a greater empathy and understanding among people sharing the same social and geographical space.

While ploughing our way through piles of interesting material in print, we ourselves have been caught in a "double bind" between literary and sociological criteria for selecting the readings. On the one hand, our aim was to assemble the texts that would give fair representation to a wide range of speakers from culturally and ethnically diverse backgrounds; on the other hand, we have made every attempt to choose the pieces that embody as much as possible the power and flexibility of language. We can only hope that in its present shape this anthology will be able to accommodate differing expectations of the students of social sciences, literature, and composition, or simply any reader who wants to be reminded of the diversity that is Canada.

The book has been arranged as a flexible tool. Although its primary thrust is directed toward mulicultural themes and their literary expression, its secondary purpose is pedagogical: the selections have been chosen also for their merit as compositional models. Their content rests firmly on the structural foundations of rhetorical form. In fact, the extended apparatus of discussion questions/writing suggestions, attached to the readings, encourages the rhetorical analysis as a way of determining the authorial purpose in writing, the reader's profile, and the sonority and effectiveness of the message. As a result, this text can not only be used as a cross-cultural thematic reader, but it can also hold inherent interest for English composition courses.

For instructors who wish to employ these selections as models of rhetorical forms and devices, we have included an alternative Contents, identifying which of two or three modes each work fits into, predominantly. Of course, many of these pieces could provide good illustrations of almost all of the modes. Some fiction, primarily narrative, has been omitted from this list.

The organization of this anthology corresponds with the goals outlined above. For practical purposes, we have divided the experience of multiculturalism in Canada contained in this volume into somewhat discrete units, though no individual selection can be isolated entirely from the themes of other units. Nonetheless, each unit has its own guiding structure, which is meant to order the rich tapestry of multicultural life into intelligible patterns. Each unit, moreover, contains a variety of genres—oral history, journalism, personal essay, letter, fiction—to identify how the cultural energy finds its outlet in different forms of expression. In addition, each unit begins with a poem that is relevant to its concerns and highlights its theme.

Furthermore, each unit begins with a brief Introduction to give context and whet the appetite of the reader. Each selection has a brief biography of the author at its beginning and Topics for Exploration at its end, designed to open the structure and content to further thought and scrutiny by the reader. After each unit, Suggestions for Further Study have been included to encourage comparative and divergent thinking, and perhaps further research into the subject. Finally, a Selected Bibliography of over twenty titles published in recent years has been included at the end of the book to facilitate reading and research in depth. It includes Canadian anthologies of short stories, essays, autobiography, and other writing related to multicultural, multi-ethnic, or immigrant experience, excluding, however, poetry anthologies and individual authors' collections (which have usually been acknowledged in the short biography preceding each reading).

Many hands and minds have applied themselves to this endeavour, and we as editors share our gratitude with pleasure. Thanks are due to John Robert Colombo and Ruth Colombo for their indefatigable mining talents, to Nancy Ennis for her patience and tenacity, to Heather McWhinney for her inception and encouragement of the project, to Anita Agar for her stimulating review, and to our families for their tolerance during the rough parts of the voyage.

Eva C. Karpinski, Seneca College, Toronto
Ian Lea, Seneca College, Toronto

PUBLISHER'S NOTE TO INSTRUCTORS AND STUDENTS

This textbook is a key component of your course. If you are the instuctor of this course, you undoubtedly considered a number of texts carefully before choosing this as the one that will work best for your students and you. The authors and publishers of this book spent considerable time and money to ensure its high quality, and we appreciate your recognition of this effort and accomplishment.

If you are a student, we are confident that this text will help you to meet the objectives of your course. You will also find it helpful after the course is finished, as a valuable addition to your personal library. So hold on to it.

As well, please do not forget that photocopying copyright work means the authors lose royalties that are rightfully theirs. This loss will discourage them from writing another edition of this text or other books, because doing so will simply not be worth their time and effort. If this happens, we all lose—students, instructors, authors, and publishers.

We want to hear what you think about this book, so please be sure to send us the stamped reply card that has been inserted at the end of the text. This will help us to continue publishing high-quality books for your courses.

CONTENTS

UNIT ONE
COMING HERE: ORIGINS

UNIT TWO
BEING HERE: UNCERTAINTY

UNIT THREE
SELF AND OTHER: LANGUAGE

UNIT FOUR
GROWING UP: EDUCATION

UNIT FIVE
DRIFTING APART: GENERATION GAP

UNIT SIX
MAPS OF MEMORY: PLACES REVISITED

UNIT SEVEN
DOUBLE BIND: CANADIAN IDENTITY

RHETORICAL CONTENTS

PROCESS ANALYSIS

DIVISION AND CLASSIFICATION

CAUSE AND EFFECT

DEFINITION

COMING HERE: ORIGINS

INTRODUCTION

"Voyages to the new world" have been the stuff of adventure since the beginning of time—even when that beginning has been forgotten. The motives have been as various as the voyagers: imperial ambition, enforced migration by slavery, transportation by charitable patrons, flight from misery and massacre, perhaps simple curiosity. In this unit we have selected from a multitude of origins, periods, and motives; no two of these voyages are alike in any of these respects.

Though their migration to this continent during the ice age has been forgotten, for the Cree Indians of Saskatchewan the most recent voyage of discovery has been through time, not space. Pat Deiter-McArthur (Day Woman) presents a brief history of five generations of her people since their first interaction with white explorers and settlers. Their culture shock is not the bewilderment of facing a new environment, but rather the impact of a colonizing force that comes upon their world from the outside. She chronicles the changes forced upon her culture by European invaders, changes whose effects her people are still experiencing.

Catharine Parr Traill—like her sister, Susanna Moodie, another pioneer of early immigrant literature—crossed the Atlantic to redeem lost status, ill-prepared though she was for the hardships ahead. Decades later, at the peak of the "child immigration movement" thoroughly documented in Kenneth Bagnell's essay, the British voyager was not only the literate gentleperson, but also the street child of the London slums who was rescued from destitution and premature death by the charitable enterprise of Victorian bourgeois philanthropists. These "Barnardo children" flourished in the rich potential of Canadian post-colonial growth. Now, a century later, the population of what was once the British Empire can still find life in one former colony more attractive than in another. Writing of the voluntary migrants who, like Traill, seek a better life in the "new world," Rohinton Mistry describes several motives that have brought these recent voyagers from the east to the west.

Not all immigration to Canada, however, has been voluntary. Carrie Best shows the role of slavery in early Nova Scotia society and the subsequent racism that Canadians usually prefer to condemn in our southern neighbours. Furthermore, there have always been many immigrants who arrive in Canada under duress, in flight. Their search for a future in Canada is less pressing than escape from their past elsewhere. War, hunger, and tyranny are the reasons they flee their homes in Europe and the so-called Third World. Miriam Rosenthal gives eloquent testimony to the motives of those who wanted to escape the genocidal chaos inflicted on Europe by Nazi Germany before and during World War II.

In the last 20 years, the plight of the refugees has become widespread. After 30 years of war, South Vietnam collapsed under invasion, and those who were imprisoned in their own country employed the most desperate means of escape by sea in dangerous vessels. Garry Son Hoan's is a single voice among thousands who survived. He gives a poignant account of his sea voyage from Vietnam, his time spent in refugee camps, and his delayed arrival in Canada with all its disorientations and frustrations.

The plight of refugees continues today (and will do so for some time, if history is any guide). Violence and misery in the world are never lacking. Helga Kutz-Harder has observed some trouble spots of the globe and assembled a brief anthology of the experiences of its women refugees. Each of them, in flight from a different catastrophe—civil war, starvation, foreign invasion—articulates the problems of culture shock in a new society to which she cannot assimilate very quickly. These women bring with them the burden of painful memories and straitened circumstances that life in Canada cannot alleviate. For them there is no voyage of return.

My Acadie
a poem in historical vignettes

My Acadie
a fragile vehicle for love
An Albatross of perfidious Sun-Kings
Belly stained by Abenakis
Brandy
Looking glasses for hides, feathers
And furs.

My Acadie
A mild messianic peasantry
Bras d'Or embracing
The Atlantis of our dreams
The rich silt of Minas Basin
At the porticos
Of the theatre of Neptune.

My Acadie
A shabby toy encased in seaweed
Gloomy majesty in deep mourning
North-South
Moving against the colonial dream
Between aimed guns in their emplacements.

My Acadie
Faithful tablecloth doubly secular
Scarcely cunning
Under the alien soup tureen
Nourished by repeated mirages
Of dense and credulous stillness
Like an age lulled to sleep.

My Acadie
Évangéline with velvet tread
With eyes repressing exile
Takes off her cowls of myth
And extends her arms to the newborn.

And cries out
—A strange likeness, lace torn—
Words tender
And awkward

— Ronald Després

Ronald Després, a French-Canadian poet, was born in 1935 in Lewisville, New Brunswick. He works as an interpreter in Ottawa. The poem reprinted here is a translation from the collection Paysages en contrebande *(1974).*

Pat Deiter-McArthur (Day Woman)

Pat Deiter-McArthur (Day Woman) is a Cree Indian deeply committed to Native history and rights. She has written two books: Dances of the Northern Plain *and* Games of the Plains Cree. *She works with the Federation of Saskatchewan Indian Nations to raise Native consciousness, improve employment conditions, and make the white-dominated Canadian establishment aware of the integrity of the native peoples. Herself a member of the "fifth generation," she examines in the following excerpt the five generations of Native people's history since the initial contact with Europeans.*

Saskatchewan's Indian People— Five Generations

I t has been about five generations since Saskatchewan Indian people have had significant contact with European settlers. The First Generation strongly influenced by Europeans were the treaty-signers. The key characteristic of this generation was their ability to have some input into their future. They retained their tribal cultures but realized that they had to negotiate with the Europeans for the betterment of future generations. They did not give up their language or religion or the political structures of nationhood. They were perceived by government as an "alien" nation to be dealt with by treaty.

The Second Generation (1867–1910) of Indian people were the objects of legal oppression by the government. This generation lived under the absolute rule of an Indian agent, a government employee. Through the Indian Act, this generation was denied their religion, political rights, and freedom to travel off their reserves. A pass and permit system was strictly adhered to on the prairies; every Indian person required a pass to leave the reserve and a permit to sell any agricultural produce. All children were required to attend residential schools run by the churches. The goals of their schools were, first, to make Christians out of their students and to rid them of their pagan lifestyles and, second, to provide a vocational education.

Tuberculosis was a major killer of Indian people during this time and contributed to decimating their population in Saskatchewan to a low of five thousand in 1910. This generation was treated as wards and aliens of Canada.

The laws which served to oppress the second generation were in place until the early 1950s. The Third Generation (1910–1945) was greatly affected by these laws and schooling. This generation can be described as the lost generation. These people were psychologically oppressed. They rejected their Indianness but found that because of the laws for treaty Indians they could not enjoy the privileges accorded to whites. This third generation was our grandfather's generation. Many Indians at this time could speak their language but would not because of shame of their Indianness. They were still required by law to send their children to residential schools, to send their sick to Indian hospitals, and to abide by the Indian agent. They rarely had a sense of control over their own lives. This generation was considered wards of the government and denied citizenship.

Our father's time, the Fourth Generation since treaty-signing, can best be described as the generation of an Indian rebirth. This generation (1945–1980) is characterized by a movement of growing awareness—awareness that being Indian was okay and that Indian people from all tribes are united through their aboriginality, historical development, and special status.

This generation saw the rise of Indian and Native organizations across Canada, the return of traditional ceremonies, and an acknowledgement of the need to retain traditional languages and cultural ways.

Indian people of this generation were given the right to vote in 1960. The pass and permit system was abandoned in the late 1930s. In 1956, Indian children could attend either residential schools or the local public schools. However, the effects of this generation being raised within an institution and their parents being raised in the same way had a severe impact on these individuals. The residential school not only taught them to suppress their language but also to suppress their feelings and sense of individualism. The continued attack on Indian languages by residential schools left this generation with an ability to only understand their language, but many were not sufficiently fluent to call their Native language their first language.

During the sixties, there was a rise in Indian urbanization, a trend that continues today. This generation also contributed to an

Indian baby boom that is estimated be eight to ten years behind the non-Indian baby boomers. The federal and provincial vote allowed Indian people to legally consume alcohol. Alcoholism, suicides, and violent deaths were on the rise for this generation.

This was a period of experimentation by both the Indian communities and the government. Unfortunately, neither side was ready for each other. The intended government goal of assimilation was besieged with problems of racism, poverty, maladjustment, and cultural shock.

Today's Indian people are part of the Fifth Generation. The fifth generation is faced with choices: assimilation, integration, or separation. Indian people are now able to intermarry or assimilate with non-Indian without the loss of their Indian status. Indian leaders across Canada are seeking a separate and constitutionally recognized Indian government. Indian government is to provide its own services within Indian reserves. Integration allows Indian people to retain a sense of their cultural background while working and living within the larger society.

The fifth generation people are the first children since treaty-signing to be raised by their parents. Many of this generation are not able to understand a native language. Their first and only language is English. This generation is generally comfortable about their Indianness without strong prejudicial feelings to others. However, this generation is challenged to retain the meaning of Indian identity for their children.

TOPICS FOR EXPLORATION

1. What is the purpose that prompted Pat Deiter-McArthur to write this essay? Who will make up her readership? What does she hope her readers will learn? What role is she playing for her audience? Although she presents the facts objectively, is she also trying to persuade?

2. In what order has the author chosen to present her materials? How has she chosen to divide her analysis? How effective is that pattern?

3. In her essay, she analyzes the impact of interactions with white culture on Native people whose first encounter with white settlers is seen as the historical threshold. What are the five steps

she identifies in this process analysis? What are the characteristics of each step? How does one step compare with another?

4. What challenges to Native people's identity are chronicled in Pat Deiter-McArthur's essay? What were some of the negative effects of European influence upon the Native population in each period she discusses? Were there any positive effects?

5. What were some methods that white governments in Canada used in order to repress Native culture? Find examples of assimilation, integration, and separation as patterns of the Native-white interactions described in the text.

6. What effect does the author of this Native history hope to have on the future (or sixth) generation of her people in light of the recent struggle for native self-determination and aboriginal self-government?

Catharine Parr Traill (1802–1899)

Catharine Parr Traill emigrated from England in 1832 and settled in the Rice Lake–Peterborough area in Ontario. Traill's experiences in "the bush" were described in The Backwoods of Canada *(1836), based on letters she wrote to her relatives in England. Her sister, Susanna Moodie, gave her version of similar experiences in* Roughing It in the Bush *(1852). Traill and her family were bankrupt members of the English gentry who emigrated to Canada to repair their fortunes; they found, however, that their cultural background had not prepared them well for the rigours of "bush farming" in the new world. Both books were designed to inform and warn prospective English immigrants who might have been misguided by exaggerated claims of Canadian developers. In the excerpt Traill introduces her readers to some of the uncomfortable realities of pioneer life.*

from The Backwoods of Canada
LETTER IX

Lake House

April 18, 1833

But it is time that I should give you some account of our log-house, into which we moved a few days before Christmas. Many unlooked-for delays having hindered its completion before that time. I began to think it would never be habitable.

The first misfortune that happened was the loss of a fine yoke of oxen that were purchased to draw in the house-logs, that is, the logs for raising the walls of the house. Not regarding the bush as pleasant as their former master's cleared pastures, or perhaps foreseeing some hard work to come, early one morning they took into their heads to ford the lake at the head of the rapids, and march off, leaving no trace of their route excepting their footing at the water's edge. After many days spent in vain search for them, the work was at a stand, and for one month they were gone, and we began to give up all expectation of hearing any news of them. At last we learned they were some twenty miles off, in a distant township, having made their way through bush and swamp, creek and lake, back to their former owner, with an instinct that supplied to them the want of roads and compass.

Oxen have been known to traverse a tract of wild country to a distance of thirty or forty miles going in a direct line for their former haunts by unknown paths, where memory could not avail them. In the dog we consider it is scent as well as memory that guides him to his far-off home;—but how is this conduct of the oxen to be accounted for? They returned home through the mazes of interminable forests, where man, with all his reason and knowledge, would have been bewildered and lost.

It was the latter end of October before even the walls of our house were up. To effect this we called 'a bee'.[1] Sixteen of our neighbours cheerfully obeyed our summons; and though the day was far from favourable, so faithfully did our hive perform their tasks, that by night the outer walls were raised.

The work went merrily on with the help of plenty of Canadian nectar (whisky), the honey that our *bees* are solaced with. Some huge joints of salt pork, a peck of potatoes, with a rice-pudding, and a loaf as big as an enormous Cheshire cheese, formed the feast that was to regale them during the raising. This was spread out in the shanty,[2] in a *very rural style*. In short, we laughed, and called it a *picnic in the backwoods*; and rude as was the fare, I can assure you, great was the satisfaction expressed by all the guests of every degree, our 'bee' being considered as very well conducted. In spite of the difference of rank among those that assisted at the bee, the greatest possible harmony prevailed, and the party separated well pleased with the day's work and entertainment.

The following day I went to survey the newly-raised edifice, but was sorely puzzled, as it presented very little appearance of a house. It was merely an oblong square of logs raised one above the other, with open spaces between every row of logs. The spaces for the doors and windows were not then chopped out, and the rafters were not up. In short, it looked a very queer sort of a place, and I returned home a little disappointed, and wondering that my husband should be so well pleased with the progress that had been made. A day or two after this I again visited it. The *sleepers*[3] were laid to support the floors, and the places for the doors and windows cut out of the solid timbers, so that it had not quite so much the look of a bird-cage as before.

After the roof was shingled, we were again at a stand, as no boards could be procured nearer than Peterborough, a long day's journey through horrible roads. At that time no saw-mill was in progress; now there is a fine one building within a little distance of us. Our flooring-boards were all to be sawn by hand, and it was some time before any one could be found to perform this necessary work, and that at high wages—six-and-sixpence per day. Well, the boards were at length down, but of course of unseasoned timber; this was unavoidable; so as they could not be planed we were obliged to put up with their rough unsightly appearance, for no better were to be had. I began to recall to mind the observation of the old gentleman with whom we travelled from Cobourg to Rice Lake.[4] We console ourselves with the prospect that by next summer the boards will all be seasoned, and then the house is to be turned topsy-turvy, by having the floors all relaid, jointed, and smoothed.

The next misfortune that happened, was, that the mixture of clay and lime that was to plaster the inside and outside of the house between the chinks of the logs was one night frozen to stone. Just as the work was about half completed, the frost suddenly setting in, put a stop to our proceeding for some time, as the frozen plaster yielded neither to fire nor to hot water, the latter freezing before it had any effect on the mass, and rather making bad worse. Then the workman that was hewing the inside walls to make them smooth, wounded himself with the broad axe, and was unable to resume his work for some time.

I state these things merely to show the difficulties that attend us in the fulfillment of our plans, and this accounts in a great measure for the humble dwellings that settlers of the most respectable description are obliged to content themselves with at first coming to this country,—not, you may be assured, from inclination, but necessity: I could give you such narratives of this kind as would astonish you. After all, it serves to make us more satisfied than we should be on casting our eyes around to see few better off than we are, and many not half so comfortable, yet of equal, and, in some instances, superior pretensions as to station and fortune.

Every man in this country is his own glazier; this you will laugh at: but if he does not wish to see and feel the discomfort of broken panes, he must learn to put them in his windows with his own hands. Workmen are not easily to be had in the backwoods when you want them, and it would be preposterous to hire a man at high wages to make two days' journey to and from the nearest town to mend your windows. Boxes of glass of several different sizes are to be bought at a very cheap rate in the stores. My husband amused himself by glazing the windows of the house preparatory to their being fixed in.[5]

To understand the use of carpenter's tools, I assure you, is no despicable or useless kind of knowledge here. I would strongly recommend all young men coming to Canada to acquire a little acquaintance with this valuable art, as they will often be put to great inconvenience for the want of it.

I was once much amused with hearing the remarks made by a very fine lady, the reluctant sharer of her husband's emigration, on seeing the son of a naval officer of some rank in the service busily employed in making an axe-handle out of a piece of rock-elm.

'I wonder that you allow George to degrade himself so,' she said, addressing his father.

The captain looked up with surprise. 'Degrade himself! In what manner, madam? My boy neither swears, drinks whiskey, steals, nor tells lies.'

'But you allow him to perform tasks of the most menial kind. What is he now better than a hedge carpenter[6] and I suppose you allow him to chop, too?'

'Most assuredly I do. That pile of logs in the cart there was all cut by him after he had left study yesterday,' was the reply.

'I should see my boys dead before they should use an axe like common labourers.'

'Idleness is the root of all evil,' said the captain. 'How much worse might my son be employed if he were running wild about the streets with bad companions.'

'You will allow this not a country for gentlemen or ladies to live in,' said the lady.

'It is the country for gentlemen that will not work and cannot live without, to starve in,' replied the captain bluntly; 'and for that reason I make my boys early accustom themselves to be usefully and actively employed.'

'My boys shall never work like common mechanics,'[7] said the lady, indignantly.

'Then, madam, they will be good for nothing as settlers; and it is a pity you dragged them across the Atlantic.'

'We were forced to come. We could not live as we had been used to do at home, or I never would have come to this horrid country.'

'Having come hither you would be wise to conform to circumstances. Canada is not the place for idle folks to retrench a lost fortune in. In some parts of the country you will find most articles of provision as dear as in London, clothing much dearer, and not so good, and a bad market to choose in.'

'I should like to know, then, who Canada is good for?' said she, angrily.

'It is a good country for the honest, industrious artisan. It is a fine country for the poor labourer, who, after a few years of hard toil, can sit down in his own log-house, and look abroad on his own land, and see his children well settled in life as independent free-holders.[8] It is a grand country for the rich speculator, who can afford to lay out a large sum in purchasing land in eligible situations; for if he have any judgment, he will make a hundred per cent as interest for his money after waiting a few years. But it is a hard country for the poor gentleman, whose habits have rendered him unfit for man-ual labour. He brings with him a mind unfitted to his situation; and even if necessity compels him to exertion, his labour is of little value. He has a hard struggle to live. The certain expenses of wages and living are great, and he is obliged to endure many privations if he would keep within compass, and be free of debt. If he have a large family, and brings them up wisely, so as to adapt themselves early to a settler's life, why he does well for them, and soon feels the benefit on his own land; but if he is idle himself, his wife extrava-gant and discontented, and the children taught to despise labour, why madam, they will soon be brought down to ruin. In short, the country is a good country for those to whom it is adapted; but if people will not conform to the doctrine of necessity and expediency, they have no business in it. It is plain Canada is not adapted to every class of people.'

'It was never adapted for me or my family,' said the lady, dis-dainfully.

'Very true,' was the laconic reply; and so ended the dialogue.

But while I have been recounting these remarks, I have wan-dered far from my original subject, and left my poor log-house quite in an unfinished state. At last I was told it was in a habitable condi-tion, and I was soon engaged in all the bustle and fatigue attendant on removing our household goods. We received all the assistance we required from ____, who is ever ready and willing to help us. He laughed and called it a '*moving* bee'; I said it was a 'fixing bee'; and my husband said it was a 'settling bee'; I know we were unsettled enough till it was over. What a din of desolation is a small house, or any house under such circumstances. The idea of chaos must have been taken from a removal or a setting to rights, for I suppose the ancients had their *flitting*,[9] as the Scotch call it, as well as the mod-erns.

Various were the valuable articles of crockery-ware that perished in their short but rough journey through the woods. Peace to their manes.[10] I had a good helper in my Irish maid, who soon roused up famous fires, and set the house in order.

We have now got quite comfortably settled, and I shall give you a description of our little dwelling. What is finished is only a part of the original plan; the rest must be added next spring, or fall, as cir-cumstances may suit.

A nice small sitting-room with a store closet, a kitchen, pantry, and bed-chamber form the ground floor; there is a good upper floor that will make three sleeping-rooms.

'What a nut-shell!' I think I hear you exclaim. So it is at present; but we purpose adding a handsome frame front as soon as we can get boards from the mill, which will give us another parlour, long hall, and good spare bed-room. The windows and glass door of our present sitting-room command pleasant lake-views to the west and south. When the house is completed, we shall have a verandah in front; and at the south side, which forms an agreeable addition in the summer, being used as a sort of outer room, in which we can dine, and have the advantage of cool air, protected from the glare of the sunbeams. The Canadians call these verandahs 'stoups'. Few houses, either log or frame, are without them. The pillars look extremely pretty, wreathed with the luxuriant hop-vine, mixed with the scarlet creeper and 'morning glory', the American name for the most splendid of major convolvuluses. These stoups are really a considerable ornament, as they conceal in a great measure the rough logs, and break the barnlike form of the building.

Our parlour is warmed by a handsome Franklin stove with brass galley, and fender. Our furniture consists of a brass-railed sofa, which serves upon occasion for a bed, Canadian painted chairs, a stained pine table, green and white curtains, and a handsome Indian mat that covers the floor. One side of the room is filled up with our books. Some large maps and a few good prints nearly conceal the rough walls, and form the decoration of our little dwelling. Our bed-chamber is furnished with equal simplicity. We do not, however, lack comfort in our humble home; and though it is not exactly such as we could wish, it is as good as, under existing circumstances, we could have.

NOTES

1. Any gathering for communal work.

2. Used here in its French-Canadian sense: "workshop."

3. Supporting beams.

4. "If you go into the backwoods your house must necessarily be a log-house," said an elderly gentleman, who had been a settler many years in the country, "for you will most probably be out of the way of a saw-mill, and you will find so much to do, and so many obstacles to

encounter, for the first two or three years, that you will hardly have the opportunity for carrying these improvements into effect.

"'There is an old saying,' he added... " 'first creep and then go.' Matters are not carried on quite so easily here as at home... At the end of ten or fifteen years you may begin to talk of these pretty improvements and elegancies and you will then be able to see a little what you are about." (Letter V).

5. That is, he placed the glass in the window-frames before putting the frames in place.

6. Fence repairer.

7. Manual labourers.

8. Those that own land without restrictions on its sale or use.

9. Moving from place to place.

10. Spirits (Latin: the deified souls of departed ancestors).

TOPICS FOR EXPLORATION

1. What is Traill's purpose in writing *The Backwoods of Canada*? Who is her audience? What effect is she hoping to have on her readers? What will her readers gain from her account?

2. What are some of the difficulties that Traill and her family encounter, according to this excerpt? How are these difficulties overcome? Find examples of loyalty and community spirit among the early settlers, as shown in her account.

3. What were some of the steps necessary to build a habitable dwelling in Traill's time? What skills must the immigrant have? How do building methods compare with those of today?

4. In the conversation between "the very fine lady" and "the naval officer" the issue of "rank" arises. What do they mean by rank? How do their attitudes toward work differ?

5. For what reasons, according to Traill, do so many immigrants come to Canada? According to the "naval officer" (and Traill),

which immigrants will do well in Canada? Who will do poorly? Why?

6. In the opening paragraphs of her letter, Traill dwells for a while on the image of oxen that become a fit symbol of survival through hard work and perseverance. Are there any correspondences between this image and her description of the ideal immigrants? How is she herself equipped with the qualities she lauds in the settlers?

Carrie M. Best

*Carrie M. Best was born in 1903 in New Glasgow, Nova Scotia; she is a
black civil rights activist and writer. In the 1940s, she launched and edited
The Clarion and The Negro Citizen, the newspapers that became the
medium for black people first in Nova Scotia, then nationwide. In 1976,
she was honoured with the Order of Canada; she also received an honorary
doctorate from St. Francis Xavier University. The following reading comes
from her book That Lonesome Road, published in 1977. It offers a
remarkable mixture of autobiography and history, a patchwork of impressions from archival records, personal experience, and black myth. These
excerpts are structured around the theme of black consciousness in Nova
Scotia and elsewhere.*

That Lonesome Road
FOREWORD

T he problems resulting from racial inequality and its limitations
have weighed heavily upon me from my earliest recollections and
increased with the years and the knowledge of the early history of
black Nova Scotians.

This knowledge has forced a schizocarpous[1] approach to a work
intended at the beginning to be historical, later biographical and still
later philosophical. Whether the story of my journey down a lonesome road into identity will be judged by either or all of these, I can
say with all seriousness, without regret, and sometimes with prideful
humility, that—by the Grace of God and Slavery I am what I am.

The internecine struggles of the 16th century and the persecu-
tions which followed, led many Europeans of various ethnic backgrounds to seek shelter outside of their own countries. The promise
of freedom brought explorers, adventurers, religious dissenters,
political refugee and criminals.

With the promise came also the need for labor to open up the
wilderness and to harvest its great wealth. By free will and by forced
migration, the New World was colonized.

To cultivate their tropical and equatorial colonies, the European settlers transported Black people from Africa and the West Indies as slaves; a forced migration to which I must look back for a starting point along an uncharted path in a search for an identity. With roots reaching deeply into antiquity, a point of beginning was at first difficult to determine and the research necessary to find one has taken a period of more than ten years.

In the month of September in the year 1787, a warrant of survey ordered by Governor Parr, granted 3000 acres of land in Tracadie, Nova Scotia, to Thomas Brownspriggs (Chief of the Blacks) and 73 other Negro men and their families. Whether they were among the Blacks who came from Montebeliard as religious dissenters in 1752 or from other areas is not known. Whether their arrival was intracontinental or transoceanic is irrelevant. It is recorded here because among the little company of Blacks who settled in Tracadie in Guysboro County were my great grandparents on both sides of my family.

The dial of the 20th Century clock had pointed towards its 3rd anniversary before I was born in New Glasgow, Nova Scotia, on March 4, 1903. Having had no control over either my date of arrival or my ethnic background, I cannot be held accountable for having arrived during a period in history when the New World was being colonized and continental migrations were at their height.

That Lonesome Road is not intended to be either an historical reference or an analytical evaluation of the period. It is a personal biography; a compilation of facts and encounters published and unpublished, and soliloquies gathered from among the sunshine and shadow of a life of involvement covering a period of almost three-quarters of a century. . . .

Emerson said "There is properly no history—only biography." That statement, if correct, may justify a permanent record of a journey down a lonesome road in search of an identity, where, like a fool, I sometimes rushed in where angels feared to tread. . . .

The system of slavery as an institution was established by France in Quebec in 1689 and by 1759, had, by the tacit permission of church and state, extended into New Brunswick and Nova Scotia.

The immense inrush of Loyalists from 1783–85 secured for the diabolical system of slavery a permanent place in British American life.

Among the great numbers of Negroes arriving in the remaining British provinces were freed men who had escaped from slavery. Protection to all such slaves was offered to all who had rendered military service and nearly every loyalist Corps, it is said, had representatives of the African race.

In 1790, the British government, with a view to facilitate the removal of certain Loyalists yet remaining in the United States, and to remove to their remaining American territory a number of other Loyalists lingering in dependence and abject poverty in Britain, passed an act "for encouraging new settlers in his Majesty's Colonies and Plantations in America." According to this Act, which was published in the several colonies, any person after August 1, 1790, a subject of the United States, removing thence to any of the Bahama or Bermuda Islands, or to any part of the Province of Nova Scotia, having first obtained a permit to reside there from the governor of the colony, was at liberty to bring with him any Negroes, household furniture, clothing, etc., the furniture, utensils and clothing not to exceed the value of fifty pounds for each White person and that of forty pounds for each Negro, the sale of any Negro or other property being strictly forbidden within twelve months.

The official lists showing the number of slaves owned by the Loyalists as recorded in the infallible records of the *Nova Scotia Historical Society—The Slave in Canada, Vol. X for the years 1896–98*, are too numerous to be recorded here.

December 11, 1783

Alexander Campbell, late a captain in the South Carolina, for and in consideration of the sum of forty pounds currency conveyed to Thomas Green Esq. late a captain in the Royal Nova Scotia of Foot, a certain Negro wench named Nancy.

Digby, 1798

In 1798, Jeremiah Northrup offered a reward through the Royal Gazette to any person who would bring to Mr. David Rudolph at Halifax, or to himself at Falmouth, "a Negro boy named James Grant, a smart likely lad"; through the same medium, Rueben Tucker of Digby sought the apprehension of a colored man named Francis Webb; and by a certificate acknowledged before a justice of the peace, James Cox of Shelburne in 1800 hired "my slave, George Cox" to Captain Samuel Mann of the brig "Greyhound" for a coasting voyage to Newfoundland and back.

Yarmouth, 1801

Several slave sales took place in Nova Scotia during the first decade of the nineteenth century.

One bill of sale is quoted by the Rev. J. Roy Campbell according to which in December, 1801, a slave owner sold for thirty-nine pounds a "certain Negro boy named Jack" born in his own house of parents "both my property." James Lent, a magistrate of the district and known as "Judge" Lent, is owner of slaves William and Dinah Berry, a daughter of whom died in Tusket at the age of one hundred and six years.

Similarly, in October, 1804, Peter Bonnett, high sheriff of the County of Annapolis, transfers from Isaac Bonnett and other administrators of the estate of Robert Dickson of Annapolis to William Robinson, his heirs, etc., in consideration of the sum of seventeen pounds, a certain Negro girl slave named Priscilla, about eight years and four months of age, being part of the "personal estate of the late Robert Dickson" and after the usual form, guarantees to the purchaser his right to the possession and services of the slave.

A recorded document, dated Truro, 1779, proves complicity with slavery on the part of the early Scottish-Irish settlers in Nova Scotia the larger number of whom had come from Pennsylvania and other middle American Provinces.

Truro, 1787
The revelation that Rev. Daniel Cock, a highly esteemed minister of the Presbyterian Church in Truro, was the owner of two female slaves excited public feelings and controversy in 1788. One of the slave women called Deal McGregor continued under Mr. Cock's roof until his death in 1805.

Cumberland County, 1792

Black Jack, slave of William Bulmer, is given his freedom on the death of his owner. In 1774, Thomas Watson, sheriff of

Cumberland Co., bequeathed to a daughter money, silver, chinaware, and a Negro girl called Sarah.

Halifax, 1760, 1762, 1775

As early as in 1760, an entry appears in the early records of the Protestant Dissenting Church, now St. Mathew's Presbyterian of Halifax, of Samuel Susannah and Elizabeth, children of William and Charity Willet, John, a "Negro servant", baptized by the Rev. John Secombe.

Seven years earlier in 1762, an entry was made in the register of St. Paul's parish of two Negro girls, Lucia and Francis, and in 1775, another of a Negro of Mr. McNamara. . . .

Halifax, February 10, 1784

A wholesale baptism of slaves with one name only took place in St. Paul's Church in Halifax on February 10, 1784. To the record, by the minister, the Rev. Dr. Breyton, is appended "Negroes christened belonging to John Wentworth Esq. (later Sir John Wentworth, Lieutenant Governor of Nova Scotia). Two weeks later, after becoming members of "the family of God", the Wentworth slaves were shipped to Dutch Guyana to serve on the estate of the Governor's "affectionate kinsmen", Paul Wentworth. The bill of lading lists 19 slaves described by Governor Wentworth as valuable, exceedingly useful, American born, perfectly stout, healthy, sober, orderly, industrious and obedient. . . .

Pictou, 1787

In 1787, Dr. James McGregor, renowned Pictou County abolitionist, purchased with his meagre funds the slaves of Matthew Harris of Pictou, a Mulatto man named Martin and a colored girl.

Dr. McGregor also secured the freedom of Harris' slaves, Diana Rhyno and her husband, George Mingo, who had served in the American War of Independence. Instances of the treatment of slaves after the southern fashion is recorded. Mr. T. W. Casey of Napanee, Ontario who writes—

"In his History of Pictou, Rev. Dr. Patterson writes of a Negro slave in Truro who was so treated by his master that several times he ran away, usually making for Pictou. On one occasion, his master, having caught him, cut a hole through the lower lobe of his ear, through which he passed the end of a whip-lash and knotting it, he mounted his horse and rode off dragging after him in that way the poor man, who shortly after died; it was believed in large measure from the treatment he received."

"Among the dwellings destroyed at Windsor, N.S., on a fateful Sunday in October, 1897, was one at which I had often looked askance at childhood, because of the story that a slave boy, killed by a blow from a hammer in the hand of his master, had been known to put in an occasional appearance there."

Mrs. J. W. Owen of Annapolis, has referred in the *Halifax Herald*[2] to the tradition that Mrs. Barclay, wife of Colonel Barclay of Annapolis, was responsible for the death of a slave through a severe whipping she had ordered him.

In speaking of slavery in the provinces, the few who have recognized its existence as an historical fact have assumed that during some one or other of the first years of the century, it became illegal through some special decision of the courts.

A final effort for relief by legislative action was made by Nova Scotia proprietors in 1808. During the sessions of that year, Mr. Warrick, member for the township of Digby, presented a petition from John Taylor and a number of proprietors of Negro servants (who were leaving their masters daily and setting them at defiance).

In consequence of these facts, they prayed for the passage of an Act for securing them their property or indemnifying for its loss.

It was no doubt with a view to such an end that Thomas Ritchie, member for Annapolis, during the same session introduced a bill to regulate Negro servants within the province.

This bill, which passed its second reading on January 11, 1808, but never became law, was in all probability the last struggle of a system which merited only death. . . .

Historians can no longer ignore the fact that slavery as an institution flourished in Nova Scotia and that the entire province was at one time a slave plantation; the severity of the climate alone preventing it from reaching the proportions of the southern United States.

Hidden in fear and shame, ignored by historians, excluded from the curriculum of the public school system, the story of slavery is nevertheless an historical fact. It is contained in the unpublished volumes of *The History That Never Was*: written by unknown authors unable to read that which they had written with their blood. The information contained in these phantom volumes grows with each succeeding generation making possible the writing of *The History That Was, The History That Is* and *The History That Is To Be*.

An incident that occurred at the close of the First World War tells its own story. A race riot erupted in the town of New Glasgow as the result of an altercation between a black and white youth. Bands of roving white men armed with clubs had stationed themselves at different intersections allowing no Blacks to go beyond that point. We had learned of the riot from our father when he came home from work. My oldest brother was at work at the Norfolk House and my mother who had been driven home by the chauffeur of the family for whom she had been working knew nothing of the situation.

Finding my younger brother, my father and myself at home and my older brother missing, my mother inquired as to why he was not home. It was dusk.

In all the years she lived and until she passed away at the age of eighty-one, my mother was never known to utter an unkind blasphemous or obscene word, nor did I ever see her angry. This evening was no exception. She told us to get our meal, stating that she was going into town to get my brother. It was a fifteen minute walk.

At the corner of East River Road and marsh Street the crowd was waiting and as my mother drew near they hurled insults at her and threateningly ordered her to turn back. She continued to walk toward the hotel about a block away when one of the young men recognized her and asked her where she was going. "I am going to the Norfolk House for my son," she answered calmly. (My mother was six feet tall and as straight as a ramrod.) The young man ordered the crowd back and my mother continued on her way to the hotel. At that time there was a livery stable at the rear entrance to the hotel and it was there my mother found my frightened older brother and brought him safely home.

Poetry is what Milton[3] saw when he went blind.

True Poetry

Who does not love true poetry,
He lacks a bosom friend—
To walk with him and talk with him
And all his steps attend.
Who does not love true poetry,
Its rhythmic throb and swing,
The treat of it, the sweet of it,
Along the paths of spring.

Its joyous lilting melody
In every passing breeze;
The deep of it, the sweep of it,
Through hours of toil and ease.
Its grandeur and sublimity,
Its majesty and might,
The feel of it, the peal of it
Through all the lonely night.

Its tenderness and soothing touch
Like balm on evening air;
That feelingly and healingly cures
All the hurts of care.
Who does not love true poetry;
Of sea and sky and sod;
The light of it, the might of it,
He has not known his God.

SOJOURNER TRUTH

Who was Sojourner Truth? What was her background and what
qualifications that enabled her to travel thousands of miles in a hostile environment, fighting, preaching, and praying for the emancipa-
tion of her enslaved people? Her parents came from the coast of
Guinea, her paternal grandmother was a Mohawk Indian woman.

She travelled in all twenty-one states, having lectured in both free and slave states which included New York, Massachusetts, Ohio, Maryland, Virginia, and the District of Columbia. Hers is an incredible, almost unbelievable story of undiluted faith and the courage and heroism that followed.

It was the diabolical scheme of the dealers in human flesh to stultify the brain of the slave that it might become incapable of reason, reflection or memory. The slave child followed the condition of the mother, and seldom had any knowledge of father or date of birth. They had first names only, and having no second name, took the surname of the owner; consequently they received a new cognomen[4] with each new owner.

Sojourner Truth counted her years from the time she was emancipated for it was then she began to live. She once remarked that it is what we accomplish that makes life long or short, adding that some have been on earth scores of years yet die in infancy.

The State of New York emancipated all slaves up to the age of forty in 1817 and in 1825 all who had reached the age of twenty. In 1827 all slaves became free.

Sojourner Truth became free in 1817 and it is assumed she was then forty years old or older.[5]

Completely illiterate but determined to learn and deeply religious, she refused to allow an adult to read the Bible or interpret its meaning for her. Only slow-reading children were permitted to read to her.

The interpretation, she maintained, came from a direct God to an open mind, unfettered from the confusing and controversial dogma of the different religious bodies of that era, many who owned slaves and remained silent during the anti-slavery conflict. An exception were the Quakers.

Sojourner's slave master refused to release her, demanding that she serve another year.

Unlike most slaves who escaped under cover of darkness, this remarkable woman chose to leave at dawn. With her infant on one arm, and all her earthly possessions on the other, she walked into the sunrise to begin a new life of freedom and adventure. History records that she sat down, fed her infant, and turning her thoughts to God, her only help, she prayed to Him to direct her to some safe asylum. It is written that she claimed that she knew the house where she was to live when she saw it.

The Quakers did not believe in slavery. They neither bought nor sold human flesh. Many of these Christians whom Sojourner called "God's Nobility" sacrificed their lives in the cause of freedom for Black people and their heroism as "conductors" on the Underground Railroad is legendary.

As expected, her former owner followed, and when she stead-fastly refused to return, he threatened to take her child as ransom until the year's servitude was paid. The Quaker in whose home she was sheltered bought her freedom and that of her child by paying her year's "wages"—twenty dollars; and five dollars for the child. The condition of the sale was that she was never to refer to him as Master. "There is but one Master" he said "and He who is *your* Master is my Master." When she asked what she was to call him, he replied "call me Isaac Van Wagener and my wife Marie Van Wagener. From that day, and until she received the name she claimed was given her by God, she was known as Isabella Van Wagener.

The life of Sojourner Truth is a revelation to all who read it and it is impossible to read and not be deeply moved by it. To those who have for any reason been denied access to Black History, it will open an entirely new world of thought. It will, above all other things, reveal the depth of cruelty and degradation to which human beings can descend. It will also prove that human beings may ascend above it, when the mind is allowed to take precedence over the body. That a women born and raised in slavery, who suffered untold humilia-tion and indignities, could travel up and down the land petitioning governments, ministering to the sick, preaching, praying, and fight-ing for her enslaved people is almost unbelievable but it is true. She was, as most slaves and newly freedmen, nameless, homeless and unlearned. So forceful a character was she, that in spite of having mothered thirteen children, it was rumored by her enemies that she was in reality a man, a rumor that caused her to undergo the indig-nity of having to publicly expose a part of her body to disprove it. Even then she was able to overcome, for having proven her sex, she reminded the large gathering that, as a slave woman, she had suck-led many white babies who were free, while her own children had been sold into slavery and whose very whereabouts were unknown to her.

WANDERING MANIAC

She was called many names—troublemaker, wandering maniac, and others. But her fame grew, and her wanderings led her from the slave cabin to the halls of Congress and this, by way of some of the largest churches in the land. And she lived to see, as she said "The Stars and Stripes replace the Scars and Stripes"—the lash and bruises of her people. She was devoutly patriotic, with an abiding love for her country.

Asked if she always used the unusual name of Sojourner she replied "No, indeed! My name was Isabella, but when I left the house of bondage, I left everything behind. Afterwards, I told the Lord I wanted another name because everybody had two names, and the Lord gave me Truth, because I was to declare truth unto the people."

The journey of Sojourner Truth, Harriet Tubman,[6] Phillis Wheatley[7] and other visible minority women of History may appear to be unrelated to a history-making journey made over three thousand years ago by another visible minority woman—The Queen of Sheba. But because the blood lines are the same it is in reality a continuation of the same journey which ended (and at the same time began) in Jamestown Harbour when a Dutch man-o-war unloaded the first cargo of Black Gold—Spanish speaking slaves to be traded for food to feed her starving crew. It is not similar to the journey of 3000 years ago, but, nevertheless, interesting to compare.

THEN AND NOW

Over three thousand years ago, fragments of her history were recorded in the Bible, the Talmud,[8] the Koran[9] and the legends of Syria, Armenia, Israel and Ethiopia.

To the people of the Tigris she was Eteyte of Azeb; in the Gospel according to St. Matthew, she was Queen of the South; to the Arabs, Bilqis; to the people of Jerusalem, she was the Queen of Sheba. But to her own people, she is, after three thousand years, Maqueda—the Beautiful, Dawn-upon-the-Land, The Panther-in-the-Blossom, the Virgin-Queen of Axum and Saba, revered ancestress of the Imperial line of Ethiopia, who buried her love in her heart, so that the gates of her kingdom might be opened to the wisdom of the true God.

. . . BUT COMELY

The *Kebra Nagast,* the *Book of the Glory of Kings* describes her as she was when first she met King Solomon; "She was sixteen, her skin the hue of raspberries crushed in curdled cream, smooth as wet silk rained upon. Her eyes were the soft brown of the antelope, her blue-black hair spread in ringlets from the brow as mountain marble, and her cheeks had the twin fingerprints of fascination. A child of rapture."

Such was the description of others but in the Song of Solomon she describes herself: "I am Black but comely, O ye daughters of Jerusalem, as the curtains of Solomon. . . . I am the Rose of Sharon and the Lily of the Valley."[10]

THE JOURNEY

And so it was as Queen of the vast land of Axum and Saba, North West of Saudi Arabia, that, once a year, her caravans laden with gold dust, ivory, hides and spices went to Sasu, famous for its gold mines, and enriched Axum and Saba by trading oxflesh, salt, and iron for red gold. The great temple of Jerusalem was being built, trade routes the Middle East and Africa were building up with closer communication between each other. It was inevitable that King Solomon should learn of the Queen of Sheba and her vast riches and she of his great fame and wisdom. With seventy-three ships and many hundreds of camels, the youthful Queen and Tamarin, her minister of Transport, set out for Jerusalem to meet King Solomon. The result of the journey is Biblical History.

Many leading historians believed that many of the tablets of Moses are preserved in the ancient church of Axum, and the Imperial House of Ethiopia traces its line directly from the Queen of Sheba and King Solomon through their son Menelik directly to Emperor Haile Selassi, Conquering Lion of Judah and recently deposed Monarch of Ethiopia. Could it be the "thin red line" called blood lines gave Sojourner Truth the nobility of soul that even Slavery could not destroy?

NOTES

1. Adjective derived from botanical noun for dry fruit that splits into single-seeded parts when ripe. Best's book consists, then, of independent—but equally nourishing—parts.

2. The *Halifax Morning Herald* newspaper, founded on January 14, 1875, became the *Chronicle-Herald* (mornings) and the *Mail-Star* (evenings) on January 1, 1949.

3. John Milton (1608–1674), an English poet, composed his epic poem, *Paradise Lost* (1667), after losing his vision.

4. Nickname.

5. Truth was born in 1797 and died in 1883. She was freed at age 20.

6. Harriet Tubman (c.1821–1913), an escaped slave, returned nineteen times to the South to lead more than 300 slaves to freedom.

7. Phillis Wheatley (c.1753-1784), first important black American poet. Author of *Poems on Various Subjects, Religious and Moral* (1773).

8. Body of Jewish civil and ceremonial law and legend.

9. Sacred book of Islam, a collection of Muhammad's oral revelations, written in Arabic.

10. The speaker in Song 1:5 and 2:1 might be Sheba; however, since the Song of Solomon is a wedding song, the speaker might also be the pharaoh's daughter who married Solomon. (See I Kings 3:1.) The Bible relates that Sheba visited Solomon (I Kings 10:1–13), but it records no romance between them.

TOPICS FOR EXPLORATION

1. What role is Best employing in this excerpt? Why is she uniquely qualified to discuss her subject? How does personal history become social history in her essay? Consider such phrases as "prideful humility" or "by the Grace of God and Slavery" and what they reveal about the author's attitude to black people's history and her own parallel quest for identity.

2. Who is Best's audience? Her readers will be informed, but will they also be persuaded? Why? How will an essay about the past affect the future of her readers?

3. Best makes a distinction between "free will" migration and "forced migration." Consider the characteristics and effects of each. How do they differ?

4. Best accumulates brief specific examples to illustrate general conditions and trends. Place names and dates often appear at the beginning of paragraphs. She also includes the contrasting long passage about Sojourner Truth. Compare the effectiveness of both methods of using examples. What are their purposes?

5. What are some examples of maltreatment of black slaves recorded in Best's documentary history? How has she used quotations? Where do they come from? Are they effective?

6. Best traces the long history of her people back to the Queen of Sheba. How does the connection to this legendary figure help her come to terms with the heritage of slavery?

7. Best's work goes beyond the boundaries of any strictly defined genre in that it incorporates historical, biographical, and philosophical fragments. Identify examples of these three modes in the reading. What can each of them contribute to the reader's better understanding of the narrative of racial inequality?

Kenneth Bagnell

Kenneth Bagnell was born in 1934; he is known as a journalist with a strong interest in the history of Canadian immigration. He grew up in a coal-mining town in Nova Scotia and now lives in Whitby, Ontario. Bagnell worked for The Toronto Star *and* The Globe and Mail, *and also as a television commentator and interviewer. He has been an editor of* The Review *magazine, where the following selection appeared for the first time. It was later included in his book* The Little Immigrants: The Orphans Who Came to Canada *(1981). In 1989, he published another book,* Canadese: A Portrait of the Italian Canadians.

Britain's Children Who Came to Stay

One day in June in the early 1920s, a small boy named Horace Weir stood nervously on the deck of an old steamer and watched the buildings of the port of Halifax begin to rise in the thick, gray mist. He was 11, a frail child who had been born into poverty in Britain and was now about to arrive in Canada to begin a new life as a farm boy somewhere in the Maritimes.

He gripped the rail and peered into the cold fog. He was worried, not just for himself and what lay ahead for him, but for his five brothers and sisters who were also on board that day. He, after all, was the oldest boy, the one to whom the others looked. He worried for them, wondering where they were headed and what awaited them. They, too, were bound for life on a farm, his brothers as chore boys, his sisters as mother's helpers, all except Beatrice, who was not quite 3 and would, he was told, be adopted. He worried most of all for her. He always had, ever since that night a year earlier when his parents, broken by illness and terrible poverty, signed over all their children to an organization in Birmingham that sent boys and girls overseas to Canada.

It was almost dark when the six Weir children came down the gangplank. In the darkness and the confusion of landing—or perhaps it was planned that way to avoid the sadness of parting—Horace Weir did not see any of his brothers or sisters to say goodbye. That same evening he was put on a train for the Annapolis Valley in Nova Scotia, where he was met by a farmer in whose home he would pass his lonely childhood and in whose fields he would work until he was an adult and able to find a job for himself.

When he reached the age of 18 and was on his own, he began to search for his brothers and sisters, though he did not know for certain where any of them were. Often people told him he should try to forget them, but he could not. Over the years he found his brothers and sisters, all but the youngest, Beatrice. But as he found them, he found as well that on that evening when they landed in Halifax their family had been broken forever. Once, after he had located one of his brothers, he put his feelings into words: "For brothers, it was not like brothers." All his life he wondered about Beatrice, who was so young, so helpless, and who had disappeared so completely. When he was in his thirties someone told him that she had been adopted by a family living in Prince Edward Island who had then moved to the United States, and so he was certain she was gone forever.

In June 1974, 50 years after he arrived in Canada, Horace Weir, who was then in his early sixties, a respected citizen and carpenter living near the Annapolis Valley community of Bridgetown, put his tools in the back of his car and began the drive home. Along the way he wondered idly if he and his wife might go the ball game or perhaps drive down the road to visit his son and grandchildren. When he reached home and turned into the driveway he was curious to notice, beneath the trees in front of the house, a man and woman. He got out of the car. The man, whom he had never seen before, spoke softly and a bit formally. He gave his name and said he was a retired officer of the Canadian services who had lived abroad for many years. Then, turning to the woman beside him, he asked Horace Weir if he had ever met her. Horace Weir looked and smiled but said no, he had not.

"Mr. Weir," the man said, "this is your sister. This is Beatrice."

He would always remember that day and how they stood there a long time, saying nothing. Then she reach out and shook his hand.

Horace Weir and his sisters and brothers came to this country in one of the most dramatic schemes in the history of immigration to

Canada, one in which more than 80,000 children, many just out of infancy, were gathered from the poor neighborhoods of Britain's cities—London, Birmingham, Liverpool, Manchester—and sent to Canada to live on farms, some in the Maritimes and Quebec, but most in Ontario and Manitoba. During the peak period of the movement, the early 1900s, scores of organizations and individuals were busily shipping children to Canada. Some of the children, those too young to work, were adopted into families, often informally, but most were expected to spend the years of their childhood working in the fields or tending the cattle in an indenture that was stern and lonely. It was a practice that in some ways revealed the dark side of early Canada.

The child immigration movement began well over a century ago, on a day in early November 1869 when a woman named Maria Rye, a British suffragette whose opinions were as strong as her personality, arrived in the pleasant Ontario farmland near what is now Niagara-on-the-Lake, bringing with her 77 children, mostly girls between five and 10, whom she planned to entrust to anyone who would take them. She had gathered the children from the slums of the east end of London, where life was a squalid enslavement to poverty, disease, and crime from which death was an almost compassionate rescue. "The sight of so many little orphans," said *The Niagara Mail and Advertiser* when they arrived, "nearly all of whom are, we believe, deprived of both father and mother, moved all hearts with sympathy." The children were housed in a former jail which had been donated to Miss Rye for use as a dormitory and distributing centre.

For people in Britain who feared for the welfare of the children in Canada, Maria Rye had an answer that would be repeated for the next 50 years by those who, like her, brought children to Canada: "Can anything I introduce them to in Canada or America be worse than that to which they are doomed if we leave them where they are now?"

In those same months another woman in London, a deeply religious social worker, Annie Macpherson, who would have an even larger influence over child immigration, wrote a pamphlet for distribution among the well-to-do in London. Her message was clear: "We who labor here are tired of relieving misery from hand to mouth, and also heartsick of seeing hundreds of families pining away for want of work, when over on the shores of Ontario the cry is heard, 'Come over and we will help you.'" Then, in the spring of the following year, 1870, Miss Macpherson and her workers chose about a hundred boys from the children's shelter she had opened and sailed for Canada. In late May she arrived with them by train in the quiet Ontario town of Belleville, where the local council met her and invited her to establish her Canadian "distributing home." Within two years she opened a second home, in the town of Galt. Then, in 1877, convinced that Quebec should not be overlooked, her sister Louisa opened a third in the village of Knowlton, not far from Montreal, from where she sent children to the farmers in the Eastern Townships for many years.

Still, though Maria Rye brought out the first children and Annie Macpherson enlarged upon her work, it was a slight, dapper young medical student who would make child immigration a phenomenon of Canadian history and, in the process, become its most famous personality. His name was Thomas John Barnardo, and the organization he founded, which still bears his name, would send over 30,000 children to Canada. From 1882 to the early 1930s there was scarcely a farming district in Ontario or Manitoba that did not have a number of Barnardo boys and girls, with their cockney accents, their pain clothes, and often, too often, their lonely and frightened faces.

Barnardo was in his mid-twenties, a medical student in London, when Annie Macpherson began her work, but he was so appalled by the hordes of homeless children that he gave up his ambitions in medicine and became a full-time child worker, opening his first hostel, in the slums of east end London, in 1870. Before long the building swarmed with boys, so many that Barnardo was forced to find new ways to accommodate the numbers who were so desperately in search of his food and shelter. Emigration was the answer, made obvious by the woman with whom he worked while still a student, Annie Macpherson. Thus, in the middle years of the 1870s, the first Barnardo children began arriving in Canada in the care of Annie Macpherson, who brought them, along with her own parties, and settled them throughout Ontario, mainly in the farming districts between Belleville and Galt.

By 1882, however, Barnardo's work and ambition grew so large that he set up his own immigration scheme, with hundreds of children arriving every spring, summer, and fall at the Barnardo Homes in Toronto, Peterborough, and Winnipeg, and at the training farm in northwest Manitoba, near the community of Russell. Barnardo, who referred to child immigration as "The Golden Bridge" and "The Highway of Hope," saw it not just as an idealistic opportunity for his children but as a necessity if he were to expand his work. As he often told his supporters, "An open door at the front demands an exit door at the back." Thus, by 1897, when he was in his late forties, a famous figure in Britain and Canada, Dr. Barnardo's Homes were sending out a thousand children a year; the number of child immigrants remained steady right up to 1914, when World War I interrupted the program.

Thomas Barnardo was a complex mix of philanthropist and individualist. After he opened his hostels in London, he could be found, night after night, combing the streets until almost dawn, searching out the homeless children who slept beside sheds and beneath bridges. Sometimes he would return to his hostel just before dawn with a dozen boys, providing them with the first food and shelter they had for weeks. Eventually parents, many of them in the workhouse, willingly gave him their children in a desperate hope that under his hand they might have a chance for a decent life in Canada. He became, while still a young man, a legend.

When he came on his visits to Canada he was greeted with something approaching awe, especially by the children he had sent out. Before each visit, his Canadian staff would send word of his coming to the thousands of children already on the farms and, on an appointed day, great numbers of them would gather either at the Canadian headquarters in downtown Toronto or, in the case of the girls, on the tree-shaded lawns of Hazelbrae, a large house donated to him in Peterborough which he set aside as the receiving centre for girls. Often after he visited Hazelbrae and had been the honored guest at an afternoon tea attended by hundreds of his girls, he would set out the next day, alone, by horse and buggy down dusty roads, a striking figure in frock coat and top hat, calling at farms along the way to visit as many children as he could. Once, he set out for an obscure village a short distance from Peterborough, hoping to visit two small girls, both under 12, who had been sent from England two years previous. "I walked down a long and beautifully shaded street," he would write of his visit that day, "and knocked at a detached, old-fashioned house, standing apart from the others and back from the road." He was met by an elderly woman, who said that since she was alone and needed the companionship she hoped he had not come to remove the children. He spoke with her a few minutes asking about the girls' manners and their willingness to work. Then he was ushered into the front parlor, where he sat alone while the woman went to bring the two children to meet their surprise visitor.

The girls were brought to him separately so that he might talk to each one privately. As each entered the parlor, silent with shyness, he stood up, removed his glasses, and extended his hand. He spoke gently, kindly and, with his incredible memory for family details, was able to recall the parents they had left and to assure them that, even if it were lonely and hard, their choice had been for the best. He asked if they went to school and to church and if they were reading the Bible—the one he had given each of them, the one bearing his likeness and signature on the frontispiece—and then, in a gesture that was as sincere as it was brief, he asked them to do their best to live the good life. Then he shook hands again and, with the girls holding back tears, he bowed, kissed the top of their heads, and left. For such children, many of them lonely and heartbroken, a visit from Dr. Barnardo, the only father some of them would ever know, was the most memorable event in their lives.

He was, as well as a visionary, an extraordinary fund raiser, so while he was able to defray some of the costs of sending children to Canada through government grants and free travel, the enormous expense of maintaining and expanding his homes, feeding and clothing his children, came from money he raised almost alone, as a preacher, writer, and, often, a showman. Every year, beginning in 1890, he rented for the annual meeting of Dr. Barnardo's Homes the great Albert Hall in London, turning the meeting into an extravaganza in which thousands of children took part, singing anthems, performing drills, and demonstrating the trades in which they were being trained in his homes—as tinsmiths, carpenters, tailors, domestics. But, with his keen sense of drama, he held the most emotional display for the end. After the songs were sung and the drills had ended, Barnardo, who always chaired the meetings, would step to the centre of the stage. He would say that now he was asking for the prayers of all people everywhere for his "dear boys and girls," those who were about to leave him for good. A trumpet would then sound, and from one side of the stage, slowly at first but with gathering pace, a line of children would enter, hundreds of them, all bound for Canada, boys in dark wool suits shouldering knapsacks and girls in long dresses carrying suitcases. Then, at the end of the long line, would come a child, usually a small girl, bearing a banner with only one word: "Goodbye." Invariably the audience was swept with emotion.

One day in the spring of 1909, a couple in Montreal, Mr. and Mrs. Godbee Brown, sat in the living room of their comfortable home, and for most of an hour they studied the pages of the recently published yearbook of McGill University. There, among the many serious likenesses of young men on their way into the professions of law and medicine, was the photograph of a young woman, a striking girl, around whom centred all their affections and ambitions. This was Theodora, their daughter, their only child, who was now graduating from McGill with honors, the vice-president of her class.

The outline of Theodora Brown's career at McGill carried beside her photograph, made no reference to her early life, but even if she had agreed to explain it, there was little she could have told. Her birth was a mystery even to her, hidden in a brief note written years earlier when she was taken by someone and given into the care of one of the child organizations in London. When she was five years old she was put aboard a steamer and sent to Canada. Since she was too young to be placed out as a mother's helper, she remained in the distributing home to which she had been sent, in Belleville, Ont. Then, one autumn day, the people who managed the home received a note from Mr. and Mrs. Godbee Brown, well-known members of St. James Methodist Church, Montreal, asking if they, who had no children, might take one of the children to raise as their own. Thus, in October 1890, Theodora was chosen by one of the leading families of church and society in Montreal, a couple whose home would include a library and conservatory, where her father would read her the classics. She would be surrounded by the advantages of affluence and the affections of a man and woman who took great joy in her arrival in their lives.

One day in winter, two years after she had come to the Browns, she saw some children rolling a snowball and ran to join them. Suddenly one of them, an older girl, shouted a remark that would affect Theodora's life in a remarkable way. "You know what? You're not Theodora Brown. You're a Home Girl. You came from the Home." Her mother did her best to explain, but for the rest of her life, as in the case of many children like her, the memory of that day would never go away. Despite all her gifts, her friends noticed a deep yearning for the past in her life, as if she were seeking to find out whose child she really was, not out of curiosity or bewilderment but to fill some void in her spirit. When she had a daughter of her own, Phyllis, she would remind the girl over and over again that she was her mother's "own flesh and blood." In 1948 her daughter, who had married and had her first child, returned to Montreal to bring Theodora Brown her granddaughter. Theodora's joy in seeing her grandchild was of a special kind. "It meant," her daughter would recall long afterward, "that she could once again say that a child was her own flesh and blood." In time, her daughter would become a student of genealogy and would spend years trying to unravel the riddle of her mother's childhood in Britain. But Theodora Brown's early life would remain the mystery of an abandoned child who had a fortunate destiny.

Other children were less fortunate. Barnardo and those who did similar work in the other organizations were often highly dedicated, but given the scarcity of funds, the multitude of children, and the small number of workers, especially in Canada, it was inevitable that misfortunes would occur. Some children would be placed in homes where they were worked too hard, deprived of normal affection and, in some cases, seldom visited by a worker from the organization that had brought them to their lonely life in Canada.

One spring in England, not long after the turn of the century, a thin, lonely boy named Fred Treacher, who had been put in one of the homes because of his father's death and his mother's extreme poverty, was taken aside by one of the workers, a kind woman whom he had come to trust, and told that soon he would be going to Canada.

When he arrived in Montreal, he was put aboard a train and taken to Toronto. There he was put on another train with a tag on his jacket saying he was destined for a farmer in a small community in Ontario known as Elmvale. The work was hard and, for a boy of 12 who had never seen a farm, very strange. For weeks the farmer tried to teach him to milk, but he could not learn quickly enough, and though the man said little, it was obvious that he was growing impatient. One night when, as usual, Fred was eating alone in the kitchen, he overheard the man telling his wife that the boy was not working out, that he was nothing but "a green Englishman." Several times the farmer, who seemed to believe that punishment would teach Fred to milk, beat him severely, so severely that the boy took to hiding in the hayloft or in a distant field, coming out only to work or to eat.

His life brightened one day when he got word from England that his brother Bert, who was only 9, was also coming to Canada to be placed on a farm. The next day, with the letter in his pocket, Fred crossed the field to a neighboring farm, to the home of a man and woman who had treated him with great kindness. They, too, had taken boys from the Home, but they treated them as sons. Would they, Fred asked, be able to take Bert? They said they would. Often after Bert had arrived in their home, Fred would cross the fields in the evenings, and there in the large, friendly kitchen he would sit at the table with Bert and his new family, saying little but somehow feeling that his own life was better, just knowing that his younger brother had been so fortunate.

Then, one late afternoon in August, Fred finished his work early and crossed the field, hoping that he might be able to give Bert a hand with the chores. He reached the house and, finding it empty, he climbed to the top of a hill overlooking the lake where Bert often went to feed the ducks. He looked down and saw four people: the farmer—who was stirring the water with a long pole—his wife, and two men he did not know. He called out, asking where Bert was. Only the woman looked up. Slowly, she said that Fred should stay where he was. She began to come toward him, but before she reached him he saw the long pole rise from the water, and on the end of it, hanging on a hook, was the small peaked cap his brother always wore.

Many years later, when he was an elderly man respected in his community and church, Fred Treacher would go back to Elmvale and find once more the small grave and marker he remembered from his boyhood. It said Bert Treacher, a Home Boy, was buried there. But what affected Fred so much were the words that were chosen to go beneath the name: "Dearly loved, Dearly missed."

What many children like Fred Treacher would remember all their lives was the work, long, hard, and unrewarding. In July 1905 a 9-year-old girl with a bright, expectant smile, Ellen Keatley, was sent by train from Halifax to a farm in the Nova Scotia settlement of Pictou county. Within a few days of arriving there, she was, though only 9, carrying sacks of potatoes to the cellar, picking boulders from the fields, carrying all the water to the house and barn, and wielding a bucksaw in a vain attempt to cut the wood. For eight years, during which she was never visited by the organization that sent her there, she rose before everyone else and retired after them. Finally, when she was reaching 18 and facing another winter without even warm clothes, she wrote the Home and asked to be removed. She was. Some, like Amy Norris, who came to Canada when she was 12, were not kept in one place very long but were shunted from farm to farm all through childhood. Sometimes it was because they were mistreated and the Home removed them; sometimes it was because the farmers were dissatisfied with them or no longer felt they needed them. Whatever the reason, the frequent moving form place to place left many of them bewildered and hurt and, they believe, unsettled for the rest of their lives. Amy Norris was moved 14 times in four years.

One of the most dramatic episodes in the entire history of child immigration came near the end, in the late twenties, just before the Great Depression delivered the final blow. A 14-year-old boy, very unhappy, was wandering through a London street one day when he spied a poster carrying a photo of a smiling farm boy and the words: "Come to Canada. Be Your Own Boss at 21." Within a matter of days, since he was old enough to emigrate on his own, he signed an agreement saying he would take whatever farm job was offered to him in Canada. Then he sailed. He was sent to a small, poor farm near Lindsay, Ont., to live with a man and his very aged mother, decent people, but neither of whom had much sympathy for the lonely, precocious boy who sat at the table in the evening writing poetry. He found his best friend, indeed his only friend, to be a local minister, Reverend Robert Simpson, who, following Sunday services, would invite him to his home, where they would talk of ethics and ideas. The boy would never forget him.

Within two years the boy came to Toronto. Since the Depression had struck and he had neither education nor skills, the only job he could find was selling doughnuts on the street in return for a bed and all the doughnuts he could eat. In a decision that would influence his life more than he could have imagined, he joined a working boys' club at Toronto's Broadview Y.M.C.A. There, two of the administrators, Murray Ross and Richard Davis, sensed in him special gifts. Davis suggested that he should completed his education—he had never gone to high school—and, as an afterthought, told him that, if he wished, the Y would give him a test to measure his intelligence to see whether he was suited to higher education.

Six weeks later he showed up in Richard Davis' office and took the test, a standard IQ test which he was given a set time to do, though of course, he was not expected to answer every question. He finished the test in just over half the time. He answered every question; virtually every answer was correct. Murray Ross, later to become the first president of York University, would never forget the astonishing paradox of that day, the shabby, homeless orphan with the rare, even spectacular intelligence. "We took the results," Ross told a friend years later, "to psychologists at the University of Toronto. They said he was literally one in a million." Within a few months, through the encouragement of Richard Davis and using textbooks at home, the boy finished his high school studies and was entered at the University of Chicago in sociology, where he completed his degree in less than three years.

Thus began the career of the man many believe to be the most brilliant sociologist Canada has yet produced, a child emigrant from Britain named John R. Seeley. He became, in time, the head of sociology at York University, Toronto, and is today associate dean at a private college in Los Angeles. Like all the others, he would never forget the loneliness and the hardship of those early years in Canada. But in the end, most of all he would remember how one person, a country minister named Robert Simpson, befriended him in his ordeal and touched his life with hope. Often, he says, he goes back in his mind to the Sunday afternoons in the manse near Lindsay, Ont., and the long conversations with the aging Presbyterian clergyman. Perhaps John R. Seeley was speaking for most of the men and women who came to Canada as he did and found one person who cared for them, when, a few years ago, he spoke to the American Academy of Psychoanalysis. Recalling the influence of one man in his life he told his audience: "I know that for brief times, on small scales, as far as an arm will reach, good people still do good things."

TOPICS FOR EXPLORATION

1. What audience is Bagnell addressing in his essay? What is his purpose in relating the events of the "child immigration movement"?

2. Bagnell begins his essay with a narrative about Horace Weir and ends with another about John Seeley. What is the purpose of this framing structure?

3. The story of Horace Weir is a specific example meant to represent a general condition. What is the social phenomenon that his case illustrates?

4. This brief history of British child migration is focussed on several public figures. Who were they and what did they do? Who began the child immigration movement? For what reasons was the movement initiated?

5. Bagnell illustrates some of the negative and positive effects of the child immigration movement. What were they? What is his opinion about the movement's legitimacy and ethical underpinnings? Was it child exploitation or a real solution to the problem of child poverty?

6. Find out from other sources what the concept of "indenture" means in the history of migrations to the new world. How is it related to the scheme involving British children, which Bagnell describes as "one of the most dramatic schemes in the history of immigration to Canada?"

Miriam Rosenthal

Miriam Rosenthal, a Hungarian-Jewish survivor of the Holocaust tragedy, is an eyewitness narrator of the Nazi atrocities in the concentration camps during World War II. Despite the horrors she suffered along with millions of others, she has, as her account amply shows, retained her integrity and humanity. At the end of her narrative, she and her family decide to leave behind Europe's anti-Semitism and settle in Canada; they carry with them painful memories that will inform their choices in Canadian life. This episode has been excerpted from an article about the Holocaust called "We the Living" by Alan M. Gould.

A Holocaust Survivor's Story

We were taken to the Miskolc ghetto, where we stayed for three weeks. They separated the men from the women. I told my husband, "I have a feeling that whatever happens, it will be very bad. So wherever they take us, you go back to Miskolc and I'll go back to the city." I had a feeling that I'd never see him again.

We were smashed into trains like animals, without food or water. After three days, we arrived at Auschwitz. In the same train was my father-in-law, mother-in-law, my sister-in-law, my husband's sister-in-law with her two babies, six weeks and two years old. We were starving. It was hot, stinking, no food. You couldn't go to the washroom. Outside, all we saw was trees and forest.

When we arrived in Auschwitz, we were so happy! Anything was better than the train! Sudenly, we see fences all over. We see SS men and soldiers and Jews in striped uniforms. The Jews ran to the trains and cried "Give the kinder to der mama!" But why? Why should we give the children to the grandparents? They had come to tell us that if we gave the children to our mothers-in-law, like my sister-in-law did, we would be saved. And the old women went to the gas with the children. If the mothers held on to their children they would die with them.

There was Dr. Mengele, in his white golves—a beautiful soldier. Left-right, left-right, his hand waved. We had to run—no time to look or talk. Thousands of people!

We came to Birkenau and were deloused. They shaved my hair and gave me a striped outfit, no underwear. I did not know then that right was life. I heard after the war that a train with my mother and sister arrived on the same day as my train from Miskolc. She was only twenty-five, and was begged to give up her year-old baby, but she would not do it. So she went to the left with my mother.

We were sent to barracks of five hundred women in Auschwitz. Older inmates told us, "You just come from Hungary? Look how fresh and healthy you are! You see that smoke there? That's your parents and sisters and brothers and children! They are dead!" "What? Are you crazy?" we asked.

It had been so hysterical when they shaved us. They put brown hair in one pile, black hair in another. I don't know what they did with it. There we were, naked. And we looked into each other's eyes—that was the mirror. We looked and started to laugh! We looked like idiots! Like monkeys! It was so terrible, and it was still funny.

I found out I was pregnant, in my fourth month. I didn't know, since no woman had a period at Auschwitz. And after four months, I felt something moving inside me, and I said to myself, "My God—I'm pregnant!" This was the worst possible thing, because every day I saw what happened to pregnant women. I already knew it meant death.

I didn't show until the fifth month, but I knew that every day I was waiting to die. Because one of these days they are going to catch me. And the hunger. There was no food. I begged for more food, and someone who knew I was pregnant would have mercy, and sometimes I'd get a peel of a potato. Each day's food was a tiny bit of margarine and a bit of bread. In the morning, black coffee. At night, soup.

I had been told, if they ask for a number of women to go on a transport out of the camp, to volunteer. And so, after about a month, they asked for five hundred to go to Plasow, another camp. It had been built in a Jewish cemetery.

It was a horrible place. People worked on mountains, like slaves in ancient Egypt, carrying stones. When we arrived a Polish Jewish Kapo named Henry Reisfeld said to me. "I can use twenty women. I will save them in my barrack for work." He had been in the camp for three years already. He was unbelievable. I'd ask him, "Why are you helping me like this?" And he said. "You look like my daughter so much—she was killed here. I'll show you the grave." He survived the war—he wrote me right after. He knew I was pregnant and he got me food—bread, more bread, anything he could. But we didn't stay there too long, maybe a few weeks. It was terrible there, but still better than Auschwitz.

One day he told me. "We got an order; you must go back to Auschwitz. Don't go back. We'll be liberated soon by the Russians." I told him that I wasn't staying. I would go back with the rest of the girls. I wasn't going to leave my friends and my cousin. And so we were shipped back to Auschwitz. He ran after our train with a pail of water throwing it onto the train. Again, selections. Again, Mengele. Left. Right. And already he was selecting weak ones and strong ones. Or those who looked pregnant. I was pretty far—my fifth or sixth month, already showing. And in front of me was my first cousin, who wasn't even married! Mengele called to her in German "You are a pig." She replied "No, I am not a pig." "Yes you are, and don't you dare talk back to me. You go the the left." And he sent her to the gas. Me, he let go. "I can't believe it," I told the girls. I was expecting to die.

Two weeks later, I was put on a transport to Augsburg, in Germany—a Messerschmitt airplane factory. Everyone was so happy! A factory! Better than Auschwitz! And this was the first time we saw other people—Germans. Political prisoners from Holland, Belgium.

We got better food than in Auschwitz. We were still hungry, but it was better. The political prisoners were allowed to go and live in the city at night. The Jews were kept in the barracks. I worked next to a Christian communist. All day on the machine, to help build airplanes.

One day, as I worked, two SS men came in to look closely at every worker. One said to me in German "You pig woman! What are you doing here! You are pregnant? Let's go! Where? Back to Auschwitz." I said good-by to my friends, who were crying. But it was a relief. I couldn't care anymore. Thank God the suffering would be over. And the fear of what would happen to the baby. But my husband didn't even know that I was pregnant! There was no one there to help.

So they put me on a passenger train. This was December, 1944. I had on big wooden shoes and no stockings, and it was snowing. The two soldiers were very decent. They knew the war was coming to an end. They bought my ticket. I had a classy trip! There were civilized people sitting all around me, and I still didn't have any hair, and I was pregnant, and I looked crazy.

People kept looking at me, and the two soldiers went out to smoke. And a German lady said. "What is happening here?"

"Don't you know?" I said to her. "I'm Jewish. They're taking me to the gas, in Auschwitz. Don't you know what is happening to the Jewish people?" She said she didn't, and was so concerned that she opened her purse and took out a piece of bread and handed it to me. The other people were all staring. They really didn't know. They were polite to me.

The train stopped after a few hours, and the men said, "Let's go. Get off the train." "What happened?" "They bombed Auschwitz. You won't be going to the gas now." "Where are you taking me?" "To Landsberg."

It was a special *lager*, a horrible camp where they worked people to death. They handed me over like a parcel, giving my number, and they left. The work camp was called Kaufring. The same setup. Barbed wire. Electrified fences. No Mengele. I saw men and women in different parts of the camp, with only barbed wire between them. Skeletons. They could hardly work anymore. An SS woman took me to a cabin. My God, what I see in this cabin! Six other pregnant women like me! I went hysterical crying, "Why are you here?"

They called us the Pregnancy Commando. Every day we worked. But we had food. The Germans knew they had lost the war. They wanted to use us as alibis—that they didn't kill infants. So we worked every day. I was in my eighth month. It was bitter cold. We worked in a laundy, to wash lice out of prisoners' clothes and hang them out to dry. Some days we had to carry dead bodies in a wagon, dump them in a big pit, and the SS would dump lime on them.

The women started to give birth—first one, then another. I was the last, the seventh. I helped the first six into the world. The midwife. There was a doctor, a Jewish prisoner. But he was skin and bones. He had been a gynecologist in Hungary. One day the SS brought him to us "He will be your doctor!" We started to laugh. He couldn't even stand up. He should help us? After the SS left the doctor said, "Children how can I help you? I have no strength left. I'm dying!" He was about fifty-five and looked terrible.

David, who was the Jewish Kapo in the kitchen, he saved our lives. He used to hide meat under the coal in a pail. He told us "Look, you have a doctor now. I'm going to fatten him up so that he should have strength to help you have the babies!" So he snuck extra food to Dr. Vadasz. He survived the war; I sent him clothes then, and wrote to him. He soon after passed away. But then the doctor said, "I have no needle, no medicine, no nothing! No diapers! No soap!" But David once stole a sheet, which he tore up for diapers.

One day, he came in with an SS man. He had been a teacher. And he wept and said, "Look, I'm an SS officer. There is no excuse. I know I am going to die. The Americans are very close. But please believe me—I have children at home, too." And under his coat, he had pieces of rags, soap. Two or three times he did this.

The doctor delivered each of the babies. I was very sick. Leslie was ten pounds—and with all that lack of food! I had forty-eight hours of labour. He was a beautiful baby with blonde, curly hair, and blue, blue eyes, and the SS men went crazy over him—he was a little Aryan! I had a very difficult delivery. The doctor told me, "Miriam I'm trying everything. I can do nothing more. Only God can help you."

Finally, my son was born. I didn't even know, on the other side of the electrical fence, where the men were, they were praying all night—psalms—for me. The whole night. Because they heard the screaming from me. I was so overwhelmed by pain, when the men yelled out, "Do you know what day is today—the day you had the baby? It's Purim! It's Purim!"

But then I was very sick. The placenta stayed in. I got fever and was unconscious. My friend who delivered six weeks before me—she now lives in Brazil, and came in for my son's wedding—she nursed Leslie. She saved my son's life, She told me later that she didn't think I would survive, so she had decided to adopt him.

And then the order came that the Americans were coming, and we had to evacuate the camp. We had to go to Dachau—to the gas—with our babies. So they started to empty the camp, but they couldn't take me, because I was so sick. Four soldiers lifted the bed and began to take me to the infirmary. But as they were walking, I started to hemorrhage, and the whole placenta came out. They ran to Dr. Vadasz, who made a cleaning.

I felt better. Leslie was being nursed by my friend. I had one more camp to go to—Dachau. We walked and walked. I had little milk and Leslie began to lose weight. We were put in an open cattle-car in April, 1945.

We saw airplanes and bombs falling. They thought we were Germans! They bombed our trains—they blew up the engine and the first two cars filled with Jews. We kept waving frantically; we are not Nazis! We are Jews! But how could they see?

The train stopped, so we thought the war was over. I tied Leslie to my neck with a piece of cloth and I jumped from a high trestle. It was near a forest, near Dachau. I ran toward a village, and a peasant woman threw bread to me.

All of a sudden, the Germans shot at us, and began to force us back to the train. I had put Leslie by a tree trunk and covered him with leaves and my body. There were bombs falling and the Germans were shooting . . . we were led back to the train. They brought a new engine and we continued toward Dachau.

Dachau is a city, and we went through it, in our open car. The train stopped in the middle of the city, across from apartments. We were held up because they could not gas the Jews fast enough—so many were being shipped in from across Europe. So we had to sit and wait. This was already early May. And the baby was hungry and I was hungry and I had very little milk.

Ever since Leslie was born, I had such a will to live again! I had a child, I must take him home, I must save him. He was beautiful! And he never cried. It's as if he knew that he was not supposed to cry. Somehow he knew.

So I got off the train. People cried out "They are going to shoot you! The war is almost over!" But I said, "I don't care! I have no milk and my baby in hungry." And I left off the train with Leslie. It was daytime. I crossed the street, went upstairs into an apartment building, knocked on the door. A German woman opened the door. "What do you want?" "I'm hungry. I need milk for my baby. We are Jewish and we are going to be gassed."

She almost went crazy. And I'll never forget that in her hallway there was a long mirror. It was the first time I'd seen myself since before the deportation from the ghetto. I had a little bit of hair. She quickly got a piece of bread and a glass of milk. She knew what was happening, since she must have seen all the trains filled with Jews every day going to Dachau. Where could they have been taking them?

I came back to the train with Leslie. The women were like animals, grabbing the bread from me. A man—a dentist—from our town—a skeleton, came to me and begged for a piece of bread. I gave him my last piece. He survived the war.

Then the train started to go. We got into Dachau at night. There was shouting and yelling and screaming: "Free! Free! You are Free!" It was American soldiers who had broken in. At four in the morning, dead bodies everywhere, chaos and American soldiers. We were screaming. One American gave me a little prayer book—I never part with it—it's in my purse even now.

The Americans wanted to take away the babies with their mothers to a home, to keep us strong. I didn't want to go. I said, "No, I want to go home as soon as I can."

One day I walked through the barracks and my husband's cousin recognized me. "Miriam! My goodness! What happened! Whose is this baby?" I told him. "Are you hungry?" he asked. "I'm going to bring you a chicken!" He wrung the neck and plucked it and cooked it and brought it to me. He laughed, "Nice and kosher—you can eat it!" Whenever I see him nowadays, he says, "Remember the chicken?" Who cared if it was kosher or not kosher, as long as you had food?

They drove me in a jeep with a doctor and a nurse from Dachau to Prague. Then I went again in a train—on the top of a coal wagon. Can you imagine? I was nursing and not nursing. I once went to the engineer and got hot water for the baby.

I finally arrived in Komarno. My brother had survived a forced labour camp. He didn't recognize me, and didn't know I had a baby. He took me back to what was left of our family home. Russians lived there—Russian soldiers.

The cousin who I met in Dachau went home before me and he met my husband. He told him, "I met your wife. She's coming home with the baby." And he said, "Yah? What baby?"

"Your Baby! He looks like your father—exactly! It's a beautiful baby!" My husband told him, "You're crazy!" Then he realized that I had probably become pregnant. He said, "Maybe a German soldier. Maybe she was made pregnant by a Nazi." It did happen in the war, of course.

And he started to walk. I don't know how many days, but he walked all the way to my city, Komarno. There was no train. His shoes were completely gone from walking. He had been in a slave labour camp during the war. Until the moment he came to my door, I didn't know he had survived. He knocked and there I stood. He just cried and cried: "He looks like my father." I told him, "You know he has your ears." One of Leslie's ears is bent, just like my husband's. Our reunion was unbelievable.

We wanted to start living like normal human beings. We had thought that after what had happened the world stopped, and everyone would be crying for us. But the Hungarians would say, "Oh look! We thought you wouldn't come back." Or, "Look—more came back than went!" Things like that. We came home broken in body and broken in soul, and that was the welcome. One day I saw a woman wearing my mother's coat walking down the street.

I wrote to my sister in Canada. They wrote back. We had to go to Cuba first. Canadian immigration wasn't open yet, and the United States wouldn't give us a permit to stay temporarily. We had stayed ten months in Paris waiting for papers, and then ten months in Havana. Then we were congratulated by the Canadian consulate: "Good luck!"

First we were in Timmins for a year, where my husband served as rabbi. From there, we went to Sudbury. We stayed sixteen years. We came to Toronto sixteen years ago, and we opened Miriam's Bookstore.

Leslie has a Ph.D. in organic chemistry, and works at Honeywell. He is married with two girls and a boy. Lilian is thirty-two, has a teaching diploma, and has taught kindergarten. Murray is doing his Master's in medieval Jewish history at McGill. He is single.

I tell you, Canadians don't appreciate where they are. To be here in this blessed country—nothing else but freedom! They don't know! To be free; to walk in the streets; you can go to synagogue, do whatever you want, speak your mind. You don't have to worry. What it means to be a person—to live like a human being! People have to learn to appreciate Canada. We have to be thankful every day we are here.

I have nightmares. Not often, but I have them. I feel that I can't find my baby Leslie, and we have to run. Again we are in the trains.

My daughter asks me, "How can you divide yourself and live still like a human being?" And I answer her, "I have to cope. You live, you work, you don't think about it." I very seldom tell my story. And this is but a nutshell of what happened.

I used to feel guilt. Not any more. Why me, I would ask, why did I come home, and not my mother, who was such a pious, honest Jew? Why me?

And the whole question comes up, about religion: why am I still religious? I am asked. And I tell them, "I brought a son back from Hell—how can I not believe in God?"

TOPICS FOR EXPLORATION

1. Whom does Rosenthal have in mind as her audience while she narrates her personal story? What is her pupose: to inform? to persuade? Does she have any other?

2. Rosenthal's narrative does not employ much commentary. Does this make her story more effective? Is commentary even necessary?

3. Rosenthal's text includes examples of the extreme bestiality institutionalized by concentration camps. How did the Nazis "dehumanize" the Jews upon their arrival at the camps? What steps were taken to destroy the prisoners' identities?

4. What were the causes and conditions that brought about these horrors in Europe during World War II? Does Rosenthal consider the causes of the suffering? Why or why not?

5. How was Rosenthal spared so often? What were the circumstances of the chance events that saved her life? Apart from the

role of pure chance in the small gestures of help extended to her, what attitude characterized those who managed to survive? How did her "will to live" endure among so many painful experiences?

6. Most of Rosenthal's story relates her imprisonment by the Nazis. Compare that with the brief description of experiences in Canada after the war. Why did she decide to immigrate to Canada?

Rohinton Mistry

Rohinton Mistry was born in Bombay, India, in 1952, and emigrated to Canada in 1975. Educated in economics at Bombay, in Toronto he worked in a bank while studying philosophy and literature at night. In 1985, he was awarded the Canadian Fiction *Contributor's Prize. In 1988, the collection of short stories from which our selection has been taken,* Tales from Firozsha Baag *(1987), was short-listed for the Governor General's Award. His novel* Such a Long Journey *won the Governor General's Award and became a national bestseller in 1991. These fictions have a strong autobiographical element and meticulous, authentic detail. Mistry's stories often reflect the tensions of Bombay life and contrast it with the exotic temptations of life elsewhere, especially in the West.*

Lend Me Your Light

> . . . your lights are all lit—then where do you go with your lamp? My house is all dark and lonesome,—lend me your light.
>
> *Rabindranath Tagore*
> *Gitanjali*

We both left Bombay the same year. Jamshed first, for New York, then I, for Toronto. As immigrants in North America, sharing this common experience should have salvaged something from our acquaintanceship. It went back such a long way, to our school days at St Xavier's.

To sustain an acquaintance does not take very much. A friendship, that's another thing. Strange, then, that it has ended so completely, that he has erased himself out of our lives, mine and Percy's; now I cannot imagine him even as a mere bit player who fills out the action or swells a procession.

Jamshed was my brother's friend. The three of us went to the same school. Jamshed and my brother, Percy, both four years older than I, were in the same class, and spent their time together. They had to part company during lunch, though, because Jamshed did not eat where Percy and I did, in the school's drillhall-cum-lunchroom.

The tiffin carriers would stagger into the school compound with their long, narrow rickety crates on their heads, each with fifty tiffin boxes, delivering lunches from homes in all corners of the city. When the boxes were unpacked, the drillhall would be filled with a smell that is hard to forget, thick as swill, while the aromas of four hundred steaming lunches started to mingle. The smell must have soaked into the very walls and ceiling, there to age and rancify. No matter what the hour of the day, that hot and dank grotto of a drill-hall smelled stale and sickly, the way a vomit-splashed room does even after it is cleaned up.

Jamshed did not eat in this crammed and cavernous interior. Not for him the air of redolent of nauseous odours. His food arrived precisely at one o'clock in the chauffeur-driven, air-conditioned family car, and was eaten in the leather-upholstered luxury of the back seat, amidst his collection of hyphenated lavishness.

In the snug dining-room where chauffeur doubled as waiter, Jamshed lunched through his school-days, safe from the vicissitudes of climate. The monsoon might drench the tiffin carriers to the bone and turn cold the boxes of four hundred waiting schoolboys, but it could not touch Jamshed or his lunch. The tiffin carriers might arrive glistening and stinking of sweat in the hot season, with scorching hot tiffin boxes, hotter than they'd left the kitchens of Bombay, but Jamshed's lunch remained unaffected.

During the years of high school, my brother, Percy, began spending many weekend afternoons at his friend's house at Malabar Hill. Formerly, these were the afternoons when we used to join Pesi *paadmaroo* and the others for our most riotous times in the compound, the afternoons that the adults of Firozsha Baag would await with dread, not knowing what new terrors Pesi had devised to unleash upon the innocent and the unsuspecting.

But Percy dropped all this for Jamshed's company. And when he returned from his visits, Mummy would commence the questioning: What did he eat? Was Jamshed's mother home? What did the two do all afternoon? Did they go out anywhere? And so on.

Percy did not confide in me very much in those days. Our lives intersected during the lunch routine only, which counted for very little. For a short while we had played cricket together with the boys of Firozsha Baag. Then he lost interest in that too. He refused to come when Daddy would take the whole gang to the Marine Dri *maidaan* on Sunday morning. And soon, like all younger brothers, I was seen mainly as a nuisance.

But my curiosity about Percy and Jamshed was satisfied by Mummy's interrogations. I knew that the afternoons were usually spent making model airplanes and listening to music. The airplanes were simple gliders in the early years; the records, mostly Mantovani and from Broadway shows. Later came more complex models with gasoline engines and remote control, and classical music from Bach and Poulenc.

The model-airplane kits were gifts from Jamshed's itinerant aunties and uncles, purchased during business trips to England or the U.S. Everyone except my brother and I seemed to have uncles and aunties smitten by wanderlust, and Jamshed's supply line from the western world guaranteed for him a steady diet of foreign clothes, shoes, and records.

One Saturday, Percy reported during question period that Jamshed had received the original soundtrack of *My Fair Lady*. This was sensational news. The LP was not available in Bombay, and a few privately imported or "smuggled" copies, brought in by people like Jamshed's relatives, were selling in the black market for two hundred rupees. I had seen the records displayed side by side with foreign perfumes, chocolates, and cheeses at the pavement stalls of smugglers along Flora Fountain.

Sometimes, these stalls were smashed up during police raids. I liked to imagine that one day a raid would occur as I was passing, and in the mêlée and chaos of the clash, *My Fair Lady* would fly through the air and land at my feet, unnoticed by anyone. Of course, there wasn't much I could have done with it following the miracle, because our old gramophone played only 78 rpms.

After strenuous negotiations in which Mummy, Percy, and I exhausted ourselves, Percy agreed to ask his friend if I could listen to the album. Arrangements were made. And the following Saturday we set off for Jamshed's house. From Firozsha Baag, the direction of Malabar Hill was opposite to the one we took to go to school every morning, and I was not familiar with the roads the bus travelled. The building had a marble lobby, and the lift zoomed us up smoothly to the tenth floor before I had time to draw breath. I was about to tell Percy that we needed one like this in Firozsha Baag, but the door opened. Jamshed welcomed us graciously, then wasted no time in putting the record on the turntable. After all, that was what I had come for.

The afternoon dragged by after the sound-track was finished. Bored, I watched them work on an airplane. The box said it was a Sopwith Camel. The name was familiar from the Biggles books Percy used to bring home. I picked up the lid and read dully that the aircraft had been designed by the British industrialist and aeronautical engineer, Thomas Octave Murdoch Sopwith, born 1888, and had been used during the First World War. Then followed a list of parts.

Later, we had lunch, and they talked. I was merely the kid brother, and nobody expected me to do much else but listen. They talked of school and the school library, of all the books that the library badly needed; and of the *ghatis* who were flooding the school of late.

In the particular version of reality we inherited, *ghatis* were always flooding places, they never just went there. *Ghatis* were flooding the banks, desecrating the sanctity of institutions, and taking up all the coveted jobs. *Ghatis* were even flooding the colleges and universities, a thing unheard of. Wherever you turned, the bloody *ghatis* were flooding the place.

With much shame I remember this word *ghati*. A suppurating sore of a word, oozing the stench of bigotry. It consigned a whole race to the mute roles of coolies and menials, forever unredeemable.

During one of our rare vacations to Matheran, as a child, I watched with detachment while a straining coolie loaded the family's baggage on his person. The big metal trunk was placed flat on his head, with the leather suitcase over it. The enormous hold-all was slung on his left arm, which he raised to steady the load on his head, and the remaining suitcase went in the right hand. It was all accomplished with much the same approach and consideration used in loading a cart or barrow—the main thing was balance, to avoid tipping over. This skeletal man then tottered off towards the train that would transport us to the little hill station. There, similar skeletal beings would be waiting with rickshaws. Automobiles were prohibited in Matheran, to preserve the pastoral purity of the place and the livelihood of the rickshawallas.

Many years later I found myself at the same hill station, a member of my college hikers' club, labouring up its slopes with a knapsack. Automobiles were still not permitted in Matheran, and every time a rickshaw sped by in a flurry of legs and wheels, we'd yell at the occupant ensconced within: "Capitalist pig! You bastard! Stop riding on your brother's back!" The bewildered passenger would lean forward for a moment, not quite understanding, then fall back into the cushioned comfort of the rickshaw.

But this type of smug socialism did not come till much later. First we had to reckon with school, school uniforms, brown paper covers for textbooks and exercise books, and the mad morning rush for the school bus. I remember how Percy used to rage and shout at our scrawny *ghaton* if the pathetic creature ever got in his way as she swept and mopped the floors. Mummy would proudly observe, "He has a temper just like Grandpa's." She would also discreetly admonish Percy, since this was in the days when it was becoming quite difficult to find a new *ghaton*, especially if the first one quit due to abuse from the scion of the family and established her reasons for quitting among her colleagues.

I was never sure why some people called them *ghatons* and others, *gungas*. I suppose the latter was intended to placate— the collective conferment of the name of India's sacred river balanced the occasions of harshness and ill-treatment. But the good old days, when you could scream at a *ghaton* that would kick her and hurl her down the steps, and expect her to show up for work next morning, had definitely passed.

After high school, Percy and Jamshed went to different colleges. If they met at all, it would be at concerts of the Bombay Chamber Orchestra. Along with a college friend, Navjeet, and some others, my brother organized a charitable agency that collected and distributed funds to destitute farmers in a small Maharshtrian village. The idea was to get as many of these wretched souls as possible out of the clutches of the village money-lenders.

Jamshed showed a very superficial interest in what little he knew about Percy's activities. Each time they met, he would start with how he was trying his best to get out of the country. "Absolutely no future in this stupid place," he said. "Bloody corruption everywhere. And you can't buy any of the things you want, don't even get to see a decent English movie. First chance I get, I'm going abroad. Preferably the U.S."

After a while, Percy stopped talking about his small village, and they only discussed the concert program or the soloist's performance that evening. Then their meetings at concerts ceased altogether because Percy now spent very little time in Bombay.

Jamshed did manage to leave. One day, he came to say goodbye. But Percy was away working in the small village: his charitable agency had taken on the task full time. Jamshed spoke to those of us who were home, and we all agreed that he was doing the right thing. There just weren't any prospects in this county; nothing could stop its downhill race towards despair and ruin.

My parents announced that I, too, was trying to emigrate, but to Canada, not the U.S. "We will miss him if he gets to go," they told Jamshed, "but for the sake of his own future, he must. There is a lot of opportunity in Toronto. We've seen advertisements in newspapers from England, where Canadian Immigration is encouraging people to go to Canada. Of course, they won't advertise in a country like India—who would want these bloody *ghatis* to come charging into their fine land?—but the office in New Delhi is holding interviews and selecting highly qualified applicants." In the clichés of our speech was reflected the cliché which the idea of emigration had turned into for so many. According to my parents, I would have no difficulty being approved, what with my education, and my westernized background, and my fluency in the English language.

And they were right. A few months later things were ready for my departure to Toronto.

TOPICS FOR EXPLORATION

1. Mistry's story is autobiographical. How does this affect the style? What methods does the author use to give weight and authenticity to his story?

2. The lunches attended by the narrator, his brother, and Jamshed at school and at Jamshed's house are symbolic of the contrast between the respective social levels of their families. How do they differ?

3. Who are *ghatis*? How do they represent the institutional injustice of Bombay? Contrast the lifestyles of the *ghatis* with those who live in the Malabar Hills.

4. How does the narrator as a young boy perceive the West? What are the symbols of its exotic luxury? Is the title Mistry's ironic comment about West? In the context of his critique of Bombay's social stratification, does the title reflect the idealized longing for Western democracies in post-colonial countries?

5. What is the meaning of the contrast among the three main characters, Jamshed, Percy, and the narrator? How do their motives differ? In the light of their desires, what different goals do they accomplish?

6. What is the process that an Indian immigrant must follow in order to come to Canada?

7. How do you understand the narrator's comment at the end that the idea of emigration has turned into a cliché for so many people in his country? In what way does the story's flashback into the past explain the growth of emigration from post-independence India?

Garry Son Hoan

as told to Eugene Buia

Letter to Vietnam *is the title of Eugene Buia's documentary film, based on the actual experience of the nine-year-old Vietnamese boy Garry Son Hoan, who in November 1978 left his parents to become one of the "boat people" running away from the communist regime. It is also the title of the book that presents the text of letters Garry wished to send to his parents, as taken from the narration of the film. Both the film and the book give an account of Garry's journey aboard a small fishing vessel, which carried him from Vietnam to the freighter* Hai Hong, *famous for transporting refugees, and to his final destination in Toronto, where he became an immigrant, among almost fifty thousand other boat people accepted by Canada.*

Letter to Vietnam

Dear Mother,

We came to a country called Canada today. We are happy to be here after so many days on the boat called *Hai Hong*. It was much bigger than the fishing boat we left in, the biggest boat I have ever seen. When I left you and Daddy in the night to go away in that small boat I was afraid and I missed you. Muy Shing said I should try not to cry. I tried, but I cried. Since that time lots of things have happened. We have been so many places. Once we left the fishing boat and went on the *Hai Hong* we thought we were saved, but many times we came to land and many times we were sent back out on the water again. I am very tired of moving but it doesn't stop. Always we are waiting to go someplace else but here in Canada, for the first time, I feel safe, almost as safe as in Saigon with you. Finally people seem happy and friendly, though I don't understand them. I am glad I have Muy Shing, Liang and My Chou here with me. We are well, but there were some hard times. No one on the *Hai Hong* was happy. Many wished to die. It frightened me very much.

There were so many people on the boat. There were old people and children even younger than me. Liang says there were over two thousand people. On the boat, think of it! We had no roof. It was hot during the day, so cold when the sun went down, and always raining. We took turns standing up at night so there would be room to lie down and sleep. I thought of our nice house in Saigon. In my head I would walk through the rooms and think of sharing food together. I was very hungry on the boat.

One place we stopped—Indonesia—we waited for one week but they wouldn't let us in. They told us there was a big American boat waiting for us out at sea to take us away. We went to look for it but it wasn't true. We were sailing again with little food or water. Then we got to a place called Malaysia. Again we waited. Liang said the problem was that there were many Vietnamese, Chinese and Cambodians already in Malaysia and there was no room, but some men did come onto the *Hai Hong* and give us food. When we sat there, very hungry and afraid, I couldn't believe it was better than being at home with you.

One day we learned that we were to land in Malaysia. Everyone was so happy. When we got to shore we all jumped and walked around, glad to be able to move again. Still it was very crowded at the camp where they kept us.

They wouldn't let us out. There was wire fence all around. It reminded me of Saigon with soldiers outside guarding us, keeping us from running away. There was no place I wanted to go. I stayed close to Muy Shing, Liang and My Chou.

When we finally landed there were still more lines. We waited to get off the boat and to go through the many lines where soldiers and officials asked us question. After we found a place to lie under a metal roof we joined many others who waited to choose clothing from a huge building filled with big piles of things to wear. We had worn the same clothes all the time we were on the boat and had lost the small bag we had with us. Muy and My picked out new things. Some of the women at the camp had needles. Some people were making wallets and shoes to pass the time and make extra money. Some of the others at the camp had escaped Vietnam with all their money. Muy and My fixed our new things to fit us. Later when we found out we were going to Canada our new clothes were not good enough to keep us warm.

The camp was much better than the boat, but everyone wanted only one thing, to have a home again. Each day we waited as Liang met again and again with the officials of different countries. He said he sometimes felt he was fighting with everyone else in the camp to win a place where we could live. In line as the men waited each day, sometimes they would grow angry. Though there were many long days we had not drowned at sea as others had. We had travelled all the way across the sea and we were alive!

At the camp Liang talked to lots of men. After many days he told us the news; we were going to Canada. Everyone says this is good. Liang and Muy Shing were very excited so I was happy too.

We too had to ride airplanes to get to Canada. Sometimes they stopped. I was afraid they would make us get off and that we would be lost again, but we continued on. On one plane a baby cried the whole time. I wanted to cry too, but this time I didn't. I fell asleep.

When I woke up we were in Canada. It was all very confusing. I don't know why everyone wanted to take pictures of us. Everyone wanted to talk to us too. People even tried to talk to me. They thought I would know English! I know I will have to learn.

We came to an army base called Longue Pointe. There are more army men and lines here. Doctors and nurses had to look at us all to know if we were healthy. We all were, but we did have some sores and sunburns from Malaysia. We are staying in places called barracks and even though many of us have to sleep in the same bed it is the nicest place we have been since home. Oh, yes! I must tell you the first thing I noticed was that this land is colder than anyplace I have ever been. We were taken to a large building to get jackets and pants. They are funny clothes that make me look fat, but they are very warm. Since Malaysia we have been given new clothes everywhere we stop. Liang says our jackets are presents from the Canadian people. Canadians are nice, but they are always asking us questions and dragging Liang off someplace to wait in line.

The planes and the soldiers of Base Longue Pointe and all the men asking questions remind me of Saigon. When the planes take off sometimes it sounds like the shells fired at Saigon and I jump, but everyone says we are safe now. I guess it is better here than there, but it is scary not knowing where you are going. The soldiers here look different than the ones in Saigon, and I don't see any guns. There haven't been any since Malaysia. The streets at this army base are quiet and Liang says we might never hear shooting again. That seems impossible, but none of the ladies or men here are hurt. They all look good. I asked Liang if there was war here too? He said no. I wonder if these men and ladies have ever heard guns? I haven't seen any children yet, but I have a friend from the *Hai Hong*, his name is Tho. I still remember my friends in Saigon; how we would sit together on the streets playing cards and hope that the soldiers would give us money to shine their shoes. Do my friends wonder where I am; have you told them? I wish I could have. I kept it a secret as you told me to. I hope you can bring some of my friends with you when you come. Can you bring my dog, Ry? You would like it here. No more shooting. I miss you.

Love,
Garry Son Hoan

This is my new Canadian name. I like it very much. I heard it in a movie.

TOPICS FOR EXPLORATION

1. Who is intended to be the actual reader of Garry's letter? Is it the same as its addressee? What is the purpose of making an ostensibly private letter public? Would it lose some of its effect if it were addressed directly to the Canadian audience?

2. Garry's letter is a simple and straightforward description of the dramatic circumstances of the boat people's escape. What is the advantage of having the events told from the point of view of a nine-year old? Is there any disadvantage?

3. Reconstruct the stages of the journey that brought Garry and other Vietnamese to Canada. What were his experiences during the passage and in the refugee camps?

4. What does Garry's letter reveal about different attitudes toward the boat people expressed by the authorities in the countries where they stopped? What kind of reception did they have? What bureaucratic obstacles did the Vietnamese refugees encounter in their quest for freedom?

5. What picture of Canada emerges from Garry's emotionally charged account? Contrast his feelings about Canada with his former experiences.

Helga Kutz-Harder

The real-life stories collected in Helga Kutz-Harder's reportage often have their source in unspeakable suffering and misery that caused their subjects to flee their homelands and become refugees in Canada.

The socio-political backgrounds of these personal experiences are varied. The Iranian Revolution of 1978, led by Ayatollah Khomeini, replaced the Shah's regime with an Islamic government that established a strict Moslem rule. It governed in a way that many people found more repressive than the Shah's reign. In 1978 in Afghanistan, a Soviet-backed military junta seized power, initiating the cycle of civil violence and guerrilla fighting that went on for ten years, until the Soviet troops were finally withdrawn, and continued even afterwards. The civil war left the country devastated and depopulated. From 1979, El Salvador, in Central America, has been the site of relentless battle between the U.S.-supported military government and the leftist popular movement. Thousands of people have been killed or "disappeared"; thousands have sought escape in refugee camps. Burundi, a small African country, has been troubled by long-term political instability that has its roots in ethnic conflicts. For years, it has been unable to escape the bloody civil war between the Hutu majority and the Tutsi ruling class. Somalia, an African republic uniting former British and Italian colonies, is subject to both drought and flood, which places this country in the so-called hunger belt. It has received international economic and technical assistance. Sri Lanka, formerly the British colony of Ceylon, has been wracked since its independence in 1948 by the violent religious, linguistic, and ethnic conflict between the majority Sinhalese Buddhists and the minority Tamils who favour an independent Tamil homeland. The politics of violence and terrorism is the island's everyday reality.

Breaking the Barriers:
Refugee Women in Canada

The stories of the refugee women I have met in Canada fill me with woe and wonder. The realities of their past sometimes defy my imagination. The courage with which they find their place in a settled society like Canada is awe-inspiring. Many of them have an aura of calm and beauty which masks the turmoil inside when they try to hold in tension the unbearable memories of the past, the spirit-defying obstacles of everyday life in a cold new country, and the tentative flame of hope which dares to believe that this is the place where their spirits can flourish.

Many of the refugee women are reluctant to talk of their past, sometimes because they are afraid of unleashing emotional despair which they may not be able to control, and sometimes because they need to bury some of the details in order to be accepted by their people here. Breaking the barriers within themselves requires as much courage as breaking the barriers between them and their new society. The stories which I have gathered here are tributes to this courage. They look inward and outward. They give us truth about ourselves, about us, and about the world in which we live together. The women and their stories are a gift to us.

YOUNG WOMAN FROM IRAN

A young Iranian man started the conversation: "Women in Iran suffer two times more than men." The young widow accompanying him continued the story. Because her husband wrote down his criticism of the government he was imprisoned. Because she was pregnant with his child, she, too was imprisoned. When he died, the authorities freed her from prison, but she found herself imprisoned by a society which shunned her because of him. She had no right to study, no right to work, no way to survive and feed a child.

She was bitter about her past: "Woman are half of a man, except when they have to go to prison the same as a man." She told me that many woman with children fill the prisons, and many women are executed. Many children lose both parents and become the lost children of Iran, because "nobody is allowed to help them."

She arrived at a Canadian airport, carrying a small daughter and "horrible memories" of family members' executions, and religious repression, especially of women. Immigration officials treated her well and gave her a hearing only two days later. She came to the meeting tired and worried. She did not know what to do when the official thundered: "Why, why, why don't you go home where you belong? Why are you coming and stealing jobs from Canadians?" In her heart she cried: "I can't go home, I would rather be executed than treated like this. I can't stop crying." She needed to believe that she would be helped, not criticized for why she was where she was.

As a single mother she knew that first of all, she must find work. But before that, she must study French because she was in Montreal.

She worried about a lot of things. What could she do with her little girl? How could she manage? How could she live if her baby became sick? She could find work in a factory, but how nice it would be to work at her own profession, even at a minimum wage.

She ended her conversation: "Women aren't refugees because of what they have done, but because of what their husbands have done." She bowed her head and, as her lustrous black hair fell over her shoulders, we wept, men and women alike. Will we ever know what keeps her going day after day?

YOUNG WOMAN FROM AFGHANISTAN

She was one of the privileged few who had ventured out of a tradition in which females are sequestered, to attend the university in Kabul. The times away from campus were still spent with women in whose company love and tradition and nurture were felt and passed on. Men were for marrying and for stability.

Then came the terror of war and the flight from danger. Her mother died in her homeland. One sister found her way to Germany. Other sisters found their way to Australia. She married a countryman along the way, and they came to Canada along with his five unmarried brothers. She and her baby daughter were the only females in the household, and she longed for women to turn to for guidance and cultural continuity.

At twenty-three she saw the advertisement for a youth training program available to anyone unemployed under the age of twenty-four. Toronto apartments are expensive, and a child needs toys and a bed and clothes and books and love. "If I don't take the program now I'll be too old for the age restriction, and when I leave my child with the sitter she cries and will not eat," she explained. At home, a mother or an aunt or sister could have helped. Here, a strange woman with strange customs cares for her child. She sobs over the telephone. I can not solve her dilemma, but I can listen to her story.

She called again recently. She has moved to the suburbs, far away from public transportation, to be able to offer her child a garden to play in. Her loneliness and alienation are intensified. I wonder how long it will be before she walks with a sense of fulfilled promise.

YOUNG WOMAN FROM EL SALVADOR

A church heard about her fear of returning to El Salvador, and quickly agreed to sponsor her into Canada. She waited eleven months in Buffalo while the Canadian authorities read through the stacks of paper and signed the right ones before she could finally end her journey. The room they provided was so warm and welcoming, and she sank into some pillows, exhausted. Eventually the young man she had met along the way found her, and became her husband.

Like most new immigrants, their monthly income was minimal, unequal to the expectations she placed on herself as a good wife. In her understanding, that included serving expensive cuts of meat and spending the day at home to protect the timing of the evening meal. Meanwhile, her sponsors ate bean sprouts and granola, and watched her weekly allowance used up in apparently inappropriate grocery bills. They advised when they could, and in time the grocery bills got lower; so did her self-esteem as a wife. She learned how to fit into the Canadian economy, but felt she was betraying her cultural values.

How do any of us know which culture should be imposed on which? Will she eventually be a Canadian Salvadorean woman, or a Salvadorean Canadian woman? Either way, she may feel as if she has failed at being a good woman.

YOUNG WOMAN FROM BURUNDI

She had been a refugee in Africa for seven years, and was relieved when Canada selected her as a government sponsored refugee, along with her four small children. She came to Montreal, fluent in French and full of hope. Two children went to school, and two children went to daycare. She was one of the lucky ones; she got a job in a factory. Factory work itself was an unfamiliar experience. She began to sense that no one wanted to talk past her black face. She tried to realize what was happening around her: "I cried in the washroom, and nobody noticed my tears when I came out. I wondered why nobody cared about me until I realized that nobody cared about anybody. Nobody even said 'excuse me' when they stepped on a toe."

Machines frightened her, and she was transferred to a simpler one. It wasn't simple, though, to be working with men for the first time in her life. She finally decided to leave her job, and was amazed that the boss was sad. She realized with surprise that he thought she had been doing a good job. He never told her!

She stayed home for a while and worried about the other women. She had never been involved in collectives of any kind, but she knew they needed each other. She went to an International Centre and told them about her worries and how they could help each other. She filled out complicated forms to create a job to help other women, and got a grant for a new job. Now she works with women and helps them from her own experience in Canada. "All those women are slaves to their culture," she said. "They forget their own possibilities."

Can we ever fully understand why they are here? Can we learn from their experience? Can we understand them as individual women? Will we ever look at them without prejudice?

YOUNG WOMAN FROM SOMALIA

She was highly skilled in Somalia: a typist and telex computer operator. But after her husband disappeared (just one of thousands) her life changed, because in Somalia a working woman needs a male sponsor. At first her uncle sponsored her, but he disappeared, too. And so she was fired, with no place to go. "The war in Somalia is an anarchist war. It is a war on women," she said. Any woman between the ages of eighteen and forty is not safe from being forcibly removed to the army camps to be raped and violated. And that's only the beginning. If her husband finds out, he kills her for the shame of it all; if they know that he has found out, they kill him, too; if he goes into hiding instead, and she won't tell where he is, they kill her.

And so she escaped to Canada, aching because she left a young baby with her sister, who couldn't come to Canada as protection for her sister: only a girl with a baby is safe from violation. And so she sacrificed her baby daughter to save her sister. Most of all she feels so alone because there are not enough Somalis in Canada to form the kind of community to which she needs to belong, in order to stand upright in the midst of the pain and the memory of the flesh and blood she left behind.

YOUNG TAMIL WOMAN FROM SRI LANKA

As a child she had heard stories of bombings from her mother. Then, one of the bombs killed her young husband, and she felt them in her soul when she realized that her unborn twins would never know their father. She was a high school teacher, and one extra-violent day her principal warned her to stay at home. Frozen with fear, three women watched while thugs ran to the back of the house with torches to burn it down—just because she was a Tamil. Only wit and the need to survive kept them moving to a temporary safe haven, a room 6'x10' for fifty people. "I still feel the scars of that burning," she said.

The nurse who helped her wash the twins asked: "When are you going home?" She remembers bursting into tears because she had no home to go to. They kept moving, sleeping with their clothes on and a bit of food nearby, ready to move when necessary. For three months they stayed in India, then they found their way to England, where a Canadian church heard about them and sponsored their move to Canada. They waited eleven more months before arriving at the welcoming church. One of the first comments from an unthinking person confused her: "You a refugee? Surely immigrant is more like it."

The sponsoring church is kind, but the trauma and depression remain. Holding her teaching skills in her memory, she wonders why only the men are easily given studying opportunities here in Canada. She shared some of her disappointments with us: "The cultural transition lies heavily on the women. The guilt for having left home is heavy." Beneath the warm smile and the classic beauty lies a lot of pain.

These refugee women will never forget the land of their birth. Without doubt, the scars of past traumas will also never be forgotten. Perhaps they did not know much about Canada before they arrived here. But now they know that Canada is their homeland. They know that the peace and safety they have found in Canada will give them a chance to start a new life. Now they have an opportunity to develop their potential and contribute their talents to the land which gave them refuge.

TOPICS FOR EXPLORATION

1. What is the author's role in "Breaking the Barriers"? How objective is Kutz-Harder's approach to her subject? Whom is she trying to reach in her audience? What is the purpose of this essay?

2. What barriers have these refugee women raised against communication about their own past? Why?

3. Why has the author chosen to concentrate on women in her essay? Why do these women symbolize the problems of their countries so well?

4. What are some of the sacrifices the women have suffered in order to emigrate from their countries? What difficulties do these refugees have in common? What problems are unique to each?

5. What are the major dilemmas that the refugee women face while adjusting to a new environment in Canada? How have their cultural origins affected the choices they have made in Canada?

6. Gender and ethnicity conspire against these refugee women, putting them always at a disadvantage. Find evidence in their stories that they have been victims of inequality in their male-dominated cultures at home. Then try to analyze their present situation in Canada so as to determine how far the double-jeopardy, associated with being both a woman and a member of a visible minority, affects their chances for a better future.

SUGGESTIONS FOR FURTHER STUDY

1. Compare the history of the "five generations" written by Pat Deiter-McArthur and the black stories of Nova Scotia by Carrie Best. How are these two distinct experiences similar? How do they differ? What causes of oppression do they reveal? What strategies do the authors use in their common attempt to reach out to the future by means of reviewing the past?

2. Compare the experiences of Catharine Parr Traill coming to Canada from the heart of the British Empire more than a century ago and those of Rohinton Mistry's immigrants arriving today from the former British colonies. How have conditions changed? What has remained unchanged?

3. In this unit there are numerous examples of political refugees. Discuss the similarities binding Miriam Rosenthal's narrative of war-torn Europe to the experiences of the refugee women and the boat people in Helga Kutz-Harder's account and Garry Son Hoan's letter, respectively. How do their stories differ?

4. Compare the main reasons for immigration as experienced by the London street children in Bagnell's essay with the journey of Garry So Hoan from Vietnam. Bagnell speaks second-hand about his subjects while Garry speaks in his own voice. What difference does it make?

5. Carrie Best quotes the records that show "complicity with slavery" on the part of some early settlers in Nova Scotia. One generation later than the events described by Best, Traill portrays similar white middle-class settlers in a favourable way. Is there any ironic clash of perspectives here? For further comparisons, you might also add Pat Deiter-McArthur's perspective.

BEING HERE: UNCERTAINTY

INTRODUCTION

Coming here is always a challenge. Sacrificing the familiar, habitual, and comprehensible—whether the sacrifice has been voluntary or necessary—leaves a void to be filled by the strange, disconcerting, and confusing messages sent by the new environment. Arrival in the new land demands patience, flexibility, and strength to assimilate a new geography and the languages and customs of those who have come before. Even for those born here, the Natives and Inuit, the experience of "being here" has been troubled by the arrival of a domineering, consumption-based white culture which they have struggled to understand and, often, to resist. Thus, "being here," for new and old Canadians alike, is marked by an uncertainty that springs from common sources: the disruption of self-definition in an alien milieu; the anxiety of livelihood and economic loss; and the blight of prejudice and racial discrimination.

Self and environment are inseparable. In a strange or unfamiliar place, even the most flexible personalities may have difficulty trying to interpret and integrate the new information they receive all the time. As a consequence, their sense of identity becomes blurry, and personal as well as cultural self-definition may pose a serious problem. Richard G. Green, in "The Last Raven," explores the impact of white norms and values upon a group of Mohawk boys. In an episode of willful destruction carried out against nature, the boys disclose their confusion about the world that has estranged them from their Native roots, but not allowed their authentic identity to emerge. Markoosie, in his fictional adventure based on his experiences as a bush pilot in the Arctic, contrasts the means of survival used by Inuit and whites while struggling against the inhospitable climate of the north. The story suggests that two cultures may not easily share customs and technologies, but—at least in the emergency portrayed in "Wings of Mercy"—they can co-operate for a common cause. In "Indigo," Yeshim Ternar probes the isolation and dislocation the two characters—a white woman and a black man—feel when confronted with their environment in Montreal, the people around them, and even each other. Their lack of definition and purpose is reflected in the sterile futility of their lives and in their inability to communicate beyond the surface experience.

Having escaped the violence or poverty of their homelands, many immigrants suffer economic problems in the new land. They strive to regain what they have lost "at home" or to gain what they have never had before. From the time of Catharine Parr Traill on, Canada has been portrayed as a land of opportunity for the industrious and ingenious. The reality of "being here," of course, is usually different at the beginning: privation, frustration, and the struggle for livelihood where the old rules of economic success might not apply. In *The Russian Album*, Michael Ignatieff recounts the difficulties of a privileged Russian family whose social and economic base was shattered by the Bolshevik Revolution of 1917. He illustrates its bewildering effects upon his grandparents: the brief sojourn in England, the hopeful migration to Canada, and the struggles for security within the new country's borders. The fate of the Ignatieffs is only one example of thousands of families scattered by war and revolution. The Irish sought self-definition in the struggle against British dominion that led to the establishment of the Irish Free State in 1922. Their long history of repression and poverty has prompted many waves of emigration to the western hemisphere. Brian Moore describes the worries and pretenses of his fictional character, Ginger Coffey, trying to establish himself in Canada. The necessity to bolster his self-image and assure his economic survival finds Coffey on the edge of desperation in a new territory where the old ploys might not work. Not all the conflicts of adjustment result in despair, however. In "Doing Right," Austin Clarke uses humour to reveal the anxieties and ambitions of the West Indian community in downtown Toronto, its inner tensions, expressed in insecurity and competition, and its distrust of the urban white society.

Perhaps the worst consequence of "being here" for visible minorities is the outrage of racism. It has taken its toll among Canadians, whether Native, black, or Asian. What is only subtly implied by Yeshim Ternar, or humorously appraised by Austin Clarke, comes under open scrutiny in Rosemary Brown's and Joy Kogawa's writing. The effects of racism upon community and individual alike—systemic injustice, personal prejudice, economic and emotional anguish—are all explored candidly. Rosemary Brown's autobiography describes the discrimination she encountered during her first days in Montreal in the 1950s. Discrimination in accommodation, education, and the workplace angered Brown and without doubt contributed to her political activism. Joy Kogawa, widely known for her novel *Obasan*, illustrates a similar difficulty of "being here" experienced by the Japanese Canadians who were imprisoned or confined in internment camps during World War II. Along with many others who were wrongfully treated, Kogawa has struggled politically to redress the injury and redeem the memory of the victims. The last chapter of her new novel, *Itsuka*, shows the Canadian government accepting responsibility for its error and making its apology to its wronged citizens.

The texts in this unit, which attempts to classify some cultural frictions and anxieties, are necessarily a limited sampling. The variety of expression can never be exhausted as long as the manifold ways of "being here" continue to articulate themselves.

Chinese Wall Writings

Notice

Fellow countrymen, read the following notice quickly:
Having amassed several hundred dollars,
I left my native home for a foreign land.
To my surprise, I was kept inside a prison cell!
Alas, there is nowhere for me to go from here,
I can see neither the world outside nor my dear parents.
When I think of them, tears begin to stream down.
To whom can I confide my mournful sorrow,
But to etch in a few lines on this wall.

— Anonymous, from Beiyang, Xinhui County,
Guangdong Province

A Mr. Lee from Taishan County, Guangdong Province, carved a poem on a
wall on 4 September 1911

Sitting alone in the Customs office,
My heart aches.
Had I not been poor,
I would not have travelled far away from my home.
I went abroad upon my brother's advice.
The black devil here is ruthless,
He forces the Chinese to sweep and clean the floor.
Two meals a day are provided
But I wonder when I will be homeward bound.

An anonymous person wrote the following:

Deserting my parents, wife and children, I come to the Gold Mountain because I am poor. I remember their words that they have tried by various means to raise a thousand and some odd dollars for my passage. I have now safely arrived but unexpectedly the people here wanted to examine my eyes, forced me to strip to the waist and to take off my pants to lay bare my body. I have much been abused and insulted because China is weak and I am poor. I always think of my parents. My dear fellow countrymen, we should return home and help build our mother country strong and rich.

The sorrow and anger of the imprisoned immigrants were vividly expressed in their poems. The following one was written in 1919:

I have always yearned to reach for the Gold Mountain.
But instead, it is hell, full of hardship.
I was detained in a prison and tears rolled down my cheeks.
My wife at home is longing for my letter
Who can foretell when I will be able to return home?

Another poem reads as follows:

I am in prison because I covet riches.
Driven by poverty I sailed over here on the choppy sea.
If only I did not need to labour for money,
I would already have returned home to China.

The above inscriptions, hidden beneath layers of paint and whitewash, were discovered in November 1977, during the demolition of the Immigration Building in Victoria, B.C. Some messages were carved on the cell walls with a sharp point; other messages were written with pen and ink. Dr. David Chuenyan Lai, at that time a geographer at the University of Victoria, man-

aged to read the inscriptions and translate them into English. They were writ-ten in traditional verse forms or in running prose. Here they appear in free forms taken from Lai's article "A 'Prison' for Chinese Immigrants," The Asianadian, vol. 2, no. 4.

The Immigration Building was built in 1908, and over the years it served a number of purposes. At one time it included cells in which Chinese immi-grants were confined until their transit papers could be processed. The "wall writing" attests to the loneliness, humiliation, pride, ambition, and confusion of the immigrants. Each Chinese dreamed that Canada would be, for him, the Gim Shan *(Gold Mountain) where he could seek—and find—his fortune. In these cells each man could only dream.*

Richard G. Green

Richard G. Green was born in 1940 in Ohsweken, on the Grand River in Ontario; he is a Turtle clan Mohawk. A frequent contributor to short fiction anthologies and magazines, he is also an editor and cartoonist. He lives on the Six Nations Reserve, and his work appears regularly in Turtle Quarterly Magazine *and the* Brantford Expositor. *He also teaches Native Studies at Mohawk College in Brantford. In 1991, his book* The Last Raven: A Collection of Short Stories by a Mohawk Author *was published by Ricara Features, a publishing company he helped to organize as a Native communications project.*

The Last Raven

Looking at Dan and Nola Goupil, you'd never guess they're married. Not that they're unworthy but she's at least two heads taller which makes you wonder how they make out physically. They subtly administer the word of God each week, while we sit in a circle trying to overcome hardness of the high-backed wooden chairs. The circle is part of a continuing plot to get us closer to God, nature, and each other by moulding us into a team of young-adult Christians. Truth is, Sunday school attendance is mandatory to play on the hockey team, which is why I'm here.

When I adjust my tie clasp, my elbow presses against the flesh of a bare-armed girl sitting beside me. She brushes at the spot as if removing bacteria, folds her hands with kindergarten precision, and places them in her lap. She knows I'm Mohawk and I know that's why she brushed off her arm. Girls outnumber boys two-to-one in this class, and none of them drives you mad with desire.

"Well, Mr. Silverheels," Nola says, her voice one octave above a whisper in true Christian fashion. "What do you think the meaning of Christ's action toward the penitent woman at the home of Simon the Pharisee was?" Hanging *Mr.* and *Miss* to surnames is supposed to elevate us to adult status, though we're expected to call Dan and Nola by their given names. When the Goupils first arrived, I labelled this a get-acquainted trick, but I accept their eccentricities, though it's weird not being called Jim.

"What?" I say. "I . . . I don't think I heard the question." I glance toward Bill Shostrom, as he flashes a devilish smile. He slouches in his chair, the lapels of his blue suit flex into a diamond shape exposing the too short length of his polka-dotted tie. His punk hair is greasy with hair-goo, and a glimmer from the ceiling lamp reflects off his forehead. If you believe opposites attract, then you know why we're chums.

Tracking the direction of my eyes, Nola says: "Now don't you tell him the answer, Mr. Shostrom." The class laughs. She turns to the fat girl beside me, who's impatiently waving an arm.

"Yes, Miss Breen."

Miss Breen leaps to her feet. "I think it's a story to remind us that even though we're constantly submerged in sin," she says, confidence rampant in her tone, "Christ loves those who love." Satisfied with her brief moment of superiority, she directs a smirk toward me as she plops her oversized buttocks back into the chair.

"I disagree," I say. I'm not sure why this blurted out, but now I'm committed to explanation. I feel tension in the wily shifting of everybody's eyes.

Dan Goupil glares at me, and a nervous hush settles over the room. He never enters class discussion, but I can see he's interpreted my remark as an attack on his wife. He removes a handkerchief, holds his plastic-rimmed glasses toward the ceiling light, and huffs on the lenses. Wiping them with a fluid motion he says quietly, "Exactly what do you disagree with, Mr. Silverheels?" A smile curls his thin lips as he scans the class. "Surely you don't challenge the love of Jesus, eh?"

"No sir," I say.

"Well I'm glad to hear that." The class translates his actions, and, suddenly, I'm in a sea of snickering faces. "Well then, Mr. Silverheels." He puts on his glasses. "*What* do you disagree with?"

"It's just that . . . well, I uh, I don't think the love of Jesus is in question here. That's the constant theme of the New Testament and is indicated in many previous occasions. I think that, by forgiving this woman of all her sins, Christ is directing a lesson of humility toward Simon."

"Humility?"

"Yes. He's raised Mary Magdalen to a level of respectability above that of His host. He's used her to show Simon that her example of love makes her superior."

"You think Christ would *use* someone for His own gain?"

"In this case, yes."

All eyes rest upon Dan. It's plain that emphasis has shifted from correct and incorrect and is now a question of vanity. To these people, Christ is their saviour; to me, He's a prophet. I realize Dan's next statement decides the outcome. He glances at his wristwatch, and I'm reminded that it's almost time for dismissal. Perhaps I'll be saved by the bell.

Nola raises her eyes above an opened Bible. "Mr. Silverheels?" she asks. "What do you think Christ means when he says, "Therefore I tell you her sins, which are many, are forgiven for she loved much; but he who is forgiven little, loves little.'"

Dan brushes dandruff specs from his lapel. Simultaneously, shuffling feet and voices penetrate from the corridor outside. Looking at me, Dan says, "I think you've misconstrued the point of today's lesson . . ."

"Dan," Nola smiles. "I think you're *both* right." Everybody closes their Bible, with a thump. "Now class," Nola continues. "Before you all run off, don't forget our house-party this afternoon. We expect to have a lot of fun, and I pray none of you will miss it."

I stand and file toward the door, a feeling of betrayal welling up inside me. If the objective of this class is participation, why haven't I been shown any mercy? Passing Dan at the doorway, I smile meekly. He squeezes my shoulder and says, "See you this afternoon." But I'm unable to answer.

On our way home, Bill and me and a skinny kid named Hartman always stop at Gimpy's Diner. Our arrangement is we keep Gimpy's shovelled in winter and he lets us in on Sundays to play a pinball machine everybody calls "The Chief." Light the 975,000 point-feather, and with Gimpy's verification you get a dollar from the "Picnic Fund" jar. In three years of play, I've won twice.

"Are you going to the Goupils' this afternoon, Jim?" Hartmann stares at my reflection in the machine's glass panel.

"Not in a million years."

"What about you, Bill?"

"I dunno. I've got a lot of homework to do."

Hartman looks back at me. "What are you going to do?"

"I don't know," I say, tearing open my collection envelope.

"Hey," Bill says. "Your parents are supposed to take mine to a lacrosse game, eh? You're not going with them, are you?"

"No," I say. "The Warriors are in last place, and they'll probably lose again. I'll probably stay home and terrorize my sister."

"Get out of the way, amateurs." Bill squeezes between Hartmann and me. "Make way for the pro."

"Speaking of girls," Hartmann says, "maybe I'll go to the Goupils' party. Linda'll probably be there."

"Nola's kid sister?"

"Yeah."

Inserting a quarter into the slot, Bill says, "Don't tell me you're in love with Linda Switzer?" He pushes the coin-return button with the heel of his hand and takes out a jackknife. "Hey Gimpy," he works the blade into the slot. "This damn thing's jammed again!"

"I wouldn't say I was in *love* with her," Hartmann says.

Gimpy walks over, scratches his belly, and pounds on the machine. To Bill, he says, "I don't know why you're the one who always screws up this machine."

"Because he's just a big *screw*-up," I say, overcome with cleverness.

"When they get older, you gotta prime 'em a bit." Gimpy kicks the machine and the coin clicks inside. Lights flash. Bells clang. The caricature of an Indian in Sioux headdress swings his tomahawk and dances backward into starting position. "There. What did I tell ya, eh?" Gimpy winks and limps back to his cleaning chores.

"I wouldn't say I was in love with her," Hartmann repeats. "But if you guys aren't going to be doing anything," he cracks a knuckle, "then I'm going to the Goupils' party."

Bill launches his first ball. "Who says we're not going to be doing anything?" He pushes a flipper button, and a wave of satisfaction sweeps his face. "We're going to be shooting drunken crows this afternoon."

According to Bill's latest plan, after our parents leave for the lacrosse game, we're going to take our fathers' shotguns on a hunting trip. Bill says the radio reported that a flock of crows has been gathering on the edge of town menacing people for several days. Because of something called jurisdictional ingress and egress over the woods they're in, nobody can do anything about removing them.

"We're going to be big heroes, eh?" Bill says, as we leave Gimpy's. "We're going to do our duty and eliminate those hazardous crows. Meet you at the bridge at two o'clock."

When my parents leave the house, my older sister curls up on the sofa and flashes her beady eyes. "*Sehksatiyohake Senta: whah,*" she says in Mohawk. She does this to aggravate me. We left the reserve when I was three, and my family seldom speaks Mohawk here in Brantford. Sometimes, when the house is full of visitors, she gets everybody going and there's a point where they all look at me and laugh. But she can't fool me. She wants me out of the house this afternoon, so she can cuddle with her boyfriend.

She's hovering around me like a fruit fly on a puckered apple, and it's impossible to get the shotgun from my parents' closet. To avoid suspicion, I put on my new maroon windbreaker and depart for the woods in street shoes.

I'm first to arrive. I sit on my favourite girder at the railway bridge listening to creek water gurgle far below. To the west, a band of nimbus gathers on the horizon, promising rain. Bill and Hartmann laugh while they goose-step the railroad ties, gleaming shotgun barrels propped between body and forearm. Bill wears a red plaid jacket and a ludicrous straw hat, whose front brim is folded flat; "BILL" is inscribed there in red paint. Two ragged pheasant feathers jut from a hatband, denoting hunting prowess. Hartmann's olive jacket has "SMITH" in stencil letters above his left breast pocket. They both notice I don't have a shotgun, but say nothing.

I step atop a gleaming rail and gingerly keep their pace, my shoes making a tap-dancer sound. We hike down the straight tracks, grateful that railroads always take the shortest, most private routes. I've never seen more than two crows in the same place at one time and believe Bill's story to be false. We turn and cross a field, their heavy boots clearing a path for me through chest-high thistles.

We march toward a stand of hemlock when Bill signals a halt. From an opening beyond us, I hear a confused hum of shufflings and scattered caws. Perched amid saplings and clusters of lobe-leafed bushes, crows occupy the centre of a U-shaped clearing. Bill and me are going to circle, leaving Hartmann stationed at the opening to block any escape attempts. To the northwest, the woods thicken, and, when we reach our position, the crows are between us and a barrier of trees.

Bill hands me a yellow box of shells and we begin. Each squawk, each shriek intensifies, and it's plain we've been detected. It's so noisy I'm forced to cover an ear.

A sea of bobbing heads covers the ground like a rippling stadium tarpaulin. Branches bend in smooth arcs to accommodate squawking occupants. The crows compete for tiny red berries; they rape the bushes and peck each other in rages of greed. One bird leaps from his branch, frantically beats his wings, and flutters to the ground. These birds aren't drunk as Bill reported; most are too bloated to fly. Smaller crows retreat to the woods beyond, but the majority continue their indulgence in spite of our presence.

Bill inserts two shells into his double-barrelled shotgun and closes it with a snap. Signalling Hartmann, he drops to one knee, cocks the hammer, and aims into a crowded sapling. I've been instructed to pass two shells into his palm and stand clear when spent castings are ejected. One hundred metres away, Hartmann slams the breech of his gun closed and raises its barrel in readiness. It's clear we've entered a world not intended for humans.

Bill's first blast shatters the air; my eardrums ring in response. Again he cocks, sights, and squeezes the trigger. *Boom!* He breaks the gun, and two casings spiral to the ground; a stench of sulphur bites my nostrils. "Shells!" he yells. I slap two cylinders into his opened palm, like an intern assisting at surgery. An unexpected blast from Hartmann's direction makes me flinch. Bill smiles.

Fluttering and squawking, the crows are in chaos. Their numbers work against them, wings become entangled, foiling attempts to fly. Where Bill has fired into loaded branches, twin holes poke through the blackness. Leaning forward, he aims at the base of a crowded bush. *Boom!* His body jerks up with the recoil of the gun. In its panic, one crow hovers above us. It flaps its wings to escape, but Bill blows it into an inkblot of swirling feathers. "Shells!" Bill shouts, waving away down-fluff. I barely hear him through the liquid hum in my ears.

Some of the crows fall to the ground, others scurry through the grass toward Hartmann. Some flap their wings, crane their necks, and scold, but remain imprisoned in their branches. Hartmann concentrates his blasts on those who manage flight, his left arm pumping with mechanical precision. Bill can hit three crows with one barrage. It's evident from his cursing that he considers it a miss if only one falls. Hartmann lowers his weapon at the black army advancing toward him. His first explosion pours through their ranks like a splash of soapy water on a ship-deck, lifting and transporting those in its wake.

Drops of rain hiss against Bill's hot gun barrel, but he continues his shooting oblivious of weather conditions. "Shells!" he yells, blowing at smoke billowing from the breech.

A thunderclap booms across the terrain. The OPP must be on their way. "It's starting to rain!" I shout, relieved at the possibility of leaving.

"Good," Bill says. "It'll muffle our shots." I hear the clink of shell casings dropping into a pile at my feet. "Come on, we've got to chase them toward Hartmann!" We advance, Bill firing once every three strides. It's like walking through a ploughed field, clods of black bodies occasionally squishing under our feet, the sensation plastic and awkward,

A crow deliriously wanders about the ground, dragging a broken wing. I stoop, hypnotized by its misery. It trips and falls forward on its side, desperately clawing at the earth for traction. I reach to help, but it pops its smooth head between twisted wing feathers into a contorted position of defence. Eyes shrivelling with betrayal, it arches its neck to peck my hand. Instead, its eyelids squeeze shut, muscles relax, and it rolls over on its back. An eyelid pops open and an empty black sphere gazes at me. I scoop up cartridges from the shell box. I drop them into my pocket, and tear the cardboard into a sheet. Covering the crow's body, I marvel at its design, reminded that things intended for a simpler function can be separated so easily from it.

When we rendezvous with Hartmann, a squadron of crows approaches head-on as if in attack formation. They are flying at eye level, their silhouettes barely visible against the backdrop of trees. In his haste to reload, Bill grabs a jammed shell casing and burns his fingertips. "Damn it," he winces. "Quick, Jim, gimmie two more shells!" He loads, waits for Hartmann and takes aim.

Their first volley flashes with the ferocity of a howitzer; two crows erased in the blink of an eye. Bill's second shot hits its target, too, but the bird's inertia carries it into his chest. Bill pushes it to the ground and squashes it with his boot. Hartmann's second burst is true, and the largest crow, bomber-sized in comparison to the others, dives to the ground. Watching the crows falling like black snowflakes, I'm amazed at Bill's and Hartmann's skill at killing. Two crows peel off in an escape manoeuvre, but Hartman's capable pump gun sweeps them into obscurity.

"We got 'em, Hartmann! We got every one of them!" Bill pushes his hat back. "Did you see how beautiful that big one rolled off and dove to the ground? Just like a Snowbird."

"Guess what, Bill? " Hartmann inspects his remaining ammo. "I hit that big one with my deer slug. You remember that deer slug I showed you?"

Bill nods. He blows at blue smoke rising from his barrels. "Heh, Jim." He slides a shell into the left chamber. "I want you to hit that crow in the tree over there." He closes the gun with a snap of authority and offers it to me.

I had hoped that Bill, consumed in his frenzy, would forget about my participation. Yet, like a substitute player sitting on the bench, I've been rehearsing all afternoon. "I'm not a very good shot," I say, not really wanting to be heard.

"Take it," Bill thrusts the weapon into my hands. "And don't miss."

I plant my feet, pull back the hammer, and raise the barrel. Raindrops poke at the shoulders of my jacket; one ricochets off the stock and splashes into my eye. I squeeze my eyelid, accept the brief sting, and shake my head. Bill sighs impatiently. Raising the front sight into the crotch of the v, I fix it on the silhouette beyond. My target twists its neck in puppet fashion against the pink colourings of the uncertain sky. I hunch my shoulder, tighten my grip, close my eyes, and pull the trigger. *Boom!*

"You missed!" Bill grabs the gun, breaks it open, blows at the chamber, and inserts one shell. "You don't sight a shotgun, stupid.

You aim it with both eyes open. And don't pull the trigger, squeeze it." Bill hands me the gun. "Don't miss this time—this is the last one."

I wipe my brow, seat the gun butt against my shoulder, and pull the hammer back, I take a deep breath, raise the barrel, and sight according to Bill's advice. Suddenly, the crow kicks away, flaps its wings, and climbs toward the horizon. I follow it and calculate its path. Hatred in the dying crow's eye nags my mind, but it's erased by my passion for success. Squeezing the trigger, I can almost see the pellet pattern sink into the feathers. "I got him," I say, exhaling. Wings spread like sagging semaphores, the crow glides down breast first, bouncing in slow motion as it hits the ground. I feel a surge of triumph. I try to push my face into a smile.

Bill slaps my shoulders. "Nice shooting," he says, taking the gun.

Sheets of rain force us into the woods seeking shelter, but sunbeams isolate the clouds and begin melting them. Each imprisoned with our own thoughts, we view black specks dotting the landscape. Blotches of blood coating tree branches, bushes, and grass begin washing away. Divots in the ground smooth their sores. Severed branches remain, permanent scars to today's memory.

When sunlight finally blasts through, we cross the open peninsula toward the tracks, the ground sucking at our feet. Bill ransacks the largest black feathers and adds them to his hatband, his singed fingertips provoking an occasional grimace. In a show of humanity, Hartmann plods across the field, finishing off dying survivors with his gun butt. I pick up a shell casing and blow on its open end, the lonely whistle recalling the dead crow's eye and its echo of emptiness.

Beneath the bridge, I wash mud from my shoes with a gnarled twig. I notices a brown spatter of blood on my pant leg. It's partially dry, and I splash cold creek water on it to prevent a stain. Gusts of wind, already frigid, push at bushes along the bank sending messages of winter to those who are listening. I gaze at Bill and his Medusa-like headdress. A felling of sardonic ridicule blossoms inside me, but humility pacifies the notion.

TOPICS FOR EXPLORATION

1. What do Dan and Nola Goupil represent for Jim Silverheels, the young Mohawk? Why does Jim feel betrayed by the Goupils when his interpretation of a Biblical passage is ignored?

2. Do you see any symbolic meaning in the argument between a Native boy and white missionaries over the message of love and humility conveyed by the story of Mary Magdalen? What do "love" and "humility" represent in the context of the encounter between Native and white cultures?

3. What is the significance of the crow-hunting expedition? What is the symbolism of this slaughter? How does Jim feel about the dying birds? What is the importance of the crow killing in the context of the Biblical discussion?

4. How does Jim Silverheels see himself as an outsider not only in the schoolroom, but also among his friends? What are the reasons for his alienation?

5. The narrator feels a sense of betrayal for the second time in the forest, when he contemplates the bird massacre. Interpret the reference to "humility" repeated in the last sentence of the story.

Michael Ignatieff

Michael Ignatieff was born in 1947; he has studied at Harvard and King's College, Cambridge. He lives in England and works for the BBC as a writer and host of programs, and is the author of drama for screen and television. His books include The Needs of Strangers *(1985), a study of social ethics, and* Asya *(1991), a spy thriller. This excerpt derives from* The Russian Album *(1987), which won the Royal Society of Literature Award in 1988. In 1917, the Russian monarchy was toppled by revolution and, with thousands of others of the privileged classes, Ignatieff's family fled to western Europe to escape the Bolshevik terror and to rebuild their lives in a new context.* The Russian Album *is Ignatieff's analysis of the émigré phenomenon, centring on several generations of his own family.*

from The Russian Album

Her oldest boys were growing up fast. They towered over her, her five sons, each thin as a rail, each over six feet, loud-voiced, ebullient, melancholy and high-minded like their father. She called them her *durachki*—her little fools. As they became men she teased the seriousness out of them as best she could. She would introduce Nick in company as 'my eldest, in comparison to whom Napoleon was a mere nonentity'. And Vladimir, with his dangling arms, vast drooping face and lop-sided grin, she would call 'my little wood violet'. They all had nicknames: Alec was Seyka, Lionel was Lino and George, her youngest, she called Giesenka.

Exile drew her closer to them. In the Caucuses they had seen her transformed into their 'tigress'. Now, greying and in her fifties, she sewed their buttons and kept aside special treats for them when they came home from school, from university, from their first jobs. She cooked and washed for them and became, as she had never been before, the physical heart of their world. And before every journey she would ask them, 'Have to seen to your digestions?'

She and Paul had drummed it into the boys that the past was past and that they must not end up like so many émigrés driving taxis and keeping their bags packed for the return journey to Petersburg. Alec, the family rebel and tease, most like his mother in looks, was the first to leave. In Kislovodsk he had become fascinated with geology and in England completed a degree at the Royal School of Mines. Soon he was off to Sierra Leone to work as an engineer in a gold mine. Nick, the family dreamer and philosopher, wanted to be a writer but his father insisted that he get a degree in something practical, so Nick soldiered his way through a degree in electrical engineering at the University of London. Blanching at the thought of settling in to suburban life, Nick answered an advertisement in a paper offering free passage, board and lodging to harvesters in Canada, and in 1924 set out for northern Alberta. Dima soon joined him, lured by Nick's promise of a job at a lumber camp making railway ties. Nick was a fantasist and Dima discovered when he arrived that there was no tie camp and no job. But they stuck it out harvesting and homesteading in the cold northern plains of Alberta.

Dima came back to England in the autumn of 1927, strong and sunburned, with stories of riding the boxcars and working in the endless fields of the prairies which reminded him of the vast plenty of old Russia. Paul was away all that winter of 1927–28 collecting money for the Red Cross and Dima ran the farm with Natasha while the younger boys, Lionel and George, completed their year at St Paul's. By the spring of 1928, Dima was determined to sell the farm. Milk prices were falling and the farm was too small to be profitable. Some of his former teachers from agricultural college came up to inspect the place and told him it was a lovely family home but hopeless as a commercial proposition. So the twenty-three-year-old Dima ordered the farm to be sold and wired his father when the deed was done. What is more, he told his father he was taking his mother and George and Lionel to Canada. If that was the case, his father replied, then he would stay on in Paris working for the Red Cross.

To this day, Dima's decision arouses passions. For Dima, the matter was straightforward: if the farm was losing money, it had to be sold. For George and Lionel, who could only dimly remember Russia as a place of terror and deprivation, Beauchamps was the only home they had ever known. Torn between a son who was certain the family would go under unless it made a break for Canada and a husband who was spending more and more time in the émigré world of Paris, Natasha decided in favour of her son. George and Lionel watched as the family wrenched itself apart. In the early summer of 1928, after the house and farm had been sold, Dima called in the auctioneers to sell off the contents of Beauchamps. The valuers came through the house and put together a catalogue and then a crowd assembled on the lawn and the bidding began. As the hammer rapped down, George and Lionel and Natasha watched their furniture being carted off and the farm animals put into other men's halters and led away. Their own remaining possessions, a tiny heap of clothes and some Russian treasures, were piled once again into Natasha's trousseau trunk and shipped down to Southampton where in September 1928 it was loaded on board the steamship *Montrose*, bound for Montreal. When the ship sailed, George, then fifteen, crawled into bed and held his mother tight to stop her from crying.

They travelled on Nansen passports, issued to stateless refugees. Lionel's and George's were stamped with a Canadian visa admitting them as agricultural labourers. When they landed in Montreal, Dima took George's boater and chucked it into the St Lawrence. 'You won't need that here!' he boomed.

Dima settled them into a cold-water flat in the Victoria Apartments in east-end Montreal. The winter of 1928–29 was a low ebb for Natasha. The money trickled away in that wretched bug-ridden apartment in the icy foreign city, and she was reduced to taking the streetcar down to Bonsecours market to bargain for cheap vegetables to feed her boys. But no matter how little money there was, she sent them to an exclusive private school, Lower Canada College. In order to pay for her sons' education, she gave up spending on herself and began gambling the money from the sale of the farm in penny mining stocks. She entered her sixtieth year, gaunt and bony with deep circles under her eyes, always dressed in the same severe ankle-length black dress fastened at the neck with one of her mother's brooches. Sometime that year Nick came back from Alberta with his fiancée, the daughter of Judge Woods from Edmonton. She remembered meeting Natasha in that dark, narrow apartment in the east end and thinking she was the most mournful and lonesome creature she had ever met in her life.

After a miserable year at school, George set off for the west coast in the spring of 1929 to find a summer job on the railways. At Grand Central Station in Montreal, Natasha pressed twenty-five dollars into his hand and warned him in her inimitable way that if he got mixed up with 'loose women' his nose would fall off. He was just sixteen and he worked all summer as an axeman on the shores of Kootenay Lake in British Columbia, cutting trees and making stakes for the right-of-way for a railbed linking the Crow's Nest pass with the Kettle Valley Railway line into Vancouver. The railbed skirted the canyon walls of the lake and an axeman had to master his trade one step from a fatal fall. George shed his St Paul's School diction for bunkhouse slang; he picked up an impressive scar on his knee during a duel of axe-throwing with an Irishman and he learned how to fight back when his mates dumped him, bedding and all, into the mountain stream at the back of the camp.

There is a picture in Natasha's album of George on the railbed at the edge of Kootenay Lake that summer of 1929. He has knotted a handkerchief and put it on his head against the heat and he is wearing a work-shirt, jeans and heavy boots. He is arm in arm with two of his workmates and he looks as tough and as happy as they do. They called him the Douk, because the only Russians they had ever met were Doukhobours, members of the reclusive religious sect who had emigrated from Russia and moved into the remote valleys of British Columbia. His boss spent his evenings going through volumes of the *Encyclopedia Britannica*, and one evening came across the article on George's grandfather, Nicholas Ignatieff. When he asked his young axeman whether they were related, George realized he was happier to be thought a decent axeman than to be a count. He came back to Montreal in the autumn, fired up as his brothers had been with the magic of the west and the feeling that he had proved himself.

Fortunately the stock-market crash of October 1929 saved him from having to return to the pickled gentility of Lower Canada College. Natasha had been trying to stretch their money by buying stocks and when the market collapsed the capital from the sale of Beauchamps was halved. By this time Nick had a job as an electrical engineer with Ontario Hydro and at his instigation the family moved to a rented farmhouse in Thornhill on the northern outskirts of Toronto. The Depression brought the family back together. Dima, who had been homesteading in the Peace River country in northern Alberta, lost his farm to a hailstorm and returned to Toronto to work as a junior instructor in soils chemistry at the University of Toronto. It was his salary that kept the family going in 1930 and 1931.

Then in 1932, Paul arrived from Paris after four years away. The Depression had dried up charitable sources for the Russian Red Cross and so his work had slowed to a trickle. He was now sixty-two and after four years in the little room at the Hôtel Ramsès in the Square des Batignolles it was time to come home. What part he had played in the émigré politics of Paris, that tangled milieu of White plotters and Red *agents provocateurs*, he kept to himself. How Paul explained his absence, how Natasha took him back, neither ever said. They made some sort of peace between themselves and settled into a succession of houses the boys rented for them in Toronto. In the photographs, they always stand a distance apart: he in his rakish fedora, his face a mask of cool charm with the hint of a smile beneath his sweeping moustache; she stooped, squinting, smiling back at the camera, with the choker around her neck and the same spare black dress.

In 1936, Dima found them some land in Upper Melbourne, a small pulp town on the St Francis River in the Eastern Townships south of Montreal, and Paul supervised the building of a little brick two-bedroomed cottage with a screen porch and a high gabled roof to plane away the snow. It stood among the dark pines above the river and they settled in to raise vegetables, to grow a garden and to await the arrival of grandchildren. Natasha continued to play the stock market on the quiet, determined to recoup the losses of 1929. Soon the drawers of her desk were full of prospectuses from companies like White Lake Gold and Porcupine Silver.

George went on a Rhodes Scholarship to Oxford in 1936. His parents did not want him to go, fearing he would be lost to them by settling in England. But his father presented him with General Ignatieff's gold watch and saw him off on the boat. Lionel went to law school at McGill.

In this new country, whose winters recalled their own, whose immensity brought back that lost immensity of their own, Paul and Natasha took out papers of citizenship and were at last able to consign their Nansen passports, emblems of homelessness, to the attic. They were too old by then to shed their accents or to take up new lives but they never tried to clamp their children within an émigré ghetto or to insist on Russian brides. All but one of the sons married outside the Russian circle. When Marjorie Adams, Florence Hargreaves, Helen Fraser and Alison Grant came into the family they stood uncomprehendingly through their own weddings at the Russian church. One by one the diamond stars on the necklace the Sultan of Turkey had given the boys' grandmother were taken off and passed along the chain of a now Canadian family. Natasha and Paul bade them all welcome to the family, she with her Garbo voice, he with his courtly attention to the feminine. The Canadian daughters had to get accustomed to Russian directness about all the things which good Canadian Protestants never mentioned in company: digestion, money and grief. These Canadian brides learned how to cook Russian dishes and listened to stories of Kislovodsk and Kroupodernitsa for clues to their husbands' moods—melancholic, hysterical, passionate and withdrawn by turns. All of the sons sought strength and practicality in their wives; they searched for and found in them also their own mother's wry irony.

In September 1939, Nick and Dima enlisted and by 1940 were with the Canadian army in England. Alec was managing explosive factories there, and George was already a junior foreign service officer at Canada House in London. Only Lionel remained behind finishing law school at McGill, living with his parents in the little bungalow in Upper Melbourne, Quebec.

It was some time in the summer of 1940, with her boys overseas and her first grandchildren just arrived, that Natasha began typing out her memoirs in the little wood-panelled bedroom at the back of the bungalow. Paul had written his own memoirs years before in England. He wrote for a public audience; she wrote for the children and grandchildren. My boys, she said, tell me I have a 'special vivid manner of expressing myself. Having no pretension to authorship, I just do it to please my boys.' She enjoyed herself that summer. Memory, she said, 'quite flew me back to my happy past'.

She used any old scrap of paper she could find—children's exercise books purchased at the Rexall drugstore in town, recipe cards, the back of grocery lists. She typed with two fingers, ignoring punctuation, writing as she spoke, in the English she had learned from governesses at Doughino, the English she knew her grandchildren would grow up speaking as their mother tongue. Back and forth across the years she scavenged, retrieving whatever she could from the darkness. The snow piled high outside in the long winters of the war. She and Paul sat by the fireplace in the sitting room listening to the radio for news of the battles. By 1943, Dima was a chemical warfare officer with the Canadian troops at the battle of Monte Cassino, and Paul and Natasha followed the news of the Italian campaign with painful attention. They listened for all bulletins about Russia, their hearts aching at the names of each town that fell.

I have a picture of them taken by Lionel in the winter of 1944. They are standing outside the cottage in Upper Melbourne, side by side in the snow on a cold winter's afternoon. They are bundled up in long winter coats that seem to pull them down into the earth. Natasha is smiling in the squinting quizzical way of hers. Her grey hair is pulled back in an untidy chignon and her long straight neck is enclosed in a black choker. Her knees are slightly bent and turned inwards, which gives her stance the awkwardness of a shy girl. Paul is standing a fraction apart, elegant as always with an astrakhan perched on his head, a carefully knotted tie and twirled moustaches. The sockets of his eyes are dark and the ridges of his cheekbones are sharp and exposed. He is not smiling. They are both wearing bedroom slippers and they stand on the flagstones, little dry islands in an expanse of white snow. Spring is months off; the darkness will soon close about the house. It is the last picture in the album.

TOPICS FOR EXPLORATION

1. In this exploration of his family history, what audience does Ignatieff have in mind? What is the purpose of studying his genealogy? What role do the old photographs from the family album play in his narrative? Why does Ignatieff focus his discussion on the mother? Is it an effective strategy?

2. Why do the émigré parents insist that "the past was past"? How important has the family past actually turned out to be for their survival in the New World?

3. What difficulties does the immigrant family face in Montreal? What jobs to the sons take in order to make a living? What keeps the family members together?

4. What similarities does the family find between Canada and Russia? What differences? How must the wives of Natasha's sons adjust to the Russian traditions?

5. In the family archives, two kinds of documents can be seen as emblems of the successive stages of their migration: the Nansen passports (issued to refugees by the League of Nations) and the Canadian citizenship papers. Explain the differences between the conditions of exile and immigration they represent.

6. In a few pages, Ignatieff describes the lives of his grandparents and their children, through the émigré years in England, the Depression in Canada, and the war in Europe. What does this brief panorama of émigré life between the wars tell his readers? Is it effective?

Brian Moore

Brian Moore was born in Northern Ireland in 1921, and in 1948 he emigrated to Canada where he worked as a journalist. He now lives in California. His many novels—including The Luck of Ginger Coffey, The Lonely Passion of Judith Hearne, Catholics, The Great Victorian Collection, The Doctor's Wife, Cold Heaven, The Colour of Blood, Black Robe, *among others—have won numerous awards in Canada, The United States, and Britain; many of them have been made into critically acclaimed films. The following excerpt comes from* The Luck of Ginger Coffey, *first published in 1960, which reflects some of Moore's own experiences as an immigrant in Canada.*

from The Luck of Ginger Coffey

Outside in the refrigerated air, snow fine as salt drifted off the tops of sidewalk snowbanks, spiraling up and over to the intersection where a policeman raised his white mitt paw, halting traffic to let Coffey cross. Coffey wagged the policeman the old salute in passing. By J, they were like Russkis in their black fur hats. It amused him now to think that, before he came out here, he had expected Montreal would be a sort of Frenchy place. French my foot! It was a cross between America and Russia. The cars, the supermarkets, the hoardings; they were just as you saw them in the Hollywood films. But the people and the snow and the cold—that woman passing, her head tied up in a babushka, feet in big bloothers of boots, and her dragging the child along behind her on a little sled—wasn't that the real Siberian stuff?

"*M'sieur?*"

The other people at the bus stop noticed that the little boy was not wearing his snow suit. But Coffey did not. "Well, Michel," he said. "Come to see me off?"

"Come for candy."

"Now, there's a straight answer, at least," Coffey said, putting his arm around the boy's shoulders and marching him off to the candy store on the corner. "Which sort takes your fancy, Michel?"

The child picked out a big plastic package of sourballs. "This one, *M'sieur*?"

"Gob stoppers," Coffey said. "The exact same thing I used to pick when I was your age. Fair enough." He handed the package over and asked the storeman how much.

"Fifty cents."

By J, it was not cheap. Still, he couldn't disappoint the kid, so he paid, led his friend outside, waited for the policeman to halt traffic, then sent Michel on his way. "Remember," he said, "that's a secret. Don't tell anybody I bought them."

"Okay. *Merci, M'sieur*."

Coffey watched him run, then rejoined the bus queue. He hoped Veronica wouldn't find out about those sweets, for it would mean another lecture about wasting his money on outsiders. But ah! Coffey remembered his boyhood, the joys of a penny paper twist of bullseyes. He smiled at the memory and discovered that the girl next to him in the queue thought he was smiling at her. She smiled back and he gave her the eye. For there was life in the old carcass yet. Yes, when the good Lord was handing out looks, Coffey considered he had not been last in line. Now, in his prime, he considered himself a fine big fellow with a soldierly straightness to him, his red hair thick as ever and a fine mustache to boot. And another thing. He believed that clothes made the man and the man he had made of himself was a Dublin squire. Sports clothes took years off him, he thought, and he always bought the very best of stuff. As he rode downtown on the bus that morning there wasn't a soul in Montreal who would say There goes a man who's out of work. . . . Not on your earthly. Not even when he went through the doorway of the Unemployment Insurance Commission and marched right up to *Executive & Professional*, which seemed the right place for him.

"Fill it out the table over there, Mr. Coffey," said the counter clerk. Nice young fellow, no hint of condescension in his tone, very helpful and natural as though this sort of thing happened to everyone. Still, pen in hand, *write in block letters or type*, Coffey was faced once again with the misleading facts of a life. In block letters, he began:

Born: May 14, 1916, DUBLIN, IRELAND.
Education: PLUNKET SCHOOL, DUBLIN. NATIONAL UNIVERSITY OF IRELAND, UNIVERSITY COLLEGE, DUBLIN.
Specify degrees, honors, other accomplishments: [He had not finished his B.A., but never mind.] BACHELOR OF ARTS . . .[Pass.] 1938.

List former positions, giving dates, names of employers, etc.: [Flute! Here we go.]

IRISH ARMY. 1939–1945. ASST. TO PRESS OFFICER, G.H.Q. COMMISSIONED 2ND LIEUT. 1940; 1ST LIEUT. 1942.

KYLEMORE DISTILLERIES, DUBLIN. 1946–1948, SPECIAL ASSISTANT TO MANAGING DIRECTOR, 1949–1953, ASSISTANT IN ADVERTISING DEPARTMENT.

COOMB-NA-BAUN KNITWEAR, CORK. 1953–1955, SPECIAL ASSISTANT.

COOTEHILL DISTILLERIES, DUBLIN.
COOMB-NA-BAUN KNITWEAR, DUBLIN.
DROMORE TWEEDS, CARRICK-ON-SHANNON.
} AUGUST 1955–DECEMBER 1955 SPECIAL REPRESENTATIVE FOR CANADA

List Present Position:

[His position as of this morning, January 2, 1956, was null and bloody void, wasn't it? So he put a line through that one. Then he read it all over, absent-mindedly brushing the ends of his mustache with the pen. He signed with a large, much-practiced signature.]

The wooden plaque in front of the young man who looked over his application bore the name J. DONNELLY. And naturally J. Donnelly, like all Irish Canadians, noticed Coffey's brogue and came out with a couple of introductory jokes about the Ould Sod. But the jokes weren't half as painful as what came after them.

"I see you have your B.A., Mr. Coffey. Have you ever considered teaching as a profession? We're very short of teachers here in Canada."

"Holy smoke," said Coffey, giving J. Donnelly an honest grin. "That was years ago. Sure, I've forgotten every stitch."

"I see," J. Donnelly said. "But I'm not quite clear why you've put down for a public relations job? Apart from your—ah—Army experience, that is?"

"Well now," Coffey explained, "My work over here as Canadian representative for those three firms you see there, why that was all promotion. Public relations, you might call it."

"I see. . . . But, frankly, Mr. Coffey, I'm afraid that experience would hardly qualify you for a public relations position. I mean, a senior one."

There was a silence. Coffey fiddled with the little brush dingus in his hat. "Well now, look here," he began. "I'll put my cards on the table, Mr. Donnelly. Those firms that sent me out here wanted me to come back to Ireland when they gave up the North American market. But I said no. And the reason I said no is because I thought Canada was the land of opportunity. Now, because of that, because I want to stay, no matter what, well, perhaps I'll have to accept a more junior position here than what I was used to at home. Now, supposing you make me an offer, as the girl said to the sailor?"

But J. Donnelly offered only a polite smile.

"Or—perhaps if there's nothing in public relations, you might have some clerical job going?"

"Clerical, Mr. Coffey?"

"Right."

"Clerical isn't handled in this department, sir. This is for executives. Clerical is one floor down."

"Oh."

"And at the moment, sir, ordinary clerical help is hard to place. However, if you want me to transfer you?"

"No, don't bother," Coffey said. "There's nothing in public relations, is there?"

J. Donnelly stood up. "Well, if you'll just wait, I'll check our files. Excuse me."

He went out. After a few minutes a typewriter began to clacket in the outer office. Coffey shuffled his little green hat and deerskin gauntlets until J. Donnelly returned. "You might be in luck, Mr. Coffey," he said. "There's a job just come in this morning for assistant editor on the house organ of a large nickel company. Not your line exactly, but you might try it?"

What could Coffey say? He was no hand at writing. Still, needs must and he had written a few Army releases in his day. He accepted the slip of paper and thanked the man. "I'll phone them and tell them you'll be on deck at eleven," J. Donnelly said. "Strike while the iron's hot, eh? And here's another possibility, if the editor job doesn't work out." He handed over a second slip of paper. "Now, if nothing comes of either of those," he said, "come back here and I'll transfer you to clerical, okay?"

Coffey put the second slip in his doeskin waistcoat and thanked the man again.

"Good luck," J. Donnelly said. "The luck of the Irish, eh, Mr. Coffey?"

"Ha, ha," Coffey said, putting on his little hat. Luck of the Canadians would suit him better, he thought, Still, it was a start. Chin up! Off he sloped into the cold morning and pulled out the first slip to check on the address. On Beaver Hall Hill, it was. Up went his hand to signal a taxi, but down it came when he remembered the fourteen dollars left in his pocket. If he hurried, he could walk it.

Or shanks' mare it, as his mother used to say. Ah, what's the sense giving Ginger any money for his tram, she'd say; he'll never use it. Doesn't he spend every penny on some foolishness the minute you put it in his pocket? And it was true, then as now. He was no great hand with money. He thought of himself in those far-off days, hurrying to school, the twopence already spent in some shop, whirling the satchel of schoolbooks around his head, stopping at Stephen's Green to take out his ruler and let it go tickety, tak, tak, among the railings of the park. Dreaming then of being grown up; free of school and catechism; free from exams and orders; free to go out into a great world and find adventures. Shanks' mare now along Notre Dame Street, remembering: the snow beginning to fall, a melting frost changing gray fieldstone office fronts to the color of a dead man's skin, hurrying as once he had hurried to school. But this was not school. School was thirty years ago and three thousand miles away, across half a frozen continent and the whole Atlantic Ocean. Why, even the time of day was different from at home. Here it was not yet midmorning and there, in Dublin, the pubs would be closing after lunch. It made him homesick to think of those pubs, so he must not think. No, for wasn't he at long last an adventurer, a man who had gambled all on one horse, a horse colored Canada, which now by hook or crook would carry him to fame and fortune? Right, then!

So shanks' mare he went across Place d'Armes under the statue of Maisonneuve, an adventurer and a gambler too, who had sailed out in sixteen forty-one to discover this promised land, and shanks' mare past the Grecian columns of a bank and do not think what's left in there, but shanks' mare alone up Craig Street, remembering that he was far away now from the wireless network of friends and relations who, never mind, they would not let you starve so long as you were one of them but who, if you left home, struck out on your own, crossed the seas, well, that was the end of you as far as they were concerned.

And shanks' mare up Beaver Hall Hill, last lap, all on his onlie-oh, remembering that any man who ever amounted to anything was the man who took a chance, struck out, *et cetera*.

But oh! he was close to the line today. Only he knew how close.

TOPICS FOR EXPLORATION

1. In this excerpt from his novel, Brian Moore gives us a glimpse into the mind and attitudes of Ginger Coffey. In your opinion, is Ginger Coffey a candidate to be a successful immigrant? Why or why not?

2. Why does Coffey buy expensive candy for Michel, the neighbourhood boy? What does this episode reveal about Coffey's character?

3. Why does Coffey consider the information on his résumé to be "the misleading facts of a life?" When executive positions seem scarce, why does Coffey inquire about a clerical job?

4. How is the use of language and humour in this brief fragment a reflection of Ginger's personality?

5. How does Moore show us the anxiety of his immigrant? Why has Coffey "gambled all on one horse, a horse colored Canada"? Summarize Ginger's attitude about Canada?

Rosemary Brown

Rosemary Brown was born in Jamaica in 1930; she came to Canada in 1950. A social activist and feminist scholar, she was involved in volunteer work and professional counselling for women and children; she also taught Women's Studies at Simon Fraser University. She was the first black woman to be elected to the British Columbia Legislature (1972). She has participated in national and international conferences on peace and human rights. She has often appeared on television; in 1987 she hosted a TV Ontario series, Women and Politics. *The following excerpt comes from her autobiography,* Being Brown: A Very Public Life *(1989), where she shares the story of her political career and private life as a struggle for dignity and human rights.*

from Being Brown

Living in Montreal, even in the relative seclusion of Royal Victoria College, the women's residence at McGill University, brought me my first contact with racism, Canadian-style. I had been raised on a diet of poems and stories about the oppression of being Black in the United States, but always there was the rider that Canada was different. Indeed, my family thought that by sending me to university in Canada they were guaranteeing that I would not have to deal with what they referred to as the 'ugliness' of prejudice while receiving a reasonably good education (not as good as I would have received in England, but certainly superior to anything offered in the United States).

I must confess that the graduates of McGill, Dalhousie and the University of Toronto I met before leaving Jamaica fed the myth of a discrimination-free Canada by never mentioning prejudice. They spoke glowingly of their Canadian friends, indulgently of their Canadian professors and lovingly of their Canadian social experience. There were many jokes about the weather, some feeble attempts to include French phrases in their conversation and great bragging about the superiority of the academic standards. The only complaint that I remember hearing concerned the shortage of Jamaican girls enrolled at the universities. The boys felt that they had to justify dating white Canadian girls while extolling the beauty and virtue of the childhood girlfriends left in Jamaica, from whom they had extracted promises of fidelity during their absence and to whom they had pledged eternal love.

I read the brochures sent to me by Royal Victoria College and McGill University avidly. I was hungry to add to my limited knowledge of Canada, which did not go much beyond the county's expanse of snow and ice, the dependence of the world on its prairies for wheat, its brave and loyal support of England during the war (unlike the Americans) and the idiosyncrasies of Prime Minister Mackenzie King (and his mother), who seemed to retain power forever.

I conjured up in my mind's eye a community of plain, simple, gentle folk who lived uneventful lives in a cold uneventful country inhabited by very few Black people and a handful of Native Indians who resided on reserves.

I was happy with the prospect of my studying in Canada; so was Roy. We both assumed that I would not have any interest whatsoever in Canadian men, that I would not be distracted by a glittering social life; I would study, complete my four years, and return to Jamaica, probably to attend the law school that was in its infancy at the University of the West Indies. In any event it was obvious to both of us that we were destined to marry and grow old together, and the four years apart would only serve to strengthen our attachment to each other.

Canada was not what I expected. Three weeks after I had settled into a double room in Royal Victoria College, the assistant warden of women called me into her office and explained that I was being given a single room, because the College had been unable to find a roommate to share the double with me. She tried to break the news to me gently, pointing out how lucky I was to secure a single room and how much more private and quiet that would be for studying. I was moved into a single room at the same rate as the double—and two white women students were immediately moved into the double room.

I was stunned! I could not believe that not one of the other students in residence had been willing to share a room with me. Other West Indian women who had been at Royal Victoria College before me shrugged the matter off as not being surprising; having had similar experiences themselves they had known all along that no roommate would be found to share my room. Every year, West Indian women, given the option, requested the cheaper double room, moved in and were later moved into the more expensive single rooms at the lower double room rate. The bureaucracy was embarrassed by the whole procedure, but had not found a satisfactory way around it. It lived in the vain hope that one year things would change and a student would be found willing to share a double room with a Black student, and so it persisted. Despite the fact that that particular form of racism worked in my favour economically, it made me angry and my anger was compounded by frustration. It eventually became clear that the experience would be typical of the prejudice I ran into during my years in residence—polite, denied and accepted.

The dining room behaviour was another example of the peculiar brand of racism practised in Royal Victoria College at that time. Whenever I entered the dining room at mealtime I would anxiously scan the tables, hoping to find a seat at a table with another Black student. If there was none available, I would look for a seat with one of the two or three white friends I had managed to make (I had made some, including Sue Curtis, whose father was the Attorney General of Newfoundland at the time). If that failed, I just sat anywhere, knowing that I would probably complete my entire meal without anyone speaking to me or including me in their conversation.

At first, because I am outgoing, a bit of an extrovert, I assumed that my tablemates were shy, so I used to initiate conversation with the person sitting beside me or across from me—the cold and unfriendly responses to these overtures soon convinced me to stop.

I was truly grateful for the people who acted as a buffer against the hurts; although they did not transform Royal Victoria College into a home away from home, they managed to give me a glimpse of that other Canada that existed beyond prejudice and discrimination. Dr. Muriel Roscoe, Dean of Women, and her assistant Marie Madeline Mottola monitored our activities to ensure that we did not withdraw into a lonely shell of self-pity, but participated in social events on and around the campus. Mike DeFreitas, the senior custodian and an early West Indian immigrant who had retired from the railroad, took on the responsibility of surrogate father. He never hesitated to chastise us for staying out late during weeknights and made it his business to meet and to know the young men who dated us. The other Caribbean women were a special source of support, and although Dr. Roscoe encouraged us not to confine our social contact to our immediate and exclusive circle, she recognized the value and necessity of the love and nurturing that we gave and received from each other.

I was neither lonely nor unhappy during my stay at McGill. The West Indian community was large, vibrant and close-knit. My closest women friends were two other Jamaicans, Patsy Chen and

Merle Darby, who had attended Wolmer's, the same private school that I had, and whom I knew well. In addition, because the ratio of male to female West Indian students was then almost three to one there was never a shortage of dates. Many of the older male students were dating white Canadians but in the early 1950s interracial dating was not as accepted as it is today and many more of the male student either refrained from doing it or did it clandestinely.

Interracial dating was absolutely taboo for West Indian women. We were all very conscious of the sexual stereotypes that we were told inhabited the fantasy world of white males, and at that time it was still very important to West Indian men that the women they married be perceived to be pure and virginal. The tragedy, of course, was that the West Indian male students internalized and accepted the white criteria of beauty and since the "only life" Black women had to live could not "be lived as a blonde," as a popular TV commercial of the time exhorted, the Black men assumed that white men saw no beauty in us, and therefore their only interest would be in our sexual availability.

Even more tragic was the fact that we Black women students (unlike our counterparts of today) shared this perception of our unattractiveness and consequently closed ourselves off from the world of white males. Tragic because the decision to do so was not based on our assessment of our worth, but on our acceptance of our male colleagues' assessment of our lack of worth.

The real excitement of my academic life at McGill was discovering Hugh MacLennan and Canadian literature. During my voracious reading years as an adolescent and teenager, I had discovered and come to love Mazo de la Roche and Lucy Maude Montgomery, and for me that was all there was to Canadian literature. I had inherited from my English high school teachers the belief that very little of value was being produced by writers in the colonies, so I had no curiosity about Canadian literature. Quite frankly I did not think that there was any.

It was with a sort of bemused inquisitiveness that in my second year I registered for the course in Canadian Literature taught jointly by Hugh MacLennan, the author, and Louis Dudek, the poet. As the works of Gabrielle Roy, Morley Callaghan, Earle Birney and Hugh MacLennan entered my life, they opened up such a rich and exciting world to me that I came to see Canada through new eyes and to develop an addiction to Canadian authors that I have never lost.

In addition, I fell in love with Hugh MacLennan. I found him a kind and inspiring teacher who found the time to talk, discuss and listen as I struggled towards a better understanding of Canadian mores, attitudes and customs. One teacher stands out in memory from my high school: Lucille Waldron (Mair), my history teacher. One teacher stands out in memory from my university years: Hugh MacLennan, my Canadian Literature professor.

The less polite face of racism remained hidden until later. Although the women who shared the residence at Royal Victoria College were content just to treat us though we did not exist, never acknowledging our presence except when necessary and then only with the minimum of courtesy, the landladies and landlords who lived in the neighbourhoods near McGill had no such inhibitions. There was nothing subtle about the racism of the landlords and ladies of Montreal. During the summer the women's residence was closed and we were all expected to return to our respective homes or seek accommodation elsewhere. Of course, my first summer in Canada, I hastened home to Jamaica and remained there until it was time to return to school. I needed desperately to be free of prejudice and discrimination, to see my family, and to reassure myself that I was still a whole and valued human being; and to assess my feelings for Roy. But by the following year, I was in love with one of the male students and wanted to spend the vacation in Montreal to be near him.

Job hunting in Montreal that summer proved to be a nightmare. My Chinese-Jamaican friend Patsy Chen secured a job immediately as a waitress at a golf and country club. Although I applied to the same club that she did and to others as well, I was never accepted. The employment counsellor kept recommending that I accept childcare jobs or light housework jobs, despite that fact that I explained I was not interested in doing housework or caring for children. She finally explained that although she had personally recommended me for a number of different jobs, only the people seeking domestic servants were interested in hiring me.

The older, wiser, senior West Indian women students, experienced in these matters, had never bothered to seek employment in Montreal. As soon as the academic semester ended, they headed for New York, where they were able to secure any type of work they wanted.

Discouraged by my job hunt, I reported to Gretchen Weston, the assistant warden in residence who was also the designated counsellor for foreign students, that I would be returning to Jamaica for the summer since I had been unable to find employment. Gretchen, who happened to be the daughter of one of the Westons of Weston's financial empire and was herself a student at McGill, was clearly upset by my report; she asked me to allow her to make some enquiries and report back to me in a couple of days. The following day she called to tell me to report to the Weston's plant in Longueil for work the following Monday.

Every summer after that I worked at Weston's Bakeries in Longueil as an office 'gopher.' I started at $35 weekly and worked my way up to $45 weekly by the time I graduated. I enjoyed those summer jobs and made some good friends, although on at least one occasion I'm sure that management regretted its generosity in creating a spot for me. One week, when I was the holiday relief for the person in payroll who computed the work hours of the employees in the plant, I was almost voted most popular person in Quebec when all the workers in the plant discovered that they had received a tremendous raise in pay—it seemed that I had multiplied when I should have added and the results brought loud rounds of applause from all the workers on the plant floor. Management quickly promoted me at the end of that week to filing letters and reports with no responsibility for payroll, although I had earlier been told that I would be working in the payroll department for three weeks.

Marie Mastrojosephs, my friend from those days, tells me that I am still spoken of kindly by many of the workers who were beneficiaries of my brief stint in payroll. And I sometimes wonder as I read about him and see him on TV news if Garfield knows how close I came to wrecking the Weston empire.

Once I had secured a job, thanks to the influence of Gretchen Weston, I had to find an apartment, and that's when I ran into the open, hostile and impolite racism of the landlords and landladies I spoke of earlier. These men and women made no secret of their dislike and distaste for Black people. They were rude, obscene and straightforward about refusing to rent us accommodation, often slamming the doors in our faces to emphasize their rejection of our request. Because I could afford it, I decided that I did not need to live in a shabby apartment near the university, so I sought better accommodations in Notre Dame de Grace and lower Westmount. It soon became absolutely clear that a line had been drawn around the university, in the nature of the U.S. 'red-lining' of a neighbourhood, encompassing approximately six blocks in each direction around McGill, that is, effectively making it a segregated neighbourhood. Blacks were not welcome as residents outside that line, except in the St. Antoine district where most of the Canadian Black families of the day lived.

The mild anger and frustration I had felt for the students in Royal Victoria College turned to hatred for the landladies and landlords of Montreal. I fell into a common, irrational habit of including all members of that group in my rage and outrage, rather than just the specific ones who had hurt me. I knew just enough French to understand the obscenities they spat at me, and various forms of the word Black were present in all of them.

Ten years after graduation, when we returned to Montreal so that Bill could complete his residency at the Allan Memorial Hospital, I found that little had changed. His white colleagues had no problems securing reasonable housing in Westmount and Outremont, while we had to settle for inferior accommodation in the poorest part of Notre Dame de Grace. By then, although the hatred had evaporated, the anger and hurt remained; we were the parents of two small children and the prospect that they would have to face similar treatment because of our decision to make Canada our home added guilt to my feelings of rage.

After that experience, I escalated my efforts to get Bill to decide to leave Canada for some other country, any other country in which our children would be free from racism. He agonized over this situation as much as I did, but always he returned to the conclusion that this was a country whose benefits outweighed the liabilities of racism, and that raising our children with self-esteem despite the experience of prejudice was a challenge we just had to face. I disagreed strongly; I wanted my children to experience my safe, loving and positive childhood, but I was not prepared to take them and return to Jamaica without Bill. So, to my rage about racism was added my anger at being powerless to control my family's choice of country of residence.

But my feelings about landlords and ladies paled in comparison to those I had about another group of people. My nightmares were filled with immigration officers. I hated and feared them because, unlike landladies and landlords, they really had my fate and my future in their hands. They had power. I thought they were stupid and cruel—petty despots who made no attempt to conceal their loathing for Black immigrants and whose sadism was uncontrolled when dealing with us.

Every year at the end of the spring semester West Indian students had to go to the immigration office to ask for an extension of our student visas over the summer. We had to lie through our teeth about not working during this time, saying that we would just be lazing about enjoying the Montreal humidity until time to resume classes in September; as students we had been issued special visas that very clearly forbade us working. Before being accepted as students we had to prove that we were financially able to attend university without needing to work or receive any financial assistance from Canada, and at the beginning of the academic year we had to show a balance of $1,000 in our bank accounts to cover the year's tuition and living expenses. The immigration officers suspected that we were lying about not working but they had no proof, and the frustration drove them into a frenzy. We had to show up at the immigration office with a passport, bank book and letter of acceptance for the fall semester at McGill. We also had to have an address and a phone number, as well as a letter of reference from a respectable member of the community, the Dean of Women for the Women, one of the lay preachers from the Student Christian Movement for the men. The officers desperately wanted to find reasons to deport us, and as we sat across from them, watching the rage struggling to erupt as they cross-examined us, we would begin to sweat. For emotional support we would go down to the immigration office in groups.

The day that I was accused of trying to secure two extensions instead of one, because I had the misfortune to show up the day after my brother, who had been down for his renewal, I thought that my world was about to explode. The agent was furious that I thought I could pull the wool over his eyes simply by changing my name from Augustus to Rosemary—after all, the surnames were the same, the colour of skin was the same, we were both students, both at McGill, both from Jamaica and as far as he was concerned, Augustus was a girl's name. I was unable to convince him that I was Rosemary and that Augustus was my brother, thus making the similarity in name, colour, etc., quite understandable—he refused to renew my visa. Two days later, accompanied by two respectable members of the community, one of them a church minister whom I had met at the Student Christian Movement, my brother and I, carrying passports, bank books, university transcripts, birth certificates and letters of acceptance to the fall semester, returned to the immigration office. This time we had a different officer, who looked at our documents, looked at us, looked at our documents, stamped the extension in my passport, yelled "next" and dismissed us without addressing a word to us. As I left, something in me snapped and I wept hysterically, right there on the steps of the building.

I used to think that nothing in my childhood had prepared me to deal with this nightmare phenomenon. I was angry at my family for raising me as though racism were a foreign unpleasantness, which I would be spared; I felt that they should have either protected me or prepared me better for this degradation.

I envied Black Americans their access to violent struggle—they could fight back. As Black students in Canada, we seemed to have no options but to rail against our treatment in private and keep our heads down in public, trying to get through the four years to graduation without incident, determined to leave this country without a backward glance or kind thought. Racism seemed to pit me against everyone, including myself—my powerlessness sent *me* into a frenzy.

I was wrong, of course; my childhood had prepared me better than I realized to deal with prejudice. Unlike Black Americans and Black Canadians, I did not become a member of a racial minority group until I was an adult with a formed sense of myself. By then, it was too late to imprint on me the term 'inferior.' I knew that all the things that we were told Blacks could not do, all the jobs that were closed to us in this country, were in fact being done ably, competently and sometimes in a superior way by Blacks at home and in other parts of the world. And I came to understand that my frustration and rage stemmed not from the attempts to make me feel inferior but from a realization of my powerlessness and vulnerability, as a foreigner, to do anything about it. My upbringing had not taught me to deal with powerlessness. I was swamped by the feeling that there was nothing I could do about employers or landlords or students or complete strangers who built fences around me and placed obstacles in my path; and I thought of what it must be like to be born Black in this country and to live all of one's life with law, media, education and every other social institution carrying and reinforcing the message of your inferiority every day of your life. I thanked God that had not been my fate and at that time I swore that no child of mine would ever be forced to endure such a fate. I was determined to leave Canada the day after writing my last exam—not even staying around long enough for my convocation.

Even as I write this, I also recall how each incident would send me racing to the West Indian community in search of succor and to drown the violence exploding in my mind in the laughter and the humour, the music, the dance and the camaraderie that I found there. Anything to forget the glares of hate, the obscene epithets, or the look that just went through me as though I wasn't there—and my own unbearable powerlessness.

When I sit around with friends and reminisce about McGill, it seems that on the surface my life was no different from that of other students. Study and party, party and study—deadlines, panic, fun, anxiety, relief, graduation. Yet in those years I changed in profound and basic ways—for I was never the same after my encounter with racial discrimination, Canadian-style. With the passage of time, the hatred faded and disappeared. But I never lost the rage at the injustice, stupidity and blind cruelty of prejudice.

TOPICS FOR EXPLORATION

1. Who is Rosemary Brown's audience? What preconceptions about her subject does she hope to dispel? What is her purpose: to inform or educate, both or any other?

2. What does Brown know about Canada before she comes? Why does Canada initially fail to meet her expectations? What is her reaction to Canadian reality?

3. Explain the meaning of "polite racism" or what Brown calls racism "Canadian-style." How was racism demonstrated during her search for jobs and accommodation? Give other examples of prejudice she had to face as a student in the early 1950s. Have these forms of racism disappeared, or is racism still a serious social problem?

4. How were black women students at that time personally affected by racial and gender stereotyping? For Rosemary Brown, what were the sources of strength and support against racism and sexism?

5. Brown compares the black situation in the United States with that in Canada. How are they different? How are they the same? How does her evaluation of the situation in these two countries compare with her childhood experience of black self-image in Jamaica?

6. How has her own past equipped her for coping with racism? According to Brown, is it advisable to raise children so as to make them aware of racism and prepare them for dealing with it?

Markoosie

Markoosie, born in 1941, is an Inuit who grew up at Resolute Bay, Northwest Territories. From age 15 he attended a government school. His novel Harpoon of the Hunter *was published first in Inuit syllabics (1967) and later in English by McGill-Queens University Press (1970), the first fiction to be published by a Canadian Inuit. "Wings of Mercy" is an excerpt from his second novel,* Wings of Mercy, *which is based on Markoosie's experience as a bush pilot. As this episode begins, an airplane carrying several people has been forced to land on an icepan in Lancaster Sound. Aboard are a boy, Seeko, who has shot himself accidentally while hunting, his father, Mannik, a nurse named Doreen Moore, and Norris Mann, the bush pilot. This chapter appeared first in* Inuttituut *(Autumn 1972).*

Wings of Mercy

In Baffin Island Fiord, Constable Swart scribbled Charlie Delta's position across a yellow message pad. Once again he tried to contact pilot Norris Mann in his stricken aircraft. There was no reply.

Norris opened the side window and tried to see ahead and below. He saw a large icepan, before the extreme cold forced his eyes shut. He pulled his head back inside and as calmly as possible fought to keep control of the aircraft.

Constable Swart continued to try and make contact with the plane without success. Then he switched his frequency and said; 'Devon Island Base. This is Baffin Island Fiord. Do you copy?' After several repeats he received an answer.

'Go ahead Baffin Island Fiord.'

'Charlie Delta has been forced down.'

'Oh my God! Did you get his position?'

'Yes, when I got his May Day, he was at latitude 74 degrees, longitude 80.'

The pilot's face lost all feeling as he strained his freezing eyeballs for a glimpse of the icepan. It was rough surfaced as he had feared.

As soon as the tires touched the ice, he pulled the power all the way back and turned off the power switch at the same time. The plane bounced once, came down hard and bounced off the ice again. It came down hard the third time and everything seemed to break apart. Norris heard a muffled cry from Nurse Moore, before he blacked out.

'Baffin Island Fiord this is Devon Island Base. Do you copy?'

'Go ahead, Devon Island Base. I hear you.'

'Did Norris say he was ditching in the water or on the ice?'

'He said he was going to try for an icepan.'

'OK. Baffin Island Fiord, we will contact National Defence for rescue service.'

'Is there anything we can do to help from this side?'

'Afraid not, we will do everything possible from here.'

Constable Jim Coleman was called to the radio shack. The radio operator outlined the situation.

'We have a downed aircraft in about here,' he explained, tracing the location on the map tacked to the wall.' There is a very slim chance that they are still alive. Norris Mann is a skilled pilot but I don't think he has had much winter experience. Nurse Moore was tending the wounded boy and I understand his father Mannik is aboard. We called National Defence for rescue service and an aircraft is on the way from Frobisher with a doctor and supplies.'

'I hope he made it to an icepan. But even so, how can a doctor get there this time of the year?' the constable asked.

'The doctor will be a member of the Royal Canadian Air Force parachute team. We are hoping he can make the jump. Those Air Force boys know their business.'

'They are our only hope,' the constable replied quietly.

'Not quite, Jim,' said the radioman. 'You could organize the Eskimo rescue party.'

'I can try that,' said the constable, still scanning the map. 'That is about two hundred miles away and four days by dog team. Keep me posted on events. I am going to the settlement and talk to the people.'

Norris slowly opened his eyes. Slowly his memory returned and the terrible realization of their predicament. His head was pounding with pain as he turned it around without moving his body. He lay beside his seat. Slowly he got into sitting position. A sharp pain shot through his left leg. His boot was torn and a trace of blood showed through, 'Broken,' he thought to himself. He found a flashlight and flicked it on.

He looked to where his passengers had been and saw the nurse prostrate over the body of Seeko while Mannik seemed to be pinned against the wall. Norris tried to stand, but his legs refused to co-operate. 'Could both be broken,' he thought, surprised at his own calmness. He dragged himself toward the nurse with his hands. She was still and did not respond when he pushed her from Seeko. The boy was still breathing. He called for Mannik and was answered by a low moan. Mannik, bleeding from a cut on his forehead, began to crawl toward him and knelt beside Seeko. 'He is still alive,' he said gratefully. Nurse Moore began to moan and then opened her eyes. 'Is everyone alright? How long have we been down?' The questions all came at once as she sought to understand the situation.

'I think my legs are broken, but there is no pain,' said Norris.

'Let me get those boots off. Have you got a knife?'

Norris pointed to the survival kit box. The nurse crawled toward the box, stopping to look at Seeko on the way. She listened to his breathing and was satisfied that his condition remained stable.

Doreen began to cut the laces on the pilot's torn boot. He clenched his teeth to keep from crying out as she removed it and the sock. A bone protruded. Quickly and skillfully, in spite of the cramped conditions, she applied a splint and bandage. She wrapped the leg in a blanket to protect it from the cold that she realized for the first time was creeping into the aircraft. She unlaced the boot from the other leg. A quick examination showed that no bones were broken but it was badly sprained and swelling. She wrapped it as best she could from the limited resources in the first aid box. Turning to Mannik she next wiped his wound clean and bandaged it.

'Anywhere else hurt?' she asked. She was relieved when Mannik shook his head and grinned.

They began to survey the damage and the full realization of their situation came to them. The aircraft door was broken off. One wing was broken and the nose buried in the snow and ice. The tiny finger of light from the flashlight disappeared in the blowing snow. How far they were from land or the size of the icepan was unknown to them. Above the wind they could hear the growing thunder of crushing ice.

'How long do you think it will be before we are rescued?' the nurse asked Norris.

He did not want to tell her that the chances were slim. He tried to be cheerful. 'It might take several days, depending on the weather. The only way to get off here will be by helicopter, and the nearest is about a thousand miles away. There is almost no daylight this time of the year. I hope they got the bearings I sent as we came down. We have to get out of here before we freeze.'

'I must build a shelter for us,' said Mannik. 'I will build an igloo.' He opened his pack and took out a snow-knife and a rifle, the hunter's tools.

When Mannik left the plane Doreen put an extra blanket around Seeko. 'I did not want to say it in front of his father, but I don't think he can live much longer without a doctor.' Norris nodded. He was thinking about it and about the food supply. He always carried emergency food—enough for one man for a week. He had a small pressure cooker and fuel for one man for two days. But there were four people. They sat in silence, listening to the beating of the wind and the distant grinding of the ice. Weak daylight crept into the plane with the cold.

Mannik returned to announce that the igloo was finished and he needed blankets to cover the floor. They could move in. He took the blankets and the heater and soon had the little shelter warm. With the help of the nurse, he moved Seeko into it first. Together they returned and helped Norris down from the plane and dragged him through the small opening.

'We will make tea first,' Mannik said, 'and then I will go and see how big this icepan is. There is a chance I might get a seal. A seal will keep us fed and provide enough fat to keep Seeko and Norris warm.' There was something in his calm and determined manner that gave strength to all of them.

Far away from the little igloo and the wrecked aircraft Constable Coleman was explaining the situation to a group of Inuit hunters.

'We have no way of knowing if they are alive. They could be on the ice and it would be impossible for a plane to land near them. That is why I am asking for volunteers to make up a rescue party. Are there any questions?' Coleman asked.

'You think they are about two hundred miles away?' asked one of the men who was called Nuki.

'Yes, but we are not sure if that is the correct position.' The constable returned to the map, and pointed to the probable spot. 'It's somewhere here, between Kikitalook and Toononik.'

'That is a lot of land and water from here,' answered Nuki. Turning to the other men for approval, he said simply: 'We will go.'

Nuki turned again to the hunters in the room and began to give instructions in their own language. 'We will start in two hours. We will need twenty men and if possible, make up fifteen dog teams. We should take the six kayaks because there is still a lot of open water. Pack enough food for a week for ourselves and the dogs. We may have to hunt later but our first job is to get to the site.' The men stood up when he stopped talking and went to their homes to prepare themselves.

Four hours after the call for help went out, an RCAF Boxcar landed on the Devon Island Base strip. The first person down the ladder was a tall man in a flight suit, carrying a bag. 'Hi!' he greeted the constable. 'I'm Doctor Carl Poole. I would like to speak to the radioman who has been talking to Baffin Island Fiord.'

Inside the radio hut over a cup of hot coffee Doctor Poole gathered all the details of the accident.

'Can you tell me what really happened. How long ago and what has been done?'

The radioman outlined the situation. 'The boy is young. He shot himself in the stomach area. The bullet is .22 calibre. The nurse said he lost a lot of blood. It has been about ten hours since the accident and we have no way of knowing what his condition is now. Just that he is somewhere out there if he is alive,' he said, pointing to the map on the wall.

Thirty minutes later the Boxcar was refuelled and again airborne. At two thousand feet they lost visual contact with the ground. The doctor studied a map with the navigator.

'Let's go up to nine thousand feet and then descend under the cloud when we get over Lancaster Sound,' the navigator said. 'That will be in forty-five minutes.'

Over the Sound, the plane dropped to 800 feet. Fog rolled up to meet them, blocking out the thousands of floating icepans, except in a few spots. For two hours they flew a pattern over the area, all eyes straining for signs of wreckage. 'There is no hope of finding them under these conditions,' the pilot said. 'We will return to base and try again later.' The big plane gained altitude and headed back to Devon Island Base.

On the icepan the three people heard the plane passing over them but they could not see it. When the sound faded away for the last time, Doreen Moore began to cry.

'At least they are looking for us,' Norris said, trying to comfort her. 'They made a good try but the clouds are too low. They will be back.'

'Don't worry, nurse,' Mannik said. 'They will come again and again until they find us. We have a saying that no matter how sadly a day ends, another new day will come to the land tomorrow.'

Inside the igloo, which was warm but cramped, Norris was making plans. 'Mannik, look in the baggage compartment of the plane. Collect all the rags or anything else that will burn. There is gasoline in the belly tank. Push up the drain valve and fill up a bottle or oilcan with it. Soak the rags and leave them outside in the open and the next time you hear a plane run out and light fire to it.'

'I will give you a hand,' said Doreen. Together she and Mannik crawled out of the igloo.

Back at Devon Island Base the pilot and navigator listened to the latest weather reports. They were not good. The meteorologist charted the path of an approaching storm. 'It is now over Melville Island and was over Prince Patrick Island yesterday. That means it is moving pretty fast. You won't have much time before you are grounded.'

The ice was rugged and made travelling slow. The barking of the dogs and the creaking of the sleds were the only sounds in the darkness. Nuki was ahead of the party, because he remembered the way from his early hunting years. They had been travelling for several hours and the dogs were growing tired when Nuki called a halt.

'We will stop a while and eat,' he said to Shinak, his closest companion.

'Are we going to keep on all night?' Shinak asked.

'We will have to go as far as the dogs can last. It is going to be rough but lives depend on us,' Nuki answered.

Inside the small igloo, the shadows of three silent people were cast upon the ice walls. They all looked anxiously at Seeko who was fighting for breath. Doreen decided she had to say the words that she hoped she would never have to say.

'Mannik,' she began, 'I have to tell you the truth. There is nothing more I can do. I don't think he will live till morning.'

Mannik looked into the eyes of the nurse and said: 'I have been expecting those words for some time. I am old enough to know when death is near.' Then he turned away and wept quietly. For many hours that was the only sound in the silent cell, while the wind mourned outside.

'Listen,' Norris said suddenly. 'Hear it? It's an aircraft up there! Quick, Mannik, light the fire!'

Norris dragged himself out after Mannik. The fire was already blazing. Norris lay on his back on the ice and looked at the sky. The clouds were patchy now and the sound of motors was getting closer.

The pilot was the first to see the pinpoint of light on the floating ice island. 'Look over there!' he shouted to his co-pilot. 'We have found them! Tell the doctor to prepare to jump. Get the engineer to prepare to drop supplies.'

The big aircraft circled wide and turned back toward the welcoming light on the ice below. They were at 700 feet with the clouds above them. It was too low for the doctor to jump and he would have to go 'blind.' Directly over the fire he turned and went up to two thousand feet and into the darkness of the clouds. The turn continued for three minutes, then he signaled for the supplies to be dropped.

'OK, Doc. If you're ready we will do that again. I will go in over the fire and then climb and circle. We can let you go at two thousand feet in three minutes.'

The doctor signaled that he was ready. He wanted to look at his watch for some reason. He went to the back of the aircraft and stood in his bulky clothes under the blue light to wait for the signal. 'I hope that is one big icepan,' he thought to himself.

TOPICS FOR EXPLORATION

1. What do we learn about living conditions in the far north? How important is environment in the drama of this story? How are the Inuit people equipped to survive there?

2. Markoosie's characters are not portrayed in depth. They are defined by their functions rather than described in detail. How effective is this approach? What does each character bring to the small group during this emergency?

3. What resources does Mannik provide in this dangerous environment? How do Nuki and his team approach the challenge?

4. This episode ends with the doctor about to parachute onto the icepan. Is this a good moment to stop?

5. How does the subject matter justify the style of Markoosie's narrative, with is sparing use of commentary and matter-of-fact attitude to the described events? How is the dramatic effect achieved?

Austin Clarke

*Austin Clarke was born in Barbados in 1934; in 1955 he came to Canada to study economics and political science at the University of Toronto. He has been visiting professor of Black Studies at such renowned universities as Yale, Duke, and Brandeis. He has held important social and political functions, including that of cultural attaché at the Barbadian Embassy in Washington, D.C. Clarke is a founding member of the Writers' Union of Canada and has served as a member of the federal government's Refugee Review Board in Ontario. He turned to writing full-time in 1963 and has since published several books, including a popular trilogy about West Indians in Toronto (*The Meeting Point, Storm of Fortune, *and* The Bigger Light*) and a memoir called *Growing Up Stupid Under the Union Jack *(1980). His most recent collection of stories is *In This City. *Our selection comes from his collection of short stories *When Women Rule, *first published in 1985.*

Doing Right

I see him and I watch him. I see him and I watch him and I start to pray for him 'cause I see him heading for trouble. Making money. "In five or six years I want to have a lotta money. Only when I have a lotta dollars will people respect me." That is all Cleveland telling me.

I had to laugh. Every time he say so, I had to laugh 'cause I couldn't do nothing better than laugh.

"Look at the Rockefellers. Look at the Rothschilds. Look at the Kennedys."

I was going to ask him if he know how they make their money. But before I could ask, he would be off dreaming and looking at the ceiling where there was only cobwebs and dust. And only God knows what was circulating through his head every time he put himself in these deep reveries concerning making lots o' money and talking 'bout the Rockefellers, the Rothschilds and the Kennedys.

I was still laughing. 'Cause the present job he had was a green-hornet job. He was a man who went to work in a green suit from head to foot, except for the shoes which was black and which he never polish. His profession was to go round the St. Clair-Oakwood area putting parking tickets 'pon people cars. Before this, he uses to be on the Queen's Park beat for green hornets.

A big man like him, over two hundred pounds, healthy and strong and black, and all he could do for eight or nine years is to walk 'bout with a little book in his hand, putting little yellow pieces o' paper on people windshields. He like the job so much and thought he doing the right thing that in the middle o' the night, during a poker game, or just dipsy-doodling and talking 'bout women, he would put back on the green uniform jacket, grabble up the peak cap, jump in the little green car that the police give him, and gone up by St. Clair-Oakwood, up and down Northcliffe Boulevard, swing right on Eglinton, gone down Eglinton, and swing left on Park Hill Road, left again on Whitmore, and all he doing is putting these yellow pieces o' paper on decent hard-working people cars. When he return, he does be laughing. I tell him he going soon stop laughing when a Wessindian lick he down with a big rock.

"I fix them! I have ticketed one hundred and ten motto-cars today alone! And the night I leff the poker game, I ticket fifty more bastards, mainly Wessindians."

I start to get real frighten. 'Cause I know a lotta these same Wessindians in them very streets where he does be ticketing and laughing. And all them Wessindians know who the green hornet is. And being as how they is Wessindian, I know they don't like green hornets, nor nobody who does be touching their cars. So I feel that any morning, when one o' these Wessindians come home from a party, or offa a night shift, and see him doing foolishness and putting yellow tickets on their motto-cars, I know um is at least *one* hand brek. Wessindians accustom to parking in the middle o' the road or on the wrong side back home. And nobody don't trouble them, nor touch their cars. And since they come here, many o' these Wessindians haven't change their attitude in regards to who own the public road and who own the motto-cars.

So whilst the boy still ticketing and laughing and putting his hands on people cars which they just wash in the car wash on Bathurst, I continue worrying and watching him.

One night just as we sit down to cut the cards, and before the cards deal, he come in grinning and saying, "I ticket two hundred motto-cars today alone!"

"One o' these days, boy!" I tell him.

"When I pass in the green car and I see him, I know I had him!"

"Who?"

"I see the car park by the fire hydrand. The chauffeur leaning back in the seat. One hand outside the car window. With a cigarette in tha' hand. The next hand over the back o' the seat. I look in the car, and when I look in, I nearly had a fit. I recognize the pipe. I recognize the dark-blue pin-stripe suit. I recognize the hair. With the streak o' grey in um. And I mek a U-turn in the middle o' the road . . ."

"But a U-turn illegal!"

"I is a green hornet, man!"

"I see."

"I size up the car. And I see the licents plate. ONT-001! I start getting nervous now. 'Cause I know it is the big man. Or the second big man in Toronto. I draw up. The chauffeur nod to me and tell me, "Fine day, eh?" I tell him, "A very fine day, sir!" And I get out. I bend over the bonnet o' this big shiny black car. . ."

"Limousine, man. A big car is call a limo."

"Well, um could have been a limo, a hearse or a automobile, I still bend over the bonnet and stick on one o' the prettiest parking tickets in my whole career!"

"The Premier's car?"

"He mek the law."

"And you think you do the right thing?"

"My legal duty. Afterwards, I did feel so good, like a real police officer, and not a mere green hornet. And I walk through Queen's Park on my two feet, looking for more official cars to ticket. And when I was finished, I had stick on *five* parking tickets in their arse. One belongst to the Attorney-General, too."

"The same man who does defend Wessindians?"

"I put one 'pon Treasurer's car, too.

Well, that whole night, all the boy talking 'bout and laughing 'bout is how he stick on tickets on these big-shots' cars or limousines. And to make matters worse for the rest o' we, he win all the money in the poker game, too. I feel now that the boy really going become important, maybe become a real police, and make money. Or else going lose a hand or a foot.

But we was feeling good, though. 'Cause the big boys in Toronto don't notice we unless um is Caribana weekend, or when election time coming and they looking for votes, or when the *Star* doing a feature on Wessindians and racism and they want a quotation. Still, we feel this green hornet is our ambassador, even if he is only a ambassador o' parking tickets. So we laugh like hell at the boy's prowess and progress.

And we does wait till a certain time on a Friday night, nervous whilst cutting and dealing the cards, to see if the boy going turn up still dress off in the green uniform, meaning that he hasn't get fired for ticketing the big-shots' cars. And when he *does* turn up, dress from head to trousers in green, we know he still have the job and we does laugh some more. But all the time I still nervous as I seeing him and watching him.

Then he start lossing weight. He start biting his fingers. He start wearing the green uniform not press, and half dirty. He start calling we, "*You* people!"

I getting frighten 'cause he had just tell me that they tek him off the Queens Park beat for good.

So, um is now that he up in St. Clair-Oakwood, and I feel he going put a ticket on the *wrong* motto-car, meaning a Wessindian car. And at least one hand brek. Or one foot. And if the particular motto-car belongst to a Jamaican, not even the ones that have locks and does wear the wool tams make outta black, green and red, I know um could be *both* foots and *both* hands!

I see him and I watch him.

"I live in Trinidad, as a police. I leff Trinidad because they won't let me ticket one hundred more cars and break the all-time record. I went to Guyana after Trinidad. I was a police in Guyana before Guyana was Guyana, and was still Demerara or BG. They make me leff Guyana when I get close to the record. Ten more tickets is all I had to ticket. From Guyana, I end up in Dominica. Same thing. From Dominica, I went to Antigua, and um was in Antigua that a fellow came close to licking me down for doing my legal duty, namely ticketing cars. In all them countries, I ticket cars belonging to prime ministers, ministers of guvvament, priests, civil servants and school teachers."

I see him and I watch him. I see him getting more older than the forty-five years he say he was born. And I see him drinking straight white rums first thing every morning lately because he say, "The nerves bad. Not that I becoming a alcoholic, I only taking the bad taste o' waking up so early and the bitterness o' disappointment outta my mouth. I am not a alcoholic, though."

But he was drunk. Cleveland was drunk drunk drunk early every day. He had to be even more drunk after he outline his plan to make money.

"Remember the Rockefellers, man!" he tell me. "This is my plan. I been a green hornet for eight to nine years now. They promise me that if I ticket the most cars outta the whole group o' hornets they would send me to training school, to be a police. First they tell me I too short. I is five-four. But most criminals is five-three. Then they tell me that my arches fallen. Jesus Christ! What you expect? After all the beats I walk in Trinidad, Guyana, Antigua, Dominica and Grenada, my arches bound to fall! And eight-nine years in this damn country pounding the beat ticketing cars! But they can't beat me.

This is the plan I got for them. Tickets begin at five dollars. Right? There is five dollars, ten dollars and fifteen dollars. Twenty dollars for parking beside a fire hydrand, or on the wrong side. Now I write up a ten-dollar ticket. And I change the ten to a forty. The stub in my book saying ten. But the ticket on the car saying ten also, which I going change from ten to a forty. Then I rush down to the place on Wellesley Street where they have all them computers. And I tell the fellow I know from Guyana something, *anything*, to get him to look up the registration for me. And then I get in touch with the owner o' the car, and subtract ten from forty, and . . ."

"You mean subtract ten years from forty!"

"You don't like my plan?"

"I think your plan worth ten years."

"Okay. What about this one? People don't lock their cars when they park. Right? Wessindians is the biggest ones. Right? A fellow don't lock his car. And um is night. And I got on my green-hornet uniform. Right? Meaning I am still in a official capacity . . . ."

I see the boy start to smile and his face spread and look like a new moon. The face was shining, too, 'cause the heat and the sureness that the plan going work this time make him sweat real bad. But I watching him. I know that Wessindians don't have much money because they does get the worst and lowest-paying jobs in Toronto. Only a certain kind o' Wessindian does have money in their pocket. The kind that does work night shift, especially after midnight, when everybody else sleeping—the brand o' Wessindian who I not going mention by name *in case* they accuse me of categorizing the race. But *certain* Wessindians, like hairdressers, real estate salesmen and fellows who know racehorses good good good, *plus* the unmentionable aformentioned brand, and the illegal immigrants, the illegal parkers, and them who hiding from the police, all them so does have money to burn, inside their cars that not locked.

The boy eyes smiling. I see dollar bills instead o' pupils. I even hear the money clinking like when a car pass over the piece o' black rubber thing in a gas station. *Cling-cling.* "Gimme three months," he say. "Gimme three months, and I going show you something."

Just as I left him, and walking 'cross Northcliffe Boulevard going to Eglinton, I see a green-hornet fellow standing up in front a man car. The man already inside the car. The man want to drive off. But the green-hornet fellow standing up in front the man car. The man inside the car honk the horn. And the green-hornet fellow take out his black book. Slow-slow. And he flip back a page. And hold down a little. And start to write down the car licents. The man honk the car agin. The hornet walk more closer. He tear off the little yellow piece o' paper. And getting ready to put it on the man brand-new grey Thunderbird. Just as the hornet was about to ticket the man for parking next to a yellow fire hydrand, the fellow jump out. A Japanese sumo wrestler would have look like a twig beside o' him. Pure muscle. Shoes shining bright. White shirt. Stripe tie. Three-piece grey suit. Hair slick back. And long. Gold on two fingers on each hand. Gold on left wrist. More gold on right wrist. The hornet par'lyzed now. A rigor mortis of fear turn the whole uniform and the hornet inside it to starch, or like how a pair o' pyjamas does look when you left um out on the line in the dead o' winter.

"Goddamn!" the man say.

"You park wrong," the hornet say.

"Who say I park wrong?"

"You park illegal."

"Who goddamn say I park illegal?"

"Look at the sign."

"Which goddamn sign?"

"The sign say *no parking* between four and six. And *no stopping anytime.* You not only park, but you stop. You stationary, too." The Indian green-hornet man's voice get high and shaky.

"Ahmma gonna give you two seconds, nigger, to take that god-damn ticket off my car, motherfucker!"

"What you call me? I am not nigger. I am Indian. Legal immigrant. I just doing my job for the City of Toronto in Metropolitan Toronto. *You* are a blasted Amurcan Negro!"

All of a sudden I see how multiculturalism gone out the window now! I start seeing all them pamphlets and television commercials that show people of all colours like we laughing together and saying, "We is Canadians." All them advertisements in *Saturday Night* and *MacLean's*, and I remember how one minister up in Ottawa say different cultures have make up this great unified country of ours. I remember it word for word. All that lick up now.

The Goliath of a man grabble hold of the hornet by the scruff of the green uniform, the peak cap fall off all like now so, the little black book slide under the car, the hornet himself lifted offa the ground by at least three inches, and shaking 'bout in the gulliver's hands, pelting 'bout his two legs like if he is a muppet or a poppet. And when I think that the man going pelt the hornet fellow in the broad road, the man just hefted him up a little more higher offa the ground and lay him 'cross the bonnet of the shining Thunderbird, holding he down like how you does hold down a cat to tickle he under his chin. And the man say, "Now, motherfucker! Is you gonna take the goddamn ticket off my Bird?"

I pass quick, bo', 'cause I know the police does be up in this St. Clair-Oakwood district like flies round a crocus bag o' sugar, at the drop of a red, green and black cloth hat; and that they does tek in anybody who near the scene o' crime, no matter how small the scene or how small the crime. And if um is Wessindians, pure handcuffs and pelting 'bout inside the back o' cruisers till they get you inside the station. And then the real sport does start! So I looking and I looking off, knowing that a green hornet, even if he look like a Pakistani or a Indian but is really a Trinidadian or a Guyanese only look a little Indian, going get help from the police. Not one police, but five carloads o' police.

All like now so, the road full up with Wessindians and other people, and these Wessindians looking on and laughing 'cause none o' them don't business with green hornets, not even green hornets that come from the Wessindies!

I pass 'long quick, bo'. I got to face the Immigration people in a week, and I don't want nothing concerning my past or present to be a stain through witnessing violence, to prevent them from stamping *landed immigrant* or *immigrant recu* in my Barbados passport! I may be a accessory before the fact. But I was still thinking of my friend, the other green hornet, so I look back to see what kind o' judgement the Thunderbird man was going to make with the Indian gentleman, who now have no peak cap, no black notebook, one shoe fall off and the green tunic tear up. And as my two eyes rested on the scene, *after the fact,* I hear the Charles Atlas of a man say, "And *don't* call the motherfucking cops! I got you covered, nigger. I knows where you goddamn live!"

I hope that this Goliath of a man don't know where my green-hornet friend does live! I hope the Thunderbird don't be park all the time up here! And I start to think 'bout getting a little message to my friend to tell him to don't put no tickets on no grey Thunderbirds or no Wessindian cars, like Tornados, whiching is Wessindians' favourite cars. And I start to wonder if he know that a Wessidian does treat a Tornado more better than he does treat a woman or a wife. And with a Wessindian, yuh can't ask his woman for a dance at a dance, unless you expecting some blows. Even if he give you permission, don't dance a Isaac Hayes or a Barry White slow piece too slow and too close, yuh. . .

I waiting anxious now 'cause I don't see the boy for days these days. I feel the boy really making money from the scheme. I walk all over St. Clair-Oakwood, all along Northcliffe, swing right 'pon Eglinton, mek a left on Park Hill Road, a further left up by Whitmore and find myself back on Northcliffe going now in the opposite direction, and still I can't rest my two eyes on the green hornet. Fellows start telling me that the boy going to the races every day on his lunch break from ticketing people cars, and betting *one hundred dollars on the nose* and *five hundred to show* on one horse, and leffing the races with bundles o' money.

I walking 'bout day and night, all over St. Clair-Oakwood, and still no sight o' the boy.

Then, *bram!* I start hearing horror stories.

"I come out my apartment last Wednesday night to get in my car, and my blasted car not there! It gone. Tow' away!" one fellow say.

A next fellow say, "Be-Christ, if I ever catch a police towing away my car!"

"I don't like this place. It too controlled and full of discipline. Tummuch regulations and laws. A man can't *breathe*. I can't go to the police 'cause I here illegal. No work permit. No job. Now, no car! You park your car, and when you come out in the cold morning to go to work at a li'l job, no fucking car!"

"I was up by a little skins one night. I tell the wife I going by Spree. I tack up by Northcliffe at the skin's apartment. I really and truly did intend to spend only a hour. Well, with a few white rums, one thing lead to the next. And when I do so, and open my eyes, morning be-Christ brek, and um is daylight. My arse in trouble now two times. Wife and wuk. I bound down the fire escape, not to be seen, and when I reach ground, no blasted car!"

Stories o' motto-cars tow'way start spreading throughout the St. Clair-Oakwood neighbourhood, just like how the yellow leaves does fall 'pon the grass a certain time o' year. Stories o' fellows getting lay off, no work permit, getting beat up, can't go to the police, in case; and fellows getting lock out by their women—all this gloom start spreading like influenza. The fellows scared. The fellows vex. The fellows angry. And they can't go and complain to the police to find out where their cars is 'cause, as you would understand, the papers not in order, yuh know! And the li'l matter o' *landed* and *recu*, and so on and so forth. . .

They can't even start calling the police "pigs" and "racists" and "criminals." And all this time, nobody can't find the green-hornet boy at all.

Well, a plague of tow'way cars rest so heavy on my mind, even though I don't own no wheels, that I get real concern. 'Cause drunk or sober, blood more thicker than water. . .

"*As man!*"

I hear the voice and I bound round. And look. I see cars. I see Wessindians. I see a police. I see a tow'way truck. And I still don't see nobody I know. But I think I recognize the voice.

"*As man!*"

I bound round again and I see the same things.

"Over here, man!"

God bless my eyesight. Um is the green-hornet man. My friend! Sitting down behind the wheel of *Do Right Towing 24 Hours.* I do so, look! I blink my two eyes. I seeing but I not seeing right. I watching, but I having eyes that see and that watch but they no watching right.

"Um, is *me*, man!"

The tow'way truck real pretty. It have in short wave radio. CBC-FM. Stereos. *And* CB. It paint up in black, yellow and white. The green-hornet boy dress off now in overalls and construction hat, cock at a angle on his head, cigar in mouth, and shades on his face, like if he is a dictator from Latin Amurca.

"Remember the plan? The plan I tell you 'bout for making money? Well, I went to my bank and get a loan for this!" He tap the door of the tow truck like if he tapping a woman. "And I had a word with a fellow who was a green hornet like me. I is still a green hornet, but I works the afternoon shift. This fellow I know, the ex-green hornet, couldn't take the abuse and the threats to his person of being a hornet, so he open a little place up in Scarborough where he *impounds* the cars I tow'way. And me and he splits the money. I brings in a car, and quick so, um lock up and impounded. If a fellow want back his car, fifty dollars! You want piece o' this action?"

I get real frighten.

"You want to get cut in 'pon this action?

"But-but-but-but. . . ."

"You see that pretty silver-grey Thunderbird park beside that fire hydrand? I watching that car now fifteen minutes. I see the fellow park it and go in the apartment building there. I figure if he coming out soon, he going come out in twenty minutes. I got five more minutes. . ."

I start getting real frighten now. 'Cause I see the car. And the car is the same car that belongst to Goliath, the black Amurcan fellow. I so frighten that I can't talk and warn my green-hornet friend. But even if I could have find words, my tow-truck friend too busy talking and telling me 'bout a piece o' the action, and how easy it is to tow 'way cars that belongst to illegal immigrants, and get money split fifty-fifty, and that to remember the Rockefellers. . .

". . .and I had to laugh one day when I bring in a Cadillac," he tell me, still laughing, as if he was still bringing in the Cadillac. "Appears that my pound friend had a little altercation or difference of opinion with a Murcan man over a car once, so when I appear with the silver-grey Caddy, he get frighten and start telling me that nobody not going to maim him or brutalize him or cuss his mother, that before anything like that happen he would go back to Guyana first and pick welts offa reefs or put out oyster pots down by the Georgetown sea wall. . . Look! I got to go. Time up!"

I see him, and I watch him pull off from beside o' me like if he didn't know me, like if I was a fire hydrant. I watch him drive up to the shiny grey Thunderbird car, not mekking no noise, like a real police raiding a Wessindian poker joint after midnight. I see him get out the tow truck, like if he was walking on ashes. I see him let down the big iron thing at the back o' the tow truck. First time in my eleven years living here as a semi-legal immigrant that I have see a tow truck that didn't make make no noise. I see him bend down and look under the front o' the Thunderbird. I see him wipe his hands. I see him wipe his two hands like a labourer who do a good job does wipe his hands. I see him go round to the back o' the Bird and bend down. He wipe his two hands again. I see him size up the car. I watch him put on the two big canvas gloves on his two hands. I watch him cock the cigar at a more cockier angle, adjust the construction hat, tek off the shades and put them inside his pocket, and I see him take the rope that make out of iron, that look like chain, and hook um on 'pon the gentleman nice, clean-and-polish grey Thunderbird.

I seeing him and I watching him. The boy real professional. I wondering all the time where the boy learn this work. He dance round to the tow truck as if only he was hearing a Barry White slow tune, and press a thing, and the Bird raising up offa the road like if um ready to tek of and fly. I see him press a next thing in the tow truck and the bird stationary but in the air, at a angle, like a Concorde tekking off. I see him bend down again to make sure that the chain o' iron hook on good. I see him wipe his hands in the big canvas gloves a next time, and I see him slap his two hands, telling me from the distance where I is watching that it is a professional job well done. I think I see the dollar bills registering in his two eyes, too! And I see him tug the chain tight, so the Bird would move off nice and slow, and not jerk nor make no noise, when he ready to tek she to the pound to *impound* she.

And then I see the mountain of the man, tipping toe down the metal fire escape of the apartment building where he was, black shoes shining in the afternoon light, hair slick back and shining more brighter from a "process" hairdo, dress in the same three-piece suit with the pin stripe visible now that the sun was touching the rich material at the right angle o' sheen and shine. And I see, or I think I see, the gentleman take off a diamond-and-gold ring two times, off his right hand, and put them in his pocket. I think I see that, and I see how the hand become big big big like a boxing glove, and I watching but I can't open my mouth nor find voice and words to tell my former green-hornet friend to look over his left shoulder. I seeing but I can't talk o' what I seeing. I find I can't talk. I can only move. A tenseness seize the moment. I do so, and point my index finger like a spy telling another spy to don't talk but look behind. But at that very moment the black Amurcan gentleman's hand was already falling on my friend's shoulder. . . .

TOPICS FOR EXPLORATION

1. Austin Clarke uses the first-person point of view to tell this story. How is it effective in reflecting the narrator's personality? The narrator speaks dialect throughout the story. Why has Clarke chosen this strategy?

2. What is the symbolic significance of "the Rockefellers, the Rothschilds, and the Kennedys" for Cleveland? By what kind of motives is he driven? Does the narrator see Cleveland's case as typical of West Indian immigrants in Canada?

3. Does the narrator approve of what Cleveland is doing as a green hornet? Why is Cleveland hostile toward West Indians? toward authority figures? For the narrator, what is the difference between ticketing cars in St. Clair–Oakwood and in the Queen's Park area?

4. During the brawl between the Indian green hornet and the "American Negro," the narrator says he sees how multiculturalism has "gone out the window." What does multiculturalism mean to him? Why is it "gone"?

5. Why won't the narrator get involved in the fight? Why don't some other people in the community complain to the police when their cars are towed away?

6. There are numerous instances of humour in Clarke's story. What comic effects are used by Clarke? What is the author's purpose in using humour?

7. Clarke ends his story in a moment of suspense. How effective is the final episode? Why does the narrator distance himself from Cleveland at the end?

8. The Caribbean community in Toronto consists largely of people of African and East Indian origin. What does Clarke's story reveal about the ways these groups perceive themselves, each other, and American blacks? Comment on the ironic meaning of the title in the above context.

Yeshim Ternar

Yeshim Ternar, a Montreal writer, was born in Istanbul, Turkey, in 1956. From 1975 to 1979, she lived in the United States; in 1980, she came to Canada. She has published fiction in Canadian, American, and European magazines; her stories have appeared in several anthologies: Telling Differences *(1989),* Other Solitudes *(1990) and* Fire Beneath the Cauldron *(1991). Her first collection of short stories is entitled* Orphaned by Halley's Comet *(1991). Her radio play,* Looking for Leonard Cohen, *was broadcast by CBC in 1992.*

Indigo

Gordon and Carol step out of the repertory theatre into the wind. They've gone to see 'Dersu Uzala' at the Conservatoire d'Art Cinématographique. Carol has seen that film once before, but it was Gordon's first.

Carol found herself crying at the same places she had cried the first time around: when Dersu's picture is being taken in the woods and the image stops, becomes a black and white photo which foreshadows a time when Dersu will be a memory. She cried there and also when Dersu and the Russian land surveyor parted ways when they reached the train tracks in the desolate Siberian plain.

The Russian yells after Dersu, calling him by name. His voice rumbles in the wind and we hear the fir trees echoing it back to us with their outstretched branches. It is a cold but sunny Siberian day. There is a hint of thaw because the ground is visible in patches.

That's where Carol cried. For the friendship, the sun, the snow, but maybe most of all for the thaw, for the sight of brown earth underneath the snow touched her. She would not admit it to anyone in Montreal but she cries every spring when she first sees the earth.

'Isn't Russia like Canada?' Carol asks Gordon as they brave the February wind on Sherbrooke Street, walking toward Carol's apartment on St. Famille.

Carol had invited Gordon for tea when the film ended.

'Sure,' he said, 'that'd be fine.' But he doesn't try to keep a conversation going while they are walking. Very few people would, Carol reassures herself, when it is so cold.

'Yes, it is, Russia is like Canada,' Gordon assents.

In Carol's kitchen, Gordon heads for a rocking chair coloured an eerie faded green as if it were once covered with moss or seaweed.

'It's perfect the way it is,' Gordon had said when he first saw that chair. 'Looks like you saved it from a shipwreck lying at the bottom of the ocean.'

'The seasons changed,' Carol had explained. 'It got too cold to go on working outdoors so I decided to leave the last bit of stripping till the spring because I don't like to use chemicals inside. Then over the winter, I got used to the way it looked.'

'Don't change it,' Gordon said then. He likes to sit in it whenever he comes for a visit.

Carol makes tea, arctic fire, which is her favourite flavour. She serves it in indigo coloured mugs. She takes out Dutch shortbread cookies from a round tin and serves them on a thick ceramic plate, also indigo with cream coloured spots.

Then she sits down in a director's chair by the kitchen window. A blue Chinese paper lantern in the living room casts a soft light into the kitchen. Carol has turned on the small light over the range. The kitchen glows.

'Would you like milk with your tea?' Carol asks.

Gordon chuckles. 'No,' he says. 'I haven't picked that up from the British yet.'

Carol gazes pensively into the mug she is holding with both hands. Then she looks up, searches Gordon's face for a sign. Gordon, always shy, will wait for her to start a conversation.

'I'm surprised every time someone answers my letters,' Carol says suddenly. 'Each time I write a letter and drop it into the mailbox, I doubt that it will go anywhere. Not because the mailmen might go on strike but because the whole world might go on strike. Half the time I think the world exists to the extent that I can imagine it. And if I didn't imagine it, it would wait still until I activated it. Isn't that scary?'

'It's Canada,' Gordon says. 'You didn't feel like this before, did you? I mean before you came to Canada. I know I didn't. I had to believe a world existed outside of Guyana. I had to believe to leave.'

'I'm scared, Gordon,' Carol says softly. 'I find myself confusing life and death more and more. I've always thought about death, even as a child, but I seem to do it more these days. I had this strange dream about it the other night. You want to hear it?'

'Sure,' says Gordon, taking a sip from his tea, leaning backward in the rocking chair.

Carol peers into her mug as if she could retrieve her dream there.

'It was the burial of a pharaoh. My best friend, a thin gentle boy and a girl, younger than I, were solemnly walking toward a burial pit. There were colourful ribbons elaborately braided into their tresses and tied to their fingers. Also, around their necks, wrists, and ankles were red and pink bands. When they walked, the ribbons in their hair and on their fingers flew in the wind. How beautiful they are, I thought in the dream.

'"You're beautiful," I said to the little girl, but she was sad. She was someone I had protected until then. "You look better than you ever looked," I said to my best friend.

'"We will be buried today" he answered.

'I knew there was no escape, but I wondered if I could help them run away. So I looked around. All I saw was the infinite sky. That is no place to hide, I thought.

'Below the sky was the burial pit with a large man-made sand dune by its side. It would soon be pushed over my best friend and the little one I had protected.

'In the dream, I didn't know if I would be buried, but somehow I was told that my duty was not to die but to mourn. This was *my* inescapable destiny as my friend's was to die. We were both bound to the same rule on the opposite sides of life. He would be buried alive to keep the pharaoh company in the next life whereas I, with some other women, would be praying from life to assist them in their journey.

'As I watched my friend go, I thought again, how beautiful and festive he looked with his ribbons flying in the wind. The wind picked up, some sand grains got into my eyes. When I rubbed my eyes and regained my sight, my best friend had already gone ahead with the little girl and disappeared in the crowd of retainers standing by the burial pit.'

'So what do you think of that?' Carol asks. 'I was so sad after that dream that I woke up and cried for a long time.'

'Hard to say,' Gordon says before taking a sip from his tea. He puts his cup down on the kitchen table, crosses his arms, and stares at Carol. Although Carol is a strong woman with wide features, she looks surprisingly vulnerable. For an instant, Gordon catches sight of her bare neck, her flesh bluish white in the indirect light as she turns to face him. He could lean over and kiss her, but he quickly changes his mind.

'Hard to say what it means,' he says. 'Maybe you miss someone you lost. You once told me about Michael. maybe you remember him subconsciously.'

Carol smiles. 'He didn't die in Egypt,' she says. 'He died in South Carolina.'

'Perhaps I didn't cry enough then, so it's all coming out now,' she continues. 'Do you know that people used to save their tears in ancient Greece?'

'How?' asks Gordon as he reaches for a cookie.

'In little glass flasks. I saw them once. Not the tears of course, the tears were long gone. Spilled over or evaporated, but the flasks remained.'

'Hm,' Gordon says, interested. 'Where was that?'

'In Adana. It was August. It's hard to imagine that kind of heat now, but it was very very hot. The kind of heat when upright objects take on a new strength only because they are standing up while the rest of the world cannot but submit and lie down.

'When I think of that day, I remember a bee buzzing defiantly and a giant amphora . . . We were coming back to the States from Teheran where Mom and Dad were stationed for the Peace Corps. My parents had decided to travel overland until England so that we could visit the historical sights on the way.

'You've never been in that part of the world, Gordon, so you wouldn't know what these museums along the Mediterranean coast look like.

'Even if it's a hot day outside, inside a museum, broken goddesses from thousands of years ago impart their marble gaze to the visitors so that you feel you're drinking from a fresh water spring just by being there, among them.

'On the second floor of this museum, I had my first encounter with the cool clarity of death.'

'Why? Because of those statues?' asks Gordon.

'No, no, it wasn't the statues. There I was, the little Protestant that I am, a miniature missionary, especially living with my set of parents, so of course a part of me wanted to restore the statues, restoring broken necklaces, make something big and beautiful out of the little relics, but it wasn't that.

'On the second floor to the left of the stairs, I was drawn to a display case. There was a marble seat across it so I sat on it and stared at the tiny glass bottles inside it. They were mostly sea green, cool. They were thicker in the base, heavier, as if the glass had slowly moved from the rim towards the bottom through the centuries.'

'Glass is liquid, you know,' says Gordon. 'It settles down through time.'

'I was wondering what those flasks had been used for. They were so small and brittle. They were too pretty to have been poison flasks whose contents courtesans or couriers would swallow if they were captured as slaves. They were too small to have been used as bottles to carry water, it would have quenched no one's thirst, not even a small child's.

'I read the inscription at the bottom of the case. It said tear flasks. Then I noticed their tiny beaks that would have fitted the tip of the tear duct.

'I imagined people saving their tears. I tried to imagine men and women doing this.

'Why should people save their tears, I thought? To make a point? To make an offering? Gifts for the dead, I reasoned. Like wine with a good meal, the ancients had offered their tears as an accompaniment to their prayers.

'I thought I should own a flask like that to save my tears, but that kind of thing isn't done anymore. Can you imagine anyone in Montreal saving their tears in blue-green flasks, Gordon?'

'No,' he answers. He clicks his tongue and shakes his head the way Montrealers do when they hear something incredulous.

'More tea?' asks Carol as she gets up from her chair to pick up the teapot and continues talking as she pours. 'They always say c'est fun. Everything's fun for the Québécois. Toujours fun.'

'But it isn't,' Gordon says.

'I can't stand it when people say that about love affairs. C'était fun. But some love affairs aren't. They are heavy, serious, real,' Carol reiterates emphatically. She sits down in her chair and crosses her legs.

'I know all about that,' says Gordon. 'It sure wasn't easy being married to my wife. For a while, it was great. I'll grant her that. She was a true Québécoise, a born Montrealer. Lots of energy, up, up all the time. Then she slid out of my sight one day and I couldn't tell if she had ever been there.

'I thought about her the other day. I was at Bar St. Laurent. I had gone in for a beer or two. I was sitting by the window. I saw this woman hitching a ride on a bicycle. She was sitting on the crossbar. She held a pair of crutches in one hand and held on to the handlebar with the other. The man she was riding with pedalled uphill furiously. They were gone in a flash. For some reason she reminded me of my wife.'

Before Gordon has a chance to grow quiet and sink into his memories, Carol's orange cat jumps on Carol's lap, shoots across the dinner table and rears for a leap from Gordon's lap, finally disappearing out of sight with his bushy tail trailing after him.

'Quite a cat, eh?' asks Carol, laughing.

'Good cat,' Gordon says, 'good cat.'

'Do you think you'll ever understand the soul of this city, Gordon?' Carol asks, trying to get his attention back. 'I have a hard time seeing Montreal as one city because it isn't. Blessings pour down on Montreal because it's so fragmented, I think. Someone once told me that a very holy rabbi who lives around Fairmount Street prays faithfully for Montreal so that it will always remain a peaceful island in a world of strife.'

'It *is* peaceful here, isn't it?' wonders Gordon. 'But I can't really find a meaning for my life here. I could sit here and talk about the first eighteen years of my life in Guyana for days on end, but the next eighteen years I spent in Canada is one fast blink. You would yawn if I tried to make a story of it.'

'That's what happens when you try to take root somewhere else, Gordon,' responds Carol. 'We've both become weird exotic plants acclimatized to the Canadian winter.'

'I wish I knew what the Québécois really think about life here. My ex-wife's father, he did something bizarre. Maybe he tried to figure out the same question.

'He was staying at the Charles Le Moyne Hospital in Longueuil for a heart bypass operation. We went to visit him the day before he was scheduled to have his surgery. He made small talk, joked with us, and I chatted as best as I could in my broken French.

'When we left, my mother-in-law stayed behind. Later, she had to leave, too, because they had to get him ready for the operation. So they gave him his sleeping pills and left him alone.

'The next morning when the nurse came to check on him, he wasn't in his bed. They looked for him all over the hospital but he was nowhere to be found.

'When the nurse did her second round, though, he was back in his bed, sleeping like a baby. They asked him where he had been, he said he didn't remember. He recalled it only after the operation.

'There is a vacant lot behind the hospital. Apparently after his wife left, he had slipped out in his pyjamas and slippers. Maybe he had a bathrobe on—it was May. He had lain on the grass, staring at the sky all night long. He never told anyone what he thought about. Neither his wife nor his daughter. He died soon after.'

'What would *you* think about if you were in that situation?' Carol asks Gordon gently.

'I don't know,' Gordon says. He draws a deep breath. 'The sounds of the bush maybe. The chorus of the birds in the morning. Maybe I would see the tall wooden houses bleached a whitish grey under the sun. I don't know.'

As he tells Carol this, Gordon remembers something else. He remembers a sweltering night in Guyana. 'Shut up, shut up,' screams his aunt. Gordon slams the door behind him so that the neighbours won't hear, but her words sail out the open window. 'Shut up, don't bring up the past. Why did you have to come back? To haunt me?'

Gordon does not hear the kiskadee or the ocean. There is no wind. He is already sick with fever. He has been back only a day, he already has a fever, and bad blood never clears.

'So what do you think *you'd* remember?' he asks Carol.

'Water, I guess I'd think about water,' she says. 'When we were in Iran, women used to gather around the fountains at sunset. They would joke with each other and talk in small groups while they waited their turn. Then the sun would set, casting a blue shadow on the whitewashed facades of the houses.'

Carol scrutinizes Gordon's face. He's handsome she thinks. They *could* be more than friends. For a moment, she imagines hugging him, spending the night with him, waking up together to look at the same snowy Montreal street from the same window.

'Talking about water,' Gordon says, as he gets up from the rocking chair. 'All that tea we drank. I got to go to the bathroom.'

He ambles down the dark hallway. Carol stares after him for a minute, then turns around and looks out the window at the snow falling on the rooftops. Her next door neighbours on the third floor, a gay couple, have gone to bed. Their lights are out but Carol makes out their black cat sitting on the window sill, staring back at her. Sometimes a squirrel scampers on the telephone wire strung between the two houses but tonight all is quiet. Carol spots a couple of sleeping pigeons, their heads hidden between their raised wings on the edge of the roof across the courtyard.

Gordon, at the other end of the house, goes into the bathroom and sits on the throne. His eye catches a glittery image on the door facing him. He blinks and looks again, this time more carefully. It's a hologram. When he shifts his gaze, he makes out a sturdy figure. First he thinks it's a guru sitting in lotus position because he knows Carol is into yoga and things like that. A guru in the bathroom? He looks again and realizes he's looking at Mr. Clean with locked arms. When he comes out of the bathroom, Gordon is still smiling.

'I'd better get going now,' he says gently. 'It's too late to catch the métro already. I hope the buses are still running.'

'They run all night.' says Carol and smiles.

Carol, holding her orange cat, waits above the stairs until Gordon closes the door behind him. Above the lace curtain that covers the glass halfway up her street door, she is able to watch him make his way down the icy outside stairs.

The snow is silvery blue. If one has the heart to take a deep breath and look straight up despite the cold, one might call the sky indigo.

Gordon, a black man in a white parka, fastens his hood tighter to keep the wind out of his ears while Carol closes and bolts her door.

TOPICS FOR EXPLORATION

1. What does Carol's reaction to the movie suggest about her character? Does the rest of the story confirm your first impression of her? What is her family background? Why has Yeshim Ternar chosen a white, middle-class, privileged American young woman as her protagonist?

2. What is the significance of Carol's dream? What does she mean when she says that her "duty was not to die but to mourn"? Why does she see herself as a "miniature missionary" when exploring the museums of the Mediterranean? How does her obsessive preoccupation with the past reflect the sterility of her present life?

3. What is the purpose of Carol's story of the "tear flasks"? How do the tear flasks relate to Carol's excessive crying at the movie in the opening section of the story? Is her story an exercise in self-pity?

4. "Do you think you'll ever understand the soul of this city?" Carol asks about Montreal. What is the soul of Montreal for Carol? For Gordon? Neither of them feels at home in Montreal. Why not? Do you think they are trying to romanticize their alienation?

5. What are Gordon's memories of Guyana? How do they compare with Carol's memories? How effective is the contrast between Gordon's silence and Carol's eloquence?

6. Carol is white and Gordon black. Is there any tension in their relationship? How do they communicate? At the end the author makes no comment on their parting. Are there any unspoken regrets between them?

Joy Kogawa

Joy Kogawa was born in Vancouver in 1935; she is a nisei, *a second-generation Japanese Canadian. After the attack on Pearl Harbor and the Japanese capture of Hong Kong in 1941, Japanese-Canadian civilians were rounded up by the Canadian government, their possessions were auctioned off, and they were transported to internment camps away from the British Columbia coast. Kogawa and her family were evacuated to Slocan, B.C., and later to Alberta. The experience of this forced migration of innocent people informs much of Kogawa's work, especially her celebrated novel* Obasan *(1981). The same theme has also recurred in her poetry and in her children's book* Naomi's Road *(1986), most recently made into a play. Kogawa has been active in the legal fight for reparations due to Japanese Canadians unfairly treated during World War II. This fragment from her latest novel,* Itsuka *(1992), which is a sequel to* Obasan, *describes the apology made to Japanese Canadians in Parliament. At the end of the excerpt is a government document of "acknowledgement," formally stating Canada's responsibility.* Itsuka *means "someday."*

from Itsuka

Dreams dreams dreams.

It begins in earliest infancy, this journey through the world's many borderlands. It proceeds through the day of the odourless fawn, past summer, into the mustier season of leaves, orchards, the harvest with its memories and dance. To be without history is to be unlived crystal, unused flesh; is to live the life of the unborn.

What I've wakened to in this new autumn day is hunger. My eyes are hungry. The palms of my hands are hungry for this square inch of space we are inhabiting today. Our bite-sized moment of life. I'm as small and as hungry as a newborn sparrow.

September 22, 1988. Ottawa.

Perhaps it's in the scheme of things that when life is most bleak, miracles break through. It's such a mystery. And so completely unexpected. I first heard about it last night. Last night was another life-time ago.

I was still at *Bridge* when Aunt Emily called around seven. Dan had just called her. She immediately called Anna and me. She couldn't call any others because it's still completely confidential. All she said was "Come over immediately. I can't tell you why." I rushed up to the apartment and found her looking around abstractedly. She packed in silence, mechanically. We tried to sleep. We were up before the alarm. Anna, looking like a blimp, came by with Brian at at 5:30 a.m., and we've been driving the four and a half hours along the 401 towards the cut-off at the Tweed highway. We're in a daze.

Our president, Mick Hayashi, Dan and others on the strategy team, unlike most of us, had felt something would have to happen following the American resolution, but over the many months and years they'd grown wary of false optimism. They did not communicate a word of hope to the rank and file. There had been so much debility and loss of morale when repeatedly, after promises of negotiations, there'd be a collapse in talks. Then suddenly, three weeks ago, the team was called to a Montreal hotel, and after a weekend of non-stop negotiating the unbelievable happened. An agreement was reached. There's to be a full acknowledgement of the injustices, individual compensation of $21,000 each to those affected (the Americans are to receive $20,000), a community fund and a race-relations foundation. It's a $350,000,000 package.

"All that? Just like that? But—was there no warning?"

The team was sworn to secrecy. They were told that if the news leaked out in any way, and if the Legion, for instance, objected, the whole thing could be jeopardized. Even now, everything could be stopped. Dan took his oath so seriously that he went north to an isolated cabin.

"It's a miracle. What happened, do you think?"

Brian thinks it's because it's election time. Plus they're copying the Americans, for sure. Maybe it's because of a few key people—like John Fraser, the Speaker of the House.

Young John Fraser, Aunt Emily tells us, was a child in Vancouver when we all disappeared. His father took him to the cenotaph in Stanley Park where Japanese Canadian veterans of the First World War were memorialized. "I fought beside those men," he told his son. John Fraser never forgot.

Whatever the reasons may or may not be, we're so used to pessimism that the fact of a settlement isn't really registering. Aunt Emily says she doesn't want to say another word until she's actually in the House and the papers are actually signed. Dan told her the whole thing is so precarious anything could still stop it.

"How do you think Nikki's going to react?" Anna asks.

Publicly?" Aunt Emily says. "She'd be a fool to oppose it. And Nikki's no fool."

"Privately, she'll break out in a rash," Brian says.

Privately, I'm wondering if Nikki is still convinced the NJCL are greedy opportunists. Vultures, I think she called us. Could there be any truth in her statement that history will condemn us and vindicate her? That, I suppose, is something none of us can know. What we as a community decide to do from this day on will reveal who we are.

Brian is familiar with the route. We take a rest break at Tweed, get to Ottawa shortly after ten, check in to a friend's house on Gilmour Avenue near the Lord Elgin Hotel, collapse for a second on our beds. And now here we are in this city, the country's capital, the four of us, walking up to Parliament Hill under the blue-white September sky.

I think of the years of labour, the rally half a year ago that Aunt Emily missed—how we walked along in the drizzle and how I wasn't feeling a whisper of hope even though I was carrying the yellow ribbons of hope, and suddenly this unbelievable, this most astonishing day.

If I were a watcher in the skies, I might notice small antlike groupings of people walking up Parliament Hill this morning, up past the Centennial flame; up the wide walk and the steps and into the lobby of the Centre Block with its high vaulted ceiling. Dan flew up last night. Others from the strategy team are here with Mick Hayashi, plus some people from the Ottawa community. Only a few passes have been arranged since it's all such a secret. We hand over our cameras and notebooks at a desk, go down the marble hall, enter the high narrow gallery above the House of Commons and look down directly on the members of Parliament facing each other from their two tiers of benches. So few members present. The speaker is on a dais to our left. To our right is the public gallery, without a single person in it. The huge chamber seems almost empty. Just a handful from our community. So little flesh, but so many ghosts.

Mick Hayashi, Dan and all the main people plus a couple of senior citizens are on the side of the gallery facing the Prime Minister. A few other people from Ottawa, Aunt Emily, Brian, Anna and I sit in the opposite balcony. Anna waves a finger to our team. Below us are the people who lead the country. We can see the top of Prime Minister Mulroney's head from the back and, opposite him, Mr. Broadbent, leader of the New Democratic Party. The leader of the Liberal Party is not present.

11:00 a.m.

The Prime Minister stands. The magic of speech begins—this ritual thing that humans do, the washing of stains through the speaking of words.

"Mr. Speaker," the Prime Minister begins. "Nearly half a century ago, in the crisis of wartime, the Government of Canada wrongfully incarcerated, seized the property, and disenfranchised thousands of citizens of Japanese ancestry. . . ." Even as I strain to hear and remember the many words, they are gone and speech is a trickster, slipping and sliding away. "To put things right," the Prime Minister says in his low voice. And again, "to put things right." And once more. "To put things right."

"Most of us in our own lives," he is saying, "have had occasion to regret certain things we have done. Error is an ingredient of humanity. So too is apology and forgiveness. We all have learned from personal experience that, as inadequate as apologies are, they are the only way we can cleanse the past so that we may, as best we can, in good conscience face the future. . . ."

In the future I know we will look back on this moment as we stand and applaud. We'll remember how Ed Broadbent crossed the floor to shake the Prime Minister's hand and we'll see all this as a distant sun, a star, an asterisk in space to guide us through nights that yet must come. The children, the grandchildren, will know that certain things happened to their ancestors. And that these things were put right.

Sergio Marchi, the Liberal Party representative, is commending our president and community "for their never-ending determination and deep belief in the cause that they carried so well for so long. Today's resolution, no doubt, is a tribute to their sense of purpose, but it is also an appropriate response to those who continue to question the legitimacy and motivation of the leadership. . . ."

I feel us wanting to jump up and cheer but we are contained. And as I look down I can see Mr. Broadbent, who was married to a nisei and knows our story from the inside. I'm glad to be on this side, facing him. He appears agitated, his hands shuffling papers, his eyes glancing up to where we sit. And then he rises and speaks and he's fighting to control his voice. "They, as Canadian citizens, had done no wrong," Mr. Broadbent says. "They had done no wrong. . . ."

This feast of words is too wonderful, too sad, too joyful. I'm numb. Aunt Emily too is listening from some great slow distance of time and space. We are seated at a banquet table that was a hope for people yesterday and will feed us with hope tomorrow. The power of this hour is being stored now in our hearts as a promise fulfilled, a vision realized, and the healing rises up to us, the healing falls about us, over the countryside, here and there, today and tomorrow, touching the upturned faces filled with the waiting and longing of all the wordless years.

The speeches end and it's all going by so fast, so fast, and we're back in the west hallway, in a room where a small throng is gathering. The signing of the agreement is happening here and I catch just a glimpse of the Prime Minister again, no more or less real than any other person as he steps into the room. The TV cameras are directed upon him and our president, smiling, shaking hands, then sitting at a table, the strategy team standing behind. A flashing of lights and cameras clicking. And it's done.

Then, like a gathering swarm of bees, politicians, staff members, the NJCL vanguard in a block, TV crews and reporters all move down the hall, the wide stairs. We walk back down the middle of the Hill to the press conference on the other side of Rideau Street. Aunt Emily is sleep walking.

We can't get into the room where the press conference is and we go with the overflow, up the crowded elevator to a sixth-floor lounge and a television screen, then back down again into the world of microphones and cameras, and catch up with Dan and the others as they walk back up to the Parliament Buildings for a reception.

I want some way to slow down the day, but the waterfall refuses to be contained in a cup and we're swept along in the swift liquid hour, into a room with tables of food, glib words, glazed eyes, cameras flashing, and Aunt Emily is standing with Mr. Broadbent and she looks stunned and not altogether coherent.

"I feel I've just had a tumour removed," one of our friends from Ottawa says to me. "Can you believe it, Naomi?"

We're in a buzz of sounds whirring about.

"Let me congratulate you, Mick. I think you've created a vaccine."

"Yes?"

"Against fatigue. A vaccine against compassion fatigue."

Cedric, Morty, Marion and Ken have just flown up from Toronto and Cedric has the most joyful tearful smile I have ever seen. he comes rushing up to me and in all that crowd he takes me in his arms. "Watch out, world," he whispers. "The mouse has roared."

I laugh. I am whole. I am as complete as when I was a very young child. Marion puts her arms around us both. "God bless us every one," she says.

Aunt Emily and Dan are talking with a man from the Secretary of State who asks Aunt Emily, "How did you feel when you heard the apology?"

Aunt Emily is in a trance and can't reply. My aunt of the so many words. How does she feel as this day speeds by? How does the grass feel in the cool autumn air? How does the sky feel? And the community across the country as it hears the news today?

Ken says, "I finally feel that I'm a Canadian." You can hear the trembling in his voice.

Aunt Emily and I look at each other and smile. We've all said it over the years. "No, no, I'm Canadian. I'm a Canadian. A Canadian." Sometimes it's been a defiant statement, a demand, a proclamation of a right. And today, finally, finally, though we can hardly believe it, to be Canadian means what it hasn't meant before. Reconciliation. Liberation. Belongingness. Home.

Anna and Brian, Cedric, Morty, Aunt Emily and I walk back to Gilmour Avenue. We let ourselves smile. "Well?" Aunt Emily asks, looking up at the sky. That's all she can say.

We make some tea and catch the TV news on every channel we can find. We gasp when we see the official shots. By focusing on the Prime Minister and the MPs behind him, the camera makes the House seem packed, when in fact, it certainly wasn't—not that it mattered. There's a brief report on the radio that Nikki was contacted in Toronto. She said she was very happy about the announcement. We all applaud and toast Nikki with our cups of tea.

The Vancouver contingent phones and we go off to meet for supper. Someone is doing an interview with Mick outside the restaurant. We go in. Wait. Mick arrives. We eat. A few Ottawa people drop by. Then Cedric and I excuse ourselves and leave, ducking past a man taking pictures. We walk hand in hand out into the evening air, up Elgin Street, along Rideau, where strangers are standing at their bus stops, waiting for their many buses, walk past and up to the grounds of Parliament Hill again. We're walking off the stage of the day with its hovering of well-wishers and the great happy crush of the press—away from the speeches, the interviews, the congratulations, the shaking of hands at the restaurant, where some people are still looking at one another, pinching themselves, asking if it's true.

We're taking time, taking time to quieten this day, to bring it back from its already past. We're stretching it out on the canvas of the night air, shaking it out like a blanket to wear.

Oh Aunt Emily, Aunt Emily, is it not the happiest day of your life? I want to remember everything. Savour it all. Our frantic search for a safety pin for the tie on Anna's skirt. The man who honked his horn on Rideau Street and waved. The pattern of sand on the Centre Block steps. Mick, our brave president, with a hand in his hip pocket as he walked briskly ahead of us. I want to etch the day onto the permanent airwaves of memory, replay it over and over until it starts to seem real. Aunt Emily, I want to be able to see you for ever and ever the way you were this morning, walking happily,

happily up the hill in your brown trenchcoat and your good walking shoes, my dear warrior aunt. I want to call all the ghosts back again to share this day that none of us can believe is happening.

In my pocket, I have the folded piece of paper that contains the government statement. I read the words again and I take them into my childhood home. I pile them like firelogs, one by one. I warm my limbs.

"As a people, Canadians commit themselves to the creation of a society that ensures equality and justice for all. . . ."

I hand the paper to Cedric and he reads it aloud as we stand looking out over the shadowy trees and bushes on the slope, to the Ottawa River below. In a month's time the leaves of the trees will change colour, and then they will fall as they've been falling for ever, year after year, each leaf with its own tiny story twirling into every other ongoing tale.

This hill is not unlike the slope to the Old Man River near Granton, though it's steeper here and the river is more wide. Sixteen years ago I stood with my uncle on the Granton coulees in the coolness of a night like this, looking down at the ocean of grass, and he said, as he always did, "Umi no yo." It's like the sea.

It's like the sea tonight, Uncle. A busy bubbling trembling sea of the almost sighted and the sometimes blind, the swimmers, the drifters, and those who don't know how to swim. We are here together, and it's enough.

Sixteen years ago this month, my uncle died. And two years later, so did my Obasan. I'm thinking of them and of the rapids, the waterfalls, the eddies in the journey to the sea, and how today we've touched the sounds of the waves on the shore, the applause, the pulse of earth's heart still beating. And I'm thinking of Uncle's words and the words of an old man in Slocan.

"There is a time for crying," they said. "But itsuka, someday, the time for laughter will come."

This is the time, dear Uncle, dear Ojisan. The dramatics, the tears and cheers, have arrived in their own way in their own time. We have come to the hour when the telling leaps over the barricades and the dream enters day.

I can hear the waves from childhood rippling outwards to touch other children who wait for their lives. I can hear the voices, faint as the far-away sound of a distant, almost inaudible wind. It's the sound of the underground stream. It speaks through memory, through dream, through our hands, through our words, our arms, our trusting. I can hear the sound of the voice that frees, a light, steady, endless breath. I can hear the breath of life.

Thank you for this.

ACKNOWLEDGEMENT

As a people, Canadians commit themselves to the creation of a society that ensures equality and justice for all, regardless of race or ethnic origin.

During and after World War II, Canadians of Japanese ancestry, the majority of whom were citizens, suffered unprecedented actions taken by the Government of Canada against their community.

Despite perceived military necessities at the time, the forced removal and internment of Japanese Canadians during World War II and their deportation and expulsion following the war, was unjust. In retrospect, government policies of disenfranchisement, detention, confiscation and sale of private and community property, expulsion, deportation and restriction of movement, which continued after the war, were influenced by discriminatory attitudes. Japanese Canadians who were interned had their property liquidated and the proceeds of sale were used to pay for their own internment.

The acknowledgement of these injustices serves notice to all Canadians that the excesses of the past are condemned and that the principles of justice and equality in Canada are reaffirmed.

Therefore, the Government of Canada, on behalf of all Canadians, does hereby:

> 1) acknowledge that the treatment of Japanese Canadians during and after World II was unjust and violated principles of human rights as they are understood today;

> 2) pledge to ensure, to the full extent that its powers allow, that such events will not happen again; and

> 3) recognize, with great respect, the fortitude and determination of Japanese Canadians who, despite great stress and hardship, retain their commitment and loyalty to Canada and contribute so richly to the development of the Canadian nation.

TOPICS FOR EXPLORATION

1. "To be without history is to be unlived crystal, unused flesh." Why does the narrator feel she is without history? Find other examples of Joy Kogawa's use of figurative language to convey the "unspeakable."

2. What are the details of the reparations offered to Japanese Canadians? Are the reparations adequate to compensate them for the losses in property, the years of hardship, and the belated recognition of the injustice done to them?

3. In her narrative, Kogawa presents real people, such as Brian Mulroney and Ed Broadbent. What is the effect of introducing historical personages into the fictional world of the novel? What does it tell us about the margin between fact and fiction?

4. "The washing of stains through the speaking of words" is what humans do, says Kogawa. Why does she believe that the "stain" may be washed clean by the government's public apology? How does the same generalization apply to her own writing and its cleansing, therapeutic function?

5. One of the characters, Ken, says, "I finally feel that I'm a Canadian." How, on this most astonishing day, has the meaning of being Canadian changed for those Japanese Canadians who were there to hear the announcement and receive the apology?

6. How does Kogawa's text celebrate the sense of purpose in the Japanese-Canadian community? How do its members view their responsibility toward the past and future generations?

7. Why has Kogawa included the government "Acknowledgement" at the end of this fiction? How effective is putting together a fictionalized account and a genuine document, both related to the same historical event? What do they contribute to each other?

SUGGESTIONS FOR
FURTHER STUDY

1. Compare Austin Clarke's fiction with Rosemary Brown's essay. What do they have in common? In what ways are they different? Is there a difference between the two central figures resulting from education, gender, or expectations?

2. Compare "racism Canadian-style" as it affects different groups such as Caribbean immigrants in Austin Clarke's story and Rosemary Brown's autobiography, and the Japanese Canadians of Joy Kogawa's *Itsuka*. What have been the consequences of racism for each group?

3. Compare the Montreal described by Rosemary Brown with the appraisal of that city by Carol in Yeshim Ternar's story "Indigo." Are both images of the city accurate? Do they contradict each other?

4. Discuss the portraits of Native Canadians as presented in Green's "The Last Raven" and Markoosie's "Wings of Mercy," How close are these characters to Native culture? How much have they been influenced by white culture, technology, and attitudes?

5. What prospects and experiences in the new land might be determined by the immigrant's expectations and his/her social background? Compare on the basis of real and fictional accounts of immigration in Michael Ignatieff's, Rosemary Brown's, Brian Moore's, Austin Clarke's, and Yeshim Ternar's writing.

6. The Chinese Canadian National Council has sought reparations for past injustices committed against Chinese immigrants to Canada. On the basis of "Chinese Wall Writing" and Joy Kogawa's *Itsuka*, compare the role that the Canadian government has played in both encouraging immigration from Asia and disenfranchising Asian immigrants.

UNIT THREE

SELF AND OTHER: LANGUAGE

INTRODUCTION

Learning to speak is like learning to think. It is possible that the way we learn to think is a direct consequence of the way language structures our thinking. Therefore, expression in one's first language is as clear and easy as the breath that generates it.

However, there is no universal spoken language that would enable us to communicate without the structures that custom enforces. Thus, the languages of the world, in their diversity, set up barriers between mental processes and their expression. Those who cross geographical barriers also cross the boundaries of language. Crossing these barriers means learning to think again in the patterns imposed by a new culture. Of course, the level of language intentionally acquired in adulthood can be either enhanced by curiosity or limited by inhibitions and fears. On the one hand, living in a foreign language can impose constraints or lead the newcomer to cling to the known; on the other hand, it can double the resources of those who dream in two vocabularies. Most of the voices in this unit think in one or several other languages while speaking in English. Most of them find unique advantages in this richness, but there are difficulties, too.

Myrna Kostash, in "Pens of Many Colours," raises the issues of ethnic identity and assimilation. She prefers the layers of expression that texture her English, but resents being "hyphenated" as a Ukrainian-Canadian author if that excludes her from mainstream literature in Canada. For her, the tension of not joining the old, English-speaking elite generates the challenge and excitement of expressing a double heritage of language in her work. For Eva Hoffman, an author who straddles English and Polish, the difficulty of being transplanted into a new cultural and linguistic context is the severing of "signifier from signified," or the word (and its associations) from the experience. She describes the frustrating ironies of learning a second language and the attendant loss of self-definition; she also explores how fluency in a language sets up a class structure. All in all, "linguistic dispossession" is a division of self from culture. Himani Bannerji has similar views. She reaches out to her childhood experiences in India with all their resonances of myth and meaning; she focusses her reminiscences on her mother and discovers that experience cannot be fully conveyed in a language in which it did not originate and which is divorced from the context that gives it meaning.

The barriers of language, then, are sometimes difficult to transcend. Genni Donati Gunn deals with the dilemma of conserving one culture while living in another. In "The Middle Ground," Rosalba wants to keep her son Claudio "from being Canadian" because she fears he will lose the Italian heritage so important to her. Nevertheless, as a teacher, she deplores the conservatism of the older generation of Italian immigrants, exemplified by the repressive cultural limits set upon her disabled student, Peppi, by his Italian parents. Garry Engkent communicates a different problem. In "Why My Mother Can't Speak English," the narrator's mother has lived in Canada for decades but has never learned English for a variety of reasons: the rigidity acquired in old age, her preference for her original culture, the limitations set by her patriarchal husband, and so on. The isolation of having one language amidst the culture of another cuts her off from the possibility of understanding Canadian customs and patterns of behaviour and interpreting them in a correct way. Engkent understands that the old woman fears to learn English because it would "change her Chinese soul," even though, in her case, language might act as a barrier to attaining Canadian citizenship.

In this unit, the contrast between the liberating articulation and hindering muteness that we observe throughout the continuum of language is indeed striking. Despite the frustrations involved in conveying the full measurement of human experience, "life is," as Himani Bannerji believes, "always more than the expression of living it."

how feel I do?

your eyes plead approval
on each uttered word

and even my warmest smile
cannot dispel the shamed muscles
from your face

let me be honest
with you

to tell the truth
I feel very much at home
in your embarrassment

don't be afraid

like you
I too was mired in another language
and I gladly surrendered it
for english

you too
in time
will lose your mother's tongue

and speak
at least as fluent
as me

now tell me

how do you feel?

—*Jim Wong-Chu*

Jim Wong-Chu came to Canada from Hong Kong in 1953; he is a founding member of the Asian-Canadian Writers' Workshop. This poem comes from his collection Chinatown Ghosts *(1986).*

Myrna Kostash

Myrna Kostash is an Edmonton author of Ukrainian background. From this double perspective she points out the ironies and paradoxes familiar to bilingual and bicultural people. She has published All of Baba's Children *(1977), a book of non-fiction dealing with Ukrainians in Canada, and* Long Way from Home: The Story of the Sixties Generation in Canada *(1980), a study of that turbulent decade. As a freelance journalist, she has written stories and articles for major Canadian magazines. Her strong interest in feminism is visible in her contribution to* Her Own Woman: Profiles of Ten Canadian Women *(1975), and in her book* No Kidding: Inside the World of Teenage Girls *(1987).*

Pens of Many Colours

Gabrielle Roy once wrote about Ukrainian Canadians that we possess "une teinte indéfinissable de rudesse et d'extrême douceur, de violente gaieté et de violente protestation". Nevertheless, she felt that we were somehow familiar to her—like the French-Canadians, she wrote, we were possessed of a "nostalgia for the past" which kept cropping up in our speech—and were relieved, therefore, of our burden as the Other, the Alien in Canadian society. Thanks to our drift away from the land and our arrival in the towns and cities where everybody else was living, we had even lost our status as a real minority group: we had, according to Roy, "completely adapted" to Canada and our "dances, picturesque costumes, and songs" had passed into the "national heritage" where they were taken up as "all of ours" by Canadians at large. And that, I suppose, is the end of the story, as Roy saw it.

I don't know when Roy wrote this essay but I would guess well before 1970, given its tone of satisfaction that the incomparably jolly and crude Ukrainians had ceased to be alien among Canadians, that our characteristics, far from marking us as strangers, reminded the writer *of her own people*, that our very ethnicity was no longer a rebuke to Anglo and Franco cultural habits but had somehow merged with them and brought us all closer together in a kind of reconciliation. I have no doubt that Roy approved of these processes. But almost everything she had to say about Ukrainians and otherness is now quite out of date. In the last 20 years, we have almost entirely "rethought" ourselves, as it were; and I for one no longer recognize myself in this romantic portrait of the wistful suburban settler and reconciler of paradoxes.

Or rather, to speak more honestly, I do recognize myself in that portrait but it is like an old photograph found in a shoebox: a momento of an earlier self that evokes sharp recall of what we once believed and cherished and what still resides within the more recent self, but like a kind of hard nut around which the layers of experience and reflection have formed a complex tissue.

I don't suppose there is any member of a minority or oppressed group—any woman, any person of colour, any ethnic—who has not dreamed of belonging—of escaping from the curse of the ghetto and entering the high streets of the city like an ordinary citizen. It is this dream that Roy speaks to—and also, let us never forget, to the fear held by our ruling classes of the unassimilated, hence unmanageable, stranger at their gates—and so the evocation of finality, absorption, closure (in a word, assimilation), is meant to be profoundly reassuring. We ethnics have deeply desired to be ordinary, to be "just" Canadians (as women have desired to be "just" human beings and homosexuals "just" men) and relieved of our role of the exotic, at best, sinister, at worst, newcomer whose job it is to provide object lessons to "Canadians" about their own superiority.

My parents' generation—the first one born in Canada—seems to have confronted this. By learning to speak English, by taking middle-class jobs, by raising children in the suburbs, they did more than just take on protective colouring. They served notice that they wished to be engaged in the general public debate and process of construction of Canadian society. They wanted to *be* there. As comforting and reaffirming as a ghetto is, its homeliness and solace have a price; exclusion, self-containment, set-asideness. If the ghetto is a sanctuary, it is because this is precisely the zone where the outside world, the big one, the mainstream one, cannot and does not wish to intrude.

For my generation, however, the question has been posed again, and it has been posed not as a polarized conflict between the either/or of assimilation and ghettoization but as the postmodern realization that we ethnic *arrivistes* live in both conditions at once. The point, suddenly, is not Roy's dream of the reconciliation of opposites but the acceptance, even cultivation, of what Eli Mandel has called the "interface" of cultures, the "dialectic of self and other" where tension at the point of contact, ambivalence, ambiguity, porousness, is the point, not resolution—the transcendence of paradox, stasis—as had been implied in the older dream. No, this new generation does not want to *overcome* the so-called problem of ethnicity but to live with it. It doesn't want to see its "problem" as having been dealt with once and for all the moment its parents adapted to the ordinary, the unexceptional. It wants to revive the extraordinary, the dissonant, the unpresentable, and juxtapose them to the civilized centre.

This is no gratuitous exercise. *This is our condition.* For as surely as the repressed material of the subconscious reasserts itself in the individual soul—as dream, obsession, metaphor—so does it come back to haunt the assimilated ethnic. To my parents' generation, it came back as nostalgia—that melancholic yearning for the unrecoverable. To an older generation of writer, as with Gabrielle Roy, it came back as a figure of speech, as though metaphor could transform the conflicted self into well-being. For my generation, though, it has reasserted itself as politics, specifically the politics of the inside agitator.

> I wanted the I to be an arrow
> of pure intent
> instead of the flesh it tears through
> I am a snake
>
> shedding my skin
> from the inside
> *(Joanne Thorvaldson, Border Crossings)*

Of course it is no accident that it is my generation which raises the creative possibilities of ambivalence and ambiguity; we are, thanks to our parents' efforts, at home in Canada. Our status as citizens is not in question. We can *afford* to cultivate tension. But we came to this tension through our own generational experience. I have written elsewhere about how the '60s experience in student movements, civil rights movements, the counterculture and the women's liberation movement have provided us the material with which to identify with the oppressed and brutalized against the violence of capitalist, post-industrial institutions and with which to identify ourselves as a group, a collective consciousness, an unalienated "we". From this experience, it was not far for the ethnic to go to embrace the "we" in ethnicity as well and, more important, to see it as a zone of resistance to the overbearing authority of the dominant culture that oppressed us as women, blacks, gays, students. For if it is true, as George Grant has said, that resistance to oppression is possible as soon as we come to know and love what is good in that which is ours, then our politics as inside agitators become a given the moment we embraced the "ethnic" in ourselves: the person with a specific history, which is to say memory, with a special sense of place—the interlocked historical narratives of Canadians *and* aliens—and with an experience of endurance and contention that did not take place only in the private fastness of the self but in all of us, together, relations.

To know all this, of course, is to know that one's condition as ethnic is one of flux, pluralities, tension. That one is simultaneously *of* this society but not at all times *in* it.

How this condition affects the place of the ethnic writer within Canadian writing is the obvious next question. How do we, living at the interface of cultures and insisting in their contiguity, and their ultimate communicability between each other, how do we write ourselves into the dominant culture? How do we become heard within the orchestrated polyphony of CanLit? It is not an obvious question, for, even when we write in English, as most of us do, we do not stand in the same relationship to language as do the anglophones.

Under these words
Are the echoes of other words

as the Polish-English poet, Maria Jastrzeska, writes. Even when English is our first language, we have all our lives heard another one (or two or three), as though these *other* sounds—strange, fragmented utterances though they be—were natural speech, one which preceded the one we now call mother English. And so we are like the young James Joyce, Irish-born, monolingual English-speaker, in conversation with his tutor from England who suddenly realizes that though they are both speaking the same language, for one of them the language has had to be *learned*—struggled for, struggled against—across generations of Celtic-speaking peasants who were forcibly dragged into English speech by violent men from a foreign place. So, my "native tongue" is a kind of gift. It is not mine by race or ancestry, it is mine only because my parents learned it. Behind *them* stand rank upon rank of peasants who never spoke a word of it, who spoke instead a language lettered by monks of Byzantium. Perhaps it is time now to speak of sister or cousin-tongues as well as of the mother?

The second problematic concerns one's designation as a writer in Canada. I had the very odd experience of finding myself entered in the *Oxford Companion to Canadian Literature* as "Kostash, Myrna, See: Ukrainian Writing". Odd, because it seems to me that, over some 20 years of writing. I have made a contribution not just as an ethnic but as a woman/feminist, an Albertan, a Canadian, a non-fictionist, organization activist, teacher—why should the "Ukrainian" component of all this activity be the one to characterize me? Odd, too, in that I have no idea what "Ukrainian writing" is supposed to mean in my case; I write only in English and address an English-speaking audience. What on earth does it take to become a Canadian writer, a contributor to and practitioner of CanLit, if not books written in Canada by a Canadian for Canadians? Could it be that, given my origins outside the Anglo-Celtic and Franco founding nations, I shall *never* be considered to belong because I wasn't there at the beginning when the naming took place? That CanLit is a category and a practice hijacked and held captive by a very exclusive gang of men and women who all come from the right side of the tracks?

In a provocative article in *This Magazine*, Rosemary Sullivan takes up the question directly, arguing that the "national story recorded in our literature is a cumulative one and it's open-ended". I take her point: that, with each wave of immigration to Canada, the "national story" acquires new plots and characters, new sounds and images, and is never told once and for all.

Any attempt to exclude some voices to privilege others—to say that CanLit is the work mainly of male Anglo-Saxons from Ontario, say—is to do grave injury to the multicultural character of our society, of our creativity even. "What would it mean if we defined Canadian literature as the literature of a multicultural nation?" she asks, in a rhetorical invitation to consider the enriching possibilities of a literature which sees itself as multilingual and multifocal, polymorphous and resounding with a thousand different memories?

It is an exhilarating vision and yet, and yet . . . I find myself skeptical and resisting. For it reminds me of that assimilated world of Gabrielle Roy with which I began, where all difference has been transubstantiated and the particular experience of ethnics at the margin of speech and audience—the experience of alienation, anger, fear, envy,—is collapsed into a generic speech called CanLit. Anybody can belong. "I'm bored with 'Canadian' being a term of exclusion," writes Sullivan, with a hint of that ennui of the ladies and gentlemen of the chateau, presented ethnics for their entertainment. For those ethnics, "exclusion" is not boring. It is painful and exciting, for it is in those "interstices" of cultures that we have become writers. In other words, we may not *wish* to belong to the club. We may wish to live with tension and distress. We may wish to remind ourselves, over and over, that we live on the wrong side of the tracks, on the edge of town.

But "town" is home, is here. This is both literal and figurative. I grew up in an ethnic and immigrant working-class neighbourhood east of downtown Edmonton and it has never occurred to me—not then, not now—that this neighbourhood was not an organic part of the city; for all its "otherness" it was nevertheless linked by roadway and workplace and commerce to the rest of the city. Similarly, the "town" in my head is a Canadian zone: I have lived in it all my life, I understand its codes and lingo, I know how to get around, it is the place where I was given birth as a writer.

So, Sullivan makes another, more crucial error: she identifies multicultural literature with immigrant literature, as though the problems of exclusion and belonging, language and speech, were present only to the newcomer, at the point of entry, as though the Canadian-born, belonging to the generic Canadian "here", had nothing to say about the multicultural condition. But we do. We ask such questions as: What is my relationship to the English language? Do my memories of ethnic custom bear on the shape of my work? Do I, as a kind of outsider, visualize Canada differently than an insider does? How shall I balance the claims of my feminist "sisters" against those of my grandparents' ghosts? Is the Old Country recoverable?

Speaking of the theme of the torn and exiled immigrant, Sullivan asks: "When one exhausts the theme of 'there', what does one have left?"

My God, woman. Everything!

TOPICS FOR EXPLORATION

1. Whom does Myrna Kostash have in mind as her audience in this essay? What is her purpose? Does her rhetoric reflect any political sympathies and preferences—perhaps for the civil rights movement or women's liberation?

2. What similarities does Gabrielle Roy see between French Canadians and Ukrainian Canadians? Why does Kostash start her essay with Roy's observations? How has the trend toward assimilation, praised by Roy, changed since 1970?

3. Kostash mentions three models of immigrant adaptation, representative of different generations of immigrants. Explain

what she means by "ghettoization," "assimilation," and "integration." How do they differ?

4. Kostash's generation wants to "revive the extraordinary, the dissonant, the unpresentable, and juxtapose them to the civilized centre." In fact, this desire can be explained in terms of the "postmodern condition" of having it both ways. How does this program correspond with the integrational model she chooses for herself?

5. What definition does Kostash give of an "ethnic" person? What are the paradoxes of an ethnic writer who has one or several ancestral languages in addition to the "mother" tongue of English?

6. Why does Kostash resent being called a "Ukrainian" author by the *Oxford Companion to Canadian Literature*? What is the place of ethnic writers within Canadian literature? Why is she sceptical about Rosemary Sullivan's description of Canadian multicultural literature?

7. What are the advantages of living "on the wrong side of the tracks" for Kostash? What does this tension generate?

Eva Hoffman

Eva Hoffman was born in Poland in 1945; her family left for Canada when she was 14 years old. After a few years in Vancouver, she went to study in the United States, where she completed her Ph.D. in English at Harvard University. She now lives in New York and works as an editor for The New York Times. *The following excerpt has been taken from her autobiography,* Lost in Translation *(1989), in which she analyzes her experience of immigration and the difficulties of living between two cultures.*

◆

from Lost in Translation

Every day I learn new words, new expressions. I pick them up from school exercises, from conversations, from the books I take out of Vancouver's well-lit, cheerful public library. There are some turns of phrase to which I develop strange allergies. "You're welcome," for example, strikes me as a gaucherie, and I can hardly bring myself to say it—I suppose because it implies that there's something to be thanked for, which in Polish would be impolite. The very places where the language is at its most conventional, where it should be most taken for granted, are the places where I feel the prick of artifice.

Then there are words to which I take an equally irrational liking, for their sound, or just because I'm pleased to have deduced their meaning. Mainly they're words I learn from books, like "enigmatic" or "insolent"—words that have only a literary value, that exist only as signs on the page.

But mostly, the problem is that the signifier has become severed from the signified. The words I learn now don't stand for things in the same unquestioned way they did in my native tongue. "River" in Polish was a vital sound, energized with the essence of riverhood, of my rivers, of my being immersed in rivers. "River" in English is cold—a word without an aura. It has no accumulated associations for me, and it does not give off the radiating haze of connotation. It does not evoke.

The process, alas, works in reverse as well. When I see a river now, it is not shaped, assimilated by the word that accommodates it to the psyche—a word that makes a body of water a river rather than an uncontained element. The river before me remains a thing, absolutely other, absolutely unbending to the grasp of my mind.

When my friend Penny tells me that she's envious, or happy, or disappointed, I try laboriously to translate not from English to Polish but from the word back to its source, to the feeling from which it springs. Already, in that moment of strain, spontaneity of response is lost. And anyway, the translation doesn't work. I don't know how Penny feels when she talks about envy. The word hangs in a Platonic stratosphere, a vague prototype of all envy, so large, so all-encompassing that it might crush me—as might disappointment or happiness.

I am becoming a living avatar of structuralist wisdom; I cannot help knowing that words are just themselves. But it's a terrible knowledge, without any of the consolations that wisdom usually brings. It does not mean that I'm free to play with words at my wont; anyway, words in their naked state are surely among the least satisfactory play objects. No, this radical disjoining between word and thing is a desiccating alchemy, draining the world not only of significance but of its colors, striations, nuances—its very existence. It is the loss of a living connection.

The worst losses come at night. As I lie down in a strange bed in a strange house—my mother is a sort of housekeeper here, to the aging Jewish man who has taken us in return for her services—I wait for that spontaneous flow of inner language which used to be my nighttime talk with myself, my way of informing the ego where the id had been. Nothing comes. Polish, in a short time, has atrophied, shriveled from sheer uselessness. Its words don't apply to my new experiences; they're not coeval with any of the objects, or faces, or the very air I breathe in the daytime. In English, words have not penetrated to those layers of my psyche from which a private conversation could proceed. This interval before sleep used to be the time when my mind became both receptive and alert, when images and words rose up to consciousness, reiterating what had happened during the day, adding the day's experiences to those already stored there, spinning out the thread of my personal story.

Now, this picture-and-word show is gone; the thread has been snapped. I have no interior language, and without it, interior images—those images through which we assimilate the external world, through which we take it in, love it, make it our own—become blurred too. My mother and I met a Canadian family who live down the block today. They were working in their garden and engaged us in a conversation of the "Nice weather we're having, isn't it?" variety, which culminated in their inviting us into their house. They sat stiffly on their couch, smiled in the long pauses between the conversation, and seemed at a loss for what to ask. Now my mind gropes for some description of them, but nothing fits. They're a different species from anyone I've met in Poland, and Polish words slip off them without sticking. English words don't hook on to anything. I try, deliberately, to come up with a few. Are these people pleasant or dull? Kindly or silly? The words float in an uncertain space. They come up from a part of my brain in which labels may be manufactured but which has no connection to my instincts, quick reactions, knowledge. Even the simplest adjectives sow confusion in my mind; English kindliness has a whole system of morality behind it, a system that makes "kindness" an entirely positive virtue. Polish kindness has the tiniest element of irony. Besides, I'm beginning to feel the tug of prohibition, in English, against uncharitable words. In Polish, you can call someone an idiot without particularly harsh feelings and with the zest of a strong judgment. Yes, in Polish these people might tend toward "silly" and "dull"—but I force myself toward "kindly" and "pleasant." The cultural unconscious is beginning to exercise its subliminal influence.

The verbal blur covers these people's faces, their gestures with a sort of fog. I can't translate them into my mind's eye. The small event, instead of being added to the mosaic of consciousness and memory, falls through some black hole, and I fall with it. What has happened to me in this new world? I don't know. I don't see what I've seen, don't comprehend what's in front of me. I'm not filled with language anymore, and I have only a memory of fullness to anguish me with the knowledge that, in this dark and empty state, I don't really exist.

For my birthday, Penny gives me a diary, complete with a little lock and key to keep what I write from the eyes of all intruders. It is that little lock—the visible symbol of the privacy in which the diary is meant to exist—that creates my dilemma. If I am indeed to write something entirely for myself, in what language do I write? Several times, I open the diary and close it again. I can't decide. Writing in Polish at this point would be a little like resorting to Latin or ancient Greek—an eccentric thing to do in a diary, in which you're supposed to set down your most immediate experiences and unpremeditated thoughts in the most unmediated language. Polish is becoming a dead language, the language of the untranslatable past. But writing for nobody's eyes in English? That's like doing a school exercise, or performing in front of yourself, a slightly perverse act of self-voyeurism.

Because I have to choose something, I finally choose English. If I'm to write about the present, I have to write in the language of the present, even if it's not the language of the self. As a result, the diary becomes surely one of the more impersonal exercises of that sort produced by an adolescent girl. These are no sentimental effusions of rejected love, eruptions of familial anger, or consoling broodings about death. English is not the language of such emotions. Instead, I set down my reflections on the ugliness of wrestling; on the elegance of Mozart, and on how Dostoyevsky puts me in mind of El Greco. I write down Thoughts. I Write.

There is a certain pathos to this naïve snobbery, for the diary is an earnest attempt to create a part of my persona that I imagine I would have grown into in Polish. In the solitude of this most private act, I write, in my public language, in order to update what might have been my other self. The diary is about me and not about me at all. But on one level, it allows me to make the first jump. I learn English through writing, and, in turn, writing gives me a written self. Refracted through the double distance of English and writing, this self—my English self—becomes oddly objective; more than anything, it perceives. It exists more easily in the abstract sphere of thoughts and observations than in the world. For a while, this impersonal self, this cultural negative capability, becomes the truest thing about me. When I write, I have a real existence that is proper to the activity of writing—an existence that takes place midway between me and the sphere of artifice, art, pure language. This language is beginning to invent another me. However, I discover something odd. It seems that when I write (or, for that matter, think) in English, I am unable to use the word "I." I do not go as far as the schizophrenic "she"—but I am driven, as by a compulsion, to the double, the Siamese-twin "you."

My voice is doing funny things. It does not seem to emerge from the same parts of my body as before. It comes out from somewhere in my throat, tight, thin, and mat—a voice without the modulations, dips, and rises that it had before, when it went from my stomach all the way through my head. There is, of course, the constraint and the self-consciousness of an accent that I hear but cannot control. Some of my high school peers accuse me of putting it on in order to appear more "interesting." In fact, I'd do anything to get rid of it, and when I'm alone, I practice sounds for which my speech organs have no intuitions, such as "th" (I do this by putting my tongue between my teeth) and "a," which is longer and more open in Polish (by shaping my mouth into a sort of arrested grin). It is simple words like "cat" or "tap" that give me the most trouble, because they have no context of other syllables, and so people often misunderstand them. Whenever I can, I do awkward little swerves to avoid them, or pause and try to say them very clearly. Still, when people—like salesladies—hear me speak without being prepared to listen carefully, they often don't understand me the first time around. "Girls' shoes," I say, and the "girls'" comes out as a sort of scramble. "Girls' shoes," I repeat, willing the syllable to form itself properly, and the saleslady usually smiles nicely, and sends my mother and me to the right part of the store. I say "Thank you" with a sweet smile, feeling as if I'm both claiming an unfair special privilege and being unfairly patronized.

It's as important to me to speak well as to play a piece of music without mistakes. Hearing English distorted grates on me like chalk screeching on a blackboard, like all things botched and badly done, like all forms of gracelessness. The odd thing is that I know what is correct, fluent, good, long before I can execute it. The English spoken by our Polish acquaintances strikes me as jagged and thick, and I know that I shouldn't imitate it. I'm turned off by the intonations I hear on the TV sitcoms—by the expectation of laughter, like a dog's tail wagging in supplication, built into the actors' pauses, and by the curtailed, cutoff rhythms. I like the way Penny speaks, with an easy flow and a pleasure in giving words a fleshly fullness; I like what I hear in some movies; and once the Old Vic comes to Vancouver to perform *Macbeth*, and though I can hardly understand the particular words, I am riveted by the tones of sureness and command that mold the actors' speech into such majestic periods.

Sociolinguists might say that I receive these language messages as class signals, that I associate the sounds of correctness with the social status of the speaker. In part, this is undoubtedly true. The class-linked notion that I transfer wholesale from Poland is that belonging to a "better" class of people is absolutely dependent on speaking a "better" language. And in my situation especially, I know that language will be a crucial instrument, that I can overcome the stigma of my marginality, the weight of presumption against me, only if the reassuringly right sounds come out of my mouth.

Yes, speech is a class signifier. But I think that in hearing these varieties of speech around me, I'm sensitized to something else as well—something that is a matter of aesthetics, and even of psychological health. Apparently, skilled chefs can tell whether a dish from some foreign cuisine is well cooked even if they have never tasted it and don't know the genre of cooking it belongs to. There seem to be some deep-structure qualities—consistency, proportions of ingredients, smoothness of blending—that indicate culinary achievement to these educated eaters' taste buds. So each language has its own distinctive music, and even if one doesn't know its separate components, one can pretty quickly recognize the propriety of the patterns in which the components are put together, their harmonies and discords. Perhaps the crucial element that strikes the ear in listening to living speech is the degree of the speaker's self-assurance and control.

As I listen to people speaking that foreign tongue, English, I can hear when they stumble or repeat the same phrases too many times, when their sentences trail off aimlessly—or, on the contrary, when their phrases have vigor and roundness, when they have the space and the breath to give a flourish at the end of a sentence, or make just the right pause before coming to a dramatic point. I can tell, in other words, the degree of their ease or disease, the extent of authority that shapes the rhythms of their speech. That authority—in whatever dialect, in whatever variant of the mainstream language— seems to me to be something we all desire. It's not that we all want to speak the King's English, but whether we speak Appalachian or Harlem English, or Cockney, or Jamaican Creole, we want to be at home in our tongue. We want to be able to give voice accurately and fully to ourselves and our sense of the world. John Fowles, in one of his stories in *The Ebony Tower*, has a young man cruelly violate an elderly writer and his manuscripts because the legacy of language has not been passed on to the youthful vandal properly. This seems to me an entirely credible premise. Linguistic dispossession is a sufficient motive for violence, for it is close to the dispossession of one's self. Blind rage, helpless rage is rage that has no words—rage that overwhelms one with darkness. And if one is perpetually without words, if one exists in the entropy of inarticulateness, that condition itself is bound to be an enraging frustration. In my New York apartment, I listen almost nightly to fights that erupt like brushfire on the street below—and in their escalating fury of repetitious phrases ("Don't do this to me, man, you fucking bastard, I'll fucking kill you"), I hear not the pleasures of macho toughness but an infuriated beating against wordlessness, against the incapacity to make oneself understood, seen. Anger can be borne—it can even be satisfying—if it can gather into words and explode in a storm, or a rapier-sharp attack. But without this means of ventilation, it only turns back inward, building and swirling like a head of steam—building to an impotent, murderous rage. If all therapy is speaking therapy—a talking cure—then perhaps all neurosis is a speech dis-ease.

TOPICS FOR EXPLORATION

1. What role does Eva Hoffman adopt when communicating with her audience? What is her purpose in describing the predicament of a person transplanted from one linguistic universe to another?

2. How does a beginner experience a new language? How do the words in a foreign language behave for a new speaker? Why is it that "the signifier has become severed from the signified"?

3. What frustrations and paradoxes are involved in learning a new language? Why does Hoffman feel that any translation from one language to another is inadequate?

4. How does social context determine the use of language? What connection does Hoffman see between the language and the underlying set of cultural assumptions? How do "class signals" affect her perception of accent? What do "self-assurance and control" in the use of language mean to her?

5. Why does Hoffman have trouble deciding which language to use in her private diary? How is Hoffman's voice a reflection of her confusion and uncertainty? In what way does her diary help her recapture her new self through writing?

6. How does Hoffman relate the initial loss of her native tongue to the loss of identity? Why does she feel she "doesn't exist at all"?

7. What are the dangers of "linguistic dispossession" that she describes? Why can it result in frustration and rage?

Genni Donati Gunn

Genni Donati Gunn was born in 1949, and has published two books of fiction, Thrice upon a Time *(1990) and* On the Road *(1991). Her story "The Middle Ground" appeared in an anthology of Italian-Canadian writing called* Ricordi: Things Remembered, *edited by C.D. Minni.*

The Middle Ground

They came to live in Vancouver after her husband died: Rosalba and her small son, Claudio—her son who, in spite of her husband's persistent teachings, grew more Canadian each year. When he was born, Giulio had made her promise to speak only Italian to the boy—a rule she insisted upon even now that he was almost six. But the boy grew more Canadian each year. He would sit on her lap and listen attentively to stories (in Italian, always in Italian) about her parents. "*Il nonno e la nonna,*" Rosalba had taught him to say. But he had no grandparents here, no olive trees and no watermelons to hug. Claudio told her the other children laughed when he told them these stories. The boy had never been to Italy. His imagined homeland was no different to him than Canada had been to Rosalba before she came. It was not his fault that he could not remember the taste of prickly-pears, persimmons and fresh fruit.

In Vancouver, Rosalba bought persimmons in a little Chinese store on Commercial Drive. But they had been picked too soon and she could not find the right words to describe their real taste.

She'd been in Canada almost ten years, had come at nineteen to live in Victoria where Giulio taught Italian Studies at the University. But Rosalba had always loved Vancouver, its mountains and ocean so close together she could almost smell the Adriatic Sea: Trieste leaning lazy against low-slung mountains, rooftops baked ruddy in the hot summers. From the viewpoint up near the Conservatory in Queen Elizabeth Park, she could almost imagine herself sitting on the stone wall of the old castle that overlooked Trieste. Only the

cobblestones were missing and the long steep hills and curved narrow roads leading to the university. In Vancouver, a different beauty:
the clumps of evergreens, cedar-shake roofs and coloured houses.
Then the downtown high-rises jutting into the sky, dwarfed by the
backdrop of mountains.

She came to Vancouver to teach Italian at a school set in Little
Italy and filled with a mixture of first- and second-generation Italian
teenagers. It had been the natural thing for her to do, now that
Giulio was gone. Many of the students came from small villages in
southern Italy and spoke only dialects. Most had never learned
proper Italian grammar. Strange that she should be the one to recreate with patience a language and a culture for strangers' children—
she, who could not keep her own son from becoming Canadian,

The changes had been subtle. Like the night he'd asked her to
read him a story in English, although she always read to him from *Il
Tesoro*. She had been raised on it herself. The thick red volume with
gold-embossed printing on the cover, the fairy-tales and jokes and
pictures—all part of her childhood. She could almost recite each
word by heart. She'd said "no," of course, and read him his favourite
story. But the next day, seized with unbearable guilt, she'd gone to a
book store and bought *Peter Pan*, in English.

And another evening, when he'd asked if they could order pizza
with pineapple on top, she'd said, "absolutely not, that's not real
pizza," and had made him one at home, the way her mother had
taught her. But later, she'd opened a can of pineapple chunks and let
him put them on top of his. She was trying to keep him Italian, but
the boy grew more Canadian each year.

In the area around Commercial Drive, a new Italy had been
established long before she came. Here, families lived the traditional
roles of their homeland. Some women were still clad in dark dresses
that reached to below their knees, their elbows covered with shawls
and cardigans. It made Rosalba think of Goya's *Disasters of War*. All
that black—black skirts, black hair, black eyes. Only the shop windows on Commercial Drive twinkled with vibrant colours.
Mannequins sporting the newest fashions from Rome smiled into
the street, eyes vacant, smooth blond bobs and turned-up noses.
Rosalba wished they didn't look so *American*. She'd always said
America when she was in Italy, even though she'd been speaking of
Canada. From across the ocean, there had been only one continent,
no differentiation between countries. She supposed it the same for
Italy. Canadians thought of Italians on one people—all born of the
same fat little dark-haired Italian Mother Earth. But she had only to
think of her youth, of the many provinces and dialects, of the ani-
mosity between North and South, water and mountains.

She had chosen Vancouver, when her husband died, because of Commercial Drive, because of the mountains and the ocean. When the insurance money came, she went house-hunting with Claudio. At first, they looked in the Italian district. Rosalba tip-toed politely from house to house. "The bathroom counters are all marble. My husband had it sent direct from Italy, you know." Windows shuttered, floors glistening, Madonnas mounted on corner altars in the hall. "And that couch belonged to my grandmother. But we're going back. I'll sell it, if you're interested." Plaster busts of Roman Emperors; outdoors, lions guarding a driveway and at the back, a clothesline to the hydro pole. "These dryers make clothes yellow." And the neighbours peering from doorsteps. "And where are you from, Signora?" All so *Italian*. After the fifth house, Rosalba hurried Claudio into the car seat and drove back to their rented apartment. Inside, she took a deep breath and leaned back on the couch. She had panicked back there, among icons, and idols; she felt she might be absorbed into their darkness, their familiarity. She waited a few days, then contacted a real-estate firm. She asked the school secretary to call for her. "It's my accent," she explained apologetically. "They think I'm stupid."

The real-estate lady showed her houses on the West Side, tall beautiful wooden houses made of bleached grey cedar and nicked with skylights that captured the dawn. She loved these monolithic structures, the white inner walls and the echo of her heels on the hardwood floors. Although she longed to live in one of these houses, she settled finally on a sturdy, squat bungalow with precise rectangular windows with nine panes in each. She bought it because of its cream stucco exterior that reminded her of the white stone of her parents' house. She bought it because it seemed more *Italian*, and this was her concession for not buying one within the Italian district.

She enrolled Claudio in first grade at the elementary school just two blocks away from their new home and made arrangements to have a babysitter take him there in the mornings and pick him up at the end of the day. She had to leave much earlier than he did, to drive across town and be settled into the classroom before her students arrived.

"Now don't you let anyone call you anything but *Claudio*," she said on the first morning, squeezing him to her and wishing she could go with him. "Repeat it slowly if they say it wrong." Rosalba hated the way people here pronounced her name "Rozelba" or "Ruzolba", as if there were no such thing as a soft *r* or *s*. Often, she tried to break it down phonetically: "Ross-al-ba," or "Row-sal-ba, like rosary," she'd say. But they forgot too soon.

At her school, she noticed Peppi Armano immediately. He had a physical disability and always entered her ninth grade class after all the other students were seated. He had large eyes—round white saucers with pupils swimming in the middle, which followed her around the classroom.

He walked slowly, painfully, his small hands grasping the combination locks on the lockers that lined the hallways. Her classroom was upstairs, and she grew accustomed to the shuffling of feet after the bell had rung. At times, she watched Peppi make his way up or down the stairs, one foot at a time on each step. She wanted to help him, to take his free hand, the one which was not so tightly clasped to the banister, and walk down with him, but she was afraid to show her concern because Peppi kept his head down and stared only at his feet. At the end of the first week, he stayed after class and stood in front of her desk until she prompted him, "Is there something I can do?" He blushed and for a moment let go of her desk with both hands, trying to stand up straight as he spoke. "About my being late," he said in a muffled, quiet voice, "I have to wait until the others have gone. It's easier when I can hold on to the lockers. My legs . . . ," he stopped and leaned against the desk and Rosalba felt tears sting her eyes. "I understand," she said. But she didn't and later, asked the Principal about it.

"Friedreich's ataxia," the Principal told her. "His parents want to buy him a wheelchair, but he won't hear of it. He's a very stubborn boy. We've talked to him on many occasions."

After that, it seemed her ears were attuned to the sound of Peppi's small feet as they dragged through the halls. She could hear lock after lock swinging on its gate after he'd passed. She imagined she could count the lockers by his steps, by his hands which clung to the round black dials. She asked the Principal if she could have a room on the bottom floor. But he said it was impossible to reroute the school for Peppi. There were too many classes, too many students, too many timetables. "We have to do what's best for the majority," he said. And Rosalba lay in bed at night and tried to think of ways to help one small boy.

She noticed that Peppi remained reserved and always a little apart from the rest of the students. On one occasion, when she organized an after-school trip to the Italian Cultural Centre to see an Italian film, Peppi did not come. She waited for him until one of the students told her that his brother had taken him home at the usual time.

Rosalba went to see Mrs. Crombie, the school counsellor, to ask about Peppi's family.

"As far as we can tell," Mrs. Crombie said, "the parents are overprotective. The boy has no friends—in fact, goes nowhere without either one of his parents or his brother. If only he'd agree to use a wheelchair." She paused. "Has he talked to you about it?"

Rosalba shook her head.

"Poor kid. Last year, we tried talking to the parents . . . but you know how it is with these families. They believe they're doing what's best for him." She tapped her pen on her desk for a moment, then looked up at Rosalba. "Why don't you talk to them? They might listen to you, if you spoke in their language." *Their language.* Rosalba noticed the choice of words. Mrs. Crombie had not said, *your language. Their language,* as if *they* were somehow different from her. She said, "It's *my* language too." And Mrs. Crombie smiled. "Yes, but you're different." Strange the concept of foreigners. And how cultures could be massed under one umbrella. Yet individuals were considered separate. She wanted to shout, "I'm Italian." But she shook her head instead and said nothing. When she was still in Italy and the tourist season began, she had thought of all Americans in the same way. She had never considered each person as separate and distinct, but rather had seen Americans as a collective of brash, loud, forward people, with bermuda shorts and cameras. And when she'd had occasion to meet one, she too had thought that one person was different. The prejudice, then, came out of ignorance, out of the stereotypes they all accepted.

"What is a Wop?" Claudio asked.

Rosalba said, "Schoolchildren often give names to things they don't understand. You are *Italian.*"

"I don't want to be Italian," Claudio said, "because Italians are Wops. And I don't want to be a Wop."

The first few weeks of school passed quickly. She was busy with marking papers, remembering names, preparing a five-minute skit in Italian to be performed for the school. I must do something about Peppi, Rosalba thought, just as soon as I'm more settled. She became aware that Claudio had started to speak English to her at home. At first, he began with a sentence here and there that she asked him to repeat in Italian, as if she couldn't understand. Two months into the school year, Claudio announced, "I'm not going to speak Italian at home any more." Rosalba pleaded with him (in Italian), "You'll forget the language," she said. Then, "If your father were alive, he'd be heartbroken." But Claudio was obstinate. "I don't want to," he said. "What's the use of it, anyway? Nobody in my school speaks Italian." And Rosalba went to bed feeling guilty and thought about what Giulio would have done in this case. Giulio would have enrolled the boy in a school in the Italian district, where he would be with other Italian children. Each day, he grew more Canadian. And she was afraid to draw him back, to make him live a life he'd never known. She noticed that her students at school were distressed, secretive, trying to cope with the mixture of cultures—their survival dependent on the separation rather than the integration of the two. Was it fair, she thought, to force them to abide by rules that made no sense here, rules which had been implemented for a different culture in a different time?

What startled her the most was that the majority of the Italians she'd met adhered to strict oppressive customs to which she had not been exposed even in Italy. They had brought with them a culture several decades old. Things changed, times changed even in Italy, but these people insisted on remaining the same. "If you stand still, you go backward." She'd read that somewhere, and now the words appeared to make much more sense.

Rosalba asked Peppi to come and see her after school.

"I'll have to phone my brother and tell him what time to pick me up."

"I'll call him," Rosalba said, "and tell him not to come."

He looked at her doubtfully. "Oh, he'll come anyway."

Peppi arrived at 4:00 p.m., after the school halls had thinned out. He stood at her desk and when she told him to sit down, he reluctantly did so. She thought that if he could have managed it, he would have run out of the room, so much did he resemble a trapped animal.

She stared at the papers on her desk and tried to find opening words. "Peppi," she finally began. "I had a talk with Mrs. Crombie."

"It's about the wheelchair, isn't it? Why does everyone talk behind my back?"

"No one is talking behind your back. We're all very concerned about you. Your parents—"

"I'm tired of their concern." His voice rose in pitch. "They always decide everything for me. Nobody asks me what I want."

She stared at him for a moment, then asked softly, "What do *you* want, then?"

"I want to—be myself," he said. "I want to do things myself. They treat me like I can't even think."

"Maybe they're trying to do what's best for you, She paused. "If you can think for yourself, then surely you must realize that a wheelchair would help you tremendously."

"I can manage just fine on my own."

She said nothing, waiting, noting the tremor in his words. "And besides, if I get the stupid wheelchair, they'll never let me out of their sight. I don't want it!"

"You know," Rosalba said after a moment. It might not be at all how you think. With a wheelchair, you'd be able to get around on your own a lot easier. For instance, you wouldn't need anyone to take you to or from school."

"Oh sure. As if they'd let me go alone." He sat, quiet, staring at his hands. "I'm not even allowed to a movie by myself. Not unless Papa drives me. It's *embarrassing*. Being watched all the time. If it wasn't for the law here, I bet I wouldn't even be allowed to go to school; they'd keep me at home always."

"Do you want me to talk to them?" she asked.

He shrugged. "I don't think it would do any good."

A few days later, Rosalba called Peppi's parents and asked them to come to the school to speak to her. She distinctly said she wanted to see them both.

They came a little past six. She'd asked the babysitter to stay late, even though Claudio had insisted that he was old enough to be left alone for a few hours. Mr. Armano was short and round and Rosalba could see that the boy's beauty came from his mother. She was dressed much older than her years. She could not have been much more than thirty, yet she carried herself like an old woman. Her hair was smoothed back into a bun at the nape of her neck, tight and shiny, making her eyes—Peppi's eyes—appear even larger and rounder that they were. Mrs. Armano kept wringing her hands. "Is something wrong?" Mr. Armano said in English as soon as he walked into the room. "Peppi did something bad? We teach him in the house. We give him the manners—"

"No," Rosalba interrupted, and spoke in Italian. "He's done nothing wrong. He's a very good student." The Armanos looked at her, puzzled. "Then why did you want us to come if there's nothing wrong?"

Rosalba made them sit in two of the desks of the classroom. She explained to them that Peppi was growing up, that he needed to spend time with people his own age. She asked them why Peppi had not come to see the film with the class.

Mrs. Armano clenched and unclenched her hands on her lap. "He's sick," she said.

"He has a *physical* disability," Rosalba said more sharply than she'd meant to, "but this doesn't mean he can't do a lot of things other boys his age do."

Mrs. Armano looked away. "But he might hurt himself—"

"Mrs. Armano, it's part of growing up. You know that. You've raised another boy."

"Yes, but Peppi is different," she said solemnly.

"Perhaps you're trying to keep him different," Rosalba concluded.

And that night, after she tucked Claudio into bed, she thought about the Armanos, about the fine line between protectiveness and suffocation, about Peppi's symbolic stand against it. She heard Claudio's voice a few days earlier:

"Mamma, don't hold my hand when we're out."

"But why not?"

"I'm too old and Jimmy says only babies hold their mother's hand."

She had told him about her family—her brothers and sisters—and how they still held hands even as adults. But he'd slipped his fingers out of hers as she talked and hooked them into the opening of his pocket. Claudio becoming more Canadian—was she, too, trying to keep him different?

She acted as mediary between Peppi and his parents, spoke to them twice more over the next month, and was finally able to convince them to agree to a compromise: they would allow Peppi to come to school alone if he used the wheelchair. It was only a small concession, but for Peppi, the first triumph of a new independence.

She watched him anxiously that first day, his hands caressing the chrome of the large new wheels. He smiled shyly at her at the end of the day, when he left her classroom with the other teens.

She sat at her desk, long after they'd all gone, and thought about Claudio and herself. She too was trying to do what was best for him. She thought of Giulio, his smile there in Trieste. He'd preserved laughter and bittersweet memories like pressed flowers of intense moments with his family and friends. He had not been rigid. He had embraced the new way of life and enriched it with the old. Rosalba remained in her classroom, thinking, until the janitor asked her to leave so he could lock up the school.

When she arrived home, she saw Claudio sitting at his little table, drawing a picture for her. "I missed you," he said in Italian and buried his face in her skirt. "I missed you too, Claudio," she answered in English. Then she took him onto her lap and told him stories of Italy.

TOPICS FOR EXPLORATION

1. Why does Rosalba's protection of her Italian memories seem meaningless to her son Claudio? Why does she want to keep him from being Canadian? What are the "subtle changes" that Claudio undergoes in becoming more Canadian?

2. Myrna Kostash defines the immigrant nostalgia as "that melancholic yearning for the unrecoverable." In what sense is Rosalba afflicted by nostalgia? What similarities and differences does she find between Vancouver and Trieste?

3. What conflicts over the use of the mother tongue may appear in immigrant families? What kind of difficulties in maintaining the mother tongue are highlighted by the story?

4. Why does Rosalba think her accent makes her sound "stupid"? Why does Mrs. Crombie mass different individuals from one culture "under one umbrella"? Prejudice and stereotyping arise out of ignorance. How do stereotypes originate?

5. Why does Rosalba doubt the validity of imposing rules "implemented for a different culture in a different time"? Why does she panic "among icons and idols"? Why might some immigrants to Canada enforce rules not even valid in their homelands today?

6. How does the part of the plot involving Peppi's oppression by his parents contribute to the unity of the story? Does Rosalba learn from this experience something that helps her settle her own problems with Claudio?

Himani Bannerji

Himani Bannerji was born in Bangladesh in 1942 and educated in Calcutta. She came to Canada in 1969. She has published two books of poetry, A Separate Sky *(1982) and* Doing Time *(1986); her short stories and essays have appeared in different Canadian magazines and feminist journals. She has also written a children's novel,* Coloured Pictures. *She teaches sociology at York University.*

The Sound Barrier

IN THE FIRST CIRCLE

Maharaja [the great king] Yayati after many years of tending his subjects as befitted the conduct prescribed by Dharma [religion], became senile due to the curse of Sukracharya. Deprived of pleasure by that old age that destroys beauty [appearance], he said to [his] sons: 'O sons! I wish to dally with young women by means of your youth. Help me in this matter.' Hearing this Devayani's eldest son Yadu said, 'Command us, great lord, how it is that we may render you assistance with our youth.' Yayati said, 'You [should] take my [senility] decay of old age, I will [take] your youth and use it to enjoy the material world [what I own] . . . one of you [should] assume my emaciated body and rule the country [while] I take the young body [of the one who has taken on the old age] and gratify my lust [for the world].'

— *The Mahabharata, Adi Parba, Chapter 75*

It is evening. I am afraid. The sun's rays are weak. That red crucible partly sunk in the clouds is only a dim reflection of itself, not a source of light or life. The plains stretch far into the distance behind me. The human dwellings, the villages and cities are far away and hidden by the rising mist and fog from the swamps where only reeds rustle in the wind and waterbirds cry disconsolately. Beside me, the little grassy glade that I stand in, is a forest—ghana, swapada-shankula—dense and full of dangerous beasts of prey. The over-hanging foliage has the appearance of clouds which hold and nourish a damp darkness. The giant trunks of the trees have grown so close together that the forest is both a prison and a fort. No foot-paths are visible since the undergrowth denies the possibility of making an inroad. Standing at this juncture, between the swamp and this forest, with darkness fast coming upon me, I am overcome with fear. What shall I do? Where shall I turn? I can neither go for-ward nor return thence from whence under the bright noon sun I began my unmapped wanderings.—Pathik, tumi ki path haray-achho? Traveller, have you lost your way?

Miraculously, she stands beside me, risen from the ground it seems, immaculate, serene, fearless because renouncing and always in the quest for truth, dressed in orange, the colour of wandering mendicants—Kapalkundala of my childhood, the female ascetic, well versed in life and death. Her ghanakunchita keshandam—long dark curly hair—cascades down her back, framing her face, as the nimbus monsoon clouds surround the full moon, her forehead, broad and generous, her gaze mild yet compelling, serene and unselfconscious. Extending her hand, taking mine in a firm but gen-tle grasp, she spoke to me.—Bhay kariona. Druta chalo. Ratri haiya ashitechhe. Jhhar ashite pare. Don't fear. Let us move quickly. The night approaches and a storm may arise.

Where? I said to her, O apparition from childhood, from behind the closed doors of homes destroyed, vanished, a long time ago, child of Bankim, vernacular spirit, where shall I hide? Where is my refuge, my shelter? Kothay jaibo? This forest is a fearful maze, populated with unknown, unnamed dangers. Where is there for me to go?

She gently pulled me towards her, while walking nimbly into the forest. In the gathering darkness I noticed that her feet were faintly luminous and suspended above the ground. Keeping her great head poised, her gaze fixed at the gnarled entrance and tremendously muscular arms of the forest, she uttered repeatedly.—Bhayang nasti. There is nothing to fear. Aisho. Come.

It is then that I noticed she had decorated her body with human bones. A necklace of skulls hung around her neck. She had made an ornament out of death—and wore it, fearless in her conviction and knowledge of life.

Where shall we go? I asked, where hide and seek shelter for the night? What will nourish us and quench our thirst?—Woman's body is both the source of uncleanliness and life, she said. So have the sages spoken. Let us go into that gate, that body, she said, to ascertain the verity of their famed masculine, Brahmin intellect and pronouncements. Let us, O daughter of woman, enter into your mother's womb, the disputed region itself, where for many months you sat in abject meditation and waiting, nourished by the essence of her life. The stree yoni—the female genitalia, the womb, the jewel at the heart of the lotus, the manipadma itself, shall be our first place of descent for the night. There we will be protected by her, who first woke you from the inert life of sole matter—and yet was herself all body. That was her first incarnation for you and your own.

But to enter into this darkness even deeper could be dangerous, I replied. It is not greater immanence, but transcendence that we seek. Our need is to move away from, rise above, this forest, the night. This horrific darkness that makes my body inert and that clouds my reason.

But her inexorable movement never ceased. We had advanced within the edge of the forest in no time. Holding me by the hand firmly Kapalkundala had borne me by her own strength. Moving as in a dream we covered what seemed many leagues. At last the movement ceased.—We have arrived, she said, here is the zone of the body. We enter now.

It is then that I noticed that the storm I had anticipated had arrived. I felt the swirling wind. It was in fact a great whirlwind. Around and around it went—a tunnel, a spiral, a vortex, with a ring of fire at its mouth. I rotated blindly within its circular motion— rose and fell. The folds of flesh around me expanded and contracted with a great force. Up and down, out and in, light and darkness, had lost all their distinctions. I went into a headlong flight, only Kapalkundala's hold on my wrist was as sinewy and unrelenting as the umbilical cord. Sometimes I heard or felt the deep reverberations of her laughter. She was amused with my fear. Finally I heard her say, open your eyes, open them as wide as you can and look around you, see who you can find, where you are. We have reached Ananada Math—The Temple of Joy.

Opening my eyes, as the darkness drifted away from my vision, I saw—Mother.

Ma ja chhillen, ja hoiachhen, ja hoiben. Mother as she was, as she has become, and as she will be.

The storm had ceased, a wonderful calm prevailed. We were in a cave, and it was suffused with light as though under water whose source was unknown to me. There were three shrines next to each other, in three niches, holding three idols, images. Mata kumari— balika—Mother, a girl, a young nubile virgin, arrested in the act of play, body poised for motion, for flight. Mata, sangihini o garbhini—mother, a woman, crushed beneath the weight of a male figure, with one hand over abdomen protecting the life within.

Mata, briddha o ekakini, mother, old and alone, a shrunken form, blind with a hand outstretched seeking pity, curled in a foetal position.

Pranum kara. Bow down, prostrate yourself in front of her, said the female ascetic, herself doing the same. Her voice held the sound of clouds on the verge of rain. Her ascetic's serene eyes were filled with tears, they silently spilled on to her bosom. Thus we stood for a long time gazing at mother in her incarnations. Finally I gave voice to my thought.

Your renunciation is not complete, Kapalkundala, I said. You still cry. The world—its beauty and pain—still move you. You still have not succeeded in giving up an attraction for the mysteries it holds.

The Sannyasini, the woman mendicant, standing at the door of the world with her begging bowl made of a skull, looked at me sadly.—You don't understand, she said, I never did give up the world, the world was taken from me. And yet I hold onto what of it I can. What it will give me.

And what is that you hold on to, Kapalkundala, I asked her, through your severe intellections and meditations?—Compassion, she said. And since compassion cannot exist without a regard for truth and memory I seek after them as well.

Compassion for whom? I asked. —For mother and thus for you and for me. Through both involuntary responses and studied practices I hope to find my salvation.

Glancing at mother's incarnations, feeling my body tear at me in three ways, I begged her—make me your disciple. Please show me the way.

She gave me no answer. Standing as still as the icons that confronted us, wrapped in her pain and meditations, she drove me to distraction and supplications. The violence of my own tears and anguish woke me and I heard a wail as I opened my eyes. I was born.

BREAKING THE CIRCLE: WRITING AND READING A FRAGMENT

Reader, you have just finished reading a piece put together by me from fragments of language, memories, textual allusions, cultural signs and symbols. It is clearly an attempt to retrieve, represent and document something. But what sort of text is it? Does it speak to you? And what does it say? You see, on the verge of writing, having written, I am still uncertain about the communicative aspect of it. I must reach out to you beyond the authorial convention, break the boundaries of narration, its progression and symmetry, and speak to you directly: in a letter, which you will answer to the author in you. And you, as much as I, will have to get engaged not only in reflections about memories and writing, but about writing in English as Asian women in Canada.

And I would like to know whether you, as much as I, feel the same restlessness, eagerness, worry and uncertainty about expression and communication that make me want to say it all and be mute at the same time. Are you also haunted by this feeling, that as an Asian woman, what you will say about yourself, selves, about *ourselves*, will end up sounding stillborn, distant, artificial and abstract—in short, not quite authentic to you or us? Are you also trying to capture alive, and instead finding yourself caught up in a massive translation project of experiences, languages, cultures, accents and nuances? Are you also struggling with the realization that you are self-alienated in the very act of self-expression?

At times you tell yourself or others tell you, that if you were a better writer, with something really worthwhile to say, with greater clarity and depth, you would not have this problem. Maybe then you would not turn away from your own articulations as the sound hits the air, or a thought hits the page. A real writer—a better writer. But upon careful consideration I have decided to dismiss this view of things. It is not skill, depth of feeling, wealth of experience or attentiveness to details—in short a command over content and form—that would help me to overcome this problem of alienation, produced by a permanent mediator's and interpreter's role. A look at much of the writings on history and culture produced by Asian writers in English reveals that the problem goes beyond that of conceptualization and skill to that of sensibilities, to the way one relates to the world, is one's own self. Literature, in particular, is an area suffering from this tone of translatedness.

It appears that we Asian immigrants coming from ancient cultures, languages and literature, all largely produced in non-Christian and pre-capitalist or semi-feudal (albeit colonial) terrains, have a particularly difficult time in locating ourselves centre stage in the 'new world' of cultural production. Our voices are mostly absent, or if present, often out of place with the rest of the expressive enterprises. A singular disinterest about us or the societies we come from, thus who we are substantively not circumstantially, is matched equally by the perverted orientalist interest in us (the East as a mystic state of mind to the West) and our own discomfort with finding a cultural-linguistic expression or form which will minimally do justice to our selves and formations. And this has not to do with language facility, or ability to comprehend, negotiate or navigate the murky waters of a racist-imperialist 'new world.'

Even for those of us who are fluent in English or our children who grew up in Canada, the problem is a pressing one. To the extent that these children are products of our homes, modulated by our everyday life inflections (though not well-versed in the languages we bring with us), they suffer from the possibility of 'otherization.' This is done by the historical separation of our worlds, understood in the context of values and practices produced by colonialism, imperialism and immediately palpable racism. All telling, then, self-expression and self-reification get more and more closely integrated. There is a fissure that cannot even begin to be fathomed between us, those with our non-Anglo Western sociocultural (often non-Christian) ambience, and others with all of these legacies. I mention religion only to enforce the view that it is a part of a totality of cultural sign and meaning systems, rather than something apart and thus easily abstracted or extrapolated.

In fact, the very vibrancy and substantiveness of the sociocultural world we come from work against us in our diasporic existence. They locate us beyond the binaries of 'self and other,' Black and white. It is not as though our self identities began the day we stepped on this soil! But, conversely, our 'otherization' becomes much easier as we do carry different sign or meaning systems which are genuinely unrelated to Western capitalist emotional, moral and social references. And this notwithstanding our colonial experience. The beyond-and-aboveness to Westernization and white man's presence, thousands of years of complex class and cultural formations (such as specialized intellectual and priestly or warrior classes: Brahmins in India, Mandarins in China, or Samurai in Japan to name a few), and struggles, with scripts, texts, and codifications, all make us an easy target of 'otherization.' The shadow of 'the East,' 'the Orient,' overhangs how we are heard, and the fact of having to express ourselves now in languages and cultures that have nothing in common with us continue to bedevil our attempts at working expressively and communicately with our experiences and sensibilities.

I have been conscious of these problems, particularly of the integrity of language and experience, ever since I have been living in Canada and trying to write creatively in English. Speaking and being heard have often involved insuperable difficulties in conveying associations, assonances and nuances. But the problem takes on an acute form with experiences which take place elsewhere both in time and space—for example, in this text—in childhood, in Bengal. They are experiences in another language, involving a person who was not culturally touched by Westernization or urbanization, namely my mother. I wanted to write something about her, which also implies about us. I was repeatedly muted and repelled by the task on many counts. First there was the difficulty of handling the material itself.

Writing about one's own mother. Who can really re-present, hold in words, a relationship so primordial, with all its ebb and flow, do justice to it—in words? Probably true of all relationship to a degree, relationship with one's parents, which is implied in one's description of them, remains the most ineffable. Suggest, evoke, recall, narrate, the whole remains greater than the sum of its parts. The task is further complicated by the rhythm of time, growth and decline. After all she and I—mother and child—grew and changed together and away, I growing older and she, old. She was at my inception, from my first day to my present. I witnessed her life and related to her from then to her death. We overlapped for a while—overtaken however by aging, disease, decay, senility, silence and the shrillness of pain, and the ordinariness and irrevocability of death. As we moved in time our perceptions of each other changed kaleidoscopically. I cannot even recall my child's vision of her, because I cannot become that child again. She was another person, I cannot recapture her feelings and views of the world; though of course in some particular way she has been mutated, fused and transformed into my present self, each 'then and there' perhaps contributing to each 'here and now.'

Death adds a further twist to it. A living relationship is simultaneously fluid and focused and anchored in an actual person. But death fractures it into memories and associations, feelings that float about looking for a real person and interactions, but finding only spurious, associative points of reference. It is a strangely alienating moment in one's life when 'mother' is no longer an appellation which evokes a response, but is transformed into an abstraction, a knowledge involving a social structure called 'the family,' its directly emotive content now consigned to 'once upon a time.' After her death it is possible to find one's mother not only in personal memory, but in associations other than human, such as nature, and of course in a myriad of social and cultural gestures and rituals. A season or a festival becomes saturated with her memories and associations. For me the autumnal festival of the mother goddess Durga, the goddess of power with ten weaponed hands, only serves to remind me of my humble, domestic mother, who infused this festival with faith, whose world was the world of Hinduism filled with gifts, food, fasting and taboos. All this—life and death—are difficult to capture, for anyone anywhere since life is always more than any expression of living it. But the very attempt to do so is infinitely more frustrating for those who have to speak/write in a language in which the experience did not originate, whose genius is alien and antithetical to one's own.

Life, I am convinced, does not allow for a separation between form and content. It happens to us in and through the language in which it actually happens. The words, their meanings—shared and personal—their nuances are a substantial and *material* part of our reality. In another language, I am another person, my life another life. When I speak of my life in India, my mother or others there, I have a distinct feeling of splintering off from my own self, or the actual life that is lived, and producing an account, description, narrative—what have you—which distinctly smacks of anthropology and contributes at times to the paraphernalia of Orientalism. The racist-colonial context always exerts a pressure of utmost reification, objectification of self and others.

The importance of language and culture in the narrative and the integrity is even more concretely demonstrated to me when speaking in India about racism experienced by me in Canada (and other places in the West). Though less sharply alienating, being ex-colonials and experiencing racism and colonialism on our own soil and abroad, there is still a difficulty in conveying the feel of things, the contribution of exact words, tone, look, etc., in producing the fury and humiliation of a racist treatment. How can a Toronto white bank teller's silent but eloquent look of contempt from a pair of eyes lurking in her quasi-Madonna (is that it?) hairdo be conveyed to a Bengali speaking, Bengali audience of Calcutta? How can the terror skinheads—their bodies, voices, clothes or shaved heads—be adequately, connotatively expressed to a society where they are totally alien forms, where a shaved head, for example, signifies penance or a ritual for the loss of parents, or the benign-ness of *bhakticult*, a cult of devotion and love?

If we now go back to the text I have produced, in a relatively direct and uncensored manner, as though in Bengali, we can perhaps see how it expresses a sensibility alien to English and the postmodern literary world that we inhabit. I need to struggle not at the level of images and language alone, but at the levels of tonality and genre as well. It is a text with holes for the Western reader. It needs extensive footnotes, glossaries, comments, etc.—otherwise it has gaps in meaning, missing edges. It is only relatively complete for those who share my history or other noncapitalist and feudal histories—a world where epics and so-called classics are a part of the everyday life and faith of the people. They may decide that it does not work as a literary piece, but will not need many footnotes to the tone, emotions, conceptualization, references and textual allusions which create this mosaic.

Let us thus begin to footnote. This device that drags a text beyond its immediate narrative confines—might offer on the one hand the danger of objectification, of producing introductory anthropology, on the other, conversely, might rescue the text from being an Orientalist, i.e., an objectified experience and expression. To begin at the beginning—the epigraph from the Indian classical epic, *The Mahabharata*—what is it doing here in this piece? An obvious explanation is that like all epigraphs it establishes a 'theme.' It expresses my relationship with my mother and even a generalization about parent-child and age-youth relations. What we see in the episode of King Yayati and his son Puru is a trade of lives, youth and age, an aging person's ruthless desire to renew his own decaying life, even at the cost of the child's and finally a young person's internalization of an aging life. A knowledge of this legend necessitates a knowledge of this epic. Now, Western scholars of classical Indian literature would know this text, but how many are they in number? I could not take these allusions or their sign system for granted as I could, for example, the Bible, or even references to the peripheries of classical Greek literature. To do so is common practice in the West; to do what I have done is perceived as somewhat artificial, a little snobbish perhaps. Yet the commonness of such an evocation is obvious to those who see our cultures as forms of living, not museum pieces. Its presence in this text signifies not a detour into the classics, but an involuntary gesture to my mother's and my grandmother's world—in fact, to myself as a child. This is what it feels like from the inside:

It's afternoon—long, yellow, warm and humid. The green shutters with their paint fading behind the black painted rusty iron bars are closed to stop the hot air from coming in. The red cement floor has been freshly mopped and now cooled by the fan that comes a long way down from high ceilings, where shadows have gathered. Somewhere a crow is cawing and I can hear the clang and chimes of brass pots as they are being washed at the tube well. I am lying on the floor on a rush mat, listlessly. I am eight, I don't go to school yet, they have captured me, and will force me to be here until the afternoon is over because they don't want me wandering around the compound in the hot sun, climbing trees and all that. I am lying there tossing and turning—sleep is out of the question. At some point my mother enters. She wanders about the room for a while searching or taking this and that, puts her silver container of betel leaves (pan) next to her pillows, loosens the tie of her sari, worn over a long slip, her 'chemise,' and lowers herself on the bed. The bed creaks. I am lying wide-eyed. She inquires—why am I not asleep? No answer follows. She does not bother to break my recalcitrant silence, lies on her side, and proceeds to chew on her pan in silence. Her breasts flop down and touch the bed. I look sideways at the dark area of her nipple visible through the chemise front. I have no breasts. My attention shifts. I look at the book lying next to her hand, which does not pick it up. I shift towards her bed—rolling on the ground—until I am just at its edge. I know the book—Kashi Das's *The Mahabharata*. It's in verse, rhymed couplets, with their neat short jingles tripping along. I already know bits of it by heart— stories of kings, queens, great wars, of children born inside a fish or springing up from the reeds, beautiful women, long wanderings through forests and other things that I don't understand and there- fore ignore. I ask her if I can read the book, since I can't sleep. She is about to insist on my sleeping instead when the door opens, and my grandmother comes in. Small, lightfooted, thin, shavenheaded, fair- skinned, still not toothless, in her saffron sari, coloured with red clay. 'Let her,' says my grandmother. Turning to me she says, 'Wait until I lie down. Let's see how well you can read. All this money on a private tutor. Let's see what the result is.'

The book is in my hand. One of the four volumes, bound in cardboard backing and covered with little purple designs on a white base, with a navy blue spine and four triangular edges. The card- board has become soft with handling, and the paper (newsprint from a popular press) slightly brown, here and there a corner is torn, scribbles by children on the inner sides of the binding, illustrations drawn over by children with pens, such as moustaches on the faces of the heroines and clean shaven ware heroes, eyes of the wicked scratched out by my justice seeking nails, and a musty smell. I sit up, lean against the bed, my mother's rather pudgy and soft hand strokes my head, fingers running through my hair, at times the gold bangles make a thin and ringing sound as they hit each other. There is a rhythm to her hand movement, it moves to the rhythm of the verse. My grandmother has assumed a serious listening expression. I read—print, until recently only black squiggly scribbles on paper, begins to make the most wonderful sounds—words, meanings, cadences tumble out of my mouth. I am enthralled. The sound rolls, flows.

Dakho dwija Manashija jinya murati
Padmapatra jugmanetra parashaye sruti.
[See the Brahmin, who is better looking than the god of love, with lotus petal eyes that touch his ears.]

Understanding and not understanding, often supplying the meaning from my own mind, I read on. The palm leaf fan that my grandmother has picked up from habit hits the ground from her slack wrist. My mother's hand has stopped. Their eyes are closed, gentle snores greet my ears. I keep reading until the end of the canto anyway.

> *Mahabharater katha amrita saman*
> *Kashiram Das bhane sune punyaban*
> [The words/stories of Mahabharat are as nectar
> Kashiram Das recites them, the virtuous listen.
> Or: those who listen to them acquire virtue
> (produced from good, sanctified deeds)]

This then for me is the world of the epic, a most humble vernacular, domestic scene, part of child's world, which of course by definition is also the mother's world, the grandmother's world, maternal older women's world. It is interior, it is private—in afternoons when menfolk and students are at work and school—women and pre-school children, thrown together, the 'good book' playing its part between a heavy lunch and a siesta. How is Orientalist scholarship to cope with this? How is my reader of here and now in Canada, whose childhood, culture and language, [are] so far away from any of this, to grasp the essence of this experience which is not only mine, but of countless children of Bengal who are at present my age in literate, middle-class homes? This is why, not only the theme but the atmosphere, the association of Mahabharata indeed of Bengali literature, is part and parcel of what I call my mother. Today recalling her, they are dredged out of my childhood together, from the sun-soaked afternoons of East Bengal, a long time ago.

TOPICS FOR EXPLORATION

1. Himani Bannerji has split her text into two large parts: the dream narrative and the commentary upon it. Why has she used this approach? What is her purpose in the second part?

2. The symbolic tale of the three incarnations of the mother may carry different meanings for Western readers than for readers from the author's own cultural circle. Try to answer for yourself the questions Bannerji asks of her imaginary reader: "What sort of text is it? Does it speak to you? What does it say?"

3. What is the symbolic importance of the female ascetic Kapalkundala appearing to guide the dream? How does Bannerji's explanation of the relationship with her mother help you understand the tale?

4. Why does Bannerji have difficulty communicating her experience of her mother? How does the relationship with her mother approximate for Bannerji her relationship with the mother tongue?

5. What problems concerning writing in English as an Asian woman in Canada does Bannerji identify in her essay? What, for her, is the "otherization" which characterizes the clash between the East and the West?

6. "Life is always more than any expression of living it." Why is communicating an experience frustrating for those who use a second language in which "the experiences did not originate"?

Garry Engkent

Garry Engkent was born in Sun Wui county of the Chinese province Guangdong, and immigrated to Canada in the 1950s. He completed his Ph.D. in English at the University of Toronto, where he now teaches creative writing and English literature. He is also working on a novel to be called A Chinaman's Chance. *"Why My Mother Can't Speak English" was first published in the anthology of Chinese-Canadian writing* Many-Mouthed Birds *in 1991.*

Why My Mother Can't Speak English

My mother is seventy years old. Widowed for five years now, she lives alone in her own house except for the occasions when I come home to tidy her household affairs. She has been in *gum san*, the golden mountain, for the past thirty years. She clings to the old-country ways so much so that today she astonishes me with this announcement:

"I want to get my citizenship," she says as she slaps down the *Dai Pao*, "before they come and take away my house."

"Nobody's going to do that. This is Canada."

"So everyone says," she retorts, "but did you read what the *Dai Pao* said? Ah, you can't read Chinese. The government is cutting back on old-age pensions. Anybody who hasn't got citizenship will lose everything. Or worse."

"The *Dai Pao* can't even typeset accurately," I tell her. Sometimes I worry about the information Mother receives from that biweekly community newspaper. "Don't worry—the Ministry of Immigration won't send you back to China."

"Little you know," she snaps back. "I am old, helpless, and without citizenship. Reasons enough. Now, get me citizenship. Hurry!"

"Mother, getting citizenship papers is not like going to the bank to cash in your pension cheque. First, you have to—"

"Excuses, my son, excuses. When your father was alive—"

"Oh, Mother, not again! You throw that at me every—"

"—made excuses, too." Her jaw tightens. "If you can't do this little thing for your own mother, well, I will just have to go and beg your cousin to . . ."

Every time I try to explain about the ways of the *fan gwei*, she thinks I do not want to help her.

"I'll do it, I'll do it, okay? Just give me some time."

"That's easy for you," Mother snorts. "You're not seventy years old. You're not going to lose your pension. You're not going to lose your house. Now, how much *lai-shi* will this take?"

After all these years in *gum san* she cannot understand that you don't give government officials *lai-shi*, the traditional Chinese money gift to persons who do things for you.

"That won't be necessary," I tell her. "And you needn't go to my cousin.

Mother picks up the *Dai Pao* again and says: "Why should I beg at the door of a village cousin when I have a son who is a university graduate?

I wish my father were alive. Then he would be doing this. But he is not here, and as a dutiful son, I am responsible for the welfare of my widowed mother. So I take her to Citizenship Court.

There are several people from the Chinese community waiting there. Mother knows a few of the Chinese women and she chats with them. My cousin is there, too.

"I thought your mother already got her citizenship," he says to me. "Didn't your father—"

"No, he didn't."

He shakes his head sadly. "Still, better now than never. That's why I'm getting these people through."

"So they've been reading the *Dai Pao*."

He gives me a quizzical look, so I explain to him, and he laughs.

"You are the new generation," he says. "You didn't live long enough in *hon san*, the sweet land, to understand the fears of the old. You can't expect the elderly to renounce all attachments to China for the ways of the *fan gwei*, white devils. How old is she, seventy now? Much harder."

"She woke me up this morning at six, and Citizenship Court doesn't open until ten."

The doors of the court finally open, and Mother motions me to hurry. We wait in line for a while.

The clerk distributes applications and tells me the requirements. Mother wants to know what the clerk is saying, so half the time I translate for her.

The clerk suggests that we see one of the liaison officers.

"Your mother has been living in Canada for the past thirty years and she still can't speak English?"

"It happens," I tell the liaison officer.

"I find it hard to believe that—not one word?"

"Well, she understands some restaurant English," I tell her. "You know, French fries, pork chops, soup, and so on. And she can say a few words."

"But will she be able to understand the judge's questions? The interview with the judge, as you know, is an important part of the citizenship procedure. Can she read the booklet? What does she know about Canada?"

"So you don't think my mother has a chance?"

"The requirements are that the candidate must be able to speak either French or English, the two official languages of Canada. The candidate must be able to pass an oral interview with the citizenship judge, and then he or she must be able to recite the oath of allegiance—"

"My mother needs to speak English," I conclude for her.

"Look, I don't mean to be rude, but why didn't your mother learn English when she first came over?"

I have not been translating this conversation, and Mother, annoyed and agitated, asks me what is going on. I tell her there is a slight problem.

"What problem?" Mother opens her purse, and I see her taking a small red envelope—*lai-shi*—I quickly cover her hand.

"What's going on?" the liaison officer demands.

"Nothing," I say hurriedly. "Just a cultural misunderstanding. I assure you."

My mother rattles off some indignant words, and I snap back in Chinese: "Put that away! The woman won't understand, and we'll be in a lot of trouble."

The officer looks confused, and I realize that an explanation is needed.

"My mother was about to give you a money gift as a token of appreciation for what you are doing for us. I was afraid you might misconstrue it as a bribe. We have no intention of doing that."

"I'm relieved to hear it."

We conclude the interview, and I take Mother home. Still clutching the application, Mother scowls at me.

"I didn't get my citizenship papers. Now I will lose my old-age pension. The government will ship me back to China. My old bones will lie there while your father's will be here. What will happen to me?"

How can I teach her to speak the language when she is too old to learn, too old to want to learn? She resists anything that is *fan gwei*. She does everything the Chinese way. Mother spends much time staring blankly at the four walls of her house. She does not cry.

She sighs and shakes her head. Sometimes she goes about the house touching her favourite things.

"This is all your dead father's fault," she says quietly. She turns to the photograph of my father on the mantel. Daily, she burns incense, pours fresh cups of fragrant tea, and spreads dishes of his favourite fruits in front of the framed picture as is the custom. In memory of his passing, she treks two miles to the cemetery to place flowers by his headstone, to burn ceremonial paper money, and to talk to him. Regularly, rain or shine, or even snow, she does these things. Such love, such devotion, now such vehemence. Mother curses my father, her husband, in his grave.

When my mother and I emigrated from China, she was forty years old, and I, five. My father was already a well-established restaurant owner. He put me in school and Mother in the restaurant kitchen, washing dishes and cooking strange foods like hot dogs, hamburgers, and French fries. She worked seven days a week from six in the morning until eleven at night. This lasted for twenty-five years, almost to the day of my father's death.

The years were hard on her. The black-and-white photographs show a robust woman; now I see a withered, frail, white-haired old woman, angry, frustrated with the years, and scared of losing what little material wealth she has to show for the toil in *gum san.*

"I begged him," Mother says. "But he would either ignore my pleas or say: 'What do you need to know English for? You're better off here in the kitchen. Here you can talk to the others in our own tongue. English is far too complicated for you. How old are you now? Too old to learn a new language. Let the young speak *fan gwei.* All you need is to understand the orders from the waitresses. Anyway, if you need to know something, the men will translate for you. I am here; I can do your talking for you.'"

As a conscientious boss of the young male immigrants, my father would force them out of the kitchen and into the dining room. "The kitchen is no place for you to learn English. All you do is speak Chinese in here. To survive in *gum san,* you have to speak English, and the only way you can do that is to wait on tables and force yourselves to speak English with the customers. How can you get your families over here if you can't talk to the immigration officers in English?"

A few of the husbands who had the good fortune to bring their wives over to Canada hired a retired school teacher to teach a bit of English to their wives. Father discouraged Mother from going to those once-a-week sessions.

"That old woman will get rich doing nothing. What have these women learned? *Fan gwei* ways—make-up, lipstick, smelly perfumes, fancy clothes—like whores. Once she gets through with them, they won't be Chinese women any more—and they certainly won't be white either."

Some of the husbands heeded the words of the boss, for he was older than they, and he had been in the white devils' land longer. These wives stayed home and tended the children, or they worked in the restaurant kitchen, washing dishes and cooking *fan gwei* foods, and talking in Chinese about the land and the life they had been forced to leave behind.

"He was afraid that I would leave him. I depended on him for everything. I could not go anywhere by myself. He drove me to work and he drove me home. He only taught me how to print my name so that I could sign anything he wanted me to, bank cheques, legal documents . . ."

Perhaps I am not Chinese enough any more to understand why my mother would want to take in the sorrow, the pain, and the anguish, and then to recount them every so often.

Once, I was presumptuous enough to ask her why she would want to remember in such detail. She said that the memories didn't hurt any more. I did not tell her that her reminiscences cut me to the quick. Her only solace now is to be listened to.

My father wanted more sons, but she was too old to give him more. One son was not enough security he needed for old age. "You smell of stale perfume," she would say to him after he had driven the waitresses home. Or, to me, she would say: "A second mother will not treat you so well, you know," and, "Would you like another mother at home?" Even at that tender age, I knew that in China a husband could take a second wife. I told her that I didn't need another mother, and she would nod her head.

When my father died five years ago, she cried and cried. "Don't leave me in this world. Let me die with you."

Grief-stricken, she would not eat for days. She was so weak from hunger that I feared she wouldn't be able to attend the funeral. At his grave side, she chanted over and over a dirge, commending his spirit to the next world and begging the goddess of mercy to be kind to him. By custom, she set his picture on the mantel and burned incense in front of it daily. And we would go to the cemetery often. There she would arrange fresh flowers and talk to him in the gentlest way.

Often she would warn me: "The world of the golden mountain is so strange, *fan gwei* improprieties, and customs. The white devils will have you abandon your own aged mother to some old-age home to rot away and die unmourned. If you are here long enough, they will turn your head until you don't know who you are— Chinese."

My mother would convert the months and the days into the Chinese lunar calendar. She would tell me about the seasons and the harvests and festivals in China. We did not celebrate any *fan gwei* holidays.

My mother sits here at the table, fingering the booklet from the Citizenship Court. For thirty-some years, my mother did not learn the English language, not because she was not smart enough, not because she was too old to learn, and not because my father forbade her, but because she feared that learning English would change her Chinese soul. She only learned enough English to survive in the restaurant kitchen.

Now, Mother wants *gum san* citizenship.

"Is there no hope that I will be given it?" she asks.

"There's always a chance," I tell her. "I'll hand in the application."

"I should have given that person the *lai-shi*," Mother says obstinately.

"Maybe I should teach you some English," I retort. "You have about six months before the oral interview."

"I am seventy years old," she says. "*Lai-shi* is definitely much easier."

My brief glimpse into Mother's heart is over, and it has taken so long to come about. I do not know whether I understand my aged mother any better now. Despite my mother's constant instruction, there is too much *fan gwei* in me.

The booklet from the Citizenship Court lies, unmoved, on the table, gathering dust for weeks. She has not mentioned citizenship again with the urgency of that particular time. Once in a while, she would say: "They have forgotten me. I told you they don't want old Chinese women as citizens."

Finally, her interview date is set. I try to teach her some ready-made phrases, but she forgets them.

"You should not sigh so much. It is bad for your health," Mother observes.

On the day of her examination, I accompany her into the judge's chamber. I am more nervous than my mother.

Staring at the judge, my mother remarks: "*Noi yren.*" The judge shows interest in what my mother says, and I translate it: "She says you're a woman."

The judge smiles. "Yes. Is that strange?"

"If she is going to examine me," Mother tells me, "I might as well start packing for China. Sell my house. Dig up your father's bones, and I'll take them back with me."

Without knowing what my mother said, the judge reassures her. "This is just a formality. Really. We know that you obviously want to be part of our Canadian society. Why else would you go through all this trouble? We want to welcome you as a new citizen, no matter what race, nationality, religion, or age. And we want you to be proud—as a new Canadian."

Six weeks have passed since the interview with the judge. Mother receives a registered letter telling her to come in three weeks' time to take part in the oath of allegiance ceremony.

With patient help from the same judge, my mother recites the oath and becomes a Canadian citizen after thirty years in *gum san.*

TOPICS FOR EXPLORATION

1. Who does Garry Engkent have in mind as his readers? What is his purpose in using Chinese words and expressions in a story written in English? Does the English-speaking reader feel left out?

2. The narrator can't read Chinese; his mother can't speak or read English. How does this inhibit their ability to relate to each other? Characterize the narrator's attitude to his mother.

3. In what way does the story illustrate that being cut off from the language of the other in the encounter between Canadians and Chinese immigrants may lead to cultural misunderstandings on both sides? How do the mother's old attitudes continue to colour her experience and expectations in Canada?

4. For what reasons has the narrator's mother not learned English? Why did his father discourage her from doing so? Why does she fear that "learning English would change her Chinese soul"?

5. Comment on the narrator's statement that he is "not Chinese enough any more" to justify both his father's double standards for men and women and his mother's stubborn refusal to learn English.

6. What requirements are necessary in order to become a Canadian citizen? Are they valid? Does language, in the final analysis, act as a hindrance to citizenship for the narrator's mother? Why not?

SUGGESTIONS FOR FURTHER STUDY

1. Myrna Kostash and Genni Donati Gunn both address the problem faced by most immigrants, namely, how to preserve one's ethnic identity under the pressure of the new, dominant culture. Discuss how they view separation (Kostash's "ghettoization"), assimilation, and integration (Gunn's "middle ground") as models of immigrant behaviour.

2. Compare the difficulties of expression in a new language as described by Eva Hoffman and Himani Bannerji. How are the problems they confront different? How do they both see the possibility of translating one's personality into a new language?

3. Genni Donati Gunn describes the difficulties in letting the past go and accepting the present. Compare the stories by Garry Engkent and Gunn. What features of their two cultures, so different in outlook, do their stories have in common?

4. Engkent's narrator has become distanced from his Chinese roots. Rosalba in Gunn's story fears a similar change in her Italian self-image. On the basis of these two stories, identify different attitudes to language and culture held by different generations of immigrants.

5. Compare how Myrna Kostash and Himani Bannerji discuss the complexities involved in being an ethnic writer in Canada. How do their concerns differ?

GROWING UP: EDUCATION

INTRODUCTION

Education imposes the information that a culture believes is necessary for its own survival and growth. Institutions of education represent the authority that a dominant culture exercises and which citizens are taught to respect. Unfortunately, where there is power there are abuses, whether conscious or not. Often in the past, and sometimes still today, Canadian schools, rooted in white, Northern European cultural assumptions, could be seen as places of institutionalized racism. The missionary movement was based on such cultural assumptions.

Perhaps the Native people of Canada have suffered most from white domination in education. Too often, the values of Native culture have been denigrated, repressed, and lost. In Pauline Johnson's story, written almost a century ago, we see the double standards imposed by white missionaries upon the Native population and in particular on an impressionable Native girl who is betrayed by the missionary family she has trusted. Here the subjugation of Native spiritual values is further complicated by personal prejudices that provoke a violent retaliation. Johnson's fiction finds a later parallel in Carol Geddes's essay, where she describes the Teslin Tlingit people's way of life as it has been transformed by contact with a European wage-based economy and especially by education in residential schools. Only when Geddes attends university as an adult does she reverse the poor self-image inflicted upon her as a Native child by her Christian missionary teachers.

Despite the repressive character of education in the service of a colonizing power, sometimes almost by default, the learning experience can be touched by growth and, perhaps, nostalgia. In Basil H. Johnston's narrative about the small northern settlement of Spanish, school extends through the summer for a group of Native boys who are not allowed to return to their families. In spite of their isolation, the rough education on the land—fishing, hunting, exploring—turns the summer camp into "home, comfort, freedom, a place of growth" for the unhappy boys.

In the three stories dealing with immigrant themes included in this unit, the classroom is central. The characters are teachers and their students, who are immigrants or the children of immigrants. Clark Blaise tells the story of an American nightschool instructor in Montreal teaching English to an assortment of new Canadians whose naïve preconceptions and surprising ambitions frustrate and irritate him—particularly since he himself has come to distrust the values of "American" assimilation. Contact with these students is an ironic lesson for him, too. Some teachers lack even this partial insight into their students' problems. Miss Vance in Janice Kulyk Keefer's "The Amores" is a rigid authoritarian whose best intentions for Agnes, the daughter of Hungarian refugees, result in pressure to succeed by Miss Vance's standards and lead to a crisis in Agnes's relationship with her widowed, hysterical mother, and a final act of rebellion against the "imperial" Miss Vance. The anxiety of Agnes's choice between the pure study of classics and the practical skills of a secretarial course can be resolved only by a liberating act of defiance.

Personal morality and the authority of the teacher often become confused. We see the subtleties of this confusion explored in Robyn

Sarah's short story in which two Jewish girls—Esther, whose father's job was to investigate anti-Semitic propaganda, and Rhoda, the daughter of Holocaust survivors who have succeeded in the West—consider the implications of a personal remark made in the classroom by their teacher. The remark is interpreted by Rhoda's parents as an anti-Semitic slur. The resultant doubt about intention and responsibility disturbs Esther and her understanding of the meaning of blame.

No matter how the purpose of education is distorted and who might be scarred by its application, it has given to many—if only by provoking them to opposition—fruitful experience and the impulse to articulate it. The process of education is as complicated as the cultures that feed it.

What Do I
Remember of the Evacuation

What do I remember of the evacuation?
I remember my father telling Tim and me
About the mountains and the train
An the excitement of going on a trip.
What do I remember of the evacuation?
I remember my mother wrapping
A blanket around me and my
Pretending to fall asleep so she would be happy
Though I was so excited I couldn't sleep
(I hear there were people herded
Into the Hastings Park like cattle.
Families were made to move in two hours
Abandoning everything, leaving pets
And possessions at gun point.
I hear families were broken up
Men were forced to work. I heard
It whispered late at night
That there was suffering) and
I missed my dolls.
What do I remember of the evacuation?
I remember Miss Foster and Miss Tucker
Who still live in Vancouver

And who did what they could
And loved the children and who gave me
A puzzle to play with on the train.
And I remember the mountains and I was
Six years old and I swear I saw a giant
Gulliver of Gulliver's Travels scanning the horizon
And when I told my mother she believed it too
And I remember how careful my parents were
Not to bruise us with bitterness
And I remember the puzzle of Lorraine Life
Who said "Don't insult me" when I
Proudly wrote my name in Japanese
And Tim flew the Union Jack
When the war was over but Lorraine
And her friends spat on us anyway
And I prayed to the God who loves
All the children in his sight
That I might be white.

—*Joy Kogawa*

An excerpt from Joy Kogawa's novel Itsuka *can be found in Unit Two.*

Pauline Johnson

Pauline Johnson was born in 1861 on the Six Nations Reserve; she died in 1913. She was the daughter of George Johnson, a Mohawk chief, and an English mother. Her stories, poems and essays were usually published in the United States, although her reputation in Canada and England was widespread and popular. Often romanticized for the taste of the reading public of her day, her narratives, nonetheless, have a realistic edge and authentically portray some of the conflicts emerging at the meeting point of Native and white societies. The following story was first published in The Moccasin Maker *(1913), a collection of articles and short stories.*

As It Was in the Beginning

They account for it by the fact that I am a Redskin, but I am something else, too—I am a woman.

I remember the first time I saw him. He came up the trail with some Hudson's Bay trappers, and they stopped at the door of my father's tepee. He seemed even then, fourteen years ago, an old man; his hair seemed just as thin and white, his hands just as trembling and fleshless as they were a month since, when I saw him for what I pray his God is the last time.

My father sat in the tepee, polishing buffalo horns and smoking; my mother, wrapped in her blanket, crouched over her quill-work, on the buffalo-skin at his side; I was lounging at the doorway, idling, watching, as I always watched, the thin, distant line of sky and prairie, wondering, as I always wondered, what lay beyond it. Then he came, this gentle old man with his white hair and thin, pale face. He wore a long black coat, which I now know was the sign of his office, and he carried a black leather-covered book, which, in all the years I have known him, I have never seen him without.

The trappers explained to my father who he was, the Great Teacher, the heart's Medicine Man, the "Blackcoat" we had heard of, who brought peace where there was war, and the magic of whose black book brought greater things than all the Happy Hunting Grounds of our ancestors.

He told us many things that day, for he could speak the Cree tongue, and my father listened, and listened, and when at last they left us, my father said for him to come and sit within the tepee again.

He came, all the time he came, and my father welcomed him, but my mother always sat in silence at work with the quills; my mother never liked the Great "Blackcoat."

His stories fascinated me. I used to listen intently to the tale of the strange new place he called "heaven," of the gold crown, of the white dress, of the great music; and then he would tell of that other strange place—hell. My father and I hated it; we feared it, we dreamt of it, we trembled at it. Oh, if the "Blackcoat" would only cease to talk of it! Now I know he saw the effect upon us, and he used it as a whip to lash us into his new religion, but even then my mother must have known, for each time he left the tepee she would watch him going slowly away across the prairie; then when he disappeared into the far horizon she would laugh scornfully, and say:

"If the white man made this Blackcoat's hell, let him go to it. It is for the man who found it first. No hell for Indians, just Happy Hunting Grounds. Blackcoat can't scare me."

And then, after weeks had passed, one day as he stood at the tepee door he laid his white, old hand on my head and said to my father: "Give me this little girl, chief. Let me take her to the mission school; let me keep her, and teach her of the great God and His eternal heaven. She will grow to be a noble woman, and return perhaps to bring her people to the Christ."

My mother's eyes snapped. "No," she said. It was the first word she ever spoke to the "Blackcoat." My father sat and smoked. At the end of a half-hour he said:

"I am an old man, Blackcoat. I shall not leave the God of my fathers. I like not your strange God's ways—all of them. I like not His two new places for me when I am dead. Take the child, Blackcoat, and save her from hell."

The first grief of my life was when we reached the mission. They took my buckskin dress off, saying I was now a little Christian girl and must dress like all the white people at the mission. Oh, how I hated that stiff new calico dress and those leather shoes! But, little as I was, I said nothing, only thought of the time when I should be grown, and do as my mother did, and wear the buckskins and the blanket.

My next serious grief was when I began to speak the English, that they forbade me to use any Cree words whatsoever. The rule of the school was that any child heard using its native tongue must get a slight punishment. I never understood it, I cannot understand it now, why the use of my dear Cree tongue could be a matter for correction or an action deserving punishment.

She was strict, the matron of the school, but only justly so, for she had a heart and a face like her brother's, the "Blackcoat." I had long since ceased to call him that. The trappers at the post called him "St. Paul," because, they told me, of his self-sacrificing life, his kindly deeds, his rarely beautiful old face; so I, too, called him "St. Paul," though oftener "Father Paul," though he never liked the latter title, for he was a Protestant. But as I was his pet, his darling of the whole school, he let me speak of him as I would, knowing it was but my heart speaking in love. His sister was a widow, and mother to a laughing yellow-haired little boy of about my age, who was my constant playmate and who taught me much of English in his own childish way. I used to be fond of this child, just as I was fond of his mother and of his uncle, my "Father Paul," but as my girlhood passed away, as womanhood came upon me, I got strangely wearied of them all; I longed, oh, God, how I longed for the old wild life! It came with my womanhood, with my years.

What mattered it to me now that they had taught me all their ways?—their tricks of dress, their reading, their writing, their books. What mattered it that "Father Paul" loved me, that the traders at the post called me pretty, that I was a pet of all, from the factor to the poorest trapper in the service? I wanted my own people, my own old life, my blood called out for it, but they always said I must not return to my father's tepee. I heard them talk amongst themselves of keeping me away from pagan influences; they told each other that if I returned to the prairies, the tepees, I would degenerate, slip back to paganism, as other girls had done; marry, perhaps, with a pagan—and all their years of labor and teaching would be lost.

I said nothing, but I waited. And then one night the feeling overcame me. I was in the Hudson's Bay store when an Indian came in from the north with a large pack of buckskin. As they unrolled it a dash of its insinuating odor filled the store. I went over and leaned above the skins a second, then buried my face in them, swallowing, drinking the fragrance of them, that went to my head like wine. Oh, the wild wonder of that wood-smoked tan, the subtlety of it, the untamed smell of it! I drank it into my lungs, my innermost being was saturated with it, till my mind reeled and my heart seemed twisted with a physical agony. My childhood recollections rushed upon me, devoured me. I left the store in a strange, calm frenzy, and going rapidly to the mission house I confronted my Father Paul and demanded to be allowed to go "home," if only for a day. He received the request with the same refusal and the same gentle sigh that I had to often been greeted with, but *this* time the desire, the smoke-tan, the heart-ache, never lessened.

Night after night I would steal away by myself and go to the border of the village to watch the sun set in the foothills, to gaze at the far line of sky and prairie, to long and long for my father's lodge. And Laurence—always Laurence— my fair-haired, laughing, child playmate, would come calling and calling for me: "Esther, where are you? We miss you: come in, Esther, come in with me." And if I did not turn at once to him and follow, he would come and place his strong hands on my shoulders and laugh into my eyes and say, "Truant, truant, Esther; can't *we* make you happy?"

My old child playmate had vanished years ago. He was a tall, slender young man now, handsome as a young chief, but with laughing blue eyes, and always those yellow curls about his temples. He was my solace in my half-exile, my comrade, my brother, until one night it was, "Esther, Esther, can't *I* make you happy?"

I did not answer him; only looked out across the plains and thought of the tepees. He came close, close. He locked his arms about me, and with my face pressed up to his throat he stood silent. I felt the blood from my heart sweep to my very finger-tips. I loved him. Oh God, how I loved him! In a wild, blind instant it all came, just because he held me so and was whispering brokenly, "Don't leave me, don't leave me, Esther; *my* Esther, my child-love, my play-mate, my girl-comrade, my little Cree sweetheart, will you go away to your people, or stay, stay for me, for my arms, as I have you now?"

No more, no more the tepees; no more the wild stretch of prairie, the intoxicating fragrance of the smoke-tanned buckskin; no more the bed of buffalo hide, the soft, silent moccasin,; no more the dark faces of my people, the dulcet cadence of the sweet Cree tongue—only this man, this fair, proud, tender man who held me in his arms, in his heart. My soul prayed to his great white God, in that moment, that He let me have only this.

It was twilight when we re-entered the mission gate. We were both excited, feverish. Father Paul was reading evening prayers in the large room beyond the hallway; his soft, saint-like voice stole beyond the doors, like a benediction upon us. I went noiselessly upstairs to my own room and sat there undisturbed for hours.

The clock downstairs struck one, startling me from my dreams of happiness, and at the same moment a flash of light attracted me.

My room was in an angle of the building, and my window looked almost directly down into those of Father Paul's study, into which at that instant he was entering, carrying a lamp. "Why, Laurence," I heard him exclaim, "what are you doing here? I thought, my boy, you were in bed hours ago."

"No, uncle, not in bed, but in dreamland," replied Laurence, arising from the window, where evidently he, too, had spent the night hours as I had done.

Father Paul fumbled about for a moment, found his large black book, which for once he seemed to have got separated from, and was turning to leave, when the curious circumstance of Laurence being there at so unusual an hour seemed to strike him anew. "Better go to sleep, my son," he said simply, then added curiously, "Has anything occurred to keep you up?"

Then Laurence spoke: "No, uncle, only—only, I'm happy, that's all."

Father Paul stood irresolute: Then: "It is—?"

"Esther," said Laurence quietly, but he was at the old man's side, his hand was on the bent old shoulder, his eyes proud and appealing.

Father Paul set the lamp on the table, but, as usual, one hand held that black book, the great text of his life. His face was paler than I had ever seen it—graver.

"Tell of it," he requested.

I leaned far out of my window and watched them both. I listened with my very heart, for Laurence was telling him of me, of his love, of the new-found joy of that night.

"You have said nothing of marriage to her?" asked Father Paul.

"Well—no; but she surely understands that—"

"Did you speak of *marriage?*" repeated Father Paul, with a harsh ring in his voice that was new to me.

"No, uncle, but—"

"Very well, then; very well."

There was a brief silence. Laurence stood staring at the old man as though he were a stranger; he watched him push a large chair up to the table, slowly seat himself; then mechanically following his movements, he dropped onto a lounge. The old man's head bent low, but his eyes were bright and strangely fascinating. He began:

"Laurence, my boy, your future is the dearest thing to me of all earthly interests. Why, you *can't* marry this girl—no, no, sit, sit until I have finished," he added, with raised voice, as Laurence sprang up, remonstrating. "I have long since decided that you marry well; for instance, the Hudson's Bay factor's daughter."

Laurence broke into a fresh, rollicking laugh. "What, uncle," he said, "little Ida McIntosh? Marry that little yellow-haired fluff ball, that kitten, that pretty little dolly?"

"Stop," said Father Paul. Then, with a low, soft persuasiveness, "She is *white*, Laurence."

My lover startled. "Why, uncle, what do you mean?" he faltered.

"Only this, my son: poor Esther comes of uncertain blood; would it do for you—the missionary's nephew, and adopted son, you might say—to marry the daughter of a pagan Indian? Her mother is hopelessly uncivilized; her father has a dash of French somewhere—half-breed, you know, my boy, half-breed." Then, with still lower tone and half-shut, crafty eyes, he added: "The blood is a bad, bad mixture, *you* know that; you know, too, that I am very fond of the girl, poor dear Esther. I have tried to separate her from evil pagan influences; she is the daughter of the Church; I want her to have no other parent; but you never can tell what lurks in *a caged animal that has once been wild.* My whole heart is with the Indian people, my son; my whole heart, my whole life, has been devoted to bringing them to Christ, *but is a different thing to marry with one of them.*"

His small old eyes were riveted on Laurence like a hawk's on a rat. My heart lay like ice in my bosom.

Laurence, speechless and white, stared at him breathlessly.

"Go away somewhere," the old man was urging, "to Winnipeg, Toronto, Montreal; forget her, then come back to Ida McIntosh. A union of the Church and the Hudson's Bay will mean great things, and may ultimately result in my life's ambition, the civilization of this entire tribe, that we have worked so long to bring to God."

I listened, sitting like one frozen. Could those words have been uttered by my venerable teacher by him whom I revered as I would one of the saints in his own black book? Ah, there was no mistaking it. My white father, my life-long friend who pretended to love me, to care for my happiness, was urging the man I worshipped to forget me, to marry with the factor's daughter—because of what? Of my red skin; my good, old, honest pagan mother; my confiding French-Indian father. In a second all the care, the hollow love he had given me since my childhood, were as things that never existed. I hated that old mission priest as I hated his white man's hell. I hated his long, white hair; I hated his thin, white hands; I hated his body, his soul, his voice, his black book—oh, how I hated the very atmosphere of him!

Laurence sat motionless, his face buried in his hands, but the old man continued: "No, no; not the child of that pagan mother; you can't trust her, my son. What would you do with a wife who might any day break from you to return to her prairies and her buckskins? *You can't trust her.*" His eyes grew smaller, more glittering, more fascinating then, and leaning with an odd, secret sort of movement towards Laurence, he almost whispered. "Think of her

silent ways, her noiseless step; the girl glides about like an apparition; her quick fingers, her wild longings—I don't know why, but
with all my fondness for her, she reminds me sometimes of a
strange—*snake*.

Laurence shuddered, lifted his face, and said hoarsely: "You're
right, uncle; perhaps I'd better not; I'll go away, I'll forget her, and
then—well, then—yes, you are right, it *is* a different thing to marry
one of them." The old man arose. His feeble fingers still clasped his
black book; his soft white hair clung about his forehead like that of
an Apostle; his eyes lost their peering, crafty expression; his bent
shoulders resumed the dignity of a minister of the living God; he
was the picture of what the traders called him—"St. Paul."

"Good-night, son," he said.

"Good-night, uncle, and thank you for bringing me to myself."

They were the last words I ever heard uttered by either that old
arch-fiend or his weak, miserable kinsman. Father Paul turned and
left the room. I watched his withered hand—the hand I had so
often felt resting on my head in holy benediction—clasp the door-
knob, turn it slowly then, with bowed head and his pale face rapt in
thought, he left the room—left it with the mad venom of my hate
pursuing him like the very Evil One he taught me of.

What were his years of kindness and care now? What did I care
for his God, his heaven, his hell? He had robbed me of my native
faith, of my parents, of my people, of this last, this life of love that
would have made a great, good woman of me. God! How I hated
him!

I crept to the closet in my dark little room. I felt for a bundle I
had not looked at for years—yes, it was there, the buckskin dress
I had worn as a little child when they brought me to the mission. I
tucked it under my arm and descended the stairs noiselessly. I would
look into the study and speak good-bye to Laurence; then I
would—

I pushed open the door. He was lying on the couch where a
short time previously he had sat, white and speechless, listening to
Father Paul. I moved towards him softly. God in heaven, he was
already asleep. As I bent over him the fullness of his perfect beauty
impressed me for the first time; his slender form, his curving mouth
that almost laughed even in sleep, his fair, tossed hair, his smooth,
strong-pulsing throat. God! How I loved him!

Then there arose the picture of the factor's daughter. I hated her.
I hated her baby face, her yellow hair, her whitish skin. "She shall
not marry him," my soul said. "I will kill him first—kill his beautiful body, his lying, false heart." Something in my heart seemed to
speak; it said over and over again, "Kill him, kill him; she will never
have him then. Kill him. It will break Father Paul's heart and blight

his life. He has killed the best of you, of your womanhood; kill *his* best, his pride, his hope—his sister's son, his nephew Laurence." But how? How?

What had that terrible old man said I was like? A *strange snake.* A snake? The idea wound itself about me like the very coils of a serpent. What was this in the beaded bag of my buckskin dress? this little thing rolled in tan that my mother had given me at parting with the words, "Don't touch much, but sometime maybe you want it!" Oh! I knew well enough what it was—a small flint arrow-head dipped in the venom of some *strange snake.*

I knelt beside him and laid my hot lips on his hand. I worshipped him, oh, how, how I worshipped him! Then again the vision of *her* baby face, *her* yellow hair—I scratched his wrist twice with the arrow-tip. A single drop of red blood oozed up; he stirred. I turned the lamp down and slipped out of the room—out of the house.

I dreamt nightly of the horrors of the white man's hell. Why did they teach me of it, only to fling me into it?

Last night as I crouched beside my mother on the buffalo-hide, Dan Henderson, the trapper, came in to smoke with my father. He said old Father Paul was bowed with grief, that with my disappearance I was suspected, but that there was no proof. Was it not merely a snake bite?

They account for it by the fact that I am a Redskin.

They seem to have forgotten I am a woman.

TOPICS FOR EXPLORATION

1. Whose point of view has Pauline Johnson used to tell her story? What effect does that have upon her narrative?

2. Discuss how the portrait of the missionary gradually unfolds in the story. How does the girl initially describe him? Why do the trappers call him "Saint Paul"? What does the missionary's behaviour reveal about him?

3. How has Johnson portrayed the incursion of missionaries into the Native community? How is the word "Blackcoat" symbolic of its sinister aspects? What steps did the missionaries use to dispossess the Cree children of their identity? What stereotypes were used to rationalize the "civilizing" mission?

4. Why does the girl's father allow her to be taken to the mission school? What does his reaction to the Blackcoat's Christian teachings reveal about the reception given to white men by Native people?

5. How is Laurence a victim of the missionary's double standard? Is Father Paul aware of his own hypocrisy? Why does he "distrust" Esther?

6. For Esther, what does the betrayal by white religion consist of? What lesson does she learn at the mission about being "a Redskin" and "a woman"?

7. Despite its indictment of Christian hypocrisy, the story relies heavily on Christian symbolism. What is the symbolic meaning of the "snake"? How appropriate is the allusion to the garden of Eden in the story's title? Can it also be read as an allegory of betrayed trust in the relationship between Native people and whites?

Robyn Sarah

Robyn Sarah was born in New York in 1949; she grew up in Montreal. She has published three books of poetry, Shadowplay *(1978),* The Space Between Sleeping and Walking *(1981), and* Anyone Skating on that Middle Ground *(1984). Her short fiction has appeared in Canadian magazines and anthologies. "A Minor Incident" won the Okanagan Short Story Award in 1989.*

A Minor Incident

For a few years beginning around when I was twelve, my father worked for a Jewish organization, a branch of it devoted to fighting anti-Semitism. To his desk came samples of printed materials against which complaints had been lodged; he had to read these and decide what action, if any, need be taken—he was a sort of filter for hate literature. Sometimes he brought it home with him in the evenings. I remember a kind of pained face he'd have, like the face of someone who has been walking all day in shoes that are too tight, and whose feet have blistered; and he might call to me from his desk in the alcove, when I was doing my homework at the dining-room table: "Esther. Come here, I want you to see something. I want you to read this. Look, look what they say about us, terrible things . . . look . . ."

But I would not; instead I'd gather up my books without a word, and go to my room and shut the door, clenching and unclenching my hands; would he call me again? Would he insist? If he did, my mother might protest to him, in a low voice, in Yiddish which I did not understand; and he would reply audibly, in English, "She's old enough. She should see it. She should know."

I do not remember being told about the Holocaust, not when, nor by whom, though it must have been one of them my father or my mother, who told me, before it was called the Holocaust, before it had a name attached to it whereby it could be handled, contained, dismissed. I do know that only a few years elapsed between the times when, waking from nightmares, I was reassured that there were no wicked witches, that there weren't any monsters, that I didn't need to be afraid because there were no such things, they were just "made up"—and the time when I knew that men in uniforms, ordinary human beings, had dashed out the brains of babies against concrete walls before their mothers' eyes, and then shot the mothers dead; and that this was not a bad dream, not a made-up story, but was the truth and had really happened. Who could accept that and need to hear more? The one image contained the Holocaust for me; in it I felt my knowledge to be complete. The rest was numbers. Say it isn't true? Say it didn't happen *really*? No, it really happened. It happened over and over.

I know now, too, that the years when I lay awake in the dark, fearful of witches, were years when the full extent of the horror was still being uncovered; in our house, years of hushed conversations in Yiddish and rustling newspapers, radio babble, grownup talk behind closed doors. My grandmother was alive, then, and lived with us; I remember her room at the end of the hall, with a smell all its own that permeated everything in it, the maroon plush chair, the chenille bedspread, the patterned Indian rug. She had her own radio, an enormous one with a wicker front, on a shelf above the bed; she had hatboxes in the closet in which were hats of crumpled felt garnished with glazed wooden cherries, curled black plumes, pearl-tipped hat pins; in her closet, too, there hung old nylons stuffed at the bottom with clove and dried orange peel; on her bureau was a glass bowl filled with rose petals. I remember that every once in a while, my mother would call her to the telephone in a tense, urgent tone, and with one hand to her heart she would go; the conversation that followed would be a trading of names, of people I did not know and of what I later realized were towns in Galicia; yes, she would say then, yes? No. No. No. And she would shake her head at my mother, who hovered listening. No. No. Her face would slacken, she would wish the caller good health in Yiddish, and good luck. "A different Charney," she would say, putting the phone down. "Not related." It was her brother she was hoping to hear from, or have news of. People with the same name, arriving in new cities, would do that then—look up the name in the telephone book, call each listing, seeking family connection, word of relatives. They would look up every spelling. Calls came to us from Charneys, Cherneys, Chierneys. To no avail.

Years passed before I understood the significance of those phone calls. That Gran hoped to hear from her brother, yes; but not why; not what might have become of him, what was more likely with each passing day to have become of him. Years, before I realized what had happened to Gran's sister, the one I knew I was named for. The sister Gran only ever described to me as the small girl whose hair she, Gran, had braided each day, as she now braided mine: Esthie, Gran's littlest sister, still a young girl when Gran came to Canada. Years, before I connected the Holocaust with my family, in a moment of shocked comprehension. That was a connection they never made for me, and why was that? A question I've never answered. Why it took so long for me to make it myself is another. There are many such questions from my childhood. The question about Mrs. Howick is one.

When I was twelve my best friend was Rhoda Kendal, quiet like me, studious and shy. We were friends more by circumstance than by our choosing, both of us having transferred from other schools (I in fourth grade, she in fifth) at the age by which girls have formed tight bonds and cliques and are not easily receptive to newcomers. I made no friends in my first year at Wilchester School, and I knew what that felt like, so when Rhoda showed up in my class the next year and I saw her standing alone and diffident in the schoolyard, I took her under my wing. She was a sweet-natured girl with a round smooth face, placid features, and dove-soft black hair that waved. She had an air about her, among the harder-edged, more socially conscious girls, of still being a child, somehow untouched by sophistication; she seemed defenseless to me in her pleated, regulation tunic—a style the other girls, myself included, had discarded in favour of the 'A-line' pleatless tunic older girls at our school were permitted to wear.

My own defenses were already in place. Close on the realization that I would not be invited into the circle, at Wilchester, came the realization that I did not want to be. I signified this by fastening my pleatless tunic with the old regulation two-button belt, declining to purchase from the office the long, shiny-threaded sash the other girls rushed, thrilled, to trade theirs for. I continued to clump around in navy-blue Oxfords even after the principal, badgered by mothers of unhappy girls, conceded to allow an alternative, more stylish shoe. In this I differed from the two or three other loners in my class: Donna, the only Gentile girl; Brina who had a mysterious illness that absented her for weeks at a time; Jana who was cross-eyed and came to school with egg on her blouse. They, like the rest, opted for sashes and loafers, hoping thus to avoid becoming targets for whispering.

I for my part might be ignored, but I was not whispered about because my marks were too good. I did not strain for this. It was my luck, I was so constituted, that term after term, effortlessly, I led the class; and it was also my luck that Wilchester was a place where that counted.

Rhoda studied much harder than I did and got "Very Goods" and "Goods" where I got "Excellents." It was indicative of her nature that she did not in the least resent me for this, but whole-heartedly admired me and exulted in my successes as if they were her own. "Gee, you make me sick!" she might say, looking at my report card, but she couldn't stop smiling. The other girls who rushed over to compare their marks with mine, subject by subject, said flattering things to me, but their voices betrayed them, barely masking bitter envy.

As my marks protected me from being targeted, so being my friend protected Rhoda. By seventh grade we were inseparable. We spent recesses together, griping about Home Economics, discussing which girls were "boy crazy." On Saturdays we exchanged our books at the library and rode the bus home to her house or mine, giggling too loudly, dropping potato chips in the aisle. At the end of the day, we would walk each other "half-way home," and the half-way might stretch to all the way, then, "I'll walk you half-way home," till it was dark out and we were giddy with the silliness of it. Looking back on it, I think that if Rhoda had not come late to Wilchester and had not met me first of all, she might have become one of the crowd—she had it in her to fit in—whereas I, even had I not come late, would have remained singular and apart. But Rhoda had a loyal heart, and though she ditched her pleated tunic and succumbed soon enough to the sash and loafers, she was staunchly my friend and stuck by me.

Rhoda's parents had been in the camps. I didn't know this at the time; I'm not sure how I know it now. Somebody must have told me, long afterwards—perhaps my mother, perhaps Rhoda herself when we ran across each other again, years later, in graduate school. There was little to show it. They had a home like other homes in that neighbourhood, a brand-new, fashionable split-level, white rugs, sunken living-room, sofas in plastic slipcovers. It was much fancier than my parents' house; the hall floor was parquet instead of vinyl tile; the bedrooms had wall-to-wall carpeting. In the bathroom a basket by the sink contained coloured, scented soap puffs for visitors; I had to ask what they were. Everything was always immaculately clean and tidy; Rhoda and her younger brother and sister, who were twins, were generally not allowed in the living-room. It was a sharp contrast to my house, where a comfortable level of clutter prevailed and everything—furniture, flooring, fixtures—had a well-used, time-worn look.

I preferred for Rhoda to come to my house because I never felt entirely comfortable in hers. Her parents (when they were around for both worked), spoke Yiddish most of the time; their English was poor, formal, and thickly accented. About them I felt a foreignness, an apart-ness, that I could not read or gauge. Rhoda's mother was not friendly like mine. She would smile at me and say hello when we came in, but she never conversed with me or drew me out, as my mother did with the friends I brought home, and she never sat down to chat with us when we fixed ourselves snacks in the gleaming kitchen; instead she would retire to another room. Once, I confessed to Rhoda that I did not feel welcome in her house, that I thought her mother disliked me; but Rhoda, stunned, told me her mother like me very much and was happy she, Rhoda, had me for a friend. "She's shy, Esther," she told me, "and she thinks her English is bad. Maybe she's afraid you'll laugh at her. I tell her all the time how brilliant you are—"

Of Rhoda's father I have only one clear memory, and it strikes me now as being an odd one. It is of a hot spring afternoon when I arrived at the house to call for Rhoda; we were going somewhere together, I don't remember where, and as I turned up the walk, Rhoda called to me from her bedroom window, "I'll be down in a sec, I'm just changing." To pass the time, I strolled around the side of the house to look at the lilacs, and came suddenly upon her father on a ladder in the driveway, shirtless, painting the garage door. He had a cap on, and for a moment I thought he was a hired worker; then he looked up from beneath the visor and smiled at me, an oddly warm, sad smile that crinkled the corners of his eyes. He was amused to see that I had not recognized him, and motioned me nearer. "Esther. So, Esther. You like my hat?"

I felt awkward and shy. It was the first time I had seen him alone, or exchanged more than a word or two with him. I can't remember the conversation we had there, in the sunny driveway, with faint breezes wafting the smells of lilac and wet paint; but I remember that the tone was kindly, gentle, sad, and oddly intimate. "It's hard, to be a Jew," I remember him saying to me in his European accent, slowly shaking his head (and my sudden, forlorn sense of discomfiture)—"You know what they say, Esther? It's hard to be a Jew."

What was the context? I cannot at all remember. And did this scene take place before, or after, the incident with Mrs. Howick? That, too, evades me.

Seventh Grade was at that time the final year of elementary school, a year in which teachers strove to prepare students for the comparative rigours to come. Our teacher, Mrs. Howick, was strict and uncompromising, but scrupulously fair. She was a short woman in her mid-forties—the bigger girls already had the edge on her—but she commanded respect in every fiber by the way in which she planted herself at the front of a classroom: square posture, legs placed slightly apart, chin erect, hands on hips. She wore pleated skirts, high-necked blouses, dark support hose, "sensible" shoes. No jewellery, no perfume—indulgences of the younger teachers on staff. Her hair, a nondescript light brown as yet unmixed with grey, was center-parted and cut short, it stood out a little from her face, giving her a severe yet slightly dowdy appearance.

I liked her well enough. She had a brisk, animated classroom style, could be salty, was not boring, gave a reasonable amount of homework, and expected us to deliver, without coddling. Her digressions, when she digressed, were interesting. She quickly recognized my abilities and acknowledged me matter-of-factly, without effusions; she also gave me to understand that it was the thoughtfulness of my answers, rather than the correctness, that she valued. "Think, think, think," she used to exhort us, "don't let anybody else do your thinking for you." Or sometimes, if she asked for a show of hands on who agreed with a particular answer: "What are you looking around at your neighbour for? I'm asking what *you* think! *You!* Never mind the others! Else you're nothing but sheep." Her words were often accompanied by so vigorous a tapping of her pointer against the blackboard or floor that the wooden stick would snap in two, the broken end bouncing off somebody's desk to the accompaniment of stifled giggles.

The comparing of marks, whenever a test was given back, was something that evoked equal vehemence from her. "Keep your paper to yourself. What do you care what *she* got? 'What did you get, what did you get?'" (she mimicked, in mincing tones). "Is that all that matters to you? Look at your *own* paper! *Read* the comments on it— do you think I write them to amuse myself? Look at your mistakes, *learn* something!" And shaking her head in exasperation: "It's marks, marks, marks, with you people—that's all you're interested in. Just like with your parents it's money, money, money. Who's got the most—isn't that true? Today it's marks, marks, marks, and when you grow up, it'll be money, money, money."

One afternoon in midwinter, as I was getting my books together to leave, she spoke to me from her desk in an uncharacteristically personal tone. "Esther, do you have a few minutes to spare? Please stay behind. I want to talk to you about something."

My heart lurched for a second, but my conscience was clear. Maybe she had plans for me for the school concert. Maybe she wanted me to help her with something. Wondering, I followed her out of the classroom—away from a group of girls who were staying for detention—and down the hall a distance. "Esther," she said then, in a confidential voice, putting a hand on my shoulder, "I don't know if you've heard that I've been accused of saying things against Jews." Her eyes looked straight into mine, transfixing me. I shook my head; I was tongue-tied.

"Esther," she repeated. "You're Jewish. You're my brightest student. Please tell me. Have you ever heard me say anything against Jews?"

Again I shook my head. My heart was pounding; I didn't know why. It flashed through my mind that I had never thought of Mrs. Howick as being non-Jewish, or as not being Jewish. I had never thought of the student body at Wilchester, a Protestant school, as being almost all Jewish, even though I knew that in our class, only Donna wasn't, and that on Jewish holidays the handful of students from all grades who showed up were pooled in one classroom and had Art all day; Donna had told us.

"Esther, you know what I say when people in the class start comparing their marks—that they want more marks just like their parents want more money? Tell me the truth. When I said that, did you ever think that I was speaking against Jews?"

No, I had not thought so, I said, completely taken aback.

"Good. I'm glad. Well, dear, some people have thought so. Your friend Rhoda mentioned it to her parents, and her parents complained. They brought it up at the P.T.A. meeting last week, and some parents were upset and called the principal." She tapped the squat heel of her shoe against the shining floor; I saw that the edges of her hair were quivering. "Esther, you know that it was *people* I was talking about, not just Jews, but the kind of person who is always wanting more than the next one; you know some people are like that, don't you?"

"Yes," I said. The tone of entreaty in her voice dismayed me.

"I wanted to ask *you*, because you're a very intelligent girl, and very mature, and because I know you and Rhoda are friends. Maybe you'll talk to her about it. Explain to her that I didn't mean it that way. Will you do that for me?

I said, "I'll try," and she patted my shoulder, gratefully, and said, "Good girl," and then I left.

That was the end of it; there was no sequel. The episode blew over without further ado; presumably, apologies were made, and the matter was allowed to drop. I did talk to Rhoda, but I don't remember what we said—only that it was a little uncomfortable, a little strained, I think she felt pulled between respect for her parents and loyalty to me; that she neither challenged my opinion nor concurred; but I don't remember. I never mentioned the affair to my own parents, who had little use for the P.T.A. and doubtless had not attended the meeting in question. At the end of the year, Rhoda and

I went off to separate high schools and gradually, as our lives diverged, lost touch with each other.

But I still sometimes think about Mrs. Howick. Though I shovelled it under at the time, I know that something opened up beneath me, that afternoon in the dim-lit school corridor, like a section of floor caving in. I see her plain, earnest, sometimes sardonic face; I remember that I liked her, and that she liked me. I hear her voice reiterating the offensive phrases and I wonder: Was it a slur, or wasn't it? And was it fair of her to ask me to decide? I could not argue with her observation as it applied to my school and neighbourhood: the kids were as a rule competitive and pushy for marks; the parents were typically brash, upwardly mobile suburbanites of the fifties. But what gave her the right to say it, and *for whom* was she saying it? "You people," she called us. And what was she asking me to uphold—the thoughtfulness of her statement, or the correctness of it? What unexamined premises of hers did my answer endorse? In retrospect I know that even as I gave her what she wanted, even as I said I had not taken her remark to be a slur, I began to wonder whether it had been; and over the years, off and on, I have gone on wondering.

At first what I wondered about was simple: if I liked her, how could she be an anti-Semite? But if she was an anti-Semite, how could I like her? Later, painfully, having allowed that both could be the case, I wondered which of us I had let down the most.

I remember coming late out of school, that winter dusk, and trudging across the empty schoolyard alone, over the bumpy, frozen crust of old footprints. Rhoda had not waited for me; there was no point, as we walked home in opposite directions. I remember how it began to snow lightly as I reached the gate, and how the snow fell thicker and thicker, in swift dizzying flakes, across my path home.

TOPICS FOR EXPLORATION

1. What does the first paragraph contribute to the unity of the story? What is "hate literature"? What is its origin and purpose? In what sense is Esther later cast in her father's role as described here?

2. Explain why to Esther the Holocaust "happened over and over." What does her grandmother stand for? What is the

relationship between the first part of the story, discussing the Holocaust and its impact upon the narrator's life, and the "minor incident" she narrates later?

3. In what areas can Rhoda and Esther be compared? How are their families different? What is the cause of the differences? How is language an issue that causes Rhoda's mother to display "shyness"?

4. Why is Mrs. Howick accused of anti-Semitism? Why do Rhoda's parents construe her remark about the parents wanting "money, money, money" to be anti-Semitic?

5. Why can't Esther decide whether Mrs. Howick's remark was a slur? Who is the victim of this misunderstanding? The story's ending raises several questions. Why does the author leave them unanswered?

6. How is the purpose of education distorted by both Mrs. Howick's remark and Rhoda's parents' response to it?

Clark Blaise

Clark Blaise was born in North Dakota in 1940 and educated at the University of Iowa's Writers Workshops, where he later taught. He has also taught in Montreal and Toronto. He has written three short story collections, Tribal Justice, A North American Education, *and* Resident Alien, *and two novels,* Lusts *and* Lunar Attractions. *His essays and stories have been published in over 30 anthologies. Blaise is married to Bharati Mukherjee, whose "Intimations" appears in Unit Six. Together they authored two books,* Days and Nights in Calcutta *(1977), about their experiences while visiting India in the early seventies, and* The Sorrow and the Terror: The Haunting Legacy of the Air India Disaster *(1987), an account of the explosion of an Air India jet in 1985.*

A Class of New Canadians

Norman Dyer hurried down Sherbrooke Street, collar turned against the snow. "Superb!" he muttered, passing a basement gallery next to a French bookstore. Bleached and tanned women in furs dashed from hotel lobbies into waiting cabs. Even the neon clutter of the side streets and the honks of slithering taxis seemed remote tonight through the peaceful snow. *Superb*, he thought again, waiting for a light and backing from a slushy curb: a word reserved for wines, cigars, and delicate sauces; he was feeling superb this evening. After eighteen months in Montreal, he still found himself freshly impressed by everything he saw. He was proud of himself for having steered his life north, even for jobs that were menial by standards he could have demanded. Great just being here no matter what they paid, looking at these buildings, these faces, and hearing all the languages. He was learning to be insulted by simple bad taste, wherever he encountered it.

Since leaving graduate school and coming to Montreal, he had sampled every ethnic restaurant downtown and in the old city, plus a few Levantine places out in Outremont. He had worked on conversational French and mastered much of the local dialect, done reviews for local papers, translated French-Canadian poets for Toronto quarterlies, and tweaked his colleagues for not sympathizing enough with Quebec separatism. He attended French performances of plays he had ignored in English, and kept a small but elegant apartment near a colony of *émigré* Russians just off Park Avenue. Since coming to Montreal he'd witnessed a hold-up, watched a murder, and seen several riots. When stopped on the street for directions, he would answer in French or accented English. To live this well and travel each long academic summer, he held two jobs. He had no intention of returning to the States. In fact, he had begun to think of himself as a semi-permanent, semi-political exile.

Now, stopped again a few blocks farther, he studied the window of Holt Renfrew's exclusive men's shop. Incredible, he thought, the authority of simple good taste. Double-breasted chalk-striped suits he would never dare to buy. Knitted sweaters, and fifty-dollar shoes. One tanned mannequin was decked out in a brash checkered sportscoat with a burgundy vest and dashing ascot. Not a price tag under three hundred dollars. Unlike food, drink, cinema, and literature, clothing had never really involved him. Someday, he now realized, it would. Dyer's clothes, thus far, had all been bought in a chain department store. He was a walking violation of American law, clad shoes to scarf in Egyptian cottons, Polish leathers, and woolens from the People's Republic of China.

He had no time for dinner tonight; this was Wednesday, a day of lectures at one university, and then an evening course in English as a Foreign Language at McGill, beginning at six. He would eat afterwards.

Besides the money, he had kept this second job because it flattered him. There was to Dyer something fiercely elemental, almost existential, about teaching both his language and his literature in a foreign country—like Joyce in Trieste, Isherwood and Nabokov in Berlin, Beckett in Paris. Also it was necessary for his students. It was the first time in his life that he had done something socially useful. What difference did it make that the job was beneath him, a recent Ph.D., while most of his colleagues in the evening school at McGill were idle housewives and bachelor civil servants? It didn't matter, even, that this job was a perversion of all the sentiments he held as a progressive young teacher. He was a god two evenings a week, sometimes suffering and fatigued, but nevertheless an omniscient, benevolent god. His students were silent, ignorant, and dedicated to learning English. No discussions, no demonstrations, no dialogue.

I love them, he thought. They need me.

He entered the room, pocketed his cap and ear muffs, and dropped his briefcase on the podium. Two girls smiled good evening.

They love me, he thought, taking off his boots and hanging up his coat; I'm not like their English-speaking bosses.

I love myself, he thought with amazement even while conducting a drill on word order. I love myself for tramping down Sherbrooke street in zero weather just to help them with noun clauses. I love myself standing behind this podium and showing Gilles Carrier and Claude Veilleux the difference between the past continuous and the simple past; or the sultry Armenian girl with the bewitching half-glasses that "put on" is not the same as "take on"; or telling the dashing Mr. Miguel Mayor, late of Madrid, that simple futurity can be expressed in four different ways, at least.

This is what mastery is like, he thought. Being superb in one's chosen field, not merely in one's mother tongue. A respected performer in the lecture halls of the major universities, equipped by twenty years' research in the remotest libraries, and slowly giving it back to those who must have it. Dishing it out suavely, even wittily. Being a legend. Being lived and a little feared.

"Yes, Mrs. David?"

A *sabra:* freckled, reddish hair, looking like a British model, speaks with a nifty British accent, and loves me.

"No," he smiled, "I *were* is not correct except in the present subjunctive, which you haven't studied yet."

The first hour's bell rang. The students closed their books for the intermission. Dyer put his away, then noticed a page of his Faulkner lecture from the afternoon class. *Absalom, Absalom!* his favorite.

"Can anyone here tell me what the *impregnable citadel of his passive rectitude* means?"

"What, sir?" asked Mr. Vassilopoulos, ready to copy.

"What about the *presbyterian and lugubrious effluvium of his passive vindictiveness?*" A few girls giggled. "O.K.," said Dyer, "take your break."

In the halls of McGill they broke into the usual groups. French-Canadians and South Americans into two large circles, then the Greeks, Germans, Spanish, and French into smaller groups. The patterns interested Dyer. Madrid Spaniards and Parisian French always spoke English with their New World co-linguals. The Middle Europeans spoke German together, not Russian, preferring one occupier to the other. Two Israeli men went off alone. Dyer decided to join them for the break.

Not *sabras*, Dyer concluded, not like Mrs. David. The shorter one, dark and wavy-haired, held his cigarette like a violin bow. The other, Mr. Weinrot, was tall and pot-bellied, with a ruddy face and thick stubby fingers. Something about him suggested truck-driving, perhaps of beer, maybe in Germany. Neither one, he decided, could supply the name of a good Israeli restaurant.

"This is really hard, you know?" said Weinrot.

"Why?"

"I think it's because I'm not speaking much of English at my job."

"French?" asked Dyer.

"French? Pah! All the time Hebrew, sometimes German, sometimes little Polish. Crazy things, eh? How long you think they let me speak Hebrew if I'm working in America?"

"Depends on where you're working," he said.

"Hell, I'm working for the Canadian government, what you think? Plant I work in—I'm engineer, see—makes boilers for the turbines going up North. Look. When I'm leaving Israel I go first to Italy. Right away-bamm I'm working in Italy I'm speaking Italian like a native. Passing for a native."

"A native Jew," said his dark-haired friend.

"Listen to him. So in Rome they think I'm from Tyrol — that's still native, eh? So I speak Russian and German and Italian like a Jew. My Hebrew is bad, I admit it, but it's a lousy language anyway. Nobody likes it. French I understand but English I'm talking like a bum. Arabic I know five dialects. Danish fluent. So what's the matter I can't learn English?"

"It'll come, don't worry," Dyer smiled. *Don't worry, my son*; he wanted to pat him on the arm. "Anyway, that's what makes Canada so appealing. Here they don't force you."

"What's this *appealing*? Means nice? Look, my friend, keep it, eh? Two years in a country I don't learn the language means it isn't a country."

"Come on," said Dyer. "Neither does forcing you."

"Let me tell you a story why I come to Canada. Then you tell me if I was wrong, O.K.?"

"Certainly," said Dyer, flattered.

In Italy, Weinrot told him, he had lost his job to a Communist union. He left Italy for Denmark and opened up an Israeli restaurant with five other friends. Then the six Israelis decided to rent a bigger apartment downtown near the restaurant. They found a perfect nine-room place for two thousand kroner a month, not bad shared six ways. Next day the landlord told them the deal was off. "You tell me why," Weinrot demanded.

No Jews? Dyer wondered. "He wanted more rent," he finally said.

"More—you kidding? More we expected. *Less* we didn't expect. A couple with eight kids is showing up after we're gone and the law in Denmark says a man has a right to a room for each kid plus a hundred kroner knocked off the rent for each kid. What you think of that? So a guy who comes in *after* us gets a nine-room place for a thousand kroner *less*. Law says no way a bachelor can get a place ahead of a family, and bachelors pay twice as much."

Dyer waited, then asked, "So?"

"So, I make up my mind the world is full of communismus, just like Israel. So I take out applications next day for Australia, South Africa, U.S.A., and Canada. Canada says come right away, so I go. Should have waited for South Africa."

"How could you?" Dyer cried. "What's wrong with you anyway? South Africa is fascist. Australia is racist."

The bell rang, and the Israelis, with Dyer, began walking to the room.

"What I was wondering, then," said Mr. Weinrot, ignoring Dyer's outburst, "was if my English is good enough to be working in the United States. You're American, aren't you?"

It was a question Dyer had often avoided in Europe, but had rarely been asked in Montreal. "Yes," he admitted, "your English is probably good enough for the States or South Africa, whichever one wants you first."

He hurried ahead to the room, feeling that he had let Montreal down. He wanted to turn and shout to Weinrot and to all the others that Montreal was the greatest city on the continent, if only they knew it as well as he did. If they'd just break out of their little ghettos.

At the door, the Armenian girl with the half-glasses caught his arm. She was standing with Mrs. David and Miss Parizeau, a jolly French-Canadian girl that Dyer had been thinking of asking out.

"Please, sir," she said, looking at him over the tops of her tiny glasses, "what I was asking earlier—*put on*—I heard on the television. A man said *You are putting me on* and everybody laughed. I think it was supposed to be funny but *put on* we learned means get dressed, no?"

"Ah—*don't put me on*," Dyer laughed.

"I yaven't erd it neither," said Miss Parizeau.

"To put some*body* on means to make a fool of him. To put some*thing* on is to wear it. O.K.?" He gave examples.

"Ah, now I know," said Miss Parizeau. "Like bullshitting somebody. Is it the same?"

"Ah, yes," he said, smiling. French-Canadians were like children learning the language. "Your example isn't considered polite. 'Put on' is very common now in the States."

"Then maybe," said Miss Parizeau, "we'll ave it ere in twenty years." The Armenian giggled.

"No—I've heard it here just as often," Dyer protested, but the girls had already entered the room.

He began the second hour with a smile which slowly soured as he thought of the Israelis. America's anti-communism was bad enough, but it was worse hearing it echoed by immigrants, by Jews, here in Montreal. Wasn't there a psychological type who chose Canada over South Africa? Or was it just a matter of visas and slow adjustment? Did Johannesburg lose its Greeks, and Melbourne its Italians, the way Dyer's students were always leaving Montreal?

And after class when Dyer was again feeling content and thinking of approaching one of the Israelis for a restaurant tip, there came the flood of small requests: should Mrs. Papadopoulos go into a more advanced course; could Mr. Perez miss a week for an interview in Toronto; could Mr. Giguère, who spoke English perfectly, have a harder book; Mr. Coté an easier one?

Then as he packed his briefcase in the empty room, Miguel Mayor, the vain and impeccable Spaniard, came forward from the hallway.

"Sir," he began, walking stiffly, ready to bow or salute. He wore a loud gray checkered sportscoat this evening, blue shirt, and matching ascot-handkerchief, slightly mauve. He must have shaved just before class, Dyer noticed, for two fresh daubs of antiseptic cream stood out on his jaw, just under his earlobe.

"I have been wanting to ask *you* something, as a matter of fact," said Dyer. "Do you know any good Spanish restaurants I might try tonight?"

"There are not any good Spanish restaurants in Montreal," he said. He stepped closer. "Sir?"

"What's on your mind, then?"

"Please—have you the time to look on a letter for me?"

He laid the letter on the podium.

"Look *over* a letter," said Dyer. "What is it for?"

"I have applied," he began, stopping to emphasize the present perfect construction, "for a job in Cleveland, Ohio, and I want to know if my letter will be good. Will an American, I mean—"

"Why are you going there?"

"It is a good job."

"But Cleveland—"

"They have a blackman mayor, I have read. But the job is not in Cleveland."

"Let me see it."

Most honourable Sir: I humbly beg consideration for a position in your grand company . . .

"Who are you writing this to?"

"The president," said Miguel Mayor.

I am once student of Dr. Ramiro Gutierrez of the Hydraulic Institute of Sevilla, Spain . . .

"Does the president know this Ramiro Gutierrez?"

"Oh, everybody is knowing him," Miguel Mayor assured, "he is the most famous expert in all Spain."

"Did he recommend this company to you?"

"No—I have said in my letter, if you look—"

An ancient student of Dr. Gutierrez, Salvador del Este, is actually a boiler expert who is being employed like supervisor is formerly a friend of mine . . .

"Is he still your friend?"

Whenever you say come to my city Miguel Mayor for talking I will be coming. I am working in Montreal since two years and am now wanting more money than I am getting here now . . .

"Well . . ." Dyer sighed.

"Sir—what I want from you is knowing in good English how to interview me by this man. The letters in Spanish are not the same to English ones, you know?"

I remain humbly at your orders . . .

"Why do you want to leave Montreal?"

"It's time for a change."

"Have you ever been to Cleveland?"

"I am one summer in California. Very beautiful there and hot like my country. Montreal is big port like Barcelona. Everybody mixed together and having no money. It is just a place to land, no?"

"Montreal? Don't be silly."

"I thought I come here and learn good English but where I work I get by in Spanish and French. It's hard, you know?" he smiled. Then he took a few steps back and gave his cuffs a gentle tug, exposing a set of jade cufflinks.

Dyer looked at the letter again and calculated how long he would be correcting it, then up at his student. How old is he? My age? Thirty? Is he married? Where do the Spanish live in Montreal? He looks so prosperous, so confident, like a male model off a page of *Playboy*. For an instant Dyer felt that his student was mocking him, somehow pitting his astounding confidence and wardrobe, sharp chin and matador's bearing against Dyer's command of English and mastery of the side streets, bistros, and ethnic restaurants. Mayor's letter was painful, yet he remained somehow competent. He would pass his interview, if he got one. What would he care about America, and the odiousness he'd soon be supporting? It was as though a superstructure of exploitation had been revealed, and

Dyer felt himself abused by the very people he wanted so much to help. It had to end someplace.

He scratched out the second "humbly" from the letter, then folded the sheet of foolscap. "Get it typed right away," he said. "Good luck."

"Thank you, sir," said his student, with a bow. Dyer watched the letter disappear in the inner pocket of the checkered sportscoat. The folding of the cashmere scarf, the draping of the camel's hair coat about the shoulders, the easing of the fur hat down to the rims of his ears. The meticulous filling of the pigskin gloves. Mayor's patent leather galoshes glistened.

"Good evening, sir," he said.

"*Buenas noches*," Dyer replied.

He hurried now, back down Sherbrooke Street to his daytime office where he could deposit his books. Montreal on a winter night was still mysterious, still magical. Snow blurred the arc lights. The wind was dying. Every second car was now a taxi, crowned with an orange crescent. Slushy curbs had hardened. The window of Holt Renfrew's was still attractive. The legless dummies invited a final stare. He stood longer than he had earlier, in front of the sporty mannequin with a burgundy waistcoat, the mauve and blue ensemble, the jade cufflinks.

Good evening, sir, he could almost hear. The ascot, the shirt, the complete outfit, had leaped off the back of Miguel Mayor. He pictured how he must have entered the store with three hundred dollars and a prepared speech, and walked out again with everything off the torso's back.

I want that.

What, sir?

That.

The coat, sir?

Yes.

Very well, sir.

And *that.*

Which, sir?

All that.

"Absurd man!" Dyer whispered. There had been a moment of fear, as though the naked body would leap from the window, and legless, chase him down Sherbrooke Street. But the moment was passing. Dyer realized now that it was comic, even touching. Miguel Mayor had simply tried too hard, too fast, and it would be good for him to stay in Montreal until he deserved those clothes, that touching vanity and confidence. With one last look at the window, he turned sharply, before the clothes could speak again.

TOPICS FOR EXPLORATION

1. Is Norman Dyer a sympathetic character? How would you describe his self-image? Are there any ironic touches in Clark Blaise's portrait of Dyer?

2. Characterize Dyer's attitude to Montreal, to the States, to his French-Canadian and immigrant students. What does the internationality of Dyer's clothing suggest? How does it correspond with his upward mobility? How does his clothing contrast with that of his Spanish student Miguel Mayor?

3. What is Dyer's motive for teaching nightschool English? What are some of the rewards? Compare his reasons for being in Montreal with those that brought his students there. How does he essentially differ from them?

4. Why does Dyer, who is American, distrust the attitudes commonly associated with Americans? Why does he like to think of himself as "a semi-permanent, semi-political exile" in Montreal?

5. Why is a country that does not enforce the learning of its language "not a country," according to Mr. Weinrot?

6. In the last paragraph, Dyer thinks that "Miguel Mayor had simply tried too hard, too fast, and it would be good for him to stay in Montreal until he deserved those clothes, that touching vanity and confidence." Comment on the idea of "deserving" expressed here. Is Dyer displaying a double standard here?

Basil H. Johnston

Basil H. Johnston, born in 1929, is an Ojibwa writer and educator. He has published fiction, translations, humour, poems, essays, reviews, and children's books; he has also worked for film and television. His academic interests focus on Ojibwa language, history, and culture. Among his titles are Moose Meat and Wild Rice, Ojibwa Heritage, Ojibwa Ceremonies, How the Birds Got Their Colours, *and* Tales the Elders Told. *He works in the Department of Ethnology of the Royal Ontario Museum in Toronto. Our selection comes from* Indian School Days, *first published in 1988.*

Summer Holidays in Spanish

We made the best and most of everything, good and bad, those of us who had to remain in Spanish, while others went home for vacation, made our summer happier and more carefree than it had any right to be.

The week before the end of the school term was like an anthill, with prefects and brothers supervising students in dusting, mopping, polishing, painting, repairing all the classrooms, toilets, refectories, corridors, chapels, and fence posts to make them fit for habitation come September. During the clean-up, the boys going home for the summer laughed constantly as they prattled about the meals that they were going to eat or what they were going to do. For the rest of us, who had nothing to look forward to, the last week was dismal.

As bad as the week might have been, it was as nothing compared to July first, when our fellow students left. We could only stare with mist in our eyes and resentment in our hearts as we watched parents from Sagamok, Cutler, Mississauga, Garden River, Birch Island, and Thessalon arrive and then leave with their sons. Then there was Dave Solomon whom we called David Plug, from his chewing tobacco habit. Poor as he was, he nevertheless walked down from the village of Spanish to come for his sons and daughters. We ached in bone and muscle to see all the "Plugs"—Orion,

Leo, Joyce, Lillian, Doris, and Eleanor—skipping on the road to freedom and happiness. All day, old cars came and went, leaving the school just a little emptier.

Of the students going home for summer, the majority went by boat. At 9:00 A.M. on the day of departure, the boys from Wikwemikong, West Bay, Sheguindah, Sheshegwaning, and Sucker Creek on Manitoulin Island lined up in the yard in front of the main entrance to the recreation hall to be counted. They then marched in two columns down to the wharf, where they boarded the *Red Bug*. After them came the girls from St. Joseph's under heavy escort of three Daughters of St. Joseph. They, too, boarded the *Red Bug* on the side opposite the boys. The *Garnier*, under command of Father Hawkins, towed the *Red Bug* from Spanish to Gore Bay, a distance of twenty miles.

By the end of the day there may have been thirty-five of us left in the school, lingering in the silence and in the shadows of the empty yard, recreation hall, and dormitory: Ojibway from Cape Croker, Saugeen, Parry Island, Byng Inlet, Chapleau, Missinabi, Golden Lake, and Temagami, and Mohawks from St. Regis and Caughnawaga.

Next morning after breakfast, we made preparations for our own summer vacation on Aird Island, two miles from the mainland. We loaded straw, bedding, clothing, and laundry bags on the democrat for delivery to the *Garnier*; we stacked pots, pans, dishes, spoons, knives, ladles, tin cans, butcher knives; beans, peas, tea, oatmeal, bread; pails of lard, beets, onions, beef, pork; a tarpaulin, sails, oars, paddles, boards, tools, flashlights, and a medical kit into crates and bags. Lastly, we lined up to be counted before boarding the *Red Bug*.

It took the *Garnier*, cruising leisurely, no more than a half-hour to tow the *Red Bug* and three punts that slid from side to side over the wash and threatened to break from their tow-lines and make off by themselves.

Hardly had the *Red Bug* touched the bottom of the sandy bay at the camp than we all leaped off to race to the lean-to that was to be our shelter at night and during rain, in order to claim and to stake out a sleeping place near a friend on the straw. During this rush, Father Hawkins and the prefects, who were to be our guardians, cooks, and doctors, said nothing, but allowed us to enjoy our freedom.

"Dis is my place. I'm gonna sleep beside my frien' here. And don' you snore and don' you piss on my blanket."

Only after we had all staked out our sleeping places did the prefect blow his whistle to summon us to work.

For the next while, we were busy unloading the *Red Bug*, willingly and cheerfully.

"Where's do you wan' dis straw, Fauder?"

"Where you put dis here pot?"

"Where you wan' us to put dis sad ol' mush?"

"Hey, Fauder, where you gonna keep de candies?"

And Father Mayhew, whom we called Joe DiMaggio, grinned as he directed the porters to deliver "peas over there" and "blankets over there" and "you know where the tarp goes."

Where the *Red Bug* was unloaded and the punts pulled on shore and tethered, the *Garnier* steamed back to the mainland, leaving us to all the comforts and freedom that only the forests, winds, waters, and rocks can provide, confer, and allow.

But before we were allowed to leave camp, there was more work to do.

This lean-to, damaged during the past year by winds, snow, and porcupines, had to be repaired. With birch-bark, leaves, boards, and driftwood, thirty-five boys soon patched all the cracks and chinks, and stopped up every hole against wind and rain. Because we constructed our beds with the same ingenuity as loons, but with far less care, they resembled a series of nests without eggs, or mice's nests. In quick order, after getting our own quarters fit for habitation, we scrubbed the picnic tables, gathered wood, pitched the tent for Father, and erected the tarpaulin above the tables.

While we were busy getting the camp in order, Father was brewing a meal in an enormous pot. Just what he was doing we did not know nor, from the results, did it appear that he knew what he was doing either, but, according to his helpers, Father opened jars of cut green beans and sauerkraut, poured the contents into the pot, then spilled peas, beans, carrots, potatoes, onions, bones, and meat into the boiling cauldron. As we left camp, Father was paddling and puddling the sludge.

At last we were free. Free of rules, free to come and go as we pleased, free to eat or go without. We got to know and cherish freedom as only those who have been denied it can know and cherish it, as only seven, eight-, nine-, ten-, eleven-, and twelve-year-old boys can exercise it.

There were channels and bays and inlets for sailing and fishing, the islands of Villiers, Passage, Otter, Jackson, Brown, and Green a quarter of a mile opposite our campsite for visiting and discovering.

Some of the boys, notably Alvin Naskewe and his brother Lloyd, my former confederates at Cape Croker, did nothing else but ride the waves and fish. With each flat-bottomed punt, equipped with only one oar or paddle, navigation of any kind was almost impossible. Even with oars, it was hard to control these crafts, which, caught by the winds, slid or slithered sideways on top of the waves. Nevertheless, Alvin and Lloyd claimed one of the better punts for their own use, or, in our own vernacular, "just hogging it, dem guys."

Now, use of these punts was supposed to be decided on a "first come, first served" basis for all the boys, but, by getting up before the others, Alvin and Lloyd were well within the rules. Because no one really envied them, no one objected. Besides, having learned the craft of sailing from their father, Enoch, they were skilled sailors and navigators, poling the punts along the shore, paddling to the islands, and even sailing with the use of their blankets or shirts whenever the winds were favourable.

During season, there were patches and patches of blueberries, which meant money. For each pail picked and delivered, we were credited with twenty-five cents, which was recorded in a little black book in the same manner as our ancestors were credited in trade for beaver pelts. At the end of the picking season, which lasted about three weeks, some of us had amassed a small fortune, accumulating as much as five dollars in our accounts.

Our only motive in picking blueberries was for money to relieve our hunger during the coming winter by bread-lard-candy trading.

There was a little candy store underneath the first-floor stairway, which was opened twice daily for fifteen-minute periods at twelve-thirty and again at six-thirty. With a small investment of two or three cents in jawbreakers, licorice twists, bubble gum, and suckers, one could drive a good bargain with his candy-loving but penniless colleagues, who congregated in the recreation hall just outside the doorway, waiting and pleading, "Gimme one, gimme one."

Except to friends, no one gave a candy away. The object was to tempt someone or several to make an offer. And luckily, there was always someone who preferred candy to bread or lard. The going rate then on the open market was seven jawbreakers for a slice of bread and five for a spoon of lard to be delivered either at the very next meal or at a time to be decided by the vendor of the candies. It was through this means that we got to eat an extra slice of bread on the odd occasion to allay our hunger.

Then there was hunting. For Charley Shoot, there was ONLY hunting. It was first and last. He was probably the only boy in camp, in the entire institution, who devoted all his time, from morning to night, to hunting rabbits, squirrels, partridges, groundhogs, beavers, skunks—whatever was worth hunting. I very much doubt that he ever went fishing or picking berries. For him, the day began at the beach picking pebbles, round ones that didn't curve. With a pocketful of ammunition, Charley would be gone for the day.

Charley preferred to hunt alone, rather than invite anyone too heavy-footed or too loose-tongued for the quietness that hunting demanded. Still, he asked me to go with him on a number of occasions, not that I was a good hunter or anything like that, but I was useful either as a decoy or as a porter, carrying extra ammunition or plucking the partridges that he killed. It was Charley's habit of walking directly through instead of going around swamps, hills, muskegs, ponds, thickets that provided us with excuses not to accompany him. Otherwise we might have gone more frequently and learned something.

Of the many hunting trips with Charley, I remember one clearly, and one only. On that morning and on that day, we were to hunt foxes, wolves, and bears, and I think he mentioned eagles and tigers. It was exciting . . . and frightening at the same time. Against whatever danger may have lurked behind rocks and stumps, I stuck right behind my partner, who, armed with a slingshot, frequently bent down to peer into the bushes or stopped to listen for some distant growl. For my part, I was busy checking which spruce or pine would offer the nearest shelter should bear or tiger come bursting out from ambush.

In front, Charley pushed on, his slingshot ready to fell bear or tiger. He stopped, held up a hand, and then knelt down on one knee. I, too, heard it. "Cluck, cluck"—the sound of the molars of bear or was it tiger? I looked around, behind, and to the front. Charley was drawing a bead upward, stretching the rubber bands of his slingshot well past his ear . . . steady . . . strong . . . dead on. On a pine limb sat an immense snowy owl, its hooded eyes half open in a kind of sultry way.

Charley fired. The eyes flew open, and the owl teetered on the limb for two moments before tumbling to the ground. He lurched to his feet, wings outspread, beak snapping, eyes rolling, unable to focus. Unsteady, as if drunk, the owl reeled from side to side.

"Got him jis where I wanted," Charley chortled. "We'll catch 'im an' take 'im back to camp . . . Gimme your belt."

I took my belt off without thinking and gave it to Charley.

"You stay in fron' o' dat owl; don't let 'im turn around. I'll sneak aroun' and catch 'im from behin' by de legs," Charley instructed me as he circled, crouching low. As if he knew Charley was up to something, that owl turned his neck, bearing his eyes upon my partner. Me, he ignored.

"Hey!" Charley stopped. He whispered loudly. "He's lookin' at me. Git 'im to turn aroun' and look at you. Do sometin'." Charley was angry.

With one hand, I held onto the waistband of my pants that were already sagging; with the other hand, I waved at the owl. I took two steps forward, calling at the same time, "Hoo! Hoo!"

The owl, perhaps perceiving the "Hoo! Hoo!" as a mating call, instantly turned. By now he had recovered most of his senses, When he saw me, he snapped his beak, then charged, half-flying, half-running. I went into reverse. With the owl gaining, I turned to sprint away. In so doing, I lost my grip on my pants, which fell to my ankles. I went sprawling. I covered my head.

In his rage, the owl pounced on my trousers, ripping at them with his claws and tearing at them with his beak, as if he were slashing at his favourite meal, the skunk.

At this moment of mortal danger, Charley hurled himself upon the owl and me. The next thing that I knew in my terror was Charley yelling, "Grab 'is neck, grab 'is head." I twisted around, got my hands on the owl's neck, and applied a choke-hold. By this time, Charley had wound my belt around the owl's legs and bound the owl's wings with his slingshot. I did not let go of that owl's neck until Charley told me to let him go.

Like big-game hunters who had bagged a trophy, we bore our prize back to camp in triumph. For all the indignity we had heaped upon him, knocking him down from his perch, wrestling with him all trussed up as a big white bundle through the forest, depositing him on a picnic table for all the boys to see, and then tying his one leg to the tree so that he wouldn't fly away, that owl stood on the picnic table with pride and looked upon us all as if he would take us all on. As if weary of the sight of us, he flew up to the limb of the maple tree directly above the picnic table.

After a couple of days, Charley untied the twine that bound the owl's leg. That owl remained in our camp for a week or more. During his stay, we fed him mice, birds, bread, fish, and scraps. But one morning the owl wasn't there. He was gone, summoned perhaps by his mate or by the spirit of the north. We twitted the prefect-in-charge, "Our owl woulda' stayed except for de mush you cook."

Even though the days at Aird Island were happier than those at the school, the loneliness was never far. The daily arrival of the *Iron Boat* with fresh supplies of bread, more green beans and "sad ol' peas," along with meat, also brought either happiness or sadness, depending on whether we received a letter or not . . . mostly loneliness and dejection.

But it was the occasional receipt of a letter from home that kindled hope and trust, and kept faith alive. At mail call, we'd congregate around the prefect who held a small packet of letters, opened and censored, in his hand. We'd wait for our names to be called.

Were we to get a letter from home, Eugene, Charley, Hector, and I would sit down together. The recipient would read it aloud to his colleagues. We didn't care about anyone's health or events at home; our sole interest in the letters that we received and the only message that we sought in the letters were the words, "You are coming home." And were they to be written, we could endure Spanish for another six months, a year even.

"Dear Brother," a letter to Eugene from his sister Delina read. "You're going to come home; you'll be home by Christmas. I've missed you, and Donald and Luke have missed you. When you come home we'll have loads of fun . . ."

Eugene just about danced for joy. "I'm going home for Christmas, I'm going to be home by Christmas; I'm getting out of here." Over and over, Eugene kept repeating the same words, and he laughed and slapped his thighs. We were glad for him, but envious, too. He was going home; we were not. Someone cared enough for him, but no one cared enough for us.

Eugene counted the days. He was even angelic in his mood and pious in his behaviour toward priests and teachers. Christmas came, but no one came for Eugene. That was the way it was.

Letters, almost every letter that arrived gave promise of going home. They gave us hope and they gave us faith to go on from season to season, from year to year. And, I suppose, they kept us in line, inspired us to obedience, lest we forfeit our chances for going home by misconduct.

Getting away from Spanish was never far from our minds. Feeling more neglected by his family after he had received a few cuffs from the prefect-in-charge for breaking an oar, Kitchi-Meeshi-Hec (Hector Lavalley) decided to run away from Spanish. Midst sobs and tears he took his leave of the camp, Aird Island, and Spanish by shaking hands with Charley and Eugene.

Instead of bidding Kitchi-Meeshi-Hec "goodbye," Charley and Eugene decided to accompany the escapee. They were not discouraged by their lack of knowledge of geography or the miles of black-fly, mosquito-infested bushes and swamps. Escape first; the details would follow. With Charley hunting along the way, there was little to worry about.

On the afternoon of the escape, Hector, Charley, and Eugene walked to the narrows at Little Detroit. At the banks of the narrows, the fugitives stood to regard the flow and pace of the current and the best manner of crossing the passage that was less than a stone's throw in width, but deep and swift. Even for strong swimmers, the crossing would have been dangerous. For Eugene, small and scarcely able to swim, it was almost impossible.

According to Eugene, Charley got the far-away look in his eyes, as if he could see something in the distance that others could not see, except that he was looking into the mass of rock on the opposite side. When the vision passed away, Charley spoke of his revelation.

They would pray for and work a miracle. Hector, almost sin-free would most likely receive the graces from Heaven to enable him to cross the narrows like St. Christopher. In the first crossing, Hector would bear Eugene; then Hector was to return for Charley.

For a while, they prayed mightily, but perhaps not with the degree of faith required for the enactment of miracles. Who of the three entertained the gravest doubt and thus aborted the miracle will never be known. It may have been Hector, who, too astounded by his nomination to imitate St. Christopher, failed to pray with the proper sanctity; it may have been Eugene for envying Hector; it may have been Charley for his inability to turn his mind from such worldly and material things as rabbits and moose long enough to dwell upon the spiritual.

At the end of devotions, which they conducted kneeling down and with great fervour right at the water's edge, Hector dropped to one knee to allow Eugene to get on his back. Even though Eugene was small and light, Hector's knees almost buckled, and he wobbled as he stepped gingerly into the water. Once he stepped into the water, set his foot on the slippery slime of the rock, there was no turning back. Hector slithered, Eugene struggled to dismount; both sank, hugging one another, and started to drift in the current out toward Shoepack Bay. Just a little way from where they fell in, Hector and Eugene ran around and scrambled ashore, feeling like wet kittens and quite a bit less pious.

They returned to camp, having abandoned plans for escape. They would tough it out. I think that that summer was the last vacation Charley, Eugene, and Hector spent on Aird Island. Thereafter, as older boys, they remained at the school helping Brothers Van der Moore and Grubb with milking and feeding livestock and getting the hay in.

There may not have been much on Aird Island, but we wrought, from what little there was and what little we had, something bigger and finer and stronger. No one could see it, but it was there; no one could express it, but it was there. It was in each of us. With every new attempt or renewed attempt to achieve, our resourcefulness grew, and, as our resourcefulness enlarged, so did our spirit of independence and passion for personal freedom. We may have been deprived, but poor in spirit we never were.

At the end of summer, maybe a day or so before the students from Manitoulin came back, we left Aird Island and everything on it and everything that it represented—home, comfort, freedom, a place of growth—to return to exile, loneliness, confinement, and a feeling of repression within the walls of St. Peter Claver.

TOPICS FOR EXPLORATION

1. What do summer holidays in the town of Spanish imply?
   Contrast the feelings of those students who are to remain there
   with those who are going home for the summer vacation.
   What is school associated with, in the boys' minds?

2. Why does Basil H. Johnston use dialect in his dialogue? He
   also uses lists or catalogues of things and places. Why?

3. Describe the first day at the camp on Aird Island. What experiences can the boys have by "visiting and discovering" the surrounding islands? Why are they happier there than at school?

4. Charley Shoot is expert in hunting with a slingshot, but prefers
   to hunt alone. The narrator might have "learned something"
   from him. What?

5. How does the captivity of the owl symbolically reflect the boys'
   situation at school?

6. Read the last sentence of Johnston's narrative and comment on
   its effect. How does Aird Island become "home, comfort, freedom, a place of growth" for the boys?

Janice Kulyk Keefer

Janice Kulyk Keefer was born in Toronto in 1952. She has published several collections of stories, including The Paris-Napoli Express, Transfigurations, *and, most recently,* Travelling Ladies *(1990). Her short stories have won the CBC Literary Competition twice, in 1985 and 1986. In addition, she has published critical monographs on Maritime fiction and on the stories of Mavis Gallant, a volume of poetry, and a novel,* Constellations *(1988). She lives in Nova Scotia.* The Amores, *Ovid's collection of love poetry, caused a scandal in ancient Rome, offended the Emperor Augustus, and resulted in Ovid's exile from Rome for immorality. In Keefer's story, the family of the protagonist, Agnes, fled Hungary after the anti-communist Revolution of 1956 was suppressed by Russian tanks.*

The Amores

In her dream she is at a railway station, an old-fashioned place with a glassed roof and wrought-iron pillars, the kind she can just remember having known in Hungary. Only she isn't a little girl, but her present age, seventeen—which makes it all the stranger that she should be dressed in a child's tam, an embroidered woollen coat whose full skirt finishes high above her knees, and ankle socks with lace-up leather shoes. In one hand she is holding on to a small suitcase, much too small for the things she will need on such a long journey—for in her other hand she grasps, as firmly as she can, a ticket the size of a blackboard, bearing the names of an endless list of stops she will have to make before she arrives at a destination whose name she hasn't yet had time to find. A conductor is blowing a shrill whistle, urging her to board before the train starts up, warning that she'll make the whole party late. She tries to explain that she can't board until her mother has come to embrace her and say goodbye. Her mother is always late, so in this dream it does not occur to her to think that Marta might have forgotten or worse— decided not to come at all. Pigeons wheel under the metal rafters, making a noise like soft thunder as the conductor begins to shout at her, shouting and shouting until Anyès thinks that his eyes will burst, splattering the round spectacles he wears. And between her fear that the man will blind himself with rage unless she obeys him and boards the now-moving train, and her grief at what her mother will feel, arriving too late at the station, Anyès leaps upon the train just as she catches sight of Marta, her hair down, wearing only a slip and bedroom slippers, so frantic has been her haste to come to her. She always wakes just after the moment at which she has slammed the compartment door in the face of the conductor, who, tumbling down to the platform besides her mother, watches her from his knees, furious, bereft, as the train smokes away.

Miss Vance's classroom had a kind of running cornice along its four walls on which were lodged each pupil's monument to their teacher's vigorous enthusiasm for her subject: a model of the Forum, columns manufactured from white-painted corrugated packing paper: *papier-mâché* replicas of shields and amphorae; plasticine reproductions of figurines and jewellery, and a copy, one foot high, of the statue of Caesar Augustus reproduced on page ninety-seven of *Living Latin.* Dust furred the replicas, the columns of the Forum had begun to crack, undergoing metamorphosis back into paste and paper under Caesar's cross-eyed gaze and warning finger, but the effect of the whole remained inspiring from ground-level, especially to the superintendents who came on their yearly rounds to assess what contribution the study of dead languages made to the acquisition of knowledge and school spirit.

You can learn everything you need to know in life from Latin and the Bible, Miss Vance could have told the inspectors—did tell each crop of students whose lot it was to learn every week a new declension, conjugation, item of vocabulary. To this day, many of those students who have gone on to become doctors, accountants, social workers, even school principals could, if ordered with the rap of a pointer to a blackboard, reproduced *bellum, belli, bello; amo, amare, amavi, amatum,* spurred into unwonted accuracy by the presentiment of Miss Vance behind them. Miss Vance with her short grey hair—clipped, not cut; her spectables restraining the overbright, overround eyes that seemed like fluorescent tennis balls glowing in darkened courts. Wearing crumbled cotton blouses, like paper bags over breasts both enormous and flattened, juiceless cantaloupes that had been squashed on the way home from market.

Mannish, they had called her—the straight skirt, always grey, the lisle stockings and lace-up, sensible shoes supporting the skinny legs that bore her up like pale, tapered columns under the massive weight of some temple roof.

Julia Vance, Anyès had learned from the flyleaf of a volume of the *Aeneid*—Miss Vance's own copy, which she had let Anyès borrow one day when the girl had quickly finished whatever translation exercise the others were still gnashing their pens over.

'To my daughter Julia, as a reward for proficiency in her studies, with the hope that she may learn from the immortal Mantuan the sublime value of selfless service.' Edward Archibald Vance. Miss Vance had often told her students about her father, his ministry, and the travels father and daughter had undertaken before the Reverend Edward Archibald had expired—not lingeringly, self-indulgently, but in his customarily efficient way—from a heart attack after Sunday service, lunch with the Missionary Society and an afternoon spent reading *The Presbyterian Herald.* She had shown them slides of the Reverend Vance standing beside a Celtic cross somewhere in County Kerry, and next to Virgil's monument, the one erected in Mantua. A large man wearing a peculiarly rigid fedora and a dog collar which made you think of the spikes bulldogs wear round their necks, such a severity of starch did it betray.

'We didn't care a hoot for mantua,' Miss Vance had said, in her loud, eager, yet authoritative voice. 'Or for Italy, if it comes to that.' And she had left the image of her father—his hand outstretched to the verses engraved on Virgil's monument—solidified on the screen; had planed her lisle-stockinged, matchstick legs wide apart before her desk, and cautioned her students about the inevitable shock, the actual disgust they would feel if they were ever unwise enough to try to travel to the land of Caesar and Cicero and Publilius Syrus. 'The only ticket there,' she had said, tapping the edition of *Living Latin* she had picked up from her desk, 'lies in these pages.'

She had been looking at the entire class when she'd begun her peroration, but on pronouncing 'pages' fixed her eyes on Agnes Sereny, who was sitting with her small feet primly together, her hands clasped on the desktop, her eyes fixed on Miss Vance's in an expression that might have been fear or reverence or perhaps just the desire to produce whatever it was that her teacher wishes to see reflected there. Shining in Miss Vance's eyes was a mixture of encouragement, admonition, and something she would not name. Stern, solid, selfless was Miss Vance's life, as befitted the daughter of such a father, a daughter who had lost her mother and shouldered responsibility for her father's well-being at an age when most girls her age would have begun to stop playing with dolls, and started to become them.

Yet in this, the fifty-third year of Miss Vance's life, the thirtieth year of her teaching, she had discovered herself capable of something she feared was love—not the passionate obedience she had shown her father, but rather, his own need to shape and control the beloved; a desire to possess, not the girl's affections, but her very nature. Had Miss Vance ever loosed her knowledge of the Classics from the water-tight compartments into which she'd deposited the rules of grammar and the laws of style, and permitted it to flood her own experience, she might have had second thoughts about the story of Pygmalion, or at least about Venus's role in the whole affair (Miss Vance could never remember the name of the marble woman come-to-life, but then you weren't supposed to—she wasn't the point of the story). As it was, she merely reassured herself with the fact that Pygmalion had got everything he wanted—it was one of the rare myths that ended happily.

She had taken Agnes to heart from the very first class. Perhaps it was nothing more than that the girl's name and her appearance went so fittingly together. Agnes—Miss Vance pronounced it with a hard 'g', even though she knew the girl's mother said 'Anyès', the way the French do, turning the very softness of the letter into an endearment. *Agnus:* the kind of hair that was not blonde but white, an impossibly pure shade that always looked as if it would melt should you touch it. A body not short (that implied a defect) but small, and skin fresh, full—as if it would spring back at your touch, like angel-food cake in the pan. Round, brown eyes: not deep, not dark, but light and clear. Sweetness, whiteness: 'lamb', Miss Vance would have called her, had she ever permitted herself to use endearments. There were aspects of Agnes' life, however, which obliged Miss Vance to treat her not as a pet, but as a child—her own.

One of these aspects was the girl's undoubted ability as a Latinist. Whereas her classmates, however brightly they began the five-year immersion into the Latin tongue, ended by baulking at the endless examples and exceptions that had to be memorized before each class, Agnes seemed to need them the way you do ground under your feet in order to stand up. On her face would appear an expression of utter serentity when she was construing difficult phrases: she didn't find Caesar's accounts of the Gallic wars at all tedious, she positively glowed when they tackled Virgil in the senior grades, and she'd shown herself particularly adept at translating the few, rigorously selected passages of Ovid to which Miss Vance allowed her students access. (Catullus and Petronius were, of course, so far beyond the pale they didn't exist, even up on the dusty, distant cornices of Miss Vance's classroom.)

But this unusual aptitude for Latin in an age when all but the best schools had axed that subject from the curriculum was not the deciding factor in Miss Vance's adoption of Agnes. It was rather the necesssity the teacher felt, faced with her pupil's background and environment, to be more than an academic instructor. In the first place, the girl was Hungarian. There were certain foreign races—the French, the German, even, precariously, the Italian—which Miss Vance could accommodate in her conception of society. Though of pure Scots-Irish stock, she did not hold with those who would not acknowledge the existence, never mind the rights and claims, of those who were not Anglo-Saxon as well as white and Protestant. But she drew the line at certain sure point: she warned her senior pupils against applying to University College, for example, because there were—so many Jews who went there: an Oakdale student would be much better off at Trinity or Victoria. And when it came to ethnic groups who didn't possess recognizable alphabets, whose language even the most rigorous phonetics could not decode, Miss Vance proclaimed not defeat but disgust.

About the Serenys she had obtained all necessary information. Agnes and her parents had escaped from Hungary after the uprising—that gave proof of virtue, daring, fortitude, however distastefully dramatic to Miss Vance's eyes. The family had established itself in a split-level suburban home some ten minutes' walk from Oakdale School: this was all unexceptionable. But a few years before Agnes made the transition from junior to senior high school, Mr. Sereny—a pharmacist with his own shop downtown—had gone bankrupt and died in much too quick succession. The suburban house had been sold, Agnes and her mother moving to a home just within the catchment area for Oakdale School, but, alas, to one of the new and crudely built apartment towers that were springing up at the extreme west of the municipality, disfiguring the skyline, which previously had only to deal with the tops of immature blue spruce and maple trees. The apartment tower smelled of boiled cabbage and suspicious spices, one of Miss Vance's junior colleagues had told her—he'd been there looking for accommodation soon after his appointment to the school and had wisely decided to lodge elsewhere. Not, however, in the low-rise, respectable apartment house in which Miss Vance lived—across from the plaza, it is true, but screened by a high wall of impenetrable shrubbery.

That shruberry protected Miss Vance from more than the sight of leather-jacketed, cigarette-spouting loafers at the plaza five-and-ten. It allowed her and the other tenants of Oakdale Manor immunity from the kinds of activity that went on in less reputable buildings than their own. For the same colleague who had rashly gone one Saturday morning to inquire about renting a bachelorette at Oakdale Towers had witnessed, right in the lobby, an embrace between a young, badly-dressed, foreign-looking man and an older woman whose too-short skirt and whose hair—peroxide-platinum—gave her away as none other than Mrs. Sereny, whom the teacher had encountered only days before at a Home and School. Luckily, Agnes hadn't been anywhere near the lobby; hopefully, might not even have been in the building, since the most scandalous thing about the whole episode, as Miss Vance understood it, was that the couple were obviously coming down from the apartment where they had spent time—perhaps the night—together. There had been a certain something about the way they clung together in that most inhospitable lobby, with its hard, narrow benches drawn up in a travesty of intimacy around a fake rubber plant. But Miss Vance had silenced her informant with a look that went like a pin through a finger.

The next afternoon she had talked to the girl while everyone else was belabouring a tricky passage Miss Vance had assigned as an impromptu translation exercise. Agnes, for whom the passage was no more difficult than the riddles on a bubblegum wrapper, sat at the long table at the back of the classroom, working on a *papier-mâché* model of an aqueduct. Miss Vance watched her silently tear strips of newspaper and then asked whether Agnes had started to make up a list of universities to which she would apply midway through Grade Thirteen next year. Agnes had looked uncomprehendingly at Miss Vance, all the while tearing strips of newspaper, and then, in her soft, unaccented yet not-quite Canadian voice, had said that she'd never thought of going on to university. There wasn't the money for that; she had her mother to think of; she would get work as a salesgirl at one of the shops in the plaza, and take a secretarial course at night, and with the two of them working they could afford a larger apartment. Miss Vance had only smiled at her, shaking her head so vigorously that Agnes thought her eyes would work loose from their sockets. The buzzer rang then, and the girl went back to her seat and left the classroom with the others.

That evening Miss Vance had checked the syllabus of her *alma mater*, a small liberal arts college in New Brunswick which had the reputation of turning out excellent classical scholars. On page eighty-two of the syllabus she found among a list of entrance scholarships exactly what she wanted: the Charles Maltman Award for Classics, to be bestowed upon a student whose exceptional ability was matched only by his financial need: there was even provisions for the student's being given summer employment tutoring deserving high school children from the local town. Miss Vance had lain awake till nearly two, plotting the campaign that would remove Agnes forever from the stink of boiled cabbage and immorality in her mother's apartment.

The Sereny's apartment smelt most often not of boiled cabbage, but of chicken paprikash, poppy-seed strudel, brandied plums. For Marta Sereny, having sold the suburban split level to help pay her husband's debts, met the rent on the apartment at Oakdale Towers by acting as cook at the *Hungarian Village*, the plaza restaurant— over-large and funereally under-lighted. She took home, in aluminum baking dishes and small styrofoam containers, the invariable leftovers from her labours, to which the plaza florist, liquor-store and bank clerks paid tribute, but which attracted few of the people who occupied the suburb's interminable brick bungalows, and who preferred to do their dining-out downtown. The *Hungarian Village* was perpetually on the verge of folding down, except that the owner, a Mrs. Lampman who lived in Rosedale, operated the whole affair as a tax write-off and was rather fond of Marta Sereny and that sweet, small, pale daughter of hers, who waitressed on weekends and was said to be doing rather well at school—in Latin, of all things.

Mrs. Lampman occasionally came to lunch at the *Hungarian Village*; over coffee and dessert she would listen to Marta's fears and hopes concerning her daughter—it wasn't healthy, all this fussing with a dead language; surely she ought to be taking something more practical, like typing and shorthand—things that would give the girl a chance in life, a chance at meeting the right sort of men—doctors, lawyers, businessmen, pharmacists . . . . Marta had begun to wring her hands as though they were strudel dough she was kneading to paper thinness. Worst of all that woman was trying to turn the girl against her own mother, against what Marta thought best for the girl's happiness. Anyès had told her—they had no secrets from one another, they were as thick as this—and Marta had crossed two rosy fingers, holding them up inches away from Mrs. Lampman's eyes.

Mrs. Lampman went on stirring too much sugar into her tepid coffee as she listened, thinking how old Marta looked—not that her skin wrinkled or sagged more than it should, but that her whole face was like a map marked with places and people forcibly abandoned, of immense distances covered, not in the best of circumstances, and with no little hardship. Marta looked tired in the same way as do small children who have been allowed to stay up far beyond their proper bedtime, and in whose heavy eyes you sense a reproach to grownups who should have known better. Her features, too, were exaggerated like a child's—her lips soft, wide, curiously stippled and crisscrossed with lines like the palm of a hand; the blue of her wide eyes pale, as though the colour had been carelessly scribbled in, her cheekbones not tilted but positively veering up to her temples. Yet it was a face that gave a blurred, attenuated impression, as though you were always seeing it through tears, which was curious, Mrs. Lampman reflected, since she could not once remember Marta having cried, or her eyes even moistening all the times she had recounted bits of her personal history—bits like chipped beads falling from a broken necklace.

That her marriage had not been a happy one, for example. Marta would put one small, plump hand against the rise of her breast—she always wore her necklines cut low—as if to gesture to, and yet conceal the cause of her marital woes. Her husband had never been able to—satisfy her. It was no wonder there was only the one child, Marta had sighed, stroking the flesh between her throat and the neck of her short black dress. And Anyès had always been so attached to her father, though God knew he hadn't ever had time for her, and as the end he made—the effect *that* had had upon the girl. . . . Though it hadn't interfered with her schoolwork, she was an A student, the kind who worked so hard she excelled. But in Latin? Come to the New World and study Latin? And that teacher—she was so masterful, so demanding, she had the girl staying up half the night to do extra projects. Anyès worshipped her, just as she had her father. It wasn't good for a child to worship anyone like that, especially when she had her own mother to help her and teach her things you didn't learn at school.

Mrs. Lampman listened without nodding or shaking her head. She said that she'd heard of the teacher in question: she possessed a marvellous reputation, had been with the school for years, had helped form the character of hundreds of children from the best families. If this Miss Vance felt that Anyès had a future as a Latin scholar, that her talents would be wasted with bedpans or carbon paper, why not let things take their course? Without waiting for an answer, Mrs. Lampman had pushed away the cold, super-saturated coffee, risen from her chair and told Marta in parting that she'd mentioned her name to a Mrs. Jablonski who needed a caterer and waitress for a birthday party she was giving in two weeks' time.

'Bitch,' Marta had hissed after Mrs. Lampman closed the door—but it wasn't clear whether she was speaking of Miss Vance or the owner of the restaurant. She went back to the kitchen and began packing up leftovers from that day's cooking. Tonight they closed early—it was her evening off and Zoltàn would be coming. They would eat the remains of the veal birds and poppy-seed *torte*, and then Anyès would do her homework while Marta and Zoltàn took the bus down to the subway station, and the subway downtown, where they would walk, arm in arm, staring into lighted jeweller's shops and the endless windows of department stores; or, perhaps they would see a Hungarian film at the Hall, and then have a beer in the Blue Cellar Room. It didn't matter what they did, so long as they stayed out long enough for Anyès to have finished her homework, taken her bath and fallen fast asleep in her bed—the foldout couch which had been moved to the spot farthest away from the paper-thin wall of Marta's bedroom. And then Marta and her lover, who had been at university in Hungary, but now worked at the *Budapest Bakery* and studied law at night school, would unlock the apartment door and creep toward the bedroom with such reverent caution that you would have thought there was a newborn asleep on the couch; would lock themselves into the bedroom and make love in a silence so cavernous, so desperate it would wake Anyès from dreams so full of loss and confusion she would have to bite down on her knuckles to keep from calling out.

Between the time that Miss Vance had first spoken to Agnes about applying for a scholarship, and the day that she'd put into the girl's hand a letter confirming that the Charles Maltman had been awarded to Agnes Sereny of Oakdale School, and the night that Anyès had finally confessed to her mother what the scholarship entailed—four years in a place far enough away that neither Marta or Anyès would be able to afford telephone calls, never mind visits to each other—Anyès began to have a recurring dream. She would be at a railway station, waiting to board a train which always tried to leave without her. Unable to fall asleep again after waking, she would switch on the lamp at the edge of the fold-out couch, pick up a book and read, hoping that the very sound of the words, undulating like waves in a shallow bay, would soothe her to sleep. *'Foelix qui potuit rerum cognoscere causas / Atque metus omnes et inexorabile fatum / Subjecit pedibus, strepitumque Acherontis avari. / Fortunatus et ille deos qui novit agrestes, / Panaque, Sylvanumque senem, nymphasque sorores . . .'* But the more she read, the more distressed she would become, as if her very fluency were mocking her. She would put down the book, realizing that Pan, Sylvanus, and the sister-nymphs meant no more to her than the plates she washed at her mother's restaurant. And then all the maxims and mottos she'd had to translate would pommel her: *Dum spiro spero*—while I breathe I hope—*Nemo timendo ad summum pervenit locum*—No man by fearing reaches the top—*Quod incepimus conficiemus*—What we have begun we shall finish. And then she had had a vision of all the mottos at the headings of all the chapters of all the Latin textbooks in the world forming the bars of a colossal cage so intricately twisted and turned that she was caught inside with no room to move even a finger.

The knowledge that she could leave the cramped apartment which had begun to seem even smaller once her mother and Zoltàn had started quarrelling, and get onto an airplane to a beautiful place—Miss Vance had shown her slides of it—hit her like a fist in the face. What use—no, what good was Latin since it had nothing to do with anything that had ever marked her life? Or was that why she had loved it so much—because it made a marble labyrinth in which she could happily lose herself, she who hadn't the slightest desire to find her way out again?

The conjunction *cum*, the Present Infinitive Active and passive Indirect Statement—they had nothing to do with the young men she had seen being shot in the streets of Budapest, the young men her father had told her she was too young to have seen or remembered, even in a nightmare; nothing to do with the last time she had seen her father—bruising her shoulder against the locked bathroom door, breaking into the room with her mother to find him in his business suit, with his hat on, stretched out in a tub of water as pink as the roses on the wallpaper. Or, worse than all of this, the last quarrel, the one they hadn't tried to shut her out from by closing the bedroom door, so that she had heard, buried under the comforter on the couch, Marta accusing Zoltàn of watching Anyès when he thought she wasn't looking, of wanting to put his hands on her, touch her, and she only a child, innocence itself. The crash of his hand against her mother's face so that she wouldn't say any more, as if saying it, not thinking it, made it true. And her own silence, hot, smothered under the comforter, knowing that her mother was right and also that she was wrong—for Zoltàn had come an hour early that evening, knowing Marta to be still at the restaurant, and had stood over her as she worked at the kitchen table (consonant stems of third declension—*corpora, corporum, corporibus*) and put his hands on her shoulder and she had let him; and had slid his hands which were large but finely shaped—she had studied them as often as she had her conjugations—light as leaves against her skin, under her sweater and over her breasts, and she had let him, having no language to ask, or refuse, or explain, even to herself, what she wanted to be happening. . . .

The night after all the nights Zoltàn had not come Anyès had woken out of this dream of a railway station to hear, not the thunderous silence of lovers, nor the black hum of heating machines and electric wires in the apartment wall, but a sound she had only heard twice before: the night that her father had decided they must try to escape from Hungary, and the night before she and her mother had moved out of their house into the apartment. The sound of her mother weeping: not pleading or resisting, but as if she were mourning her own fate; as if she knew already what such travel would cost her, and that she didn't have the means to pay.

Anyès had pulled a sweater over her night-dress and walked soundlessly to her mother's room. The light was on, the door ajar— dull lamplight haloing its edges. Anyès knocked, and walked inside. Dressed only in her slip, her mother was sitting on the bed, whose covers she had not even bothered to turn down. Beside her was a bottle of brandy, nearly empty, the stars on its label tarnished, forlorn. Marta had looked up at her daughter, rubbing the skin above her breasts as she did so, the pink satiny slip cutting into flesh which Anyès saw was too soft, too white, too full to be touched without hurting. Wordless, Marta held out her arms to her daughter, wrapped them round the girl's small and delicate shoulders, drawing her in as if Anyès were an infant to be put to the breast, fed and comforted; as if her daughter's tears were milk spurting from Marta's nipples, soaking them both. 'Don't leave me, I have nothing, don't leave me, my love, my darling Zoltàn—Anyès—Zoltan.'

Anyès reached up and gently loosened her mother's arms around her, lay her down and then pull the flimsy blankets over her; twisted the cap back on to the brandy bottle, turned out the light and sat on the edge of the bed, holding her mother's hand until she heard the slow, shuddering breath of Marta, sleeping.

Miss Vance had proposed the presentation: Agnes had an obligation, she stressed, to mark the occasion of her winning of the scholarship with a demonstration, not only of her own scholastic capacities, but also of the intrinsic value of Classics in the classroom. Agnes would speak during the last Latin class of the year, on an author of her choice. The principal, the Guidence Counsellor, the Student Teachers would all be invited to hear an exposition on the principal merits of the author in question, and a few well-chosen words of confidence in and gratitude for all that the Latin tongue could bestow upon its conscientious students.

Agnes had chosen Ovid—against Miss Vance's wishes (she favoured Virgil, something from the *Eclogues*, perhaps). If it had to be Ovid, the *Baucis and Philemon* from *The Metamorphoses*, Miss Vance had suggested, would be the best choice. Agnes had agreed— at any rate, there was no further discussion, and Miss Vance was confident enough of Agnes' submissiveness (the Eastern European heritage being good at least for something) not to interfere with the girl's construing of that one safe story from Ovid's libidinous pen. And so Agnes was permitted to spend the last month of Latin class in the library, preparing her presentation.

The library was dimly lit—Mrs. Paulson, the school librarian still had vivid memories of blackouts and rationing back in her native England. Classical literature was shelved in a crepuscular cor- ner which the school's architect had originally intended as a broom closet. And so Anyès felt for, rather than looked out, the volumes she needed for her exposition; and so she came upon the volume of Ovid that had somehow got squeezed behind the *Metamorphoses* and the *Tristia*—a different sort of book, with soft leather covers and a crested bookplate inside the cover: *ex libris* J.L. Stanhope.

Mrs. Paulson could have explained to Agnes that the book had not got lost behind the other volumes, but had been palced there deliberately. The library had received quite a generous donation of books from the late Mr. Stanhope, who had owned the farmland which was now the suburb of Oakdale, and whose large stone house, visible from the library's window, had become a Christian Science Reading Room. Among the books had come some text in precarious, if not actively pernicious taste. Mrs. Paulson had not conferred with Miss Vance, whom she disliked in the way she always had the sort of roly-poly clown toy which, no matter how often you knock it over, always comes up grinning back at you. She couldn't bear the thought of throwing out books with perfectly good bind- ings, so had simply hidden them away. After all, they were printed in a foreign language, and she doubted whether the vocabulary lists to be found in *Living Latin* would permit even the most resourceful student to make much of this poet's dalliance with Corinna, that poet's address to Lesbia.

Yet in this case—Anyès Sereny's happening to have chanced upon that supple, leather-bound version of the *Amores*—Mrs. Paulson had gravely erred. For the text was a dual Latin-English version, and the translations were lively indeed—so lively that Anyès sat for the whole of each Latin class with them, and even returned at the end of the school day to devour first the English, then the Latin of each poem, utterly unaware of the rush-hour traffic returning faithful husbands from city to suburb; of the sunset's garish reflection in the windows of the Christian Science Reading Room; of the fact that Miss Vance expected her to help with repairing plasticine models, and that her mother was waiting for her to deal with dirty dishes and accounts at the *Hungarian Village*.

The afternoon of the presenation for Miss Vance, Agnes Sereny had taken her place at the podium in front of the class, oblivious to the emphatic boredom of her fellow students, all of whom had by now the same natural repugnance for anything Latin as they'd have for objects in a mortuary. Yet as she began to speak they actually listened—not to Agnes' account of Ovid's life but to the conviction that beat like little wings through her words, carrying her out of the classroom into some higher, richer air. And when Agnes started to read what Miss Vance had announced as *Baucis and Philemon*, that tale of marital devotion and fidelity, they'd leaned forward in their absurdly child-sized desks as if taking in a sermon from a different kind of mount.

> In summer's heat, siesta time
> I lay relaxed upon my couch.
>
> One shutter closed, the other ajar
> let in a sylvan half-light . . .
>
> And then, Corinna—her thin dress loosened,
> long hair parted, falling past the pale neck—
>
> lovely as Semiramis entering her wedding bower,
> or Lais of the many lovers.
>
> I pulled away her dress: she fought to keep it
> though it didn't hide much,
>
> yet fought as one with no wish to win.
> Victory was easy, a self-betrayal.
>
> There she stood, faultless beauty
> before my eyes, naked.
>
> Such shoulders and arms—
> Nipples firmly demanding attention—

Miss Vance, erect at her desk, but gasping for breath as if something had been holding her underwater for so long she thought she'd surely drown: 'I think you've gone as far as good taste will permit. Sit down!'

On Agnes Sereny's face an expression no longer somnolent, serviceable, but vivid, naked as the look in Miss Vance's eyes as she abruptly dismissed the class, requesting Agnes to stay behind. The girl stood behind her seat in the front row while the classroom emptied, until teacher and pupil were left alone with the array of patched and peeling replicas over their heads. Miss Vance was still seated at her desk; she did not even look at Agnes, but took off her spectacles and began rubbing her eyes with the heels of her hands, pressing them like a second pair of eyelids into her face. Looking at her, Anyès felt the same shock of perception she'd had in seeing her father for the last time—knowing that it was the last time, that there was suddenly an immeasurable distance between them.

Miss Vance at last pulled her hands from her eyes, put on her spectacles and looked at the girl for a long while. Whatever she'd meant to say, the words come out as this:

'The one time, the only time I ever did something I knew was wrong, was the time I skipped a class at university. My "friends" dragged me off to a movie. *Ecstacy* it was called, or some such poppycock— it was supposed to be very daring. But all I could think of was the work I should have been doing in class—of what my father would say if he knew. I hated every minute of it. And I never did a thing like that again. Ever.'

Anyès made no answer. As Miss Vance took off her spectacles again and covered her eyes the girl thought of her mother as she'd seen her that night—dishevelled, exposed. She knew, suddenly, that she was free of them both: that she could never again give them whatever they needed from her—and that they knew this, too. There was no call for any valediction. She picked up her papers, her pencil case, the library copy of *The Amores* and walked from the classroom as if out of a dream—in a hurry, as though she had a train to catch.

TOPICS FOR EXPLORATION

1. Why does the author begin her story with Agnes's dream? What does it reveal about Agnes's character? How does it prepare us for what follows?

2. Characterize Miss Vance as a "worshipper" of the dead Empire. What was her father's role in influencing her attitude toward the Empire? How is her love of imperial Rome related to her attitude toward non-WASP cultures and languages? Would you call her views ethnocentric?

3. Why does Miss Vance need to "shape and change and control" Agnes? How is her desire to mould her pupil connected with her sense of cultural superiority?

4. Analyze the relationship between Agnes and her mother. Why does her mother feel that Latin in worthless in practical life and a secretarial course is more appropriate for Agnes?

5. What does Latin represent for Agnes? What are the implications of her winning the classics award in New Brunswick?

6. How does Agnes's sexuality express itself in the story? In what sense does it jeopardize the relations between Agnes and her mother? Agnes and Miss Vance?

7. Why does Agnes choose *The Amores* as her presentation exercise? How does she come to feel free of both her teacher and her mother? What does this freedom mean?

8. How have repressive personal morality and the authority of the teacher become confused in Miss Vance?

Carol Geddes

Carol Geddes is from the Tlingit Nation in the Yukon. She graduated from Concordia University and has worked for the National Film Board. She has made several films, including Doctor, Lawyer, Indian Chief. *Her writing and films often describe the problems that aboriginal women face in both Native and white society. "Growing Up Native" was first published in* Homemaker's Magazine *in 1990.*

Growing Up Native

I remember it was cold. We were walking through a swamp near our home in the Yukon bush. Maybe it was fall and moose-hunting season. I don't know. I think I was about four years old at the time. The muskeg was too springy to walk on, so people were taking turns carrying me—passing me from one set of arms to another. The details about where we were are vague, but the memory of those arms and the feeling of acceptance I had is one of the most vivid memories of my childhood. It didn't matter who was carrying me— there was security in every pair of arms. That response to children is typical of the native community. It's the first thing I think of when I cast my mind back to the Yukon bush, where I was born and lived with my family.

I was six years old when we moved out of the bush, first to Teslin, where I had a hint of the problems native people face, then to Whitehorse, where there was unimaginable racism. Eventually I moved to Ottawa and Montreal, where I further discovered that to grow up native in Canada is to feel the sting of humiliation and the boot of discrimination. But it is also to experience the enviable security of an extended family and to learn to appreciate the richness of the heritage and traditions of a culture most North Americans have never been lucky enough to know. As a film-maker, I have tried to explore these contradictions, and our triumph over them, for the half-million aboriginals who are part of the tide of swelling independence of the First Nations today.

But I'm getting ahead of myself. If I'm to tell the story of what it's like to grow up native in northern Canada, I have to go back to the bush where I was born, because there's more to my story than the hurtful stereotyping that depicts Indian people as drunken welfare cases. Our area was known as 12-mile (it was 12 miles from another tiny village). There were about 40 people living there—including 25 kids, eight of them my brothers and sisters—in a sort of family compound. Each family had its own timber plank house for sleeping, and there was one large common kitchen area with gravel on the ground and a tent frame over it. Everybody would go there and cook meals together. In summer, my grandmother always had a smudge fire going to smoke fish and tan moose hides. I can remember the cosy warmth of the fire, the smell of good food, and always having someone to talk to. We kids had built-in playmates and would spend hours running in the bush, picking berries, building rafts on the lake and playing in abandoned mink cages.

One of the people in my village tells a story about the day the old lifestyle began to change. He had been away hunting in the bush for about a month. On his way back, he heard a strange sound coming from far away. He ran up to the crest of a hill, looked over the top of it and saw a bulldozer. He had never seen or heard of such a thing before and he couldn't imagine what it was. We didn't have magazines or newspapers in our village, and the people didn't know that the Alaska Highway was being built as a defence against a presumed Japanese invasion during the Second World War. That was the beginning of the end of the Teslin Tlingit people's way of life. From that moment on, nothing turned back to the way it was. Although there were employment opportunities for my father and uncles, who were young men at the time, the speed and force with which the Alaska Highway was rammed through the wilderness caused tremendous upheaval for Yukon native people.

It wasn't as though we'd never experienced change before. The Tlingit Nation, which I belong to, arrived in the Yukon from the Alaskan coast around the turn of the century. They were the middle-men and women between the Russian traders and the Yukon inland Indians. The Tlingit gained power and prestige by trading European products such as metal goods and cloth for the rich and varied furs so much in fashion in Europe. The Tlingit controlled Yukon trading because they controlled the trading routes through the high mountain passes. When trading ceased to be an effective means of survival, my grandparents began raising wild mink in cages. Mink prices were really high before and during the war, but afterwards the prices went plunging down. So, although the mink pens were still there when I was a little girl, my father mainly worked on highway construction and hunted in the bush. The

Yukon was then, and still is in some ways, in a transitional period—from living off the land to getting into a European wage-based economy.

As a young child, I didn't see the full extent of the upheaval. I remember a lot of togetherness, a lot of happiness while we lived in the bush. There's a very strong sense of family in the native community, and a fondness for children, especially young children. Even today, it's like a special form of entertainment if someone brings a baby to visit. That sense of family is the one thing that has survived all the incredible difficulties native people have had. Throughout a time of tremendous problems, the extended family system has somehow lasted, providing a strong circle for people to survive in. When parents were struggling with alcoholism or had to go away to find work, when one of the many epidemics swept through the community, or when a marriage broke up and one parent left, aunts, uncles and grandparents would try to fill those roles. It's been very important to me in terms of emotional support to be able to rely on my extended family. There are still times when such support keeps me going.

Life was much simpler when we lived in the bush. Although we were poor and wore the same clothes all year, we were warm enough and had plenty to eat. But even as a youngster, I began to be aware of some of the problems we would face later on. Travelling missionaries would come and impose themselves on us, for example. They'd sit at our campfire and read the Bible to us and lecture us about how we had to live a Christian life. I remember being very frightened by stories we heard about parents sending their kids away to live with white people who didn't have any children. We thought those people were mean and that if we were bad, we'd be sent away, too. Of course, that was when social workers were scooping up native children and adopting them out to white families in the south. The consequences were usually disastrous for the children who were taken away—alienation, alcoholism and suicide, among other things. I knew some of those kids. The survivors are still struggling to recover.

The residential schools were another source of misery for the kids. Although I didn't have to go, my brothers and sisters were there. They told stories about having their hair cut off in case they were carrying head lice, and of being forced to do hard chores without enough food to eat. They were told that the Indian culture was evil, that Indian people were bad, that their only hope was to be Christian. They had to stand up and say things like "I've found the Lord," when a teacher told them to speak. Sexual abuse was rampant in the residential school system.

By the time we moved to Whitehorse, I was excited about the idea of living in what I thought of as a big town. I'd had a taste of the outside world from books at school in Teslin (a town of 250 people), and I was tremendously curious about what life was like. I was hungry for experiences such as going to the circus. In fact, for a while, I was obsessed with stories and pictures about the circus, but then when I was 12 and saw my first one, I was put off by the condition and treatment of the animals.

Going to school in Whitehorse was a shock. The clash of native and white values was confusing and frightening. Let me tell you a story. The older boys in our community were already accomplished hunters and fishermen, but since they had to trap beaver in the spring and hunt moose in the fall, and go out trapping in the winter as well, they missed a lot of school. We were all in one classroom and some of my very large teenage cousins had to sit squeezed into little desks. These guys couldn't read very well. We girls had been in school all along, so, of course, we were better readers. One day the teacher was trying to get one of the older boys to read. She was typical of the teachers at that time, insensitive and ignorant of cultural complexities. In an increasingly loud voice, she kept commanding him to "Read it, read it." He couldn't. He sat there completely still, but I could see that he was breaking into a sweat. The teacher then said, "Look, she can read it," and she pointed to me, indicating that I should stand up and read. For a young child to try to show up an older boy is wrong and totally contrary to native cultural values, so I refused. She told me to stand up and I did. My hands were trembling as I held my reader. She yelled at me to read and when I didn't she smashed her pointing stick on the desk to frighten me. In terror, I wet my pants. As I stood there fighting my tears of shame, she said I was disgusting and sent me home. I had to walk a long distance through the bush by myself to get home. I remember feeling this tremendous confusion, on top of my humiliation. We were always told the white teachers knew best, and so we had to do whatever they said at school. And yet I had a really strong sense of receiving mixed messages about what I was supposed to do in the community and what I was supposed to do at school.

Pretty soon I hated school. Moving to a predominately white high school was even worse. We weren't allowed to join anything the white kids started. We were the butt of jokes because of our second-hand clothes and moose meat sandwiches. We were constantly being rejected. The prevailing attitude was that Indians were stupid. When it was time to make course choices in class—between typing and science, for example—they didn't even ask the native kids, they just put us all in typing. You get a really bad image of yourself in a situation like that. I bought into it. I thought we were awful. The whole experience was terribly undermining. Once, my grandmother gave me a pretty little pencil box. I walked into the classroom one day to find the word "squaw" carved on it. That night I burned it in the wood stove. I joined the tough crowd and by the time I was 15 years old, I was more likely to be learning against the school smoking a cigarette than trying to join in. I was burned out from trying to join the system. The principal told my father there was no point in sending me back to school so, with a Grade 9 education, I started to work at a series of menial jobs.

Seven years later something happened to me that would change my life forever. I had moved to Ottawa with a man and was working as a waitress in a restaurant. One day, a friend invited me to her place for coffee. While I was there, she told me she was going to university in the fall and showed me her reading list. I'll never forget the minutes that followed. I was feeling vaguely envious of her and, once again, inferior. I remember taking the paper in my hand, seeing the books on it and realizing, Oh, my God, I've read these books! It hit me like a thunderclap. I was stunned that books I had read were being read in university. University was for white kids, not native kids. We were too stupid, we didn't have the kind of mind it took to do those things. My eyes moved down the list, and my heart started beating faster and faster as I suddenly realized I could go to university, too!

My partner at the time was a loving supportive man who helped me in every way. I applied to the university immediately as a mature student but when I had to write Grade 9 on the application, I was sure they'd turn me down. They didn't. I graduated five years later, earning a bachelor of arts in English and philosophy (with distinction). . . .

Today, there's a glimmer of hope that more of us native people will overcome the obstacles that have tripped us up ever since we began sharing this land. Some say our cultures are going through a renaissance. Maybe that's true. Certainly there's a renewed interest in native dancing, acting and singing, and in other cultural traditions. Even indigenous forms of government are becoming strong again. But we can't forget that the majority of native people live in urban areas and continue to suffer from alcohol and drug abuse and the plagues of a people who have lost their culture and have become lost themselves. And the welfare system is the insidious glue that holds together the machine of oppression of native people.

Too many non-native people have refused to try to understand the issues behind our land claims. They make complacent pronouncements such as "Go back to your bows and arrows and fish with spears if you want aboriginal rights. If not, give it up and assimilate into white Canadian culture." I don't agree with that. We need our culture, but there's no reason why we can't preserve it and have an automatic washing machine and a holiday in Mexico, as well.

The time has come for native people to make our own decisions. We need to have self-government. I have no illusions that it will be smooth sailing—there will be trial and error and further struggle. And if that means crawling before we can stand up and walk, so be it. We'll have to learn through experience.

While we're learning, we have a lot to teach and give to the world—a holistic philosophy, a way of living with the earth, not disposing of it. It is critical that we all learn from the elders that an individual is not more important than a forest; we know that we're here to live on and with the earth, not to subdue it.

The wheels are in motion for a revival, for change in the way native people are taking their place in Canada. I can see that we're equipped, we have the tools to do the work. We have an enormous number of smart, talented, moral Indian people. It's thrilling to be a part of this movement.

Someday, when I'm an elder, I'll tell the children the stories: about the bush, about the hard times, about the renaissance, and especially about the importance of knowing your place in your nation.

TOPICS FOR EXPLORATION

1. According to Geddes, what contradictions are involved in growing up Native in Canada? Why does she think that exploring these contradictions is necessary and fruitful?

2. What advantages does Geddes identify that compensate for the "sting of humiliation and the boot of discrimination" felt by Natives in Canada?

3. Discuss the impact of white civilization upon the way of life of Yukon Native people. What different means of survival have they been trying to adopt? What problems do they face?

4. What conditions existed in the schools in Whitehorse? What methods did the white teachers use to humiliate Native students? How has this tratment affected Native self-esteem?

5. What was the turning point for Geddes in reclaiming her sense of self-worth?

6. What are the "plagues of a people who have lost their culture"? How does the self-government movement offer "a glimmer of hope"?

7. Contact between white people and Native people is usually seen as a one-way process, with the dominant white culture imposing its norms upon the natives. How does Geddes visualize the possibility of influences running in the opposite direction? What traditional Native values could enrich white lives as well?

SUGGESTIONS FOR FURTHER STUDY

1. Compare the account of the Holocaust given in Robyn Sarah's fiction with the factual narrative by Miriam Rosenthal in Unit One. How is the experience different for Sarah's narrator who has only heard about that tragedy and for Rosenthal who witnessed it firsthand? How is it similar?

2. What have the effects of Christian missionaries been upon Canadian Natives? Compare the role of missionary schools in Pauline Johnson's story, Basil H. Johnston's narrative, and Carol Geddes's essay.

3. Compare motives for hunting in Basil H. Johnston's narrative with those in "The Last Raven" by Richard G. Green in Unit Two. How does the capture of the owl compare with the slaughter of the crows? How is the dignity of these birds responded to?

4. What "mixed messages" are sent to Natives by white culture? How do they affect young people's self-image? Compare the treatment of this problem in the works by Carol Geddes and Pauline Johnson.

5. Compare the images of the teachers presented in the stories by Janice Kulyk Keefer, Clark Blaise, and Robyn Sarah. How do they confuse private morality with their professional ethics and purpose as educators?

DRIFTING APART: GENERATION GAP

INTRODUCTION

Children often choose to define themselves in opposition to their parents. A gap that opens between generations can be filled with recriminations, regrets, indifference, guilt, or sadness. The stress of this estrangement, though necessary for maturation, is increased if the parents are immigrants who cherish the traditional "home culture" they bring with them while their children, by contrast, adopt the assimilated or dominant culture of the new country. Parental preferences in language, food, and religion, and the cultural memories the parents transmit may be met with distrust and left behind. Later, perhaps, they may be appreciated. Sometimes the parents, consciously or not, perhaps pressured by cultural and educational demands or economic needs, encourage their children to yield their ethnic language and customs and to embrace, to a lesser or greater degree, the opportunities for success offered by conforming to the majority culture. However they are expressed, the generational changes cannot be avoided.

Each cultural group responds to the defection of its children in different ways that are specific to itself. In her autobiographic narrative, Loretta Jobin, a Cree author, savours the uniqueness of a rapidly disappearing culture: the Cree language (now lost to the young ones), Native food delicacies unfamiliar to the young, and memories of a way of life, now alien, on the reserve. Jobin's parents left their relatives and the reserve in order to give their children the chance for an education—they were accommodating to the relentless incursion of white culture; her old father, however, recalls a heritage which she can only reconstruct at one remove. In contrast, in Frank G. Paci's story "Mancuso's and Sons," the father is determined to pass on the Italian family tradition of bread baking that threatens to be interrupted. The symbol of craft passed from father to son is disturbed by the son's injury, which does not permit him to support the arduous profession of baking in the old manner, and by the mother's stubborn refusal to allow her "weak" son into apprenticeship.

Among the factors that can contribute to conflict between generations, lack of strong communication is central. In two stories in this unit, fathers confess their bewilderment about what motivates their children and feel the children slip beyond their control. In "Waiting," Janette Turner Hospital, an Australian-Canadian writer, describes the interminable waiting in an Indian airport from three different points of view: that of an Indian father who reflects on the attitudes of his distant daughter now living in Vermont; that of a pompous, frightened Indian airline ticket official; and that of a white woman stunned by a culture shock and about to leave India. A gallant gesture by the Indian father permits a momentary contact with the white woman, which, vicariously, reopens the relationship with his "Americanized" daughter. In Neil Bissoondath's story "Insecurity," a father of East Indian origin, living on a Caribbean island and troubled by racial and political unrest, finds it necessary to safeguard his money by transporting it secretly to his son who attends university in Toronto. However, he gradually discovers the same growing gap between himself and his son as he had felt with his own father. His desire for his son to be "independent" has, ironically, resulted in the father's being "left behind."

The breach between generations is often so great that communication is obscured, confused, or lost. In his memoir of his father, Mordecai Richler talks about the differences that separated them and admits that his perception of his father remains full of "unresolved mysteries." Time has softened, but not clarified, the sad tension between them. Like Richler, Isabel Vincent in her essay describes her distance from her own roots. The assimilation of her Portuguese parents into the Canadian mainstream is incomplete, but Vincent has removed herself so far from her ethnic community in Toronto and "Canadianized" herself so thoroughly that she is once turned down for a newspaper job because, ironically, she is perceived as too "Anglo-Saxon."

Confrontations between the generations cannot be resolved by the capitulation of either side; inevitably, there will be a drifting apart as each generation defines itself anew, against the values of the previous one and in response to the needs of its environment. Nevertheless, as the authors in this unit have shown, the memory of these rites of passage can continue to explain us to ourselves and our children.

Tara's Mother-in-law:

What kind of place you've brought me to, son?
Where the windows are always closed
And the front door it is always locked?
And no *rangoli* designs on porch steps
To say please come in?
How can you expect Lakshmi to come, son?
You think she'll care to enter
Where the same air goes round and round?
She "the lotus-seated consort
    of him who reposes
    on the primeval ocean of milk?"
You think they'll bless this food
    three days old
    you store in cans and ice-cupboard?

Son, son, it gives me great joy
to see you so well settled,
children and wife and all.
Though my hairs do stand on end
When your wife holds hands with men
And you with other men's wives.
But I am glad, son, I really am
That you are settled good good
And thought to bring me all the way
To see this lovely house and car and all.

But I cannot breathe this stale air
With yesterday's cooking smells
going round and round
Son, cooking is an everyday thing
Not a Sunday work alone
And son, cooking should smell good
The leaping aromas
    of turmeric and green coriander,
    and mustard seeds popped in hot oil
    that flavour food, not stink up the air.

Open the windows, son.

I am too used to the sounds
    of living things;
Of birds in the morning
Of rain and wind at night,
Not the drone of furnace fan
    and hiss of hot blasts
    and whoosh whoosh of washing machine.

Open the windows, son,
And let me go back
    to sun and air
    and sweat and even flies and all
But not this, not this.

—*Uma Parameswaran*

Uma Parameswaran came to Canada from Madras in 1966 to study at the University of Winnipeg. The poem reprinted here was published in Shakti's Words: An Anthology of South Asian Canadian Women's Poetry, *edited by Diane McGifford and Judith Kearns (1990).*

Loretta Jobin

Loretta Jobin was born in Saskatchewan in 1948. She decided to become a writer at the age of eight, when she first read the poetry of Pauline Johnson. She has lived in different Canadian cities and now makes her home in Edmonton. She divides her time between her family and a career in journalism. The reserve described in her memoir is the Red Pheasant Reserve that her parents came from.

The Winds of My Youth

I never lived on the reserve, but at least once a year we would make the twenty-five mile trip in my uncle's truck to visit our relatives. It was hard to hear above the sound of the wind in the back of the pickup, but that never stopped us from talking. Every once in a while, I would turn to look in the cab to see my parents talking and laughing with my uncle. I was glad that they had allowed me to sit in the back with my older brothers and sisters. We counted the hawks circling in the sky and kept our eyes open in a contest to see who could spot the most coyotes or deer, but I liked best to watch the gophers scurrying in the fields. Mother always said she thought they were suicidal, for it seemed that they would wait until a vehicle was in front of them before deciding to race across the road.

When we reached the hills, the landscape behind us looked like an aerial photograph, and Ken spotted the old Indian residential building where our father had gone to school. I had often seen this large, white building from our attic window. It looked so forgotten, sitting on the hill in the distance, almost obscured by the tall poplars surrounding it.

"Did you know Dad was born in these hills?" Winston asked of anyone who might be listening.

"He was not!" replied Ken, who never liked to agree with anything our oldest brother said. "He was born on the reserve."

"Shows how much you know!" Winston shouted back. "The reserve wasn't even around when Dad was born," he added matter-of-factly.

I guessed that was true, for my father was quite old. He was born at a time when Indians still wore Hudson's Bay blankets wrapped around their shoulders and moccasins on their feet. My father had often told us that, as a small boy, he wore his long hair in braids and had a pierced earring dangling from his ear lobe. He also told us that he had seen the last of the buffalo roaming the plains. He was born in 1892, so if he said he saw the last of the buffalo I, for one, believed him. I believed everything my parents told me. Yvonne spotted the old fort in the distance, and this started us talking about all our relatives who we thought must have died in this area.

The steeple of the post office, the tallest building in our town, slowly faded out of sight. Shortly after, we reached the turn-off to the reserve and bounced around in the back of the truck as we drove over the bumpy roads. I stood up to wave at the children playing in the yards of the homes we passed. Most of the houses were small, and there was usually a truck or tractor parked in the driveways. It was early, so I knew most of my uncles would be working in the fields, bailing hay or threshing.

"Sit down Lulu, before you fall down!" Winston shouted at me.

I sat down, feeling bad that I had made him cross. I guess he was afraid I might fall out of the truck, but I was six years old and knew better.

We would have been made to feel welcome at each house we passed, but my father wanted to go straight to the house of his only sister. Ken was the first one out of the truck and raced up to my aunt and uncle, who met him at the door.

"Tansay," he said in his deep voice, while shaking their hands. He was ten and didn't like to be seen kissing, although that was what we were taught to do.

Yvonne and I laughed when Winston said, "Ha! That's the only Cree word he knows."

When the rest of us entered my aunt's small kitchen, I noticed the kettle already boiling on the wood stove. News travelled fast on the reserve, especially when visitors from town were expected.

I studied my aunt, who resembled my father, as she talked in Cree to my parents. They were both fair, and, although she was two years younger than her brother, her hair was bone white, while his looked like a mixture of salt and pepper. I watched as she reached into the cupboard for the cups for tea, and soon she was placing bannock on the table at which we sat. As she fried up choke-cherries in grease, I knew my parents' mouths would be watering, for this was a delicacy to them. It made my stomach turn, and I wondered how I could get out of eating. I knew it was bad manners to refuse the food put before me, but I hated the feel of the crushed pits mixed in together with the berries.

I said as humbly as I could, "No thank you, Aunty. I'm not hungry," although I was starving.

I felt that everyone knew I was lying, for mother had often told me my face was very easy to read. If they did, no one said anything.

Hearing a car door slam, I raced to the living-room window to see who had pulled up. It was my aunt and uncle with their seven children. They weren't really my aunt and uncle; they were just cousins, but because they were older that's what we were taught to call them.

I stared at my many cousins as they straggled into the house. Some had dark skin with big, brown eyes, others had fair skin, and one even had red hair and freckles. I don't know why I found this so unusual, for it was the same in my family. My father was fairer than my mother and even had green eyes. He always said the white blood that ran through our veins was strong. As I stared, I noticed the high cheek-bones, characteristic of the Indian race, prominent on everyone's face.

My aunt's neat but small house was crowded, and, after being warned not to go near the open well, we were sent out to play. I walked carefully as I stepped over the broken boards of the step and looked up to see my aunt's yard strewn with bikes. We had many relatives on the reserve, and as soon as we were spotted driving by young cousins had jumped on their bikes and rode through the fields to beat us there. Soon, I knew my uncles would hear of our visit and leave the fields to say hello and grab a quick cup of tea with my parents.

One cousin had ridden over on his horse and asked me if I wanted to ride it.

"Sure," I said, trying to sound brave.

But, I was happy to hear Winston say, "Honey, you're too little, you might get hurt."

That started my cousins giggling, for they had learned how to ride almost before they learned how to walk. Not only that, but sometimes they even drove their fathers' cars and tractors down the dirt roads of the reserve. When they started laughing and talking in Cree to one another, I was sure they were making fun of me. Winston must have seen the tears welling up in my eyes, for he said, "Hop on," while jumping on the horse. Ken boosted me up, and I held tightly on to Winston as we rode around the field on the other side of the driveway. I was scared of horses, because I had once been kicked by one of my father's Clydesdales that he kept in town. We never got to ride those horses, because they were used for pulling the wagon while he delivered water to the townspeople.

Later, Winston talked one cousin his age into going riding with him to a part of the reserve known as Pasquak. That was where he had been born, along with my older sisters, Mary, Elsie, and Amy. The reserve was large and Pasquak a fair distance from my aunt's house. I knew he had to ride through fields and over hills, and by the time he got back I expected his clothes would be full of burrs and spear grass. If he took shortcuts around the sloughs, I thought he might also get wet and probably get into trouble with my mother. Or, if the horse stumbled in a badger or a gopher hole, he might get hurt. "Be careful, Winnie," I said, just as he started galloping away.

I learned later when he returned from his ride that all that was left of the small house was the root cellar upon which it once sat.

I tired of trying to play with my cousins, who shied away from me. Yvonne was older than me and didn't like me hanging around her, so I went into the house instead. I sat down in a corner on the wood floor, hoping that no one would notice me. Anyway, I loved to listen to my aunts and uncles speak of old times with my parents. They were fluent in both Cree and English and often switched while speaking. My parents sometimes spoke Cree at home, especially when Mary and Elsie were home, for they could also speak Cree, and I guess I picked up a few words. I was glad when I heard a familiar word or phrase, because then I could figure out what they were talking about.

My father started telling the story about how he used to have to take his blind grandfather for walks as a young lad. He said the old man would be feeling the ground before him with his cane as he held on to my father's shoulder with his free hand. My father shook his head as he recounted how he would purposely lead his grandfather through all the gopher holes in sight and how he'd laugh when the old man stumbled and fell.

I smiled as I watched my old aunts dressed in their calico skirts, with bright kerchiefs tied around their heads. They would raise their hand to their mouths while uttering, "Mah!" in their disbelief at my father's naughtiness. Everyone laughed at his story, which set the mood for their favourite pastime. They were known for their storytelling as well as their teasing, especially my uncles, Gavin and Tom. How often I had watched my brother Ken stomp away after they called him "Little Mad Bull," because of his quick temper. Earlier, one of my small, dark cousins had bent her head to hide the tears after being called "a lighter shade of chocolate brown." Perhaps, they teased us in preparation for being called names by the white people, but, whatever the reason, we were used to it. We learned early that the worst mistake we could make was to get angry, for this only sent my uncles into fits of laughter and made them tease all the harder.

Uncle Tom also liked to tease my mother. She was his oldest sister, and he enjoyed getting her riled.

"Remember the first time Lilly had to give a urine sample to the doctor?" he laughed, while asking no one in particular.

"That's enough, Tom," my mother replied sharply, embarrassed at the memory of her naïveté about the white culture when first moving to town.

Uncle Tom pretended not to hear her, and said, "Oh, dear! Didn't you save a sample each day for a month in a large bottle?"

"Wah, Wah, Tom!" my aunt cut in and, acting as though her next remark would erase mother's embarrassment, said, "She only saved it for a week!"

Uncle Peto interrupted the story to say, "I remember as a little girl you used to hunt down all the ant hills in the area and knock them down with a stick, Lilly."

Mother laughingly told them how she was mesmerized by the army of ants. She said she couldn't believe how the smaller ants could carry much larger captives on their backs with seemingly no problem and she would knock the large ant off with her stick, thinking she was doing the captor a favour.

"You always were a good hunter, Lilly," Aunt Hazel said, jokingly.

Uncle Lennox said, "It's true, Lilly was a good hunter," and then told how she used to shoot ducks and snare rabbits to feed her younger brothers and sisters when times were tough.

We heard often about how times were tough, especially during the depression.

"Neechas?" someone asked my father. "Do you remember that house we were helping you build before you got married?"

"Uh, Uh", my father replied. "That would have been a beautiful house."

I had heard this particular story many times. It was the largest house on the reserve and was being built on a hill, and it offered a grand view of the prairies below. My father had worked hard to buy the lumber and panes of glass for the many windows. The day before my parents' wedding, a freak cyclone ripped the shingles from the roof and shattered the windows, only moments after the men had found safety. They had no money left to rebuild.

My mother said, "I guess my vanity was nipped in the bud," as she recalled how they had to start their life together in the small house at Pasquak.

The room turned quiet for a moment at the recollection. Soon, the talk turned somber, as they recalled the many people who had passed away over the years. One uncle, they said, had buried four of his children after a bout of the flu. That made me sad. I liked better listening to the happy memories, especially mother's favourite, which was Christmas when the reserve was blanketed in snow. There was never much money for presents, she would tell me, but happy times were had wishing relations good health and wealth for the new year. She said it was so nice to drive down the road and hear the bells on the approaching sleighs jingle in the crisp night air. They would meet at a certain house and dance until the wee hours of the morning. Her father would play all the favourites, such as "Rubber Dolly," on his violin, and my uncles would accompany him on their guitars. I also liked to hear of the time when mother had barely enough time to hitch the horses and throw her four small children on a buck board to escape a grass fire burning out of control. The reserve held many memories for my parents—some good, some bad.

My father broke the silence by telling the joke about the Indian who went into the store asking for kiddely beans.

The white store owner said, "You mean kidney beans, don't you?"

The Indian looked at him in surprise and replied, "I said kiddely, diddle I?"

This started a round of jokes told mainly in Cree. If one were exceptionally funny and could be repeated in English without losing its humour, my parents would repeat it for my older brother, who by this time had come in the house. That is, if it were meant for young ears.

Long after the sun sank over the horizon, we would hop once again into the back of the truck. We would wave and shout goodbyes to our relatives and prepare ourselves for the chilly ride home. As we rode in the dark, we could see the shape of the hills and the scattered clumps of bushes silhouetted in the moonlight.

I never knew life on a reserve. When my oldest sister reached school age, my parents enfranchised, realizing the reserve could not offer hopes of a decent education for their children. Leaving relatives and a familiar way of life behind, they packed their meager belongings and moved to a small town.

Our house was on the outskirts of the town, close to the highway and the grain elevators. It was a wooden two-storey structure, with boards weathered grey from the many years of being stripped by wind, snow, and rain. Untrimmed caraganas bordered three sides of the front yard, and only a few patches of grass grew in the sandy soil among the weeds. The backyard faced the town, and from our attic window we could peer across the open fields into the hills and see the winding road leading to the reserve.

TOPICS FOR EXPLORATION

1. Although Lulu has never lived on the reserve, she is captivated by the memories this place holds for her parents and relatives. Why?

2. Find any examples of the gap separating the generations that grew up on the reserve and those who, like Lulu, have been raised in towns. What features of her father's childhood seem strange to Lulu?

3. Why are delicacies enjoyed by the elders disliked by the young children?

4. Ken, Lulu's brother, knows only one Cree word. What is the significance of this? What do the younger children lose because they have no Cree?

5. Telling stories about members of the family has a good effect on family unity. What effect does it have on the young Lulu?

6. Why did Lulu's family move off the reserve? What is implied by the symbolic location of her parents' house "on the outskirts of the town"? What exactly is the contrast between the town and the reserve? Try to justify the author's ambivalent feelings about the reserve.

Frank G. Paci

Frank G. Paci was born in Italy in 1948, and came to Canada in 1952. He was an English teacher for several years in Sault Ste. Marie and Toronto. In 1988–89 he was writer-in-residence at York University. He has published three novels, The Italians, Black Madonna, *and* The Father; *three other novels are awaiting publication. His works are characterized by a thematic consistency: they all explore the life of Italian immigrant families, especially the impact of immigration upon their self-image and personal well-being.* "Mancuso's and Sons" *has been taken from* The Father, *first published in 1984.*

Mancuso's and Sons

In the kitchen his father spoke to him like a grownup as he was having his coffee.

"I started to work when I was nine years old," he said in Italian. "My father owned the only bakery in the town in the Abruzzi. We only made large loaves of rough bread that weighed 4 kilos. Large loaves taste better because they take longer to bake, and therefore more flavour and aroma are in the oven. Then, after I got my papers as a master baker, I made my special kind of bread. The people in the town called it *Orestepane*. Bread named after me, you understand. When my father had to stop working because of arthritis I was the only baker there. If I didn't bake bread no bread was sold. But then, in the army in Rome, the officers made me make lighter pasty bread I didn't like. We called it black bread because of the black shirts. Then, when I was a prisoner of war in North Africa, I almost went crazy because I didn't have anything to do most of the time. Many soldiers went crazy, Stefano. It was a bad time. Our nails didn't grow and our hair fell out because we didn't have any vitamins. Friends of mine died of starvation and pneumonia and jaundice—much worse than your hand."

Stefano sipped his cocoa and listened intently. He had never heard his father speak so long, except for the time they went fishing at Echo Bay. Stefano didn't ask any questions. He was content just to listen. "How can the fish bite a worm that talks so much," he recalled his father saying.

His father wore a white short-sleeved shirt and white pants. They were immaculately clean and looked soft from repeated washings. Every third day Maddelena washed a batch of his whites. They hung like cut-outs on the line: shirt, pants, shirt, pants.

His father's black hair glistened with brilliantine. He had a handsome face, with smooth pale skin and a cleft on his chin. Stefano had heard his mother say jokingly that the only reason she married him was that he looked like Valentino and her father. He had never seen Valentino, but his grandfather, whose picture was in his parents' bedroom, did look a little like his father. Oreste, though, had gentle and kind eyes. Stefano had rarely seen him angry. Even when he had to discipline them Stefano could tell his heart wasn't in it. Maddelena had to goad him into using his belt. When he hit, though, it hurt.

Oreste was his most cheerful in the mornings when he was in the bakery whistling or singing while baking bread with Amelio. "Bread can't grow," he'd say, "under the hands of a sad man." Then he'd go on delivery in the Ford station-wagon. Besides fishing, he liked to play cards with his friends at the Marconi Hall, just a couple of houses up the street.

"People are funny here," Oreste would say, shaking his head. "They don't like their work at the steel plant. In Italia life is more important, you understand. To work is to live."

When they finished their breakfast they went through the side door of the kitchen and into the storage-room of the bakery. Oreste had told him the bakery had been built just after the First World War. The previous owner had been old Giuseppe, the Marchegian. Stefano was too young to remember much of him, except that he used to give him pieces of bread. His dad worked in the bakery alongside the old man until Giuseppe had to retire. There was no-one in his family to take over the business, so it had passed into Oreste's hands. Afterwards, for almost a year, the old man couldn't stay away from the bakery. Oreste would let him come and help out. Giuseppe passed on all his methods and treated Oreste like a son. When the old man died his father closed the bakery for three days. He hung a black wreath on the door and stayed at the Marconi for a long time.

At the front of *Mancuso's and Sons* was the shop where Maddelena sold the bread. The loaves were piled just behind the large plate-glass window and behind the counter. They made an assortment of crusty breads in various sizes. Above the counter was a sign with the varieties sold and the prices. His father's specialty was a large loaf with a shiny brown crust and a long cut on the top.

Behind the storage-room it was like a cave. There was a large hearth oven made of bricks on one side and a long counter on the other. Except for a small mixing-machine everything was done by hand.

Oreste explained a few details about the nature of dough and how it had been left to rise during the night. In a few minutes Amelio DiLabio came through the back and they were ready to start. Amelio was a short squat Calabrian who was the only other person working with his father. As soon as Amelio saw him his face lit up.

"*Bravo*, Stefano! You learn the business now, hey?"

Stefano smiled and stood to the side. Oreste took out a white paper cap from his back pocket and put it on. Stefano saw his father turn his face away for a moment, as if he had something in his eye. Then he made the sign of the cross.

Amelio was beaming. "*Vieni qui*, Stefano. I show you how to light the oven."

After he lit the oven he said, "The oven is the most important part of the bakery, Stefano. This is an old oven made of bricks, see. The stone inside is important for the taste. We make our bread just like the Romans did thousands of years ago."

Stefano listened in awe.

Oreste said, "People were making bread before they could write."

Afterwards they dumped a large pan of dough onto the counter and started to make bread. Amelio cut chunks of dough and weighed them on a flat scale while Oreste shaped them into loaves. They worked fast without talking, conscious of his presence. Then Amelio started to whistle. He had such a sharp clear whistle that Stefano took notice of him more closely.

In no time it was very warm in the small room. The clean yeasty smell of the dough was strong and made Stefano a little giddy. He looked at the sliced dough with the small bubbles at the side. Something made him reach out to touch it.

Amelio laughed heartily. "Good, hey. Just like the body of a woman. You'll know soon."

He had close-cropped brown hair and a ruddy face, with broken veins all over—and reminded Stefano of a cartoon character.

"Your father and I," Amelio went on, his face, lighting up like a Christmas tree, "we bake bread for a long time. The best bread in the West End. . . . in the country. And this dough—" he brought the end of his cupped fingers to his lips and kissed them with an exaggerated show of emotion—"I say it to you right now, is better than any woman."

Oreste laughed. "Better than any woman you know, that's for sure."

Throwing his head back like an opera singer, Amelio suddenly broke into song. "*Oy Marie, Oy Marie . . .*"

"Stefano," his father called out to him. "Come up here beside me."

Stefano watched closely as his father kneaded the hunks of dough. His hands worked fast at the beginning—punching down the roughness, poking and rolling the unformed chunk and sprinkling flour over it. But as the loaf began to take final shape he slowed down and took greater care. Stefano noticed the long tapering fingers of his father's hands. Whitened with flour they moved with slow, deft movements, as if caressing the dough. At the end he dipped a small brush in a jar that contained a yellowish liquid and brushed the top of each loaf.

"This is my secret method," his father said proudly. "It is responsible for the special crust of *Mancuso's and Sons.*" He paused as he took a knife and cut a long slash on top of each loaf. "Crust is the soul of the bread, figlio mio. Never forget. In this country they don't believe in crust.

"Daddy, what's in the jar?"

Oreste looked attentively at him and smiled. But he didn't answer.

Carefully he placed each loaf on a tray. Every so often Amelio put the loaves into the oven on a flat wooden board with a long handle shaped like a paddle. In a while there was a delicious smell in the room.

"See how it's done, Stefano," Oreste said. "You have to touch it a certain way. With the heel of your palms. Then the fingers. Add a little flour. Don't let it get too pasty. But just right. There, see. There's nothing better to eat in the world than bread. But good bread, not the stuff they make over here. Like those soft mushy rolls and the hamburger buns and the sliced paste they call sandwich bread. *Mannaggia America*, they don't know bread at all in this country!"

Stefano was surprised by his father's outburst. Amelio laughed good-naturedly, but Oreste gave him a long look and cursed a few times in Italian.

Finally his father put a hunk of dough in place and said, "Try it yourself, Stefano. Put some flour on your hands first."

All activity stopped. It didn't take him long to realize why. Since his accident his mother had fussed over him so much he hadn't been allowed to do much of anything. Certainly not to play games with the other kids. Or to work in the bakery.

With his left hand he cautiously started to knead the dough. His ears burned with embarrassment. He could feel their eyes on him. It made him so self-conscious of his deficiency he wanted to run and hide. Only the persistence of some inner voice kept him rooted to the spot. The dough was tougher than he thought. He couldn't put much pressure on it with one hand alone. Awkwardly he brought his deformed hand up to the counter and used it to keep the roll in place.

"*Bravo*, Stefano!" his father cried out.

Stefano turned and saw the fierce look of joy on his father's face.

"*Bravo!* Oreste cried out again, shaking his fist in the air.

Stefano returned the look. His heart was bursting with happiness.

Soon he was shaping the tough dough into something resembling a loaf of bread. Amelio started to sing again and his father whistled as he went about his business. Without any further need of instruction Stefano continued making loaves. When he had four done he stepped back and surveyed his work.

"Ready for the oven?" Amelio called out.

Stefano didn't know what to say.

"Brush them first," his father instructed.

Stefano dipped the brush and coated his loaves with his father's secret formula. It had an eggy smell.

"Here," Amelio came up to him. "This is what we did in the old country with our very first loaf." He rolled two long sticks of dough.

"Which one is your first?" he asked Stefano.

Stefano indicated the smallest of the four loaves. Amelio very carefully made an S and an M on top with the sticks of dough.

"Now you'll know," his father said, taking a towel and mopping his forehead. "We keep the first loaf to remind us of the care we put into it. So that every one after will have the same care."

They were standing in silence when his mother appeared on the scene. She was in her blue robe. Her long red hair was uncombed.

Stefano looked at her in triumph. He was about to show her the loaf he had made when he noticed the way she was regarding Oreste. Amelio stepped back and looked after the oven. Oreste looked at the floor.

His mother came up to him and took his hand. She didn't even notice what he had done. She was looking all along at Oreste, not at him.

"I told you, didn't I?" his mother said in an angry tone.

Oreste looked up bewildered.

"Aw, Maddelena, what harm will it do?" he said.

"He's too delicate, I told you."

"When I was nine—"

"Oh, shut up, when you were nine!" she lashed out at him.

Stefano had to hold himself back from crying. She was holding his good hand so firmly that she was crunching the knuckles.

Oreste shook his head and gave Stefano a pitiful look.

"He has to learn sometime," he said with annoyance.

"Learn what?" she snapped.

"To work with his hands."

"*Ma, stai zitto, ignorante!*" she yelled at him. "Can't you see?"

Stefano's ears burned with embarrassment. No-one looked at him. He put his deformed hand behind his back.

He could feel his mother trembling with rage. He tried to break free of her hold, but she only held him tighter, hurting his hand. Oreste kept silent, staring at the floor like a student who had done something wrong at school.

"Daddy," Stefano pleaded, as if his father needed a little coaxing.

But Oreste wouldn't look up to face him. Stefano couldn't understand why he didn't just speak out and tell her to go back in the kitchen where she belonged. They had work to do.

"Daddy," he called out again.

He was afraid to say anything more in case the fish wouldn't bite.

But before anything else could happen his mother whisked him out of the bakery and into his bedroom. His clothes were removed and his hands washed of flour. He was put back to bed. Somehow he was too numb to cry.

When he came home from school that day he found a loaf of baked bread in his room. It had a shiny crust with his initials on the top. He kept it hidden for seven days until his mother found it and threw it away because it had hardened into stone.

TOPICS FOR EXPLORATION

1. Oreste relates his life experiences to the theme of baking bread. How is the baking of bread symbolic of the heritage passed from father to son? Consider the legacy of old Giuseppe to Oreste and the situation of Stefano and his father.

2. In a way, the narrative shows Stefano's initiation into the traditional art of baking bread. Try to reconstruct the steps he has to learn in the process of bread making.

3. Stefano's injury is a central theme in the story. Why is it important for Oreste that his son learn to bake bread? Why is it important to his mother that he *not* bake?

4. Characterize the father/son relationship in the story. What do you think it was like prior to the episode described here? Why is there a gap between them? How is a new bond formed between them?

5. What traditional view of gender roles does the family in the story represent? Why does the mother come between her husband and her son?

Janette Turner Hospital

Janette Turner Hospital, born in Australia in 1942, has also lived for extended periods in the United States, England, and India. She settled in Canada in 1971 after spending four years as a librarian at Harvard University. She has lectured on English literature to audiences as diverse as university students, high school pupils, and prison inmates. Among her books are the novels The Ivory Swing, The Tiger in the Tiger Pit, Borderline, *and* Charades, *as well as* Dislocations, *a collection of short stories. Her fiction focusses on the experience of people moving across cultures, caught between different visions of the world. "Waiting" was her first story ever to be published; it appeared in* The Atlantic Monthly *in 1978.*

Waiting

Mr. Matthew Thomas owed his name and faith, as well as his lands, to those ancestors of lowly caste who had seen the salvation of the Lord. (It had been brought to South India by St. Thomas the Apostle, and by later waves of Portuguese Jesuits, Dutch Protestants, and British missionaries.) Now, heir of both East and West, Matthew Thomas sat quietly in one of the chairs at the crowded Air India office, waiting for his turn. It was necessary to make inquiries on behalf of a cousin of his wife, and although his wife had died ten years ago, these family obligations continued. The cousin, whose son was to be sent overseas for a brief period of foreign education, lived in the village of Parassala and could not get down to Trivandrum during the rice harvest. Mr. Matthew Thomas did not mind. He had much to think about on the subject of sons and daughters and foreign travel, and he was glad of this opportunity for quiet contemplation away from the noisy happiness of his son's house.

It was true that he had been waiting since nine o'clock that morning and it was now half past three in the afternoon. It was also true that things would have been more pleasant if the ceiling fan had been turning, for it was that steamy season when the monsoon is petering out, and the air hangs as still and hot and heavy as a mosquito net over a sick-bed. But the fan had limped to a halt over an hour ago, stricken by the almost daily power failure, and one simply accepted such little inconveniences.

Besides, Mr. Thomas could look from the comfortable vantage point of today back toward yesterday, which had also been spent at the Air India office, but since he had arrived too late to find a chair it had been necessary to stand all day. At the end of the day, someone had told him that he was supposed to sign his name in the book at the desk and that he would be called when his turn came. Wiser now, he had arrived early in the morning, signed his name, and found a chair. He was confident that his turn would come today, and until it did he could sit and think in comfort. Mr. Thomas was often conscious of God's goodness to him in such matters. All the gods were the same, he reflected, thinking fondly of the auspicious match which had just been arranged for the daughter of his neighbour Mr. Balakrishnan Pillai. Lord Vishnu; Lord Shiva; the Allah of his friend Mr. Karim, the baker; the One True God of his own church: all protected their faithful. He did not dwell on paradox.

God was merciful. It was sufficient.

The problem which demanded attention, and which Mr. Thomas turned over and over in his mind, peacefully and appraisingly as he might examine one of his coconuts, concerned both his married daughter in Burlington, Vermont, and the white woman waiting in another chair in the Air India office.

Burlingtonvermont, Burlingtonvermont. What a strange word it was. This was how his son-in-law had pronounced it. His daughter had explained in a letter that it was like saying Trivandrum, Kerala. But who would ever say Trivandrum, Kerala? Why would they say it? He had been deeply startled yesterday morning to hear the word suddenly spoken aloud, just when he was thinking of his daughter. Burlingtonvermont. The white woman had said it to the clerk at the counter, and she had been told to write her name in the book and wait for her turn.

This is a strange and wonderful thing, he had thought. And now he understood why God had arranged these two days of waiting. It was ordained so that he would see this woman who came, it seemed, from the place where his daughter was; so that he might have time to study her at leisure and consider what he should do.

He thought of Kumari, his youngest and favourite child. What did she do in Burlingtonvermont? He tried to picture her now that she was in her confinement, her silk sari swelling slightly over his grandchild. A terrible thought suddenly presented itself to him. If she had no servants, who was marketing for her at this time when she should not leave the house? Surely she herself was not . . . ? No. His mind turned from the idea, yet the bothersome riddles accumulated.

She was in her third month now, so he knew from the four child-bearings of his own wife that she would be craving for sweet mango pickle. He had written to say he would send a package of this delicacy. *Dear daddy*, she had written back, *please do not send the sweet pickle. I have no need of anything. I am perfectly happy.*

How could this be? It was true that her parents-in-law lived only five kilometres distant in the same city, and her brother-in-law and his wife also lived close by, and of course they would do her marketing and bring her the foods she craved. Of course, they were her true family now that she was married. Even so, when a woman was in the family way, it was a time when she might return to the house of her father, when she would want to eat the delicacies of the house of her birth.

He could not complain of the marriage. He was very happy with the marriages of all four of his children. They had all made alliances with Christian families of high caste. He had been able to provide handsome dowries for his daughters, and the wives of his sons had brought both wealth and beauty with them. God had been good. It was just a little sad that his elder daughter's husband was chief government engineer for Tamil Nadu instead of Kerala, and was therefore living in Madras. But at least he saw them and his grandchildren at the annual festival of Onam.

It was four years since he had seen Kumari. The week after her wedding her husband and his family had returned to America, where they had been living for many years. Only to arrange the marriages of their sons had they come back to Kerala. The arrangements had been made through the mail. Mr. Thomas had been content because the family was distantly related on his wife's side and he had known them many years ago, before they had left for America. Also the son was a professor of chemistry at the university in Burlingtonvermont, which was fitting for his daughter who had her B.A. in English literature. So they had come, the wedding had taken place, and they had gone.

For four years Mr. Matthew Thomas had waited with increasing anxiety. What is a father to think when his daughter does not bear a child in all this time? Now, as God was merciful, a child was coming. Yet she had written: *Dear daddy, please do not send the sweet pickle. I am perfectly happy.*

It had been the same when he had expressed his shock at her not having servants. *Dear daddy*, she had written, *you do not understand. Here we are not needing servants. The machines are doing everything. Your daughter and your son-in-law are very happy.* Of course this was most reassuring, if only he could really believe it. He worried about the snow and the cold. How was it possible to live with such cold? He worried about the food. The food in America is terrible, some businessmen at the Secretariat had told him. It is having no flavour. In America, they are not using any chili peppers. And yet, even at such a time as this, she did not want the sweet pickle. Could it mean that she had changed, that she had become like a Western woman?

He looked steadily and intently at the white woman in the room. Certainly, he thought, my daughter will be one of the most beautiful women in America. White women were so unattractive. It was not just their wheat-coloured hair, which did indeed look strange, but they seemed to have no understanding of the proper methods of beauty. They let their hair fly as dry and fluffy as rice chaff at threshing time instead of combing it with coconut oil so that it hung wet and glossy.

The woman was wearing a sari, which was, without question, better than the other Western women he had sometimes seen at the Mascot Hotel; those women had worn trousers as if they were men. It was amazing that American men allowed their women to appear so ugly. True, he had heard it said that women in the north of India wore trousers, but Mr. Thomas did not believe it. An Indian woman would not do such a thing. Once he had seen a white woman in a short dress, of the kind worn by little girls, with half her legs brazenly showing. He had turned away in embarrassment.

Mr. Thomas was pleased that the woman from Burlington-vermont was wearing a sari. Still, it did not look right with pale skin and pale hair. It is the best she can do, he concluded to himself. It is simply not possible for them to look beautiful, no matter what they do.

The thing that was important, and must now be considered, was what to do with this manifestation sent by God. The woman from Burlingtonvermont perhaps had all the answers to his questions. Perhaps she could even explain the matter of the sweet pickle. But what to do? One did not speak to a woman outside of the family. And yet why else would it have been arranged that he should have two days to observe this very woman? God would also arrange the solution, he thought simply. He had only to wait.

As he continued to study that strange pale face an amazing thing happened. A tear rolled slowly down one cheek and fell into the soft folds of the sari. Mr. Thomas was shocked and looked away.

After a little while, he looked back again. The woman seemed to be holding herself very tightly, as still as death, he thought. Her hands were clasped together in her lap so rigidly that the knuckles showed white. Her eyes were lowered, but the lashes glistened wetly. It must be a matter of love, he thought. Tragic love. Her parents have forbidden the match. For what other reason could a young woman, scarcely more than a girl, be weeping? Then his name was called and he went to the counter.

At the counter, Mr. Chandrashekharan Nair consulted the timetables and folders which would answer the queries of Mr. Matthew Thomas. He handled his sheaves of printed information reverently, occasionally pausing to make a small notation in ink in one of the margins, or to dignify a page with one of his rubber stamps. It always gave him a sense of pleasurable power. It was so fitting that the Nairs, who had from ancient times guarded the Maharajah of Travancore and defended his lands, should be as it were the guardians of Kerala in this modern age, watchmen over all the means of entry and egress.

It had given him particular pleasure to announce the name of Mr. Matthew Thomas. It was like the pleasure which comes after a summer's day of torpid discomfort, when the air is as damp and still as funeral bindings, until the monsoon bursts in a torrent of cool blessing. Just such a salvific release from several days of tension had come when he passed over the name of Miss Jennifer Harper to announce instead that of Mr. Matthew Thomas.

Life was distressingly complicated at the moment for Chandrashekharan Nair, who was twenty-six years old, and who owed his present position to his master's degree in economics as well as to his uncle who was a regional manager for Air India. The trouble was that two years ago, when he was still a student at the University of Kerala, he had joined one of the Marxist student groups. Well, in a sense joined. They had been an interesting bunch, livelier than other students. Mostly low-caste of course, even Harijans, not the sort of people one usually associated with, and this gave a risqué sense of exhilaration. But the leaders had all been decent fellows from the right families—Nairs, Pillais, Iyers. They read a bit too much for his liking, but the demonstrations had been rather fun, milling along Mahatma Gandhi Road in front of the Secretariat, confusing the traffic, making the withered old buffalo-cart drivers curse, jeering at the occasional American tourist. It was a student sort of thing to do. He had not expected that they would hang on to him in his way. It was beginning to become very embarrassing.

Of course he was all for progress. He agreed that more had to be done for the poor people. He felt that when he had his own household he would not expect so much from the *peon* as his father did. They really should not make the boy walk five kilometres each noontime to take young Hari's lunch to him at college, he though. It was too much for a twelve-year-old boy.

In theory, he also agreed with the Marxists about dowry. Nevertheless, when he had studied so hard for his master's degree, he felt he could expect a *lakh* of rupees from his bride's family. That was simple justice. He would be providing her with security and prestige. He had *earned* the money. Strictly speaking, it was not dowry. Dowries were illegal anyway. It was simply that a girl's family would be embarrassed not to provide well for her, and a bridegroom from a good family, with a master's degree into the bargain, had every right to expect that they provide for her in a manner suited to his status.

Chandrashekharan Nair's marriage, and his *lakh* of rupees, was all but arranged. There was one slight problem. The girl's family was raising questions about his associations with the Marxists. His father had assured them that this had been the passing fancy of a student, wild oats only, but they wanted something more, a public statement or action.

Chandrashekharan Nair was nervous. One of his cousins, who had held an influential position in the Congress party of Kerala, was now under attack in the newspapers. It was possible that he would have to stand trial for obscure things, and his career would be ruined. It did not seem likely that the Marxists would regain total power in Kerala, but they were becoming stronger all the time and one should not take chances. It was not wise to be on record for any political opinion, for or against anything. One should always appear knowing but vague, erudite but equivocal.

Chandrashekharan Nair leafed through the problems in his mind day after day as he leafed through the papers on his desk. The girl's family was waiting. His own family was waiting. His father was becoming annoyed. It was simply not fair that he should be forced into such a dangerous position. Three days ago some of his former Marxist friends had come to the office. They were jubilant about the Coca-Cola business, and had just erected near the Secretariat a huge billboard showing Coca-Cola bottles toppling onto lots of little American businessmen who were scattering like ants. There was to be a major demonstration and they wanted him to take part.

All of Chandrashekharan Nair's anxiety became focused on the American girl who had walked into his office yesterday. It was her fault, the fault of Americans and their Coca-Cola and their independent women, that all these problems had come to plague his life. And then the glimmer of a solution appeared to him. He would make a public statement about Coca-Cola. He would praise the new Indian drink and the name chosen for it. He would mention Gandhi, he would say that this nonviolent method, following in Gandhiji's footsteps, was the correct political way for India. All this was quite safe. Moraji Desai and Raj Narain were saying it in the newspapers every day. The girl's family would be satisfied. But he would also say a few carefully ambiguous words about American businessmen that would please the Marxists. And as he slid easily over Miss Jennifer Harper's name, he thought with a surge of delight of how he would tell his Marxist friends in private of his personal triumphant struggle with an imperialist in the Air India office.

He saw the tear run down Miss Jennifer Harper's cheek and frowned with disgust. He felt vindicated. Integrated. Both Hindu and Marxist teachings agreed: compassion and sentiment were signs of weakness. The West was indeed decadent.

Jennifer Harper concentrated all her energy on waiting. There is just this one least ordeal, she promised herself, and even if I have to wait all tomorrow too, it must come to an end. I will not let the staring upset me. There is just this last time.

After months of conspicuous isolation as the only Western student at the University of Kerala, she was leaving. She wondered how long it would be before her sleep was free of hundreds of eyes staring the endless incurious stare of spectators at a circus. Or at a traffic accident. If one saw the bloodied remains of a total stranger spread across a road, one watched in just that way—with a fascinated absorption, yet removed, essentially unaffected.

She looked up at the counter with mute resignation. Surely her turn would come today. Inadvertently, she became aware of the intent gaze of the gentleman who had arrived next after her that morning. He also had waited all yesterday, but it did not seem to ruffle him. Nor did he show any sign of the exhausted dejection she had felt. Time means nothing to them, she thought with irritation. She decided to meet his gaze evenly, to stare him into submission.

He did not seem to notice. Her eyes bounced back off a stare as impenetrable as the packed red clay beneath the coconut palms. She felt as stupid and insignificant as a coconut, a stray green coconut that falls before its time, thuds onto the unyielding earth, and lies ignored, merely something for the scavenger dogs. It was intolerable. She could feel tears pricking her eyes.

Damn, damn, damn, she thought, pressing her hands together with all the force of her desire not to fall apart from the heat, the exhaustion, the dysentery, the inefficiency, the interminable waiting. Just this one last little thing, she pleaded with her self-respect. Then a name was called, and the impertinent staring gentleman went to the counter. They had missed her name by accident. But what would be the good of attempting to protest? Communication would be a shambles. The clerk would be confident that he was speaking English but would be virtually unintelligible. He would understand almost nothing she was trying to explain. Then she would try her halting Malayalam, but all her velar and palatal *r*s and *k*s, and those impossible *d*s and *t*s, would get mixed up, and the people in the room would stare and giggle. Better to wait. He would soon notice that he had omitted a name.

There was a blare of loudspeakers passing the office. No one paid any attention to it. Every day some demonstration or other muddled the already chaotic traffic of Trivandrum's main road. If it was not the Marxists, it would be the student unions of the Congress party or the Janata party marching to protest each other's corruptions. Or it would be the bus drivers on strike, or the teachers picketing the Secretariat, or the rubber workers clamouring for attention, or perhaps just a flower-strewn palanquin bearing the image of some guru or deity.

The blast from the loudspeaker was so close that those at the counter could not hear one another speak. There was a milling crowd at the Air India doors, which gave way suddenly to the pressure of bodies. Mr. Chandrashekharan Nair blanched to see several Marxist leaders. He was going to have to make some snap decision that might have frightening repercussions for the rest of his life. He breathed a prayer to Lord Vishnu.

Mr. Matthew Thomas, who knew that the ways of God were inscrutable but wise, felt that something important was about to happen and waited calmly for it.

Jennifer Harper thought with despair that the office would now be closed and she would have to come back again the next day.

The student leader made an impassioned speech in Malayalam, which culminated in a sweeping accusatory gesture toward Jennifer. She rose to her feet as if in the dock. The student advanced threateningly, glared, and said in heavily accented English: "Imperialists out of India!" In equally amateur Malayalam, and in a voice from which she was unable to keep a slight quiver, Jennifer replied, "But I am not an imperialist."

There was a wave of laughter, but whether it was directed at her accent or her politics she could not say. Several things happened so quickly that she could never quite remember the order afterward. First, she thought, the gentleman who had stared so hard stepped between herself and the student, protective.

At the same time, the clerk at the desk had said, with a rather puzzling sense of importance, that he was especially arranging for the American woman to leave the country as quickly as possible. At any rate, she was now in a taxi on her way to the airport with nothing but her return ticket and her pocket-book. Next to the driver in the front seat was the gentleman who had defended her. She was thinking how sweet and easy and simple it was to sacrifice the few clothes and books, the purchased batiks and brasses, left back at the hostel. But the gentleman was saying something.

"My name is Matthew Thomas and I am having a daughter in Burlingtonvermont. I am hearing you say this place yesterday, and I am thinking perhaps you know my daughter?"

She shook her head and smiled.

"My daughter . . . I am missing her very much. . . . She is having a child. . . . There are many things I am not understanding. . . ."

They talked then, waiting at the airport where the fans were not working and the plane was late. When the boarding call finally came, Jennifer promised: "I will visit your daughter, and I will write. I understand all the things you want to know."

Mr. Matthew Thomas put his hands on her shoulders in a courteous formal embrace. She was startled and moved. "It is because you are the age of my daughter," he said, "and because you go to where she is."

Mr. Chandrashekharan Nair watched the plane circle overhead. He was on his way to the temple of Sree Padmanabhaswamy to receive prasadam and to give thanks to Lord Vishnu. He had just made a most satisfactory report of the incident to the newspaper reporter, and had been able to link it rather nicely to the Coca-Cola issue. It was a most auspicious day.

The ways of God are truly remarkable, thought Mr. Matthew Thomas as he left the airport. To think that the whole purpose behind the education of his wife's cousin's son had been the answer to his prayers about Kumari.

Jennifer Harper watched the red-tiled flat roofs and the coconut plantations and the rice paddies dwindle into her past. "Oh yes," she would say casually in Burlington, Vermont. "India. A remarkable country."

TOPICS FOR EXPLORATION

1. Generally speaking, each person in the story represents a different cultural background: Jennifer Harper comes from the West; Chandrashekharan Nair from the East; and Matthew Thomas is "heir of both East and West." What different cultural values and attitudes do they exemplify? How do their cultural preconceptions colour their perception of the others?

2. What is the purpose of having a varied point of view in "Waiting"? What does each of the three perspectives contribute to the reader's understanding of the situation in the story?

3. Why is waiting not a problem for Matthew Thomas? Why does Jennifer attract his attention? How does his desire for communication with her result in a protective gesture?

4. What is Chandrashekharan Nair's attitude to Jennifer? What are his views of the West? How does he turn his position in the Indian bureaucracy to his advantage?

5. How does Jennifer Harper feel about being a Western woman in India? Why does she promise to visit Thomas's daughter and send a letter? Can she explain the West to him? Can she help to bridge a gap between Thomas and his daughter?

6. Of the three portraits emerging from the story, which do you find the most sympathetic? Are all three characters treated with irony? If so, why?

7. Some "politically correct" critics nowadays raise their opposition to "voice appropriation," which apparently occurs when a writer represents the position of a person from another culture, just as Janette Turner Hospital does in creating her two Indian characters. How convincing is this argument to you? What are the risks involved in advocating political correctness for all writers?

Mordecai Richler

Mordecai Richler was born in 1931, in a Jewish neighbourhood in Montreal. His grandfather immigrated to Canada from Galicia in 1904 and worked as a street peddler. Richler spent several years travelling and living in Europe, notably in London, England, from 1957 to 1972. In 1968–69 he was writer-in-residence at Concordia University. He now lives close to Montreal. His large literary output includes such novels as The Acrobats, Son of a Smaller Hero, A Choice of Enemies, The Apprenticeship of Duddy Kravitz, Cocksure, Joshua Then and Now, *and* Solomon Gursky Was Here. *He has also published books for children and several volumes of essays, including the controversial book attacking Quebec nationalism,* Oh Canada! Oh Quebec! *The essay reprinted here comes from* Home Sweet Home: My Canadian Album *(1984).*

My Father's Life

After the funeral, I was given my father's *talis*, his prayer shawl, and (oh my God) a file containing all the letters I had written to him while I was living abroad, as well as carbon copies he had kept of the letters he had sent me.

> December 18, 1959: "Dear Son, Last week I won a big Kosher Turkey, by bowling, when I made the high triple for the week. How I did it I do not know, I guess I was lucky for once, or was it that the others were too sure of themselves, being much better at the game than I am."

> February 28, 1963: "This month has been a cold one, making it difficult, almost impossible to work outside. Yes! it's been tough. Have you found a title for your last novel? What can you do with a title like this? 'UNTIL *DEBT* DO US PART'?"

His letter of February 28, 1963, like so many others written that year, begins, "Thanks for the cheque." For by that time we had come full circle. In the beginning it was my father who had sent checks to me. Included in the file I inherited were canceled checks, circa 1945, for $28 monthly child support, following the annulment of my parents' marriage. A bill dated January 15, 1948, for a Royal portable, my first typewriter; a birthday gift. Another bill, from Bond Clothes, dated August 21, 1950, on the eve of my departure for Europe, for "1 Sta. Wag. Coat, $46.49."

My own early letters to my father, horrendously embarrassing for me to read now, usually begin with appeals for money. No, *demands*. There is also a telegram I'd rather forget. March 11, 1951. IMPERATIVE CHECK SENT PRONTO MADRID C O COOKS WAGON LITS ALCALA NR 23 MADRID. BROKE. MORDECAI.

Imperative, indeed.

I was also left a foot-long chisel, his chisel, which I now keep on a shelf of honor in my workroom. Written with a certain flourish in orange chalk on the oak shaft is my father's inscription:

Used by M.I. Richler

Richler Artificial Stone Works

1922

De La Roche Street

NO SUCCESS.

My father was twenty years old then, younger than my eldest son is now. He was the firstborn of fourteen children. Surely that year, as every year of his life, on Passover, he sat in his finery at a dining-room table and recited, "We were once the slaves of Pharaoh in Egypt, but the Lord our God brought us forth from there with a mighty hand and an outstretched arm." But, come 1922, out there in the muck of his father's freezing backyard on De La Roche Street in Montreal—yet to absorb the news of his liberation, my father was still trying to make bricks with insufficient straw.

Moses Isaac Richler.

Insufficient straw, *NO* SUCCESS, was the story of his life. Neither of his marriages really worked. There were searing quarrels with my older brother. As a boy, I made life difficult for him. I had no respect. Later, officious strangers would rebuke him in the synagogue for the novels I had written. Heaping calumny on the Jews, they said. If there was such a thing as a reverse Midas touch, he had it. Not one of my father's penny mining stocks ever went into orbit. He lost regularly at gin rummy. As younger, more intrepid brothers and cousins began to prosper, he assured my mother, "The bigger they come, the harder they fall."

My mother, her eyes charged with scorn, laughed in his face, "You're the eldest and what are you?"

Nothing.

After his marriage to my mother blew apart, he moved into a rented room. Stunned, humiliated. St. Urbain's cuckold. He bought a natty straw hat. A sports jacket. He began to use aftershave lotion. It was then I discovered that he had a bottle of rye whiskey stashed in the glove compartment of his Chevy. My father. Rye whiskey. "What's that for?" I asked, astonished.

"For the femmes," he replied, wiggling his eyebrows at me. "It makes them want it."

I remember him as a short man, squat, with a shiny bald head and big floppy ears. Richler ears. My ears. Seated at the kitchen table at night in his Penman's long winter underwear, wetting his finger before turning a page of the *New York Daily Mirror*, reading Walter Winchell first. Winchell, who knew what's what. He also devoured *Popular Mechanics, Doc Savage,* and *Black Mask.* And, for educational purposes, *Reader's Digest.* My mother, on the other hand, read Keats and Shelley. *King's Row. The Good Earth.* My father's pranks did not enchant her. A metal ink spot on her new chenille bedspread. A felt mouse to surprise her in the larder. A knish secretly filled with absorbent cotton. Neither did his jokes appeal to her. "Hey, do you know why we eat hard-boiled eggs dipped in salt water just before the Passover meal?"

"No, Daddy. Why?"

"To remind us that when the Jews crossed the Red Sea they certainly got their balls soaked."

Saturday mornings my brother and I accompanied him to the Young Israel synagogue on Park Avenue near St. Viateur. As I was the youngest, under bar-mitzvah age, and therefore still allowed to carry on the Sabbath, I was the one who held the prayer shawls in a little purple velvet bag. My father, who couldn't stomach the rabbi's windy speeches, would slip into the back room to gossip with the other men before the rabbi set sail. "In Japan," my father once said, "there is a custom, time-honored, that before he begins, a speaker's hands are filled with ice cubes. He can shoot his mouth off for as long as he can hold the ice cubes in his hands. I wouldn't mind if the rabbi had to do that."

He was stout, he was fleshy. But in the wedding photographs that I never saw until after his death the young man who was to become my father is as skinny as I once was, his startled brown eyes unsmiling behind horn-rimmed glasses. Harold Lloyd. Allowed a quick no-promises peek at the world and what it had to offer, but clearly not entitled to a place at the table.

My father never saw Paris. Never read Yeats. Never stayed out with the boys drinking too much. Never flew to New York on a whim. Nor turned over in bed and slept in, rather than report to work. Never knew a reckless love. What did he hope for? What did he want? Beyond peace and quiet, which he seldom achieved, I have no idea. So far as I know he never took a risk or was disobedient. At his angriest, I once heard him silence one of his cousins, a cousin bragging about his burgeoning real estate investments, saying, "You know how much land a man needs? Six feet. And one day that's all you'll have. Ha, ha!"

Anticipating Bunker Hunt, my father began to hoard American silver in his rented room. A blue steamer trunk filling with neatly stacked piles of silver dollars, quarters, dimes. But decades before their worth began to soar, he had to redeem them at face value. "I'm getting hitched again," he told me, blushing. He began to speculate in postage stamps. When he died at the age of sixty-five I also found out that he had bought a city backlot somewhere for $1,200 during the Forties. In 1967, however—riding a bloated market, every fool raking it in—the estimated value of my father's property had shrunk to $900. All things considered, that called for a real touch of class.

I was charged with appetite, my father had none. I dreamed of winning prizes, he never competed. But, like me, my father was a writer. A keeper of records. His diary, wherein he catalogued injuries and insults, betrayals, family quarrels, bad debts, was written in a code of his own invention. His brothers and sisters used to tease him about it. "Boy, are we ever afraid! Look, I'm shaking!" But as cancer began to consume him, they took notice, fluttering about, concerned. "What about Moishe's diary?"

I wanted it. Oh, how I wanted it. I felt the diary was my proper inheritance. I hoped it would tell me things about him that he had always been too reticent to reveal. But his widow, an obdurate lady, refused to let me into the locked room in their apartment where he kept his personal papers. All she would allow was, "I'm returning your mother's love letters to her. The ones he found that time. You know, from the refugee."

That would have been during the early Forties, when my mother began to rent to refugees, putting them up in our spare bedroom. The refugees, German and Austrian Jews, had been interned as enemy aliens in England shortly after war was declared in 1939. A year later they were transported to Canada on a ship along with the first German and Italian prisoners of war. On arrival at the dock in Quebec City, the army major who turned them over to their Canadian guards said, "You have some German officers here, very good fellows, and some Italians, they'll be no trouble. And over there," he added, indicating the refugees, "the scum of Europe."

The refugees were interned in camps, but in 1941 they began to be released one by one. My father, who had never had anybody to condescend to in his life, was expecting real *greeners* with sidecurls. Timorous innocents out of the *shtetl*, who would look to him as a master of magic. Canadian magic. Instead, they patronized him. A mere junk dealer, a dolt. The refugees turned out to speak better English than any of us did, as well as German and French. After all they had been through over there, they were still fond of quoting a German son of a bitch called Goethe. "Imagine that," my father said. They also sang opera arias in the bathtub. They didn't guffaw over the antics of Fibber McGee 'n' Molly on the radio; neither were they interested in the strippers who shook their nookies right at you from the stage of the Gayety Theatre, nor in learning how to play gin rummy for a quarter of a cent a point. My mother was enthralled.

My father was afraid of his father. He was afraid of my unhappy mother, who arranged to have their marriage annulled when I was thirteen and my brother eighteen. He was also afraid of his second wife. Alas, he was even afraid of me when I was a boy. I rode street-cars on the Sabbath. I ate bacon. But nobody was ever afraid of Moses Isaac Richler. He was far too gentle.

The Richler family was, and remains, resolutely Orthodox, followers of the Lubavitcher rabbi. So when my mother threatened divorce, an all but unheard-of scandal in those days, a flock of grim rabbis in flapping black gabardine coats descended on our cold-water flat on St. Urbain Street to plead with her. But my mother, dissatisfied for years with her arranged marriage, in love at last, was adamant. She had had enough. The rabbis sighed when my father, snapping his suspenders, rocking on his heels—*speaking out*—stated his most deeply felt marital grievance. When he awakened from his Saturday afternoon nap there was no tea. "Me, I like a cup of hot tea with lemon when I wake up."

In the end, there was no divorce. Instead, there was an annulment. I should explain that in the Province of Quebec at that time each divorce called for parliamentary approval. A long, costly process. A lawyer, a family friend, found a loophole. He pleaded for an annulment. My mother, he told the court, had married without her father's consent when she had still been a minor. He won. Technically speaking, I used to brag at college, I'm a bastard.

Weekdays my father awakened every morning at six, put on his phylacteries, said his morning prayers, and drove his truck through the wintry dark to the family scrapyard near the waterfront. He worked there for my fierce, hot-tempered grandfather and a pompous younger brother. Uncle Solly, who had been to high school, had been made a partner in the yard, but not my father, the firstborn. He was a mere employee, working for a salary, which fed my mother's wrath. Younger brothers, determined to escape an overbearing father, had slipped free to form their own business, but my father was too timid to join them. "When times are bad they'll be back. I remember the Depression. Oh, boy!"

"Tell me about it," I pleaded.

But my father never talked to me about anything. Not his own boyhood. His feelings or his dreams. He never even mentioned sex to me until I was nineteen years old, bound for Paris to try to become a writer. Clutching my Royal portable, wearing my Sta. Wag. coat. "You know what safes are. If you have to do it—*and I know you*—use 'em. Don't get married over there. They'd do anything for a pair of nylon stockings or a Canadian passport."

Hot damn, I hoped he was right. But my father thought I was crazy to sail for Europe. A graveyard for the Jews. A continent where everything was broken or old. Even so, he lent me his blue steamer trunk and sent me $50 a month support. When I went broke two years later, he mailed me my boat fare without reproach. I told him that the novel I had written over there was called *The Acrobats* and he immediately suggested that I begin the title of my second novel with a B, the third with a C, and so on, which would make a nifty trademark for me. Writing, he felt, might not be such a nutty idea after all. He had read in *Life* that this guy Mickey Spillane, a mere *goy*, was making a fortune. Insulted, I explained hotly that I wasn't that kind of writer. I was a serious man.

"So?"

"I only write out of my obsessions."

"Ah, ha," he said, sighing, warming to me for once, recognizing another generation of family failure.

Even when I was a boy his admonitions were few. "Don't embarrass me. Don't get into trouble."

I embarrassed him. I got into trouble.

In the early Forties, my father's father rented a house directly across the street from us on St. Urbain, ten of his fourteen children still single and rooted at home. The youngest, my Uncle Yankel, was only three years older than I was and at the time we were close friends. But no matter what after-school mischief we were up to, we were obliged to join my grandfather at sunset in the poky little Galliciander *shul* around the corner for the evening prayers, a ritual I didn't care for. One evening, absorbed in a chemistry experiment in our "lab" in my grandfather's basement, we failed to appear. On his return from *shul*, my grandfather descended on us, seething, his face bleeding red. One by one he smashed our test tubes and our retorts and even our cherished water distiller against the stone wall. Yankel begged forgiveness, but not me. A few days later I contrived to get into a scrap with Yankel, leaping at him, blackening his eye. Oh boy, did that ever feel good. But Yankel squealed on me. My grandfather summoned me into his study, pulled his belt free of his trousers, and thrashed me.

Vengeance was mine.

I caught my grandfather giving short weight on his scrapyard scales to a drunken Irish peddler. My grandfather, Jehovah's enforcer. Scornful, triumphant, I ran to my father and told him his father was no better than a cheat and a hypocrite.

"What do you know?" my father demanded.

"Nothing."

"They're anti-Semites, every one of them."

My grandfather moved to Jeanne Mance Street, only a few blocks away, and on Sunday afternoons he welcomed all the family there. Children, grandchildren. Come Hanukkah, the most intimidating of my aunts was posted in the hall, seated behind a bridge table piled high with Parcheesi games one year, Snakes and Ladders another. As each grandchild filed past the table he was issued a game. "Happy Hanukkah."

My grandfather was best with the babies, rubbing his spade beard into their cheeks until they squealed. Bouncing them on his lap. But I was twelve years old now and I had taken to strutting down St. Urbain without a hat, and riding streetcars on the Sabbath. The next time my father and I started out for the house on Jeanne Mance on a Sunday afternoon, he pleaded with me not to disgrace him yet again, to behave myself for once, and then he thrust a *yarmulke* at me. "You can't go in there bareheaded. Put it on."

"It's against my principles. I'm an atheist."

"What are you talking about?"

"Charles Darwin," I said, having just read a feature article on him in *Coronet*, "or haven't you ever heard of him?"

"You put on that *yarmulke*," he said, "or I cut your allowance right now."

"O.K., O.K."

"And Jewish children are not descended from monkeys, in case you think you know everything."

"When I have children of my own I'll be better to them."

I had said that, testing. Sneaking a sidelong glance at my father. The thing is I had been born with an undescended testicle and my brother, catching me naked in the bathroom, had burst out laughing and assured me that I would never be able to have children or even screw. "With only one ball," he said, "you'll never be able to shoot jism."

My father didn't rise to the bait. He had worries of his own. My mother. The refugee in the spare bedroom. His father. "When you step in the door," he said, "the *zeyda* will ask you which portion of the Torah they read in *shul* yesterday." He told me the name of the chapter. "Got it?"

"I'm not afraid of him."

My grandfather, his eyes hot, was lying in wait for me in the living room. Before a court composed of just about the entire family, he denounced me as a violator of the Sabbath. A *shabus goy*. Yankel smirked. My grandfather grabbed me by the ear, beat me about the face, and literally threw me out of the house. I lingered across the street, waiting for my father to seek me out, but when he finally appeared, having endured a bruising lecture of his own, all he said was, "You deserved what you got."

"Some father you are."

Which was when I earned another belt on the cheek.

"I want you to go back in there like a man and apologize to the *zeyda*."

"Like hell."

I never spoke to my grandfather again.

But when he died, less than a year after the annulment of my parents' marriage, my mother insisted it was only proper that I attend his funeral. I arrived at the house on Jeanne Mance to find the coffin set out in the living room, uncles and aunts gathered round. My Uncle Solly drove me into a corner. "So here you are," he said.

"So?"

"You hastened his death; you never even spoke to him even though he was sick all those months."

"I didn't bring on his death."

"Well, smart guy, you're the one who is mentioned first in his will."

"Oh."

"You are not a good Jew and you are not to touch his coffin. It says that in his will. Don't you dare touch his coffin."

I turned to my father. Help me, help me. But he retreated, wiggling his eyebrows.

So many things about my father's nature still exasperate or mystify me.

All those years he was being crushed by his own father, nagged by my mother, teased (albeit affectionately) by his increasingly affluent brothers and cousins, was he seething inside, plotting a vengeance in his diary? Or was he really so sweet-natured as not to give a damn? Finally, there is a possibility I'd rather not ponder. Was he not sweet-natured at all, but a coward? Like me. Who would travel miles to avoid a quarrel. Who tends to remember slights—

recording them in my mind's eye—transmogrifying them—finally publishing them in a code more accessible than my father's. Making them the stuff of fiction.

Riddles within riddles.

My father came to Montreal as an infant, his father fleeing Galicia. Pogroms. Rampaging Cossacks. But, striptease shows aside, the only theater my father relished, an annual outing for the two of us, was the appearance of the Don Cossack Choir at the St. Denis Theatre. My father would stamp his feet to their lusty marching and drinking songs; his eyes would light up to see those behemoths, his own father's tormentors, prance and tumble on stage. Moses Isaac Richler, who never marched, nor drank, nor pranced.

Obviously, he didn't enjoy his family. My mother, my brother, me. Sundays he would usually escape our cold-water flat early and alone and start out for the first-run downtown cinemas, beginning with the Princess, which opened earliest, continuing from there to the Capitol or the Palace, and maybe moving on to the Loew's, returning to us bleary-eyed, but satiated, after dark. Astonishingly, he kept a sharp eye out for little production errors. Discovering them filled him with joy. Once, for instance, he told us, "Listen to this, Clark Gable is sitting there in his newspaper office and he tells Claudette Colbert he will be finished typing his story in an hour. But when she comes back and we are supposed to believe an hour has passed, *the hands on the clock on the wall haven't moved. Not an inch.*" Another time it was, "Franchot Tone is in this tank in the desert, you're not going to believe this, and he says 'O.K., men, let's go. Attack!' And they attack. But if you look closely inside the tank just before they push off, the fuel gauge is indicating EMPTY. No gas. Get it?"

The Best Years of Our Lives overwhelmed him.

"There's a scene in there where Fredric March burps. He's hung over, he drinks an Alka-Seltzer or something, and he lets out a good one. Right there on screen. Imagine."

My mother was fond of reminding me that the night I was born, my father had not waited at the hospital to find out how she was, or whether it was a boy or a girl, but had gone to the movies instead. What was playing, I wondered.

My father didn't dream of Italy, where the lemon trees bloomed. he never went for a walk in the country or read a novel, unless he had to, because it was one of mine and he might be blamed for it. Bliss for him was the Gayety Theatre on a Saturday night. My father and a couple of younger brothers, still bachelors, seated front row center. On stage, Peaches, Anne Curie, or the legendary Lili St. Cyr. My father, rapt, his throat dry, watching the unattainable Lili simulating intercourse with a swan as the stage lights throbbed, then trudging home through the snow to sit alone at the kitchen table, drinking hot milk with matzohs before going to sleep.

We endured some rough passages together. Shortly after the marriage annulment, I fought with my father. Fists flew. We didn't speak for two years. Then, when we came together again, meeting once a week, it wasn't to talk, but to play gin rummy for a quarter of a cent a point. My father, I began to suspect, wasn't reticent. He didn't understand life. He had nothing to say to anybody.

In 1954, some time after my return to Europe, where I was to remained rooted for almost two decades, I married a *shiksa* in London. My father wrote me an indignant letter. Once more, we were estranged. But no sooner did the marriage end in divorce than he pounced: "You see, mixed marriages never work."

"But, Daddy, your first marriage didn't work either and Maw was a rabbi's daughter."

"What do you know?"

"Nothing," I replied, hugging him.

When I married again, this time for good, but to another *shiksa*, he was not overcome with delight, yet neither did he complain. For after all the wasting years, we had finally become friends. My father became my son. Once, he had sent money to me in Paris. Now, as the scrapyard foundered, I mailed monthly checks to him in Montreal. On visits home, I took him to restaurants. I bought him treats. If he took me to a gathering of the Richler clan on a Sunday afternoon, he would bring along a corked bottle of 7-Up for me, filled with scotch whisky. "There'll be nothing for you to drink there, and I know you."

"Hey, Daddy, that's really very thoughtful."

During the Sixties, on a flying trip to Montreal, my publishers put me up at the Ritz-Carlton Hotel, and I asked my father to meet me for a drink there.

"You know," he said, joining me at the table, "I'm sixty-two years old and I've never been here before. Inside, I mean. So this is the Ritz."

"It's just a bar," I said, embarrassed.

"What should I order?"

"Whatever you want, Daddy."

"A rye and ginger ale. Would that be all right here?"

"Certainly."

What I'm left with are unresolved mysteries. A sense of regret. Anecdotes for burnishing.

My wife, a proud lady, showing him our firstborn son, his week-old howling grandchild, saying, "Don't you think he looks like Mordecai?"

"Babies are babies," he responded, seemingly indifferent.

Some years later my father coming to our house, pressing chocolate bars on the kids. "Who do you like better," he asked them, "your father or your mother?"

In the mid-Sixties, I flew my father to London. He came with his wife. Instead of slipping away with him to the Windmill Theatre or Raymond's Revue Bar, another strip joint, like a fool I acquired theater tickets. We took the two of them to *Beyond the Fringe*. "What did you think?" I asked as we left the theater.

"There was no chorus line," he said.

Following his last operation for cancer, I flew to Montreal, promising to take him on a trip as soon as he was out of bed. The Catskills. Grossinger's. With a stopover in New York to take in some shows. Back in London, each time I phoned, his doctor advised me to wait a bit longer. I waited. He died. The next time I flew to Montreal it was to bury him.

TOPICS FOR EXPLORATION

1. Why does Mordecai Richler begin this portrait of his father by quoting excerpts from his father's letters? How has their relationship come "full circle" in regard to money? At the end he says "my father became my son." Why?

2. What is the significance of "No Success" inscribed on Richler's father's chisel? What are some examples of his "reverse Midas touch"?

3. How has Richler portrayed himself as a young man? Is he cruel or kind? How does he express his ambivalent feelings about his father? What has the distance of time told him about their relationship? In what way could the writing of this commemorative essay help the son come to terms with the memory of his father's life?

4. What was the relationship of Richler's father with his own tyrannical father? With his wife and children? Why were

Richler's parents unhappily married? What were the complaints of Richler's mother concerning his father?

5. Why does Richler say he has "no idea" what his father wanted? Why does he assume that his father "didn't understand life"? Does Richler ever understand the "unresolved mysteries"? Why not?

6. What similarities and contrasts between Richler and his father are developed in the text? To what degree does the author identify with his father?

7. How far does this essay illuminate different attitudes among different generations of Montreal Jews? What do we learn about successive waves of Jewish immigrants to Canada? Contrast the experience of refugee Jews leaving Europe during World War II with those of Jews in earlier migrations.

Isabel Vincent

Isabel Vincent is the South American correspondent for The Globe and Mail, *based in Rio de Janeiro. This selection was originally published in* The Globe and Mail *in December 1990.*

Finding a Nationality That Fits

We started to become Canadian the day my mother got her first pair of pants.

They were gray-green gabardine with a high waist, and came wrapped in tissue paper in an Eaton's box. My mother reluctantly modelled them for my brother and me, all the while declaring that she couldn't imagine ever feeling comfortable with the stretchy cloth hugging her hips. Portuguese women didn't wear pants, only the *canadianas* dared wear anything so revealing. But in the same breath she'd rationalize that she spent too much money not to wear them, and besides they'd probably be warm in the winter.

That was in 1975, a few years after my family had made the big break and moved from the poor immigrant enclave of Kensington Market to the more upscale neighborhoods of North York, where pockets of European immigration were just beginning to emerge. We were pioneers in a way. My father had been among the first wave of Portuguese immigrants to Canada in the early fifties, working a bleak stretch of railroad near Port Arthur—now Thunder Bay, Ont.—to earn enough money for my mother's passage across the Atlantic. My mother arrived sea-sick in Halifax in 1955, and took a slow train to Toronto, where she joined my father in a roach-infested flat on Nassau Avenue in the Market.

My mother still speaks of those early *sacrifícios*: living in a cold climate with cockroaches and mutely shopping for groceries, pointing out items to a local shopkeeper because she couldn't speak English. Her language skills were so tenuous that she once interpreted a greeting from an Orthodox Jew who lived in the neighborhood as an offer to buy my brother.

In those days, Toronto police used to disperse small crowds of Portuguese men who lingered too long outside cafes. Despite a burgeoning group of immigrants, there were few Portuguese speakers, even in the market.

But by 1975, the market became a Saturday-morning diversion for us, a place to shop for salted cod and fresh vegetables. To the hearty Portuguese immigrants who still worked in the factories and construction yards, and rented windowless basements in the market, we were on our way up. After all, there were very few Portuguese families north of Eglinton Avenue. Although we lived in a mostly Jewish and Italian neighborhood, we were finally becoming Canadian. Or so I thought.

I learned English in my first year of school. Multiculturalism was just beginning and hyphenated Canadians were beginning to flourish. I played with Italian-Canadians, Lithuanian-Canadians and Chinese-Canadians, but at that time nobody—especially suburban 7-year-olds—seemed able to pronounce "Portuguese-Canadian," so I told people I was Greek; it was easier to say. My brother went even further, changing his name to something faintly Anglo-Saxon, so his teachers and classmates wouldn't get tongue-tied around those sloshy Portuguese vowels and embarrass him. It seemed a very practical idea at the time, and I reluctantly followed suit.

But we still had problems, and didn't seem to belong. We never quite fit into the emerging Portuguese community, growing up around the parish of St. Mary's Church and the Toronto branch of the popular Benfica soccer club on Queen Street West. We were strangely aloof with our compatriots, most of whom had emigrated from the Azores, and whose guttural form of Portuguese we had difficulty understanding. My brother and I balked at heritage-language classes and remained passive spectators at the annual religious processions.

But if we had trouble dealing with our peers in downtown Toronto, in North York we were not much better off. My mother and aunts spoke disparagingly of the *canadianas*, Canadian women who (they were sure) knew nothing about how to keep a clean house or cook a decent meal. My mother taught me to cook and sew, and she and my aunts teased my brother, saying someday he'd marry a *canadiana* and would end up doing all his own housework.

For all her predictions, my mother was delighted to find out that she had been wrong. My brother, a physician, did marry a Canadian, but he doesn't do much of the housework. These days, my mother's biggest problem is pronouncing the name of her new grandson, Matthew Loughlin MacLean Vincent.

As I grew older I developed a nostalgia for my Lusitanian past, and tried desperately to reintegrate into the community. But I soon grew to hate the hypocrisy of some of my compatriots, most of whom were immigrants who chose to spend several years working in Canada, only to retire to the Portuguese country-side and build their palatial retreats with the fat pensions they collected from the Canadian government. Like my father, who learned English quickly and severed ties with his homeland, I became a staunch Canadian. I could sing *The Maple Leaf Forever* before I was 10, and spent my childhood years in French immersion. I became so good at masking my heritage that a few years ago when I applied for a job at a Toronto newspaper I was turned down because I was perceived as being too Anglo-Saxon.

"If you were ethnic, I'm sure they would have hired you on the spot," the wife of the paper's managing editor told me a year later.

But for most of my life being Portuguese seemed to me a liability. And then my mother bought that important first pair of pants. For a while it seemed that my life had changed. I was proud of my mother: she was becoming like all of the other mothers in the neighborhood.

But my excitement was short-lived. A few days later, she decided they just wouldn't do. She carefully wrapped them back up in the tissue paper, placed them in the cardboard Eaton's box, and returned them to the store.

TOPICS FOR EXPLORATION

1. The motif of Isabel Vincent's mother's first pair of pants functions as a framing device here. In what way does it highlight the major differences between the author and her mother?

2. What range of responses to her new country does Vincent register among different generations of Portuguese immigrants? What is the significance of moving from Kensington to North York?

3. Vincent doesn't feel quite Canadian, but she also feels estranged from the Portuguese community. Why? What methods has Vincent used to "Canadianize" herself?

4. What is the irony that Vincent is turned down for a newspaper job because she is perceived as too Anglo-Saxon?

5. In her school years and then in her career, has the author perceived her ethnicity as an obstacle, an asset, or both? Does she ever resolve the ambiguity of her feelings about her ethnic heritage and her desire to belong to the WASP establishment?

6. The title of this essay may suggest that nationality is something that can be fitted and changed at will, like an article of clothing. Does the rest of the essay maintain that view?

Neil Bissoondath

Neil Bissoondath is of East-Indian origin. Born in Trinidad in 1955, he came to Toronto in 1973 to study French at York University. He received the McClelland and Stewart Award for fiction in 1986. He has published Digging Up the Mountains: Selected Stories *(1985) and two novels,* A Casual Brutality *(1988) and* The Innocence of Age *(1992). He is now working on his second collection of stories. Bisoondath is the author of a controversial essay on racism, called "I'm Not Racist, But . . . ," which has been reprinted in several anthologies.*

Insecurity

"We're very insecure in this place, you know." Alistair Ramgoolam crossed his fat legs and smiled beatifically, his plum cheeks, gouged by bad childhood acne, quivering at the effect his words had had. "You fly down here, you look around, you see a beautiful island, sun, coconut trees, beaches. But I live here and I see a different reality, I see the university students parading Marx and Castro on the Campus, I see more policemen with guns, I see people rioting downtown, I see my friends running away to Vancouver and Miami. So you can see, we are very insecure down here. That is why I want you to put the money your company owes me into my Toronto bank account. It is my own private insurance. The bank will notify me the money has been deposited and the government here won't notice a thing."

Their business concluded, the visitor pocketed Mr. Ramgoolam's account number and stood ready to leave. He asked to use the phone. "I'd like to call a taxi. My flight leaves early in the morning."

"No, no." Mr. Ramgoolam gestured impatiently with his plump arm. "Vijay will drive you into town. You're staying at the Hilton, not so?"

The visitor nodded.

"Vijay! Vijay!" Mr. Ramgoolam's silver hair—stirred, the visitor noticed, by the slightest movement—jumped as if alive.

Vijay's voice rattled like a falling can as it came in irritated response from the bowels of the house. "Coming, Pa, coming."

The tick-tock of Vijay's table tennis game continued and Mr. Ramgoolam, chest heaving, bellowed, "Vijay!"

Still smiling beatifically, Mr. Ramgoolam turned to his visitor and said, "So when you'll be coming back to the islands again?"

The visitor shrugged and smiled. "That depends on the company. Not for a long time probably."

"You like Yonge Street too much to leave it again soon, eh?" Mr. Ramgoolam chuckled. The visitor smiled politely.

Vijay, rake thin and wild-eyed, crawled into the living room.

Mr. Ramgoolam saw the visitor to Vijay's sports car, the latest model on the road. "You won't forget to get the letter to my son, eh? Remember, it's Markham Street, the house number and phone number on the envelope. You won't forget, eh?"

"I won't forget," the visitor said. They shook hands.

Mr. Ramgoolam was back in his house before the gravel spat up by the tires of the car had settled. He followed the tail-lights through a heavily burglar-proofed window—Vijay was speeding again, probably showing off; he'd need another talking to. Nodding ponderously, he muttered, "We're very insecure in this place, yes, very insecure."

Alistair Ramgoolam was a self-made man who thought back with pride to his poor childhood. He credited this poverty with preventing in him the aloofness he often detected in his friends: a detachment from the island, a sneering view of its history. He had, he felt, a fine grasp on the island, on its history and its politics, its people and its culture. He had developed a set of "views" and anecdotes which he used to liven up parties. It distressed him that his views and anecdotes rarely had the desired effect, arousing instead only a deadpan sarcasm. He had written them down and had them privately published in a thin volume. Except for those he'd given away as gifts, all five hundred copies were collecting dust in cardboard boxes under the table-tennis board.

Mr. Ramgoolam had seen the British when they were the colonial masters and he had attended the farewell ball for the last British governor. He had seen the Americans arrive with the Second World War, setting up their bases on large tracts of the best agricultural land; and he had seen the last of them leave, the Stars and Stripes tucked securely under the commander's arm, more than twenty years after the end of the war. He had seen the British, no longer masters and barely respected, leave the island in a state of independence. And he had seen that euphoric state quickly degenerate into a carnival of radicals and madmen.

His life at the fringe of events, he felt, had given him a certain authority over and comprehension of the past. But the present, with its confusion and corruption, eluded him. The sense of drift nurtured unease in Mr. Ramgoolam.

He would always remember one particular day in late August, 1969. He had popped out of his air-conditioned downtown office to visit the chief customs officer at the docks. As an importer of foreign goods and wines, Mr. Ramgoolam made it his business to keep the various officials who controlled the various entry stamps happy and content. On that day, he was walking hurriedly past the downtown square when a black youth, hair twisted into worm-like pigtails, thrust a pink leaflet into his unwilling hands. It was a socialist tract, full of new words and bombast. Mr. Ramgoolam had glanced irritatedly at it, noticed several spelling mistakes, crumpled it up, and threw it on the sidewalk. Then he remembered he was a member of the Chamber of Commerce Keep-Our-City-Clean committee and he picked it up. Later that evening he found it in his pants pocket. He smoothed it out, read it, and decided it was nothing less than subversion and treason. At the next party he attended, he expounded his views on socialism. He was told to stop boring everyone.

Not long after the party, riots and demonstrations—dubbed "Black Power" by the television and the newspaper—occurred in the streets. Mr. Ramgoolam's store lost a window pane and the walls were scribbled with "Socialism" and "Black Communism." The words bedevilled the last of Mr. Ramgoolam's black hairs into the mass of silver.

As he watched the last black stripe blend in, Mr. Ramgoolam realized that, with an ineffectual government and a growing military, one night could bring the country a change so cataclysmic that the only issue would be rapid flight. And failing that, poverty, at best.

He had no desire to return to the moneyless nobility of his childhood: pride was one thing, stupidity quite another, and Alistair Ramgoolam was acutely aware of the difference.

He began looking for ways of smuggling money out of the island to an illegal foreign bank account. A resourceful man, he soon found several undetectable methods: buying travellers' cheques and bank drafts off friends, having money owed him by foreign companies paid into the illegal account, buying foreign currency from travellers at generous rates of exchange. His eldest son was attending university in Toronto, so it was through him that Mr. Ramgoolam established his account.

The sum grew quickly. Mr. Ramgoolam became an exporter of island foods and crafts, deflating the prices he reported to the island's government and inflating those he charged the foreign companies. The difference was put into the Toronto account. Every cent not spent on his somewhat lavish lifestyle was poured into his purchases of bank drafts and travellers' cheques.

The official mail service, untrustworthy and growing more expensive by the day, was not entrusted with Mr. Ramgoolam's correspondence with his son. Visitors to or from Toronto, friend or stranger, were asked to perform favours.

Over the years, with a steadily developing business and ever-increasing foreign dealings, Mr. Ramgoolam's account grew larger and larger, to more than forty thousand dollars.

He contemplated his bankbooks with great satisfaction. Should flight be necessary—and the more time passed, the more Mr. Ramgoolam became convinced it would—there would be something to run to beyond bare refuge.

The more insecure he saw his island becoming, the more secure he himself felt. From this secure insecurity a new attitude, one of which he had never before been aware, arose in him. The island of his birth, on which he had grown up and where he had made his fortune, was transformed by a process of mind into a kind of temporary home. Its history ceased to be important, its present turned into a fluid holding pattern which would eventually give way. The confusion had been prepared for, and all that was left was the enjoyment that could be squeezed out of the island between now and then. He could hope for death here but his grandchildren, maybe even his children, would continue the emigration which his grandfather had started in India, and during which the island had proved, in the end, to be nothing more than a stopover.

When the Toronto account reached fifty thousand dollars, Mr. Ramgoolam received a letter from his eldest son. He reminded his father that Vijay would be coming to Toronto to study and that the fifty thousand dollars was lying fallow in the account, collecting interest, yes, but slowly. Wouldn't it be better to invest in a house? This would mean that Vijay—Mr. Ramgoolam noticed his eldest son had discreetly left himself out—would not have to pay rent and, with the rapidly escalating property prices in Toronto, a modest fifty-thousand-dollar house could be resold later at a great profit.

His first reading of the letter brought a chuckle to Mr. Ramgoolam's throat. His independent-minded son, it seemed, was looking for a way of not paying rent. But then he felt a ripple of quiet rage run through him: his son had always made an issue of being independent, of making it on his own. Paying for the privilege, Mr. Ramgoolam thought, was the first requisite of independence. He put the suggestion out of his mind.

Later that night, just before bed, he read the letter aloud to his wife. This had long been their custom. She complained continually of "weakness" in the eyes. As he lay in bed afterwards, the words "great profit" stayed with him.

His wife said. "You going to buy it?"

He said. "Is not such a bad idea. I have to think."

When he awoke at four the next morning for his usual Hindu devotions, Mr. Ramgoolam's mind was made up. He walked around the garden picking the dew-smothered flowers with which he would garland the deities in his private prayer room and, breathing in the cool, fresh air of the young dawn's semi-light, he became convinced that the decision was already blessed by the beauty of the morning.

After a cold shower, Mr. Ramgoolam draped his fine cotton dhoti around his waist and prayed before his gods, calling their blessings onto himself, his wife, his sons, and the new house soon to be bought, cash, in Toronto. It was his contention that blessed business dealings were safer than unblessed ones.

He spent the rest of the morning writing a letter to his son, giving instructions that before any deals were made he was to be consulted. He didn't want any crooked real estate agent fooling his son, Toronto sophisticate or not. He also warned that the place should be close enough to Vijay's school that he wouldn't have to travel too far: a short ride on public transportation was acceptable but his son should always remember that it was below the station of a Ramgoolam to depend on buses and trains.

That was an important point, Mr. Ramgoolam thought. It might force his independent son to raise his sights a little. He probably used public transportation quite regularly in Toronto, whereas here on the island he would not have heard of sitting in a bus next to some sweaty farmer. The letter, Mr. Ramgoolam hoped, would remind his eldest son of the standards expected of a member of his family.

The letter was dispatched that evening with the friend of a friend of a friend who just happened to be leaving for Toronto.

A week passed and Mr. Ramgoolam heard nothing from his son. He began to worry: if *he* were buying a house, you could be sure *he'd* have found a place and signed the deal by now. That son of his just had no business sense: didn't he know that time was money? A week could mean the difference of a thousand dollars! Mr. Ramgoolam said to his wife, "I just wish he'd learn to be independent on somebody else's money."

He was walking in the garden worrying about his money and kicking at the grass when Vijay shouted from the house, "Pa, Pa! Toronto calling."

Mr. Ramgoolam hurried in, his cheeks jiggling. "Hello." It was the real estate agent calling.

The operator said, "Will you accept the charges?"

Accept the charges? Mr. Ramgoolam was momentarily unsettled. "No." He slammed the phone down. He glared at Vijay sitting at the dining table. "What kind of businessman he is anyway? Calling collect. He's getting my money and he expects me to pay for his business call? He crazy or what, eh?" Incensed, he ran out into the garden. Every few minutes, Vijay could hear him muttering about "cheapness."

The telephone rang again half an hour later.

This call was from his son and, luckily, not collect. The first thing Mr. Ramgoolam said was, "Get rid of that cheap agent. I don't trust him. Get someone else."

The son agreed. Then he asked whether his father would be willing to go above fifty thousand, to, say, sixty or sixty-five. Only such a sum would assure a good house in a proper location. Less would mean a good house, yes, but a long way on public transportation for Vijay.

Mr. Ramgoolam pictured Vijay riding on some rickety bus with a smelly fish vendor for company. He broke out in a cold sweat. "Now wait a minute . . . awright, awright, sixty or sixty-five. But not a cent more. And close the deal quickly. Time is money, you know."

Time dragged by. Nothing was heard from Toronto for a week. Mr. Ramgoolam began to worry. What was the no-good son of his up to now? Wasting time as usual, probably running off somewhere being independent.

Another week went by and Mr. Ramgoolam began brooding over the house in Toronto. He couldn't get his mind off it. He stopped going to the office. Not even prayer seemed to ease his growing doubts. Wasn't it better to have the cash safely in the bank, slowly but surely collecting its interest? And what about Vijay? The money for his schooling was to have come from that account: now he'd have to take money with him, and Mr. Ramgoolam hadn't counted on that. Above all, the house was going to cost ten to fifteen thousand more than the Toronto account contained; that was a lot of money to smuggle out. Would it mean a mortgage? He hated mortgages and credit. He hated owing. Buy only when you could pay; it was another of his convictions.

After three more days and a sleepless night, Mr. Ramgoolam eased himself out of bed at 3:30 a.m. He might as well pray. It always helped, eased the mind however little.

There was very little light that morning and the flowers he collected were wilted and soggy. He stubbed his toe on a stone and cursed, softly, in Hindi. The cold shower felt not so much refreshing as merely cold.

He prayed, his dhoti falling in careless folds, his gods sad with their colourless flowers.

When he finished he wrote a quick letter to his son, ordering him to leave all the money in the bank and to forget about buying a house. He couldn't afford it at the present time, he said.

He signed it and sealed it. He wondered briefly whether he should telephone or telegram but decided they were both too expensive. The next problem was to find someone who was going to Toronto. That was easy: the representative of his biggest Toronto client, the one staying at the Hilton, would be coming to his house this evening to finalize a deal and to get the Toronto account number. He could take the letter.

Five days passed and Mr. Ramgoolam heard nothing from his eldest son. Once more he began to worry. Couldn't the fool call to say he'd got the letter and the money was safe? He spent the morning in bed nursing his burning ulcer.

On the morning of the sixth day the call came.

"Hello, Pa?" His son's voice was sharp and clear, as if he were calling from across the street. "You're now the proud owner of a house in Toronto. The deal went through yesterday. It's all finalized."

Mr. Ramgoolam's jaw fell open. His cheeks quivered. "What? You didn't get my letter?"

"You mean the one the company rep brought up? Not yet. He just called me last night. I'm going to collect the letter this evening before the ballet."

"Be-be-be-fore the ballet?" Mr. Ramgoolam ran his pudgy fingers down the length of his perspiring face. He could feel his heart thumping heavily against the fat in his chest.

"Yes, I'm going to the ballet tonight. Good news about the house, eh? I did exactly as you told me, Pa. I did it as quickly as possible. Time is money, as you always say."

"Yes-yes," said Mr. Ramgoolam. "Time is money, son, time is money. We're very insecure in this place, you know."

His son said, "What?"

"Nothing," Mr. Ramgoolam ran his hand, trembling, through his hair. "Goodbye." He replaced the receiver. The wooden floor seemed to dance beneath him and, for a moment, he had a sense of slippage, of life turning to running liquid. He saw his son sitting in the living room of the Toronto house—sitting, smiling, in a room Mr. Ramgoolam knew to be there, but the hardened outlines of which he could not distinguish—and he suddenly understood how far his son had gone. Just as his father had grown distant from India; just as he himself had grown even further from the life that, in memory, his father had represented and then, later in life, from that which he himself had known on the island, so too had his eldest son gone beyond. Mr. Ramgoolam had been able to picture the money sitting in the bank, piles of bills; but this house, and his son sitting there with ballet tickets in his hand: this was something softer, hazier, less graspable. He now saw himself as being left behind, caught between the shades of his father and, unexpectedly, of his son. And he knew that his insecurity, until then always in the land around him, in the details of life daily lived, was now within him. It was as if his legs had suddenly gone hollow, two shells of utter fragility.

There was only one thing left, one thing to hold on to. He hurried to his room and, brushing his wife aside, dressed quickly. Then he swallowed two hefty gulps of his stomach medicine and called out to Vijay to drive him to the office.

TOPICS FOR EXPLORATION

1. What is the "different reality" of the sunny Caribbean island that Alistair Ramgoolam sees? What makes the island very "insecure" from his point of view?

2. What are the steps of colonial development that Ramgoolam has witnessed in his lifetime? What does "Black Power" represent for the island?

3. What methods does Ramgoolam use to smuggle money out of the island? What are the legal and moral implications of smuggling money? Do you find him to be a morally ambivalent character? Does Neil Blissoondath treat him with irony?

4. Does Ramgoolam understand his son in far-off Toronto? How are their attitudes different? Why does he suddenly realize that his son has "gone beyond" him as he has gone beyond his roots? Is the generation gap viewed as necessary? Can the cycle ever be broken?

5. Ramgoolam believes that independence is a privilege that has to be paid for. Explain the irony of this statement in reference to both the father/son relationship in the story and the situation on the island.

6. How is the idea of "secure insecurity" put into practice by Ramgoolam? What does he finally learn about the source of insecurity that has been haunting him?

SUGGESTIONS FOR FURTHER STUDY

1. Compare the use of foreign words and expressions by Isabel Vincent, F.G. Paci, and Mordecai Richler. Portuguese, Italian, and Yiddish vocabulary respectively appears in the texts written by these authors, usually without translation. What functions do foreign phrases have in their texts?

2. Compare Loretta Jobin's account of the Native reserve with Richard G. Green's view of growing up in the half-world of aboriginal and white cultures. What features of Native self-image do they share? What effect has white culture had upon their different environments?

3. Both Paci's narrative and Genni Donati Gunn's story "The Middle Ground" explore the effects of cultural origin upon the children of immigrant Italian parents. What do the two selections have in common with regard to parental authority, childhood self-determination, and the willingness of both parents and children to compromise?

4. Compare the effects that the parents in Mordecai Richler's memoir and Neil Bissoondath's story have upon their children. Richler's piece presents the son's view while Bissoondath's presents the father's. How has point of view affected the way the "other" is perceived? How is the "mystery" of the father in Richler's memoir and the son in Bissoondath's story portrayed?

5. Isabel Vincent describes the difficulty of "letting go" of a cultural habit or custom. How does this compare with the preservation of tradition in Paci's story?

6. Compare the distance between parent and child as described in Bissoondath's "Insecurity" and Janette Turner Hospital's "Waiting." On what levels does this distance exist? How are the distances similar for both. How are they different?

MAPS OF MEMORY: PLACES REVISITED

INTRODUCTION

In voyages from the old world to the new and from the past to the present, the old world of the past is not abandoned; it resides in memory of place: its intimate geography, the particular images of times past, and the experiences lived there. Sometimes "the map of memory" is all that remains, if the actual landscape has been destroyed by violence or utterly transformed by time. Those who remember have themselves changed in their journey from the past. Although scenes from childhood that they revisit in memory might be bathed in a nostalgic glow, when they revisit them in fact with adult perceptions, the collision of memory and actuality can often result in bewilderment, alienation, or even anger.

A vivid reminiscence about a formative landscape, now lost to time and change, can still affect the adult narrator. The importance of Frobisher Bay to the Inuit author Alootook Ipellie, as a crossroads of the north and a crossroads of his personal landscape, is the substance of his essay "Frobisher Bay Childhood." The impact of white culture in terms of money, food, and entertainment is strong, but the values of Inuit culture nonetheless remain sound in this warm and humorous recollection. The famous French-Canadian author Gabrielle Roy has a similar response to her childhood experiences in the French settlement of Saint-Boniface, Manitoba. For Roy, like Ipellie, her childhood town on the prairies was a meeting place for the immigrant populations of the world; this experience of "the disparity of the species" has had a lasting effect on her views as a writer. Roy writes of the "divided love" of the Québécois who have transported their culture to other parts of Canada, but can never forget their roots in their own landscape. Finally, the landscape of Manitoba itself—the hills, the prairie, the horizon—have a significance for Roy which she cannot abandon.

The losses of the past and the alienation of the present occur in two fictions where the main characters try without success to regain, even reconstruct, the past. C.D. Minni recognizes the changes that time has made in the Italian-Canadian real estate mogul Vitale and in the landscapes of his youth. After a painful separation from his Canadian wife and a 23-year absence from Italy, he returns to the Rome of his university days and the hill village of his youth, trying to recapture their vitality in himself, but the choices of his adult life have placed them beyond his reach. Likewise, in Kristjana Gunnars's "Mass and a Dance," the past cannot be successfully assembled by the narrator. The Icelandic village of her youth has been broken up and its inhabitants scattered throughout the world. A reunion in the church of the abandoned village cannot cure the alienation of the young woman who does not feel at home in the Manitoba of the present and who cannot reconstruct the peaceful security of the Iceland of her past.

Visits to the scenes of childhood can often provoke a troubling clash of memory and present experience. This can lead to disenchantment, despair, or rage. In "Intimations," Bharati Mukherjee contrasts her early childhood experiences in the crowded scenes of India with both her childhood and adult experiences in the West. When in 1973 she and her husband Clark Blaise pay a visit to modern India, she discovers that the gap between privilege and poverty has widened considerably. There is a disturbing division between the wealthy, who isolate themselves in their guarded compounds, and the increasingly violent masses outside. The "coming class confrontation" of the author's childhood is arriving.

Dionne Brand, in "St. Mary's Estate," revisits the plantation where she was born. Her memory enlivens the scenes of her visit where her grandfather had been overseer for twenty years. The contrast between black poverty and white affluence on this former slave plantation—the blacks crowded into slave barracks even today and the white mansion inhabited only two months a year—sharply renews the latent resentments of Brand's childhood. Things have not changed as much as they should.

The maps of memory may be accurate or faulty; they may survey landscapes that never existed or that have been reshaped by time. Without them we could not orient ourselves in the past or retrace the way that has brought us here. If we lose or misread our memory of the places of our past, we can sometimes lose our direction in the present.

Letters & Other Worlds

*'for there was no more darkness for him and, no doubt
like Adam before the fall, he could see in the dark'* [1]

My father's body was a globe of fear
His body was a town we never knew
He hid that he had been where we were going
His letters were a room he seldom lived in
In them the logic of his love could grow

My father's body was a town of fear
He was the only witness to its fear dance
He hid where he had been that we might lose him
His letters were a room his body scared

He came to death with his mind drowning.
On the last day he enclosed himself
in a room with two bottles of gin, later
fell the length of his body
so that brain blood moved
to new compartments
that never knew the wash of fluid
and he died in minutes of a new equilibrium.

His early life was a terrifying comedy
and my mother divorced him again and again.
He would rush into tunnels magnetized
by the white eye of trains
and once, gaining instant fame,
managed to stop a Perahara[2] in Ceylon
—the whole procession of elephants dancers
local dignitaries—by falling
dead drunk onto the street.

As a semi-official, and semi-white at that,
the act was seen as a crucial
turning point in the Home Rule Movement
and led to Ceylon's independence in 1948.

(My mother had done her share too—
her driving so bad
she was stoned by villagers
whenever her car was recognized)

For 14 years of marriage
each of them claimed he or she
was the injured party.
Once on the Colombo docks
saying goodbye to a recently married couple
my father, jealous
at my mother's articulate emotion,
dove into the waters of the harbour
and swam after the ship waving farewell.
My mother pretending no affiliation
mingled with the crowd back to the hotel.

Once again he made the papers
though this time my mother
with a note to the editor
corrected the report—saying he was drunk
rather than broken hearted at the parting of friends.
The married couple received both editions
of *The Ceylon Times* when their ship reached Aden.[3]

And then in his last years
he was the silent drinker,
the man who once a week
disappeared into his room with bottles
and stayed there until he was drunk
and until he was sober.

There speeches, head dreams, apologies,
the gentle letters, were composed.
With the clarity of architects
he would write of the row of blue flowers
his new wife had planted,
the plans for electricity in the house,
how my half-sister fell near a snake
and it had awakened and not touched her.
Letters in a clear hand of the most complete empathy
his heart widening and widening and widening
to all manner of change in his children and friends

while he himself edged
into the terrible acute hatred
of his own privacy
till he balanced and fell
the length of his body
the blood screaming in
the empty reservoir of bones
the blood searching in his head without metaphor
—*Michael Ondaatje*

Michael Ondaatje was born in 1943 in Ceylon (now Sri Lanka). In 1954, he moved to England, and in 1962 emigrated to Canada. His books include Running in the Family, *a fictionalized autobiography, the novels* Coming Through Slaughter *and* In the Skin of a Lion, *and several collections of poems. His latest novel,* The English Patient *(1992), has been awarded both the Governor General's Award and the Booker Prize.*

NOTES

1. Translation from Alfred Jarry's *La Dragonne* (1943), cited in *The Banquet Years* by Roger Shattuck (1955).

2. Religious ceremony celebrated by a parade.

3. Capital of the British colony of the same name. (Aden is now the capital of Southern Yemen.)

Alootook Ipellie

Alootook Ipellie, a talented Inuit writer and graphic artist, was born in 1951 in Frobisher Bay (now Iqaluit) in the Northwest Territories. He was educated in Iqaluit, Yellowknife, and Ottawa, where he now lives. He has worked as a CBC announcer and producer, and has been editor and contributor to different Inuit magazines, including Inuit Today *and* KIVIOQ Inuit Fiction Magazine.

Frobisher Bay Childhood

When anyone asks me where I was born, I usually answer, 'Frobisher Bay,' but I never can tell them exactly where my birthplace was. I always say, 'Somewhere down the bay.'

But Frobisher Bay is the place where I grew up. My most vivid childhood memories are still strongly rooted in this town. It is the place where I suffered my set-backs and experienced my triumphs. Although they may not know it, the people I grew up with are still dear to me. They really are an extension of my own life. For this reason I will always come back to Frobisher no matter where I live on this earth. Sometimes, one's roots are sacred to a person.

I remember the first time I went to school. It was in a small red and white metal building, which was the Anglican Church at that time. I was about eight years old then, and we had only one teacher—she was a lady. It was a chilly winter day with the sun shining from the sky above. I had no idea why we were called together in the church. The first day we played a few games and it was cold inside, so we had our parkas on. Round and round we went holding hands together, until finally the game was all over. It was actually the first day of my education; the *Quallunaaq* feeling had entered my heart.

I cannot say exactly how I felt at the time, but I am quite sure I enjoyed it. I remember there was a machine inside the church that made a noise; I found out later that this sound came from a round disc inside a box with a top that opened and closed. I learned that the discs were records and that the box was a 78 r.p.m. record player with a handle on the side that you had to wind in order to make it play. This was very new to me at the time and another extraordinary addition to my knowledge of the new things the white man was bringing to our little town.

Many of the essentials for living came in by freight ships when the ice broke up in late July. The sight of these great vessels entering the world where we lived made thrills go through our hearts. If a ship came while we slept, the elders wasted no time telling us the news.

'Wake up boys, there is a big umiak anchored in the bay.' We got up, rushed out the door, and looked at the enormous vessel that was already unloading its cargo into the barges.

Our ship that came to Frobisher was the Hudson's Bay Company ship, bringing the year's goods to the stores. When it arrived, most of the Inuit in town went to help unload the barges. This was during high tide and everyone worked as a unit, just like a circus setting up the big tents and other things to get ready for the opening night. There was laughter among the people, a sign of happiness which never seemed to stop as long as the ship stayed. The way they worked together was truly beautiful; they reminded me of a large family. No matter how old or young they were, they were there carrying things, big or small, both day and night.

At low tide, when there wasn't much work to do, the Hudson's Bay Company staff members brought out hot tea and pilot biscuits for everyone. We were hungry by then and as soon as the paper cups were handed out, we scrambled to reach into the large teapot as if it was our last chance. It was a thrill to be among these people; my own Inuit brothers and sisters. I looked at them as truly wonderful human beings, enjoying their day together. But soon there would be a time to end all this when the ship left to go to other settlements in the North. It was time now to get paid.

This was a day of joy, when everyone lined up to receive their money. It was usually only a dollar for each day and night that they helped in the unloading of the cargo. Even a few bills satisfied them, although they had worked hard for at least a whole week. There were no feelings of being underpaid or cheated; they merely took what they were given. And the very same day, most of them were completely broke again. They loved to spend money on goods of all kinds. Fascination was in their eyes when they saw certain things for the first time, and they thought to themselves, 'I must buy this thing—it is so beautiful and different.'

In those days I remember that the United States had an Air Force base in Frobisher Bay. We, as Inuit kids, would go over to their base to wait outside their kitchen in hopes of being offered something to eat. We often succeeded and the smell of their food was like nothing that we had ever smelled before.

There came a time when at least once a day I would start to dream of having tons and tons of *Quallunaaq* food right in our little hut. Even if all of the food could not go in, I would think of becoming a genius at storing food and somehow get it all in there.

One day when a group of us were just outside the Hudson's Bay store in the base area, a number of guys came out of the store and got in their jeep. As the jeep started up one of them threw us what looked like paper money. We scrambled for it like hungry pups . . . only to find out that it was play money made for the game of Monopoly. We looked up at the guys on their jeep and they were laughing their heads off. We nearly cried in disappointment.

I can remember one day I picked a fight with one of the students at lunch hour. The boy was one of those who was always causing trouble with other children and teachers. I distinctly had the feeling that I could beat him easily that day. I was feeling very strong and all my friends cheered me on. It was as if we were fighting for the heavy-weight boxing championship of the world. All the kids made a 'ring' around the two of us and we crashed into each other without a bit of hesitation, fists flying and muscles bulging from our arms! We grabbed each other's parkas and wrestled to the ground and up again. We swung our arm like sledge-hammers towards the opponent's head and made noises like only fighters made! I heard the crowd around us shouting words of encouragement and it was clear that the majority were rooting for me. It was important that I did not suffer a defeat in front of my friends. I fought hard but in the end, I received a bleeding nose and cried. Luck was not with me that day and it was good that my old friends were still my old friends. I never fought again after that.

There was a community hall in Apex Hill, which is about three miles from Frobisher Bay, and I remember they used to have a free movie for everyone on Sunday nights. Those of us who did not have very much money to throw around could not pass up the chance to see a full length movie free. So we would walk to Apex and back to see the shows that were often filled with action.

When the first movies came to our land, a whole new world was introduced to the Inuit. Our eyes would open up in fascination when the lights went out to start a movie. When the first frame appeared on the screen, we started to live in a world of fantasy.

The walks back home were as entertaining as the shows. Everyone got a big kick out of what they saw and amused themselves by reminiscing about the action-filled parts of the movie. Some of us would re-enact the roles of the movie stars and we had fun entertaining each other.

When we got back to Frobisher after the movie we'd find a deck of cards and start playing. My group of buddies played cards at least once a week like 'hard-nosed' gamblers. We would take our places and decide who was to deal the cards first and then go on to the serious business of winning as many games as we could. There was no cheating, and we played until one of us won everything the other players had.

What we were playing for were pictures of Hollywood stars.

Probably every kid in town had a movie idol in those days and pictures of these movie stars were considered as valuable as any good wristwatch or bicycle. So we never missed an opportunity to look through any magazines and newspapers that we could find around town. If we happened to find one good picture of John Wayne or Tony Curtis, it was as if we had found a gold nugget worth at least a couple of hundred dollars. Photographs of stars from western movies were without a doubt the most sought after because they were worth the most at the card table.

Next came the sword-clanking stars like Kirk Douglas or Steve Reeves. And there were the strongmen—like Tarzan, Hercules and Sampson. They were big heroes when I was an Inuit child. The photographs of clowns like Jerry Lewis, Bob Hope and the Three Stooges were also popular. So were Laurel and Hardy, and that timid knee-shaking character, Don Knotts.

The quality and the size of the pictures were very important. A good photo of John Wayne was worth two poor ones of the same star. Colour pictures were worth a few times more than black and white—no matter what condition they were in. The pictures of the stars in newspapers were considered good bargains but they were not as crisp as the magazine pictures and did not last long. Most of us could not get photographs from magazines so we had to resort to movie advertisements in the newspaper and newspapers were very scarce in our town in those days.

I can remember many times when my pockets would bulge with magazine photographs after a successful day of playing cards. They were valuable to me, so I could not afford to leave them around at home where they would not last for two minutes. I took great care not to crumple them. If I did, they would not be worth much when we started playing cards. So they were a bit of trouble to me because I could not move around the way I wanted to, and sitting down was always a problem. If I sat down many times during the day, I would find out that some of the faces of the movie stars were completely wiped out because of all the rubbing they were going through. A picture without a recognizable face was worth not a penny at the card table.

Clipping out photographs of movie stars was 'big business' for us as Inuit children. A good collector would naturally be considered the one to beat at the card games that would last for several hours. If he happened to be little greedy about his collection we had all the more pleasure when we won his precious pictures.

These are a few memories of my childhood in Frobisher Bay. Life in the Arctic is changing fast and Frobisher has changed along with its people. If Frobisher has a distinct character today, it is that it has become 'home' to many Inuit from other communities in the North. On any given day in Frobisher you might meet an Inuk who had come from a town as far away as Port Burwell in the east or from Tuktoyaktuk in the west. There were Inuit from Northern Quebec, from the High Arctic, from the Central Arctic or the Keewatin. Today there is no surprise in meeting an Inuk from Alaska or even from Greenland, on the streets of Frobisher Bay. Who knows, maybe one day we will begin to see whole families coming in from Siberia to live in Frobisher Bay!

TOPICS FOR EXPLORATION

1. For whom has Ipellie written this autobiographical sketch? How much will his audience know about his subject? What is his purpose in discussing his childhood in Frobisher Bay?

2. In one of the opening paragraphs the author says that "one's roots are sacred to a person." How does his essay support this statement?

3. How much space in this essay is devoted to showing the contacts between the Inuit and *quallunaat* (white people)? What was the Inuit experience of money? How did the Inuit entertain themselves?

4. What is the significance of the fistfight?

5. For Ipellie, Frobisher is the crossroads of the north. Why does its sense of space have a big impact on his view of the north?

6. Analyze the relationship between the loose structure of this story and the working of memory on which it seems to rely.

Gabrielle Roy

Gabrielle Roy, a distinguished Canadian writer, was born in 1909 in Manitoba, and moved to Montreal when she was 30. She received several literary awards, including the 1957 Governor General's Award for Rue Deschambault *(translated as* Street of Riches*), the Prix David (1971), the Molson Prize (1978), and the Canada Council Prize for Children's Literature (1979). Among her other books are* Bonheur d'occasion *(translated as* The Tin Flute*), the first Canadian work to win a major French literary award, the Prix Fémina;* La Petite Poule d'eau *(translated as* Where Nests the Water Hen*);* Alexandre Chenevert *(The Cashier);* La Montagne secrète *(The Hidden Mountain);* La Rivière sans repos *(translated as* The Windflower*); and* Ces enfants de ma vie *(translated as* Children of My Heart*). Gabrielle Roy died in 1983. "My Manitoba Heritage," first published in the review* Mosaic, *was translated by Alan Brown.*

My Manitoba Heritage

I

My maternal grandparents came from a little, lost region in the foothills of the Laurentians, north of Montreal. One fine day they left everything that had been their life to answer the call of the West and become homesteaders in Manitoba. They were no longer young—they had reached middle age, in fact—and it was a decision with no return, and a tremendous adjustment in their lives.

They travelled by railway, and then from St. Norbert, which at the time seems to have been a kind of caravanserai for French-Canadian settlers heading south, they started off one spring morning in their wagon filled to the ridge-pole, across the wild plain, following a faintly marked trail toward the rolling Pembina mountains. According to my grandfather, their irregular profile was supposed to console his wife for the loss of her native hills—but the very opposite happened: the sight of these pretentious little humps was to sharpen her regret at ever having left the steep slopes of her youth. This was the beginning of generations of divided love in our family, divided between prairie and mountain: a heartbreak, as I wrote in *The Road Past Altamont*, but also an inexhaustible source of dreams, of confidences, of leavings and "travellations" such as few people knew to the extent we did, a family that was horizon-bound, if there ever was one. And of course it is in their divided loves that artists and others find their hurts and treasures.

At the time of our family epic, my mother was a lively girl with a vivid imagination. Any voyage would have delighted her, for she had never been away from home, except for the occasional jaunt with her father from St. Alphonse to the big market on the square in Joliette. How can one imagine the effect of the prairie opening out before her without end and without reserve, wide as the sky which until then she had seen clipped by the crests of hills like the disconnected curves of a jigsaw puzzle. Now here was a sky that stretched all the way across from one sweet horizon to the other.

She never recovered from her emotions during that trip, and would tell about it all her life. To the point where my own childhood also fell under its spell, as my mother launched again into the old story, holding me on her knees in the big kitchen rocking chair; and I would imagine the pitching wagon and the accompanying rise and fall of the horizon as in a ship at sea.

Later, when I read Chekhov's *The Steppe* I felt myself in exactly the same atmosphere as in my mother's story. Everything was there: the rapture at the sight of the great, flat expanse of land, inviting as an open book and yet obscure to the mind; the touching unexpectedness, in this monotonous unfolding landscape, of the least sign of human presence—in the Russian story the windmill, visible from so far and for so long; in my mother's version, the roof of a house appearing at last in the distance of this uninhabited country—and even the feeling that this elusive horizon, constantly calling, constantly retreating, was perhaps the symbol and image of the ideal in our lives, or of the future as it appears to the eyes of our youth, full of promises that will always be renewed.

Once at their destination, which my grandmother called the "barbarian lands," although a number of her compatriots were already established there, she and my grandfather went about the task common to all settlers: recreating what they left behind.

Soon they had their steep-roofed houses, their sculptured cabinets, their bench beds, their kneading troughs and their spinning wheels; with their speech, still pure and picturesque in those days, their "Jansenist" faith, as people would say now, forgetting perhaps to what extent its severity was tempered by the shy tenderness of their hearts; with the grim cross in dark wood on the bedroom wall, but also the gaiety of their violins; and with all these and their memories and traditions, they built on this land in Manitoba, to the sound of the wind and the high, rustling grass, a new parish similar in all things to innumerable villages in Quebec.

My grandfather, the moving spirit behind this venture, I knew only through stories, which perhaps distorted his true face as much as they revealed it, as each raconteur painted him in his own image. Yet I often find him alive in myself at those odd moments of the soul when we seem to be acting in perfect liberty in our dreams and wanderings, but are really closely in harmony with the spirit of some ancestor. It is perhaps through him that I am still so deeply moved by the great elusive horizon, and especially the setting sun, from which came the clearest call.

My grandmother's tall figure hovers over my first memories like the grain elevators of the west, those towers rich in wheat and aroma and the magic of my childhood.

If she lived now, amid the preoccupation with self-fulfilment for women, my grandmother would likely be director of some big business or heading up a Royal Commission on the status of women. In her day, her talents were fully occupied from dawn till dusk making soap or cloth or shoes. She also concocted herbal remedies, dyes for her cloth and splendid designs for her rugs. I believe there still exist a few pieces of her homespun linen as resistant as her own willpower. In that "barbarous land" she succeeded in ruling, seldom giving in to it but often bending it to her own strong nature, having as little as possible to do with all these foreigners around her, these English and Scots, but re-baptizing in French all things and places they had named before her arrival.

For example, the neighbouring village of Somerset, where she had to go for her more serious shopping: on a fine autumn day she'd be sitting high in her buggy, reins in hand, looking very fine in her black bonnet and wide skirts spread across the width of the seat.

"Well, good-bye. I'm going shopping in *Saint-Mauricette.*"

What would she have thought, she who created saints whenever she felt like it, of this age of ours which has unmade them by the dozen? Or of this ecumenism which has the audacity to bring together what she saw fit to keep asunder?

On second thought, I imagine she would have ended up rejoicing, not at the diminution in the communion of saints but at the growth in that of the believers.

II

The eldest daughter of this proud woman was my mother, and she lived, so to speak, in order to conciliate the opposing tendencies of her parents, from whom she inherited qualities in equal doses, for she was frightened yet infinitely attracted by the unknown. The longer she lived the more her self-confidence won out over her circumspection. In her were best united our family's two fond attachments: for Quebec, where she was born and of which she had the treasury of memories that only a child's ardent imagination could have kept safe; and for Manitoba, where she had grown up and loved and suffered. Perhaps the most successful lives are those that seem destined to bring about a meeting of such neighbouring ways which otherwise would run parallel forever. It seems to me now that her life was spent in trying to bring things together. First and foremost, her poor children who were so different in character; then the neighbours; and, finally, everyone. She lived in love for what was, is and will be.

Toward the end of her life, sick and very old but still full of the great wish of her life to see the sites and beauties of the world, she was anxious to make a farewell visit to Quebec to see some distant cousins again, she said, to call on this one or that one; but I suspect that the real purpose of her trip, perhaps unknown to herself, may have been to climb to the top of a Laurentian hill to listen to the wind in a tall pine, just to see if it sang as it had when she was a child.

In the little cemetery of Saint-Mauricette, I have also seen her, her face sad and serious, suddenly bend down angrily to pull out a weed from the grave of my grandmother, who in her lifetime had never tolerated a weed either in her flower beds or in her existence.

The place to which you go back to listen to the wind you heard in your childhood—that is your homeland, which is also the place where you have a grave to tend. Though I chose to live in Quebec partly because of the love for it which my mother passed on to me, now it is my turn to come back to Manitoba to tend her grave. And also to listen to the wind of my childhood.

Long before it was time for my mother's grave, before marriage, before the time for bearing children, when love was, for her, like the beautiful Manitoba horizon, a prospect of the most delightful mirages, a man was already making his way toward her through the years, following the mysterious paths of fate: he, too, had left Quebec, emigrated to the States, and in a variety of jobs had forged an experience as broad as life. A self-made man, he was now on the verge of returning to Canada, but via Manitoba.

They must have met at one of those evenings when Quebecers got together, evenings loud with singing, with memories, and talk about old Quebec. Perhaps on that first evening my father, who was gifted with a fine voice, charmed the girl with one of those old ballads I myself later heard him sing: *Il était un petit navire*, or *Un Canadien errant*, sad, sweet songs to which he brought a disconcerting sincerity, as if they were a barely veiled admission of his own uprooted state.

They liked each other, this dark-haired girl with the sparkling eyes, the soul of gaiety, and the blond man whose blue eyes were heavy with an indefinable melancholy, as if the struggle to educate himself and rise above the fate of so many like him at the time had made him over-sensitive to unhappiness.

They married, as people did then, for life, for better and for worse, accepting in advance the children God would choose to "send" them. Not only would they accept them, they would exhaust themselves to give them a better life than they themselves had had, richer and more enlightened. What was more, and as if this effort was not enough, they intended to transmit intact to their children the ancestral faith and language which in those days went together.

But against what odds! A material existence which by itself was difficult to ensure; children which it would have been more reasonable not to have; and now this stubborn determination, in the face of common sense in a continent where almost everyone spoke English, to preserve those words that bear from one generation to the next a people's continuity, a people's soul. The surprising thing is that they met this challenge perhaps better than their descendants who are in many ways infinitely better off.

III

My father had become a civil servant, assigned to settling immigrants on the virgin lands of Saskatchewan and, later, Alberta, a task which he carried out admirably, full of a paternal care for these bewildered souls whose confusion he understood from his own bitter times of test and sacrifice before he managed to achieve his present level. My parents had eleven children. Three died young. The elder ones were already scattered when I came into the world, the "last little one," as I was called for a long time. This was in Saint-Boniface, in the short street called Deschambault, whose gentle rusticity I tried to convey in my book *Street of Riches*. Did I succeed? Is it possible to record in a book the spellbinding powers of childhood, which can put the whole world inside the tiniest locket of happiness?

We lived with our backs to the town—a very quiet little town, serious, going about its business, its loudest noise being the church and convent bells—and facing the open spaces. These "open spaces" were nothing but lots which faded off into brushland and, for me, prefigured the truly open prairie. In places it was interrupted by small circles of trees, often stunted oaks which for as long as I can remember made me think of the chance encounter of travellers crossing the plain, who had gathered 'round for a moment to swap their news. The fact that the oaks stayed on the same spot day after day, and that their circle was never altered, did not hinder my fancy: they were people telling their stories of the world and all that they had seen and done.

In fact, Deschambault Street was a place where one lived one-third in France, one-third in Quebec, and to a great extent in our own personal fancies which changed with the seasons or the arrival of a new neighbour, or perhaps took shape from our contemplation of the infinite spaces that began where the street ended.

Saint-Boniface breathed, prayed, hoped, sang and suffered in French, but it earned its living in English, in the offices, stores and factories of Winnipeg. The irremediable and existential difficulty of being French-Canadian in Manitoba or elsewhere!

Yet it was perhaps at this time of my childhood that French life in Manitoba was at its purest, in a fever of discussions, demonstrations and visits of encouragement from Quebec, and a fervour which did not succeed in destroying the obstacles. The draining-off to Quebec of our educated young people, who found no way of living in French, had not yet reached its peak; it was to result later in a cruel impoverishment of our community. On the contrary, we received almost constant reinforcements from Quebec, in small groups: a new notary, a new teacher, a printer, a doctor. Some help also came from France. When, in 1928, I went to take over my first class in the little village of Cardinal, it happened that at least half my pupils were from Brittany or the Auvergne. For me it was as if I had spent that year in the *Massif central* or some retreat in the Morbihan. I had every opportunity to learn certain richly regional expressions. How marvellous, when one went to teach in a village, to receive more than one gave! The same was true of Notre-Dame-de-Lourdes, Saint-Claude and other predominantly French Manitoba villages.

Whether their origins were humble or elevated, these immigrants of French nationality or language, Walloon, Italian, a few Flemings, as they mixed in among us, enriched our French life and culture with vitality and a most distinctive originality.

Strange as it may seem today, I owe to Manitoba the good fortune of having been born and raised in a Francophone area of exceptional fervour. No doubt it was the fervour of a frail group fraternally united in its numerical fragility and its threatened ideal to build a common front.

I suppose that this enthusiasm, like a wick turned too high, could not burn forever. But its light was there—long enough to illuminate some lives.

IV

As soon as the Red River was crossed and we were in Winnipeg, it was another world. Even today the crossing of the Provencher Bridge from Saint-Boniface to Winnipeg is for me like going from the particular to the general. I know that the contrast between the two is less marked; but in those days, almost without noticing it, we made the transition from our life, somewhat turned inward on itself, to the manifold, strange, torrential and nostalgic human flood that made up Manitoba's population and came from all parts of the earth. This was the second marvellous gift I received from that province: to have glimpsed while still very young the pied disparity of the species—along with the realization that we are basically very much alike. Without having to travel, I could see the peoples of the earth parade before my eyes. I had only to stroll through the Canadian Pacific railway station to see women in white kerchiefs, their gaze so distant it was surely fixed on the other end of the world; or whole families with their bundles, their eyes dulled with boredom, sitting in a circle on their trunks, waiting for lord knows what; or patriarchs with long beards, happed in strange capes, followed by their families in Indian file along the wide sidewalks, as if they were picking their way through a mountain pass. I have said these things time and again, and can do no more than say them again every time I write about Manitoba, because for me the sight of these bewildered people, which the province offered me when I was very young, has become inseparable from my feelings about life.

At first my mother was startled and fascinated by this motley crowd of humanity that flowed almost past our door. In comparison to their lives, our own now seemed settled and secure, at least with some roots, she liked to emphasize. But the fascination was stronger than her mistrust. Soon she took her youngest children by a Red River cruise boat to see the Ukrainians at St. Andrews, and from the deck we would watch, perhaps a little ashamed, as the women, gleaning, trying to straighten their aching backs, would shield their eyes from the sun to stare at us, the do-nothings who had no better way to spend their time than watching others work. She also took us to see the Icelanders in Gimli; or we would simply cross the narrow River Seine, a stone's throw from home, to hear the mass "in Belgium," as we used to say.

The *Arabian Nights* of my childhood were made up of these excursions into Little Wallonia, Little Ukraine, Little Auvergne, Little Scotland, Little Brittany, wherever they were in Manitoba, and also the nearly exact replicas of Quebec scattered over the plain. This already, no doubt, gave me that un-anchored feeling, the drifting sensation of casting loose from habit which, with the slight anxiety it produces, is unequalled for making us want to see and seize and hold everything new, if only for a moment.

My father, home from long expeditions among the settlers, always brought fresh news about "his" unruly Doukhobors, "his" quiet Ruthenians, "his" devout Mennonites. His settlements now extended almost to Medicine Hat, each more surprising than the last, so that you'd think his tales were taken from certain pages by Gogol. This is perhaps why, when in later years I read *Dead Souls*, I was not as astonished as some western readers. Tchitchikov's adventures seemed somehow familiar to me. What was comical, singular and improbable was just as familiar to me as the dull, believable and everyday aspect of life. I even had to learn to tone down certain elements of the reality that lay behind some stories so that people wouldn't think I was overdoing things shamelessly.

This brings me to the essential thing Manitoba brought me. My father's stories, the little trips we took with my mother, the Manitoba backdrop where the faces of all the peoples of the world were to be seen, all this brought the "foreigner" so close to me that he ceased to be foreign. Even today, if I hear a person living only a few miles away described as a "stranger," I cannot help feeling an inner tremor as if I myself had been the victim of an insult to humanity.

Either there are no more foreigners in the world, or we are foreigners all.

But the most enduring thing Manitoba gave me was the memory of its landscapes. I have travelled quite a lot. Occasionally I have been happy elsewhere and managed for a moment to feel at home in the gentle range of the Alpilles, or, odder still, in a certain small village in Epping Forest, Essex, where I ended up one day by utter chance; and there's a corner of the Isle of Rhodes, in Lindos, where at times I thought I might like to live, among the bougainvilleas and the women all in black seen against the whitest walls in the world, and the little interior gardens made of simple pebbles arranged with such grace that they compose exquisite mosaics.

At last it was the St. Lawrence, the link with our most remote Canadian past, but still a living, moving sea lane, always flowing toward the future. I live near enough to the river to see it from my window at all times, and I never grow weary of it, especially in the country, in Charlevoix, where it is twenty-two miles wide and comes and goes in regular, ample tides like the beating of creation's very heart. The "sea" drops, as they say here, and my own heart knows a kind of letdown; it rises, and my sad being finds a fresh departure.

But all these are adult loves, reflected on and sought after. My childhood love is the silent sky of the prairie, fitting the soft, level earth as perfectly as the bell cover on a plate, the sky that could shut one in, but which, by the height of its dome, invites us to take flight, to fly to freedom. My love encompasses the special silhouette, two-walled, of our grain elevators, their blue shadow like a cutout against a sky blurred with heat, the only thing on a summer day that reveals from afar the existence of the villages on this flat immensity; the mirages of those torrid days when the dryness of roads and fields throws up from the horizon illusory waters trembling between land and sky; the small clumps of trees, the bluffs gathered in a circle as if to chat in the desert about the wide world; and the infinite human variety of that countryside.

When I was young in Manitoba, one of our favourite outings was a trip to Bird's Hill. What was so attractive about it then? From the level plain there arose, for no apparent reason, a singular, long, sandy crest, the shore, one would have said, of some ancient lake, dry for centuries and turned to land, grass and market gardens, except in certain parts where brush allowed the persistence of wild life, and where one heard the plaintive cry of birds. No doubt it was a former strip of water left behind by the Sea of Agassiz since that immemorial time when Manitoba, almost entirely under water, was not even a dream. We would stay there, full of respect and astonishment. Perhaps we had an inkling that this strange crest of sand was uniting ages before our very eyes, the ages we call "past," those yet to come, the new, the old, those that persist, those that overturn, those we think dead, those we call "today," and that all these times were in truth no more than a second on the great dial.

Bird's Hill is perhaps my most sacred memory of Manitoba: on the shore of long-vanished waters, these ancient fossils, these dreams of youth, this unshakeable confidence in the far-off horizon.

You know how it fools us, this Manitoba horizon! How many times, as a child, have I set out to reach it! You always think you're about to arrive, only to see that it has retreated slightly, kept its distance once again. It is really a great signpost of life which an invisible hand mockingly maintains beyond our reach. As we get older, we grow a little discouraged and we even suspect that there is a supreme ruse behind all this, that we will never reach the horizon's perfect curve. Sometimes, however, we feel that others after us will undertake the same mad venture and that this horizon, still so far away, is the circle of mankind, full and united at last.

TOPICS FOR EXPLORATION

1. What is the "divided love" Gabrielle Roy's family has experienced that she considers in her second paragraph? What is the effect of the two images, the prairie and the mountains, on her imagination? How do these two geographic representations reflect the opposing qualities in her grandparents?

2. Roy's account catches the archetypal appeal of the experience of pioneers and homesteaders. How does she manage to add an almost epic dimension to her family history?

3. What cultural features do the Québécois transport with them to Manitoba? How do they recreate "what they have left behind?" What legacy do they pass from one generation to the next?

4. What is the "irremediable . . . difficulty of being French-Canadian in Manitoba or elsewhere"?

5. From what parts of the world did inhabitants of Saint-Boniface come? In what way has Roy's early exposure to a culturally diversified environment changed her attitude to such words as "homeland," "foreigner," or "stranger"?

6. Roy often compares her experiences to literature—her own and others'. How do these literary allusions associate Saint-Boniface with the scattered cultures of the world?

7. What other places in the world does Roy compare with her "childhood love," the Manitoba landscape? How does Bird's Hill typify the primordial quality of Manitoba? What does the horizon symbolize for Roy?

Bharati Mukherjee

Bharati Mukherjee was born in Calcutta, India, in 1940. She has studied in Montreal and now lives in Iowa City, in the United States, with her husband Clark Blaise (one of whose stories can be found in Unit Four). She has published two novels, The Tiger's Daughter *(1972) and* Wife *(1975); two collections of short stories,* Darkness *(1985) and* The Middleman and Other Stories *(1988); and, with Blaise, two volumes of non-fiction,* Days and Nights in Calcutta *(1977) and* The Sorrow and the Terror: The Haunting Legacy of the Air India Disaster *(1987).*

Intimations

My life, I now realize, falls into three disproportionate parts. Till the age of eight I lived in the typical joint family, indistinguishable from my twenty cousins, indistinguishable, in fact, from an eternity of Bengali Brahmin girls. From eight till twenty-one we lived as a single family, enjoying for a time wealth and confidence. And since twenty-one I have lived in the West. Each phase required a repudiation of all previous avatars; an almost total rebirth.

Prior to this year-long stay in India, I had seen myself as other saw me in Montreal, a brown woman in a white society, different, perhaps even special, but definately not a part of the majority. I receive, occasionally, crazy letters from women students at McGill accusing me of being "mysterious," "cold," "hard to get to know," and the letter writers find this mysteriousness offensive. I am bothered by these letters, especially by the aggressive desire of students to "know" me. I explain it as a form of racism. The unfamiliar is frightening; therefore I have been converted into a "mystery." I can be invested with powers and intentions I do not possess.

In a life of many cultural moves, I had clung to my uniqueness as the source of confidence and stablity. But in India I am not unique, not even extraordinary. During the year, I began to see how typical my life had actually been, and given the limited options of a woman from my class and from my city, how predictably I had acted in each crisis. And I see how, even in the West, I have acted predictably. My writing is a satellite of my marriage and profession; I have chosen, or fallen into, the role of bourgeois writer, limited to a month of writing in a year, or one year of writing for every seven of teaching. The American alternative, *Mama Doesn't Live Here Anymore*, remains unthinkable.

Only the first eight years were spent in Ballygunge, in a flat crowded with relatives, and friends of relatives who needed a place for sleeping and eating while they went to college in the city, and hangers-on, whose connection with my family I did not have the curiosity to determine. I was not happy in that joint family. Perhaps some of my mother's frustration seeped down to me. People say that I look very much like her. Certainly I am, like her, a collector of resentments and insults, and am stubbornly unforgiving. I suspect that in those early years, it was more important to me to retain my position as my father's favorite daughter (he has written a poem about me, titled "Treasure of the Heart") than it was to imitate, in proper fashion, the personality of my mother. But I am sure that from her I learned only to feel relief when we could close the door of our bedroom and shut out the forty-odd relatives.

It was a small room after the corners and sides had been filled with the bulky firniture of my mother's dowry. Two beds—one was the bridal four-poster, the other was a simple *chowki*—were pushed together for the five of us, two adults and three daughters. I recall that because of shortage of space, my father used to store an untidy pile of scientific books and journals on the bridal bed itself and that we children had to be careful not to kick the books in our sleep. In a household where no one kept his opinions to himself, this room was our shrine of privacy.

Sometimes there were invasions by cousins or younger uncles. Once my mother, sisters, and I returned from our customary afternoon visit to Southern Avenue to find that my eldest sister's British-made painting book and paintbox, which she had won as a school prize, had been vandalized. Another time, the lock of the wooden cabinet in which my mother kept her jewelry and small cash savings had been forced open, and some money was missing. I was taught to think of these episodes as an assault on our desire to maintain slight separateness within the context of the joint family, rather than expressions of mischief by relatives.

Within the small perimeters of that room, it became clear to me that if I wished to remain sane I should not permit myself to squander my affections on too many people or possessions. With overpopulation of that sort, possessions and relationships could at best be fragile. I learned also to be always on my guard, and because I was small, shy, and the second youngest in the family, to stay in the background, out of danger's reach. During communal meals, when all the children sat on the floor of the corridor surrounding an inner courtyard, I did not demand the prized items—eyes and brain of carp—because I knew that if I set myself no goals, there could be no defeat. I had, I felt, and intimate knowledge and horror of madness. There was a mad aunt in the family, and during a long stay that she, her husband and four children inflicted on us (because there was some natural disaster, probably a flood, in the part of East Bengal where they lived), I had seen her chase her husband with an ugly piece of firewood. I cannot recall if I had actually seen her hit her husband on the head with the firewood before I was hustled off by my mother into the privacy of our bedroom, or if the aunt had only been standing, weapon poised, about to hit him. I did not think of the uncle, whom I disliked, as the victim. But I thought of madness as grotesque, and shameful, for I had been told by my parents that if too many people came to know about the craziness in the family, it would be hard to marry us daughters off. I resolved immediately to fight in myself the slightest signs of insanity.

I was released from all that terrifying communal bonding by a single decisive act of my father's, shortly after my eighth birthday. Because of certain circumstances in the pharmaceutical company that he and his partner, a Jewish immigrant from the Middle East, had set up, circumstances that he did not explain to his daughters though he probably did to his wife, he brought home colorful brochures one day of an all-first-class boat on the Anchor Line, and within weeks we left the joint family, and Calcutta, in order to make a new start in London.

We were happy in Britain and Switzerland where my father worked on his research projects, and where we went to school and were remarkable for our good manners as well as our intelligence, and where my mother took night courses in flan baking and basket weaving. But my parents did not make for themselves a new life. The partner followed my father to London, for a while installed us in a company flat at the corner of Curzon and Half Moon streets, vacationed with us in Montreux, and was, I suspect, persuasive about his plan for the pharmaceutical company in Calcutta. And so, after almost three years abroad, we returned to Calcutta, not quite where we had left off, and certainly not to Ballygunge and the joint family.

That period abroad is the only time I have felt perfectly bilingual. It was a time of forgetting Bengali and acquiring English until I reached an absolute equilibrium. But that gradual erosion of the vernacular also contained an erosion of ideas I had taken for granted. It was the first time I was forced to see myself not reflected in people around me, to see myself as the curiosity that I must have seemed to the majority—a skinny brown child, in stiff school uniform and scarred knees, who could not do cartwheels. The sense that I had had of myself in Ballygunge, of being somehow superior to my cousins, was less destructive than this new sense of being a minority on account of my color. I felt I was a shadow person because I was not white. We were an extraordinarily close-knit family, but since I had been brought up to please, I felt I could not burden my parents with these anxieties. It would have made them unhappy, and I could not bear to do that. I could count only on myself for devising strategies of survival in London, our adopted city. I became less passive than I had been among relatives and friends in Ballygunge: I began to regard facility in English as my chief weapon for bending my own personality and for making friends among the British.

In sacrificing a language, we sacrifice our roots. On returning to Calcutta, we found that our image of ourselves had changed radically. It was not at all a question of money. *Jethoo*, my father's oldest brother, owned rice mills and lumber mills in Assam, but he would not be comfortable outside Ballygunge. But to us, the thought of re-entry into that closed, conspiratorial joint-family world was unbearable. So we sublet a flat in fashionable Chowringhee, the break from the joint family being facilitated by a quarrel between my mother and another relative. We changed schools too, from the Anglicized Bengali school on the edge of Ballygunge to the most renowned girls' school in Middleton Row, a school where, it was rumored, Indian children had for a long time been denied admission. And in our new school, the foreign nuns treasured us for our faintly British accents which had survived the long homeward journey.

From our return to Calcutta after the false start in Europe until the middle of 1959, we lived in the compound of the pharmaceutical factory which my father and his partner had set up in Cossipore, on the outskirts of the city. My parents now refer to that phase of our lives as "the good days." I thought of the compound walls as the boundaries of a small constitutional monarchy in which my sisters and I were princesses. We presided at factory functions, such as sports events, religious celebrations, variety shows for workers, and looked on that as our necessary duty.

The pharmaceutical company had bought out the garden house and estate of a refined Bengali gentleman after whom a street had been named in happier times, but whose fortunes had now declined completely. His botanical gardens—full of imported rarities—were cut down and cleared, the snakes scared away, the pools filled, the immense Victorian house converted into a production plant for capsules, syrups, and pills. I saw the conversion as a triumph of the new order over the old, and felt no remorse. Nothing would return me to the drabness and tedium of Ballygunge.

For me, being part of the new order meant walking under arches of bougainvillaea with my sisters and a golden spaniel we had acquired immediately after moving in, while neighbors gawked at us from their rooftops. We were inviolable and inaccessible within our walled compound. To our neighbors, we were objects of envy, and probably freaks. There were screening devices to protect us: gates, guards, internal telephones. We were at home to only those we wished to see; others could be sent away from the front gate. Having been deprived of privacy in early childhood, I carried my privacy to an extreme; I did not even learn the names of the streets around the factory.

Every day we shuttled between this fortressed factory compound and the school compound in an old gray Rover, once owned by a British executive who had decided independent India was no longer the best place for him. Our privacy was guaranteed on these trips by a bodyguard who looked like Oliver Hardy. The ride from Cossipore to Middleton Row and back is very long, and the cityscape unusually unpleasant. I learned very quickly, therefore, to look out of the window and see nothing. During those rides, my sisters and I talked endlessly about the kinds of men we wanted to marry, and memorized passages from Shakespeare or from the Gospels for the morning's quizzes. My older sister, who is four years older than I and currently is a childless, working wife in Detroit, was the most romantic among us. She said that she did not care about money, but that the groom would have to have excellent table manners and be perfect at ballroom dancing. My younger sister and I knew what she meant by that: She wanted a "Westernized" groom who had studied abroad, and who could command for her a "Westernized" life-style in a pretty flat on Park Street or Chowringhee. Like us, she did not want to lapse into the self-contained vernacular world of Ballygunge.

During this period we were once visited by some female relatives of Mr. D. Gupta, former owner of the garden house that we had converted into a factory. My father aranged for the visiting women to be taken on a guided tour of the plant and then to have tea with us. It was intended by my father to be, and therefore was, an amiable occasion. We sat on the Georgian and Jacobean imported furniture that my parents had extravagantly selected from auction houses on Park and Free School streets, and we listened to the niece of the former owner describe how pretty the chute of colored syrups and capsules had been. It was amiable because the old and new orders had treated each other couteously. Confrontations would come later, and my sisters and I would one day not long after that tea, on our return from school, have to walk through a crowd of striking employees who had blocked our car and who carried placards we were too well-brought-up to read. This tea among the women of the former and current owners was an acknowledgement of another sort: the vulnerability of individual heroes or families in the face of larger designs. Having a street named after oneself was no permanent guarantee of dignity or survival.

That is why, on this 1973 trip back to India, when a newer order has replaced us within the walls of that same compound, I chose not to visit the factory, nor to walk once more under the flowering arches where my sisters and I dreamed about our "Westernized" grooms and "Westernized" life-styles. On this latest trip, I was told that the neighborhood around the factory had become dangerous, and that during the recent Naxalite agitations, workers had been beaten up and that a chemist I recalled well had been knifed in the head a block and a half from the factory gates.

For me the walled factory compound, the guards at the gate office, the bodyguard inside our Rover, the neighbors staring at us from the rooftops, are now emblems. We were typical of a class in the city. There was surely nothing ignoble in our desire to better our condition. In a city that threatens to overwhelm the individual who is passive, there was nothing immoral in self-protection. But we had refused to merge with the city; we had cleared the snakes and shrubberies; we had preoccupied ouselves with single layers of existence— getting ahead, marrying well—and we had ignored the visionary whole. And now, years later, those of us who left and settled in far-off cities like Detroit and Montreal, as well as those of my school friends who stayed and who now live in flats on Park Street or own houses on Rawdon Street, are paying for having scared the snakes and gutted the shrubberies.

My parents moved out of Calcutta long ago. But the impulse to erect compound walls, to isolate and exclude, appears all around me in Calcutta in 1973. My friends live in mansions that the British had built in less volatile times to separate themselves from the bazaars and settlements of the natives. These mansions, even now, are fronted by spacious lawns, gravel driveways, enormous gates with wooden watch posts, and one or more uniformed guards. The guards are not always alert on the job. One rainy July morning as we swung into the driveway of the home of a managing director of a former British firm, we caught the guard urinating against the compound wall.

The cry these days is more for protection than for privacy, and this cry is more shrill than I have ever heard. The women who live in these mansions and whom I meet very regularly for lunch and charity work, study groups and cocktails on the lawn, tell me about the "troubled times" when everything was "topsy-turvy" because the Naxalite gangs took over. With manicured nails jabbing the air, they describe to me how the Naxals scared the guards, sometimes invaded the compounds, threw gravel against the bathroom windows, tore up the lawns by playing soccer. One elegant young woman wearing a delicate pink nylon sari and Japanese pearls (it is hard for me to adjust to this new image, for I had last seen her as a pig-tailed schoolgirl with socks that kept sliding into her shoes) wants me to know that "the troubled times" are not over yet, that what I am seeing is simply a lull before the coming class confrontation. I do not disbelieve her; it is a common conviction all over Calcutta. A woman I had met a week before is now hiding out with her family in the house of another friend in order to avoid what she calls "mischievous acts"—acid bombs? sieges? kidnappings?—by striking employees in her husband's firm.

Here in Calcutta, my friends go out into the city in groups, beautiful women in well-waxed cars, and they pack pills for lepers for Mother Teresa. They supervise sewing workshops for destitute women, even clean streets in front of photographers and journalists in order to save and beautify Calcutta. "CALCUTTA IS FOREVER" announces a billboard on Ballygunge Circular Road, paid for by the Beautification Committee. "KEEP YOUR CITY CLEAN AND DESCENT" mocks a less-professional effort near Free School Street. They have made their commitment to this decayed and turbulent city. In exchange, they want protection for themselves and their children.

To protect oneself is to be sensible, I am told. It is a city-wide obsession. Even the Scholar's Guest House where Clark and I stay and which is run by the Ramakrishna Mission, a religious Hindu order, is set apart from the street by high walls. Outside the walls are the accoutrements of Ballygunge life: hawkers, beggars, loiterers, squatters, sleepers, cows and pariahs, cars, taxis, buses, mini-buses, cycles, rickshaws, bullock carts, and heedless pedestrians. Inside there is greenery, flowers, a studied calm. The *durwan* at the gate sits on a stool and separates the two worlds. He has a register and pencil to keep track of all visitors. But still the brutal world invades the mission, and brass gas rings disappear from the secondary kitchen, and dissatisfied employees demonstrate on the edge of the judiciously kept lawn.

We do not seem to have heeded the message of the anonymous sculptor from Deoghar. We have confined ourselves to single obsessions. We have protected our territory, and posted uniformed servants to keep out the confusions of the city. We have forgotten that the guard himself is in an ambiguous position and that his loyalties may be fragile. In a city like this, an elderly relative tells me as he chews an endless mouthful of betel nuts, *You just can't be too careful. If you relax for a second, someone will snatch your gold necklace or your purse.* He advises me against certain doctors—there have been stories about nearly any doctor that I mention. *That man is too black, That man is unmarried, Never go to a doctor alone.* But to be so wise, I would like to answer, is also to distort.

Out there beyond our walled vision is a reality that disgusts and confounds the intellect, and a populace that is too illiterate, too hungry, too brutish, to be gently manipulated. Or, just as confounding, a populace too gentle to be brutishly commanded. The odds against survival for an individual are enormous, and rewards, at best, are uncertain.

Merge, commands the Deoghar sculptor, *there are no insides and outsides, no serpents, no gods.*

But at this time, we who consider ourselves more intelligent, more politically conscious, more sophisticated, more charming than the ancient stoneworker, know that to merge, to throw in our lot with Calcutta, is also to invite self-destruction. If we take down the compound walls and remove the ceremonial guard who relieves himself in the street and picks his nose while opening the gates to visitors, what will happen to our children?

It is at this point that I separate myself from the chorus of my old school in Calcutta. My sons will return to Montreal at the end of the year, study very little, ski a little more, watch Saturday cartoons on TV, and inherit the promises of the New World.

For the children of my friends who have chosen to remain in Calcutta, the range of future possibilities is infinitely more frightening. Though we never discuss it, we all know that this city will yield its rewards only to the strongest, the smartest, or the most powerful.

TOPICS FOR EXPLORATION

1. How does Bharati Mukherjee see herself in Montreal? What does she explain as "a form of racism"? What are the effects upon her self-esteem of being a minority child in England? What "strategies of survival" does she use?

2. What is Mukherjee's childhood "shrine of privacy"? Why is it necessary? What are its advantages? How does it compare with the family compound they inhabit after their return from England?

3. What are the "old and new orders" in the India of Mukherjee's childhood? How are they vulnerable to change?

4. Mukherjee's memoir vividly records certain post-colonial tensions in independent India. How does she evaluate her experience of growing up between the dreams of "Westernized" lifestyles and the "vernacular" world of poverty and overpopulation? What is the price she suggests she is paying for her family's desire to better their conditions?

5. What situation does Mukherjee encounter in India after years of absence? How, in 1973, do the privileged "isolate and exclude" others for their own self-protection? Who will be the opponents in the "coming class confrontation"?

6. There are two worlds in India. What does the world "outside" the gates consist of? How do the people "inside" respond?

7. Why can't Mukherjee identify with the local executives' wives and share their obsessive concern with security?

C.D. Minni

C.D. Minni was born in 1942, in Bagnole del Trigno, Italy, and grew up in Vancouver. A writer, critic, and editor, in 1985 he published a collection of short stories based on the theme of immigrant adaptation to the new country, titled Other Selves. *He also edited an anthology of Italian-Canadian Writing,* Ricordi: Things Remembered *(1989) and co-edited* Writers in Transition: The Proceedings of the 1st National Conference of Italian-Canadian Writers, *which appeared in 1990. C.D. Minni died in 1989. The story included here is reprinted from* Ricordi: Things Remembered.

Changes

By three o'clock, Friday, Vitale had talked to his last client. He locked up his office early.

"Goodbye, Miss Elliott."

The girl looked up from her typewriter, squinting through large, rimless glasses. "Goodbye, Mr. Di Pietro, and *bon voyage.*"

Outside, it was snowing again, goose-feather flakes. Traffic moved sluggishly, but he had plenty of time to catch his flight. He had packed the night before. The two suitcases waited, like orphans, in the middle of the front room.

The house was empty, silent. He almost expected to find another note by the telephone. *No point in discussing the reasons again. Jennifer.*

He phoned Tina, his sister, to check up on his kids; they were out in the snow. She must have held the receiver up to the window, for he could hear their yelling.

Not to worry, she said.

He dialed for a taxi.

The Calgary airport was bustling, but Toronto that evening was bedlam: baggage, children, tearful relatives. There were embraces as the CP Air flight was announced. Half the city's Italians, it seemed, were going back for Christmas.

By three o'clock, Monday, he was on the train to Rome. He had decided not to spend time in Milan after all; the city had few memories for him. He'd been there scarcely one year, the ink still wet on his lawyer's diploma, before Canada and family ties had lured him away.

It was drizzling and cold when he came out of Rome's Stazione Termini. Several Fiat cabs were parked under the street lamps. The driver of one solicited him as he stood in the rain.

"*Tassi?*"

Vitale ran for it. The driver threw his suitcases into the back and flipped the meter lever to "on." He was a paunchy man, his hat askew, a cigarette hanging from his lips.

He was taking a roundabout way to their destination to increase his fare, but Vitale didn't mind the tour; that was what he had come for. *A rest, the doctor said. A change of scene.*

They passed the Coliseum and headed towards the Sant' Angelo bridge. Vitale looked up at the archangel over the circular fortress that had once been Hadrian's tomb and was almost relieved to see it there, in the moonlight.

By the time they reached Piazza Trilussa, in the Trastevere district, the rain had stopped. The driver let him off the fountain. Vitale looked for other remembered landmarks. The statue of the poet Trilussa still leaned on one elbow. Beyond the square was a walled sidewalk along the river, where he saw the student walking; above, the skyline was crowded with bell-towers and cupolas.

He picked up his suitcases and walked the rest of the way to the *pensione.* Twenty-three years, but he recognized the owner; he was the same small, bald man, his remaining hair gone completely white.

Vitale asked for Room II, if possible.

The owner—Vitale remembered his name now, Carlo, and the wife's, Luisa—seemed surprised. *Certo*, certainly. It was the off season. He could have almost any room.

Vitale signed the register with his gold-plated fountain pen, asked after the Signora Luisa.

The owner peered over his glasses at this *americano* in a white cowboy hat. Vitale explained that he had roomed there as a student at the university before emigrating.

"Ah, *sì.*" The old man rummaged in the attic of his memory. "I seem to remember. . . ." But he didn't, probably had him confused with someone else. Luisa, he said, was dead these three years.

He took a key and came around to help him with his suitcases.

Entering his room was a step into the past. The same venetian blinds, flowered wallpaper, cracked mirror. The same Modigliani print on the wall. He opened the bathroom door, and yes, found the student, soaking in the tub. The hot water relaxed him; it made him drowsy.

The knock on the door startled him—"Is anyone home?" And a woman's teasing laugh, clear and high-pitched. Luisa.

Dead, these three years.

"*Scusa*," the owner apologized, looking at the towel around his midriff, the wet footprints on the ceramic floor. "*Scusa*, your receipt."

Vitale dressed again and went out, looking for the small *trattoria*, where the student always ate, settling his account at the end of the month. *O Cavalluccio*. A white stallion pranced above the big, spiked, double doors, three steps down from the pavement.

The proprietor put a flask of white Frascati in front of the law student, and took his order: *il piatto caldo*, the cheap, hot pasta dish. He was only a postman's son and had to be careful with his meagre allowance.

Where was the guitar player who used to go from table to table, singing ballads for the price of a meal?

He wore a red sash from which hung a tin cup. Strangers were his best patrons, and he had already spotted the blond girl with the young law student. It was the first time he had brought her there.

"*La biondina?*"

She gave her name, Elvira, and Vitale threw a coin into the cup.

The man strummed his guitar, found the right key, and burst into a somewhat bawdy song about a girl named Elvira and unrequited love. Vitale had heard it before. The lyric was always the same; only the name of the girl changed. It never failed to produce smiles around the room, however.

That night he dreamed. He was riding in a horse cab with a girl—Elvira? Jennifer? He couldn't be sure in the dark. She was angry. They had been fighting again.

"Is it something I've done?"

"No," she whispered, face averted. She did not want entanglements. "Try to understand."

He didn't.

Instead he took the job in Milan to forget, and then in Calgary, farther away.

Vitale lay awake a long time, thinking of Jennifer—all the times she had called him too conservative, a fascist. *I've changed, he pleaded. Changed? she screamed with a laugh he didn't like. Only on the outside!* He had tried to understand, really had, couldn't, then would lose his temper.

He was out early, sipped a coffee in a bar, then took a taxi to the university. It was deserted for the holiday. He walked most of the morning around the campus—a thin student with a green scarf, shoulders hunched against the cold.

He paused under the leafless trees, blew on his hands, then turned for the law library. It was open. He went in, and found Elvira at a table, surrounded by books.

He sat and just watched her: elbow poised on the table, the head inclined long-lashed to the page, left hand absently sweeping back her blond hair, which she wore long, over her thin, blue shoulder. She loved the law with a passion, she said.

One of the sacrifices of the move to Canada had been his career. He'd gone into real estate, made money, but. . . . He shrugged. He'd done it for his family, of course. Jennifer had never denied that he had been good to her. *But only with things!*

In the end, however, she had asked just for her car, her potted plants, and some money. He thought of her living with that man, that yuppie.

The librarian was staring at him. He became conscious, suddenly, of his attire—cowboy hat and high-heeled boots. Could she help him? No, no, he was just leaving.

He was due in Villa on Thursday.

He took the first afternoon bus and settled to read a newspaper. Across the aisle from him sat two fat women bundled in overcoats. One had a raffia bag on her lap, a veritable cornucopia from which she drew mandarins, biscuits, and candy to bribe her two small boys on the seat behind.

The bus climbed higher into the Apennines, the driver leaning on his horn at every hairpin curve. It stopped to let a flock of sheep cross the road. The landscape was bleak—grey fields, leafless trees, smoke from farm chimneys. Grey, stone villages, and in the distance the snow-covered peaks of La Majella (height: 2797 metres, the mountains here as rugged as the Alps).

He must have dozed over his newspaper, for the bus was over the watershed now and was descending. It began to rain, flat drops on his windshield. He waited for the first glimpse of Villa, like a black and white postcard: stone towers and ramparts against a metallic sky.

The bus continued to descend towards the river, and then climb again, through olive groves, over a stone bridge, past the tiny cemetery with its twin pines, and into town.

It was already dusk. Street lights blinked on. The station was by the post office. A small crowd had collected to meet the bus. As he waited for his suitcases, hat under one arm, someone asked if he was the telephone inspector; they were waiting for the telephone inspector.

In the post office, a blind man sold lottery tickets from a booth. Men in galoshes smoked or argued politics. A radio blared.

His father was at one of the wickets, a tall, spare man in a faded, brown jacket, white mustache, and eye-shield. They embraced. It attracted attention. He was recognized, surrounded. Someone pumped his arm. Luigino, Villa's soccer champion. Did he know. . . ? Of course, they'd gone to school together. They laughed that he'd been mistaken for the inspector. In that *cappellaccio*, hat!

They walked home together, he and his father, and he described his trip and gave news of the rest of the family. (All of them well. They send their love.) His heels caught on the cobblestones, and he stumbled. His father offered to take one of the suitcases. No, no, he'd manage.

His mother came from the kitchen when she heard voices, drying her hands on her apron, face flushed from the stove. She was baking. An aroma of vanilla and liqueurs filled the house. She hugged him. How was he? Was he hungry? She sliced a thick piece of *panettone* while his father fetched up a decanter of wine, fresh from the keg. As if he were a boy again, home from school.

They knew he would be coming alone and did not ask about Jennifer and the children. He was grateful for that, as he sat there happily watching his mother bake.

After dinner, the house filled with relatives and neighbours. His father brought up another decanter of wine, and they drank, gossiped, and joked into the night.

He was tired when he went up to bed, but content. He fell, for once, into a dreamless sleep.

He woke to the cries of a vendor in the street below. Morning. He threw back the heavy quilt and went to the window. Through the slats in the wooden *persiane*, shutters, he could see the street. A fierce wind rattled a tin can along the cobbles, and a few old women in thick black shawls were on the way to church, shoulders bent against the cold.

He showered, then plugged in his electric razor. His eyes met, like strangers, in the mirror as he combed his still luxuriant shock of black hair. In school, he'd been called Vitalis. Later, when he told Jennifer, she thought the story was funny.

Dressed, he went down for breakfast, pausing on the stairs when he heard voices.

Esaurimento nervoso, nervous breakdown. *Ma il perche?* The reason? And his mother's angry retort: what kind of woman leaves her children?

They changed the subject when he entered. His mother had prepared hot bread rolls with orange jam and tiny cups of espresso.

It was snowing on the mountains all around them, his father said, and rubbed his hands together.

After breakfast he went out. He wandered towards the heights above the town, the oldest part. He passed through the gate, all that remained of Villa's walls, and entered the Middle Ages. The tortuous streets narrowed and climbed in steps, but cobbles had been replaced like missing teeth, and the centuries sand-blasted from the rough, stone exteriors of houses. He looked up, at new wooden shutters and iron balcony railings painted green or red or blue.

He no longer knew these streets, and they did not seem to know him.

What was he looking for?

Half-way up, he reached a small square with an arcade of shops. They were closed, but he saw in windows clocks and boots, souvenirs and postcards, fruit and cheeses. At the far end, where a street descended from the castle, was Café Villa. An ancient vine grew from the dirt floor and, in summer, spread a canopy of cool foliage over the outdoor tables. The student sat in the shade, sipped iced coffee and watched village girls fetching water from the public fountain at the centre of the square, copper urns expertly balanced on their heads, gay-coloured dresses blown by the wind.

The café was closed. He stopped only a minute there, sitting at a table on the concrete floor below a plastic covering. He looked at the fountain. The water was turned off.

Above him was the ruin of the castle. He was surprised to find an iron picket fence around it and surprised that the gate was secured with a padlock. A sign advertised the times of tours. From April to October only.

But, as in a dream, he was through the gate—a 12-year-old running through the courtyard in games of tag or war, or searching for secret passageways and hidden treasure.

Somehow these memories had become more precious as he grew older.

Changed? Only on the outside!

He turned right, following a street from the parapet of which he could look down on the roofs of the town, smoke billowing from chimneys, and farther along found the shortcut, a steep flight of stairs carved into the granite of the mountain, which brought him down.

His mother had prepared a heavy afternoon meal, and the three of them lingered at the table companionably until his father glanced at his wrist-watch and stood up; he was due at the post office.

Vitale fetched his overcoat too. He strolled down to the main piazza. The afternoon was already dark enough for the street lights to blink on. In a gift shop, he bought a Pulcinella toy, the clown dressed in a green court jester's outfit and mounted on wheels so that it clapped a pair of cymbals as it moved. For his son. And a doll dressed in a traditional peasant costume for his daughter. He had these wrapped and packed to mail but, crossing the square to the post office, changed his mind; he'd bring them back himself.

It began to snow.

On the way home, the student heard the *zampognari* even before he turned the corner. He came upon a scene like an antique greeting card: the pipers playing carols in the yellow puddle of a street lamp, snow falling. A crowd had gathered around them, and people stood in doorways and at windows.

Each Christmas the pipers left their herds on the lonely, windy hills of Abruzzi and came down into the streets of towns. They were dressed in traditional shepherd costumes—short black capes, vests and leggings of sheepskin, and rawhide shoes with thongs around the legs and curled-up, pointed toes. They travelled in twos. One played a *zampogna* or kind of primitive bagpipe; the other a reed instrument like an oboe.

They held out their hats for tips, picked up coins thrown from windows, then moved on, followed by children.

His parents' house was full of family and friends. His mother had set up a side-table with *hors d'oeuvres*, bread, rolls, and wine bottles. Carols played from the stereo. He played the polite host, opening bottles, pouring wine, making himself useful with a towel on his shoulder. He was given small parcels to take back to mutual friends in Calgary. The slowness of the mails, you know. But why was he leaving so soon? In three days? He had just arrived.

Tired of explaining the reasons—his kids, his office, the difficulty of getting flight reservations around New Year—he was glad to escape to midnight mass. It was, he reflected, his first time in a church in years. At some point he had stopped going—too busy buying, selling, winning.

When he returned, the house was silent. In the kitchen embers still glowed in the fireplace. Bottles were empty, dishes stacked. He tiptoed upstairs. Yes, the game had been different. He had set out to win by the new rules, and he had won big. He lay in bed and counted his assets: two hotels, one paid for; a ski lodge; 453 acres of land; a half-share in a movie theatre; a pub; and a fine restaurant.

He was back in Calgary for the New Year. The invitation to the party was among the pile of letters, cards, and flyers inside his door.

He went.

The guests were his usual friends—accountants, agents, builders. The conversation ranged from business to sports to politics. It got louder as the liquor flowed.

A woman said something about Reagan's Star Wars programme. He recognized her vaguely, replied politely.

He was passed another Scotch.

How was his holiday?

It seemed, now, as if he had never been away.

"Five minutes," someone called.

"Four!"

Andy Williams was on TV from Times Square.

They began the countdown.

Outside, horns and banging pots.

She kissed him. There was liquor on her breath.

He left early.

Drunk, he made his way back to his car. He had parked on the road at the side of the house, and across the driveway the subdivision ended in empty fields and, beyond, the prairie.

He stumbled on the snowbank.

Something moved ahead of him. A small animal? He raised himself on one knee and reached out to grab it, but it moved away. He chased it, but whenever he got close, it jumped away from him.

He flailed his arms, stumbled, fell in the knee-deep snow.

He was unsure what it was, as it escaped across the prairie, or even if it had been there at all.

TOPICS FOR EXPLORATION

1. What is the purpose of Vitale's visit to Rome at Christmas? What does he hope to find after 23 years of absence?

2. Traversing space for Vitale also means traversing time. Several times he sees "the student" (his former self) in familiar settings. What does the use of time shifts contribute to our understanding of the protagonist?

3. Vitale's journey to his hometown, Villa, is a journey to the past; his parents treat him "as if he were a boy again, home from school." What present problem intrudes upon the nostalgic happiness?

4. Compare the modest home of his parents to the "assets" he has accumulated in Canada. Think as well of the contrast between

the Christmas Party in his parents' home and the New Year's party in Calgary. Vitale "had set out to win by the new rules, and he had won big." What has he lost?

5. The whole narrative is based on Vitale's point of view, yet we learn very little about his emotions. Evaluate his relationships with others—his wife Jennifer, his children, and his parents. What are the possible reasons for his mid-life crisis? Does he really undergo any "changes" in the course of the story?

6. How effectively does the final scene bring out a sense of emptiness and futility in Vitale's life? What does the "small animal" he sees on the snowdrift represent? Is there any attempt to solicit the reader's sympathy for Vitale?

Kristjana Gunnars

Kristjana Gunnars was born in Iceland; she teaches at Okanagan College. From 1989 to 1990, she was writer-in-residence at the University of Alberta in Edmonton. She has published several volumes of poetry. Her first collection of short stories, The Axe's Edge, *came out in 1983; her first novel,* The Prowler, *was published in 1989.*

Mass and a Dance

The ground crackled when she walked. It was frozen snow, not ice. Minus thirty-three. Smoke from all the chimneys filled the town of St. Norbert. The air was white. The sky was white. The sun was white. She had learned to like this place from constant use. The corner store, the little post office, the crude statue of Mother Mary across from the Catholic church. All the dedications in this tiny French Manitoba village to the battles of the Metis. History invaded by Winnipeg suburban developments: brand new single storey homes erected in droves over the summer. When the wind blew, whole walls of the unfinished constructions collapsed. It was not a pretty village but it had that edge of ruined history about it. An old village cradled by a bend in the Red River that insinuated: you may have lost but you're still here.

That's the whole point right there, she thought as she walked along the suburban street on her way home. To be *still here*. The thought stung her. She was placid enough yet maddened by a sense of inescapable grief: a grief like the atmosphere of the earth. Something so fundamental she knew she could not come out of it. A grief that comes to people when they know something that had life is irretrievably lost. It was not a person: it was a history. Is this how the native Indians feel, she asked herself, when they have lost territories to encroaching civilization? Or people who have lived in tiny railroad hamlets out on the prairie, when the railroad cuts service to them and the hamlet dies for lack of use? Do they feel like this?

She came to Canada because it was somehow no longer feasible to live in the town she came from. It was territory now laid waste. Since she could not stay there, she decided to quit the country altogether, refusing the daily reminders of loss: the cold rain, the northern wind, the midnight sun. She grew up in the Vestfjords of Iceland, a desolate region far in the north-west of a desolate island in the North Atlantic. Life was never easy there but, when modernity invaded the island, new urban centres sucked people out of little hard-won villages and emptied them. She thought of modern civilization as a trashcan into which everything gets thrown.

What is still called Sléttuhreppur, "Plains District," was once the northernmost inhabited region of the Vestfirdings. In nineteen forty nearly five hundred people lived there. Ten years later it was a ghost fjord. The sun rose over Hornbjarg mountain, illuminated the water in the bay, and no one saw. The church in Stadur was a ghost church. Small, wooden, white, four windows on each side and a tiny bell tower facing the sea. No one rang the bell. The Vestfirdings were gone.

She looked around her in the St. Norbert winter. It was so silent, she seemed to have lost her hearing. All she could see were bi-level houses squarely facing the sun. The crunch of her footsteps seemed to come from inside a tunnel. A bird screeched. When she looked, there were only barren branches and the bird was gone.

She still did not know why all the Vestfirdings deserted Sléttuhreppur. Most of them went to the capital city in the south. Some went abroad: Greece, America, Spain. When they were gone, thinking they had improved their lot in life, they discovered they missed their northern Arctic environment. Services were cut so there was little hope of re-establishing a community. Instead they staged a *reunion*. The previous summer. She came along with all the others. There would be a dance and a mass in the church. There was a chartered coach to Stadur in Adalvík and on the way they picked up Jakob, the priest from Isafjördur, to bless them at the end of the weekend.

The last time she was in the little church was at her confirmation. There were several very young angels draped in white from head to toe. They made a holy procession down the aisle, their black psalters clutched to their chests. They knelt before the altar, hands folded, looking up. The priest placed his hand on her head. Her elaborate hairdo went down. She forgot about the blessing: her only thought was that the priest did not understand the matter of hairdos.

On Advent Sunday they always lit the candles and then they were angels holding candles. Now Hákon the composer brought a choir to sing for them. They sang a choral work he had composed: *The Gravestone Suite*. Hákon had gone to the graveyard and written chants of the inscriptions on all the tombstones. When he conducted his choir, he stood on a table so they could all see him. After Advent mass there was coffee in the community room. Hákon again got up on the table. He stood among the coffee cups and the choir sang a chant for the food.

For the reunion mass in Stadur, all the old relics were brought back and put in their former places. There must have been eighty people. No one could bring the organ on the coach, so Reynir the organist played the accordion instead. In the evening, Reynir the organist played his accordion for the dance.

At the dance many women wore the national costume. Black skirts, black vests, white aprons and black caps with long tassels. By midnight they were all tipsy. By two in the morning these black swans all had to taken to the coach. They were smiling obliviously. She left the dance at seven next morning. Dawn had long passed. The coach driver was waiting. Passengers were impatient. Some were draped over their seats, others curled into balls. An elderly Sléttuhreppur farmer had imprisoned her in conversation in the community kitchen on the topic of education. Everyone thought they were doing something else. When she came out and realized the communal mistake, she was too embarrassed to correct it.

She crawled into her coach seat and went to sleep. The elderly farmer's son, whom she had a crush on as a teenager, had disappeared. He had long, dark blond locks and an athletic body. She used to frequent soccer matches just to look at his body. She went to men's swimming competitions for the same reason. He had not shown up for the reunion: they said he was somewhere in South Africa. After gymnasium in the city he went to college in America where he met an education student from South Africa, married her and went into the South African bush while she did research on the education of native tribes.

Meanwhile she found herself in the dead of winter in the Canadian prairie. Manitoba. Stalled cars with their hoods up littered the highway in this cold. They stood abandoned, collecting a coating of ice. Schoolchildren rolled like balls out of the yellow schoolbus and trundled home, packed in snowsuits, scarves and moonboots. They had trouble walking straight bundled up as they were.

She wondered whether her *bitterness*, that must be the word, over the *dissolution* of her birth community had something to do with the young farmer's son who had seemed to her the ideal of northern beauty. That they were *forced* to part company: forced to be the captives of *distance*?

There were moments when she appreciated the scattered clouds as they conspired with the frost to block out the sun. Every cloud over the prairie had a south-eastern lining, in gold. On days like this, all seemed to her discontinuity. No single train of thought remained steady. Stories were broken into flakes: of memory, of history, of ice. Sometimes it snowed. She had never been able to relate a story from beginning to end in this place. Not even to herself. Yet life seemed to fall into patterns: obvious patterns, sometimes so startling she wondered who designed them.

The place she now lived in seemed to her a place without beginning. Without end. Without rise and fall. It was something else. She did not understand the ground she walked on, the air she breathed. Was this what they meant by the word *alien*? Alien: a person who does not understand the place she is in. Snow was falling on the St. Norbert streets. Snow is a story that breaks off from heaven and falls down at random, she thought. Snow longs to be whole again. It longs for its origins and cannot remember when it was together. It has fallen on an unknown country. If there is a little wind, the snowflakes dance during their descent.

She recalled walking home from school, across the mountain. She was fifteen. There was a blizzard. Thick snowflakes filled the entire air, rushing from one mountain to another. She could not see. The road was no longer visible. She did not know whether she was walking into the desert tundra, forever to perish, or home. There was fear. Wanderers had been lost in these mountains since time immemorial. Their bones had been found in the spring, lying among the sheep. Suddenly headlights appeared behind her out of the snow. A car door opened and she was pulled in. Saved. She looked to see who her rescuer was: it was Fleming, the Danish fellow. Once again, bad luck.

The church in Stadur was cold the afternoon mass was again sung in Adalvík, after twenty years of standing empty. The day everyone arrived together in a coach for a reunion. People wore skin-lined jackets in the pews because there was no heat. A small kerosene camp heater stood on the floor in front of the altar. Jakob the priest prayed from behind the small communion railing. On the walls, the oil lamps tried to compete with the sun that never sets in the Arctic.

The wooden walls of the church had become attuned to silence. They echoed the silence of desertion. People could tell there were ghosts: and the curious sensation that *they themselves were the ghosts come to haunt the place where they once lived*. Reynir sat in the first pew, against the wall by the window. He had his accordion in his lap. People sang from little black hymnals with woollen sweaters draped around their shoulders. On the lectern a frayed guestbook lay open and blank. No names were written in the pages for twenty years. The stairs up to the choir loft creaked.

She sat in the second pew on the eastern side. Next to her sat a man who had become her lover when they met in Greece: the writer who had settled in Athens. Hákon the choir director looked back over his shoulder. He was a friend of the writer's other lover, the violinist who had moved to Austria. There would be talk of triangles and quadrangles. She played dumb, for lack of a better idea. Halldór the red cheeked schoolteacher sat behind them. He had taught them geometry when they were children.

She liked the way the snow fell in Canada. It did not come straight down but meandered in the air for a long time before settling. She watched one snowflake float in spirals, then up a bit, to the left, up again, down. This could go on for ten minutes before the flake joined the others on the white bundle below. At night scrapers in St. Norbert amused themselves by scraping the streets. They scraped down to the pavement and left mountains of packed snow cakes in front of the houses for the inhabitants to rid aside in the morning with useless tin shovels that folded under the impact of hard ice.

At the Adalvík reunion, after the mass people hung about outside the church. Wild angelica flowers reached up to their knees. A number of people were standing looking at the water in the bay. One by one the riplets gently licked the stones on the shore. Around the church, old gravestones leaned with the weather into the mountains.

The first time a rumour came that she would go to America occurred when she was eight. She told her friend Sjöfn. They had a game of exchanging all their clothes, including underwear and socks. Sjöfn pulled her into the street and pushed her in front of all passers-by crying out: *she's going to America.* Sjöfn pushed her into Jói's grocery store and announced: *she's going to America.* The customers turned and looked at her. She was standing in her white jacket, embarrassed, playing imbecile for lack of a better idea. Many years later she got a letter from Sjöfn, posted in Ohio. She looked for a return address but found none. Evidently Sjöfn herself had gone to America.

It was said that Reynir the organist was a lucky piece of driftwood on the beach of the Vestfirdings. He was handy with several musical instruments and could, at one go, play for both the mass and the dance. The dance that night was held in the schoolhouse at Saebólsgrundir. Reynir pumped the accordion without pause all night. Like the midnight sun, he would not set.

They got their dance partners by marching halves of verses. The man who had the last two lines to go with her first two lines turned out to be Halldór the schoolteacher. Once again, bad luck. He was fond of the Polka and they danced the Polka for an hour. Then she sat down in the hall among the smiling black swans: the elderly women in their national costumes, seldom worn any more. She felt out of place in her white dress, purchased in Toronto.

She went outside during a lull in the dancing. A number of Adalvíkings had gathered on the grass tufts where the mountains began to rise a short distance away. It was the middle of the night but still as bright as day. A feeling of dusk pervaded the silent air. Reynir had taken his accordion out and Baldur, the priest's grandson, had brought a guitar. They were singing. Their mismatched voices sounded clearly in the stillness and echoed across the valley below.

It was a little chilly. She made her way across the tufts slowly, savouring the fresh air. Adalvík: where she liked to be alone among the singing of the ghosts. They did not see her. Many were busy covering up the left ear, the one facing the wind.

Those were the tufts of grass she ran across one day when she was eleven, very fast. She had the sudden notion she wanted to be on the next Olympic swimming team and started training the same day. She ran the six kilometers from home to the sulphuric swimming pool and swam for two hours without stopping, racing from one end to the other. Then she ran the six kilometers back. She did not get as far as the Olympic team: she got sick instead and lay in bed all next day. That was her at eleven.

How the snow in St. Norbert was floundering, undecided whether to go back up or come down for good. The flakes blew in swirls and patterns in the gentle gusts of wind. Oblivious to the cold, they swam about in the air.

The streetkeepers came and broke the peaceful quiet of this French-Canadian town. Clamorous machines lumbered up and down the road with scathing noise. Those monsters left mountains of brown snow cakes behind them. Children in moonboots who came out of yellow schoolbuses could barely climb over the ice mountains to get home. They wiggled up on their tummies, thick arms and legs clinging to protruding ice shelves. She stood on the other side watching. In case one of these little balls missed its footing. But they all made it over, like diligent winter ants.

As she stood the singing of the Adalvíkings swirled in her head. It was still the middle of the night and the Adalvíkings were singing under the open sky. The sun, which had been sleeping on top of Hornbjarg mountain for a while, began to rise. Suddenly the eastern sky, the sea, the stones, the hair of the singers became drenched in gold. It was for this moment everyone had come back, she thought. *For this moment when the sun begins to ascend and the earth becomes a stone garden drenched in gold.*

The Adalvíkings were singing fatherland songs. They started up on something from *Hákon's Graveyard Suite.*

Sun sinks in the sea
Showers the mountain peaks with gold
Swans fly full of song
South toward the warm wind
Blossoms gently sway
Smile in tender oblivion
When this evening peace descends
The most beautiful of all is Adalvík.

That was from the tombstone of Einar the poet.

TOPICS FOR EXPLORATION

1. Those who left Iceland for warmer climates "discovered they missed their northern Arctic environment." Why? How did they deal with the need to re-establish the abandoned community in the Vestfjords?

2. What are the main character's feelings about modern civilization and its impact on small communities? Why is she bitter that the dissolution of her birth community in Iceland has forced people to part company? Who are the "captives of distance"?

3. What special meaning is attached to the place of one's origin? Why doesn't the main character "understand the ground she walked on" in Manitoba? How does she define alienation? What concrete symbol does she find to express her sense of alienation?

4. What is the significance of the mass and dance in the empty Icelandic church abandoned twenty years before? What do they tell us about the way memory functions in the minds of those who attend? How does the story's fragmented structure reinforce the theme of discontinuity?

5. The story has two settings: the town of St. Norbert in Manitoba and the woman's hometown in Iceland. What are her dominant impressions of these two places? What mood is created by the description of these places?

6. What is the significance of "going to America"? What effect has being in "America" (that is, in St. Norbert, Manitoba) had on Gunnar's protagonist?

7. Gunnar's story reads like an elegy, that is, a mournful tribute to her lost country. How does the ending contribute to that effect?

Dionne Brand

Dionne Brand, born in 1953 in the Caribbean, has lived in Canada for over twenty years. She has studied English and philosophy at the University of Toronto, and has also done postgraduate work in the field of education. From 1990 to 1991, she was writer-in-residence at the University of Toronto. She has published six books of poetry, the most recent of which is No Language Is Neutral *(1990). She co-authored* Rivers Have Sources Trees Have Roots—Speaking of Racism, *and edited* No Burden to Carry: Narratives of Black Working Women in Ontario 1920s to 1950s. *Our selection comes from her first collection of short stories,* Sans Souci and Other Stories *(1988).*

St. Mary's Estate

St. Mary's Estate was further on. Past the two rum and grocery shops, past Miss Dot's, past the savannah, past Miss Jeanne's parlour—paradise plums in large bottle jars. Then a piece of bush. Then St. Mary's.

Most of it is still there I notice, as the jeep misses the St. Mary's entrance and drives a little way on to Schoener's Road, the dried-out river bed in which duennes used to play all night, or so the story goes. I tell my sister this is where the spirits of dead unchristened children used to live, duennes, calling children in the evening to come and play. Our friend, driving the jeep, asks if I want to write down the correct spelling of the name of the road. I tell him it does not matter. I have known that road and that dry river bed for thirty-four years with a mixture of fear and curiosity, though I've only ever stood this distance from it. The story might still be true. The trees and the stones have been preserved in my head with their sign of silence, yellowness and eerie emptiness. When we look toward the river bed, the three of us, we look as if we're watching something or someone. Not emigration, not schooling, not brightly lit cities have managed to remove the shapes of duennes in the river bed by Schoener's Road. Not even Schoener, probably a Dutch privateer, with all his greed and wickedness, debauchery and woman-burning, not even he could remove the shapes of duennes in this river bed, by putting his strange name to it. It is still quiet, waiting for dusk for duennes to come out calling to play whoop.

The jeep turns around. The two male passengers of a truck leaving Schoener's Road stare at us as the vehicles negotiate passage. Then the jeep turns right into the gravelled entrance of St. Mary's. There is still a white sign board on a post, now leaning into the ditch at the entrance, now woodlice eaten. The letters are worn, but officious and distant; painted a long time ago, they survive like the post. A vigilant reminder and a current record of ownership and property. At this point you can see the sea straight ahead, in back of the house where I was born. This entrance gives you a sense of coming home, the same sense I've always had upon seeing it. The eyes light on the completeness of the scene it guards. There are two long barracks, one on each side of the gravel road. In front of the right barracks there is a great tamarind tree, now a little shrivelled but still protecting the place underneath, dirt swept clean, where people, mostly men, used to gather and play cards, drink rum and talk. Of the two barracks this one still houses people. All that is left of the other are the nine to twelve thick white pillars which it stood on once and the triangular moving roof under which copra is put to dry. Bush has overgrown the floors and the walls have been removed, perhaps from fire, or perhaps from ancient wear, sunk into the ground. That's where Cousin Johnny used to live. He was deaf and did not speak. He made beautiful soups and mouth-watering coconut bakes and saltfish. The whole compound would smell sweetly of his bakes on a Saturday evening.

The jeep eases along for another fifty yards; my eyes rest on the place, old and familiar like watching the past, feeling comfortable and awestruck at once. Then too, resentful and sad. A boy atop the left barracks stops raking the copra to watch us. No one else is about. The air is very still, yet breathing, a breeze, quiet and fresh, blowing from the sea. The sea here too, is still. A country beach, a beach for scavenging children, thinking women, fishermen. The sea is not rough or fantastic, nothing more stupendous than an ordinary beauty, ever rolling, ever present. The kind of sea to raise your eyes to from labour. This must have been the look toward the sea that slaves saw as they pulled oxen, cut and shelled coconut, dug provisions from the black soil on the north side of the road. This must have been a look of envy.

There used to be a big well near the tamarind tree. Plait Hair and Tamasine used to live over there, in the third place of the back row of the right barracks. She had seventeen children; he plaited his hair, refusing to cut it. He worked hard, always in silence, his cheeks sucked in. Tamasine was a big red woman, as big as Plait Hair was slight and wiry. The walls separating each quarter of the barracks from the other did not go up to the roof, so everyone could hear what was going on in the other. Each quarter was one room. People used to wonder how Plait Hair and Tamasine had seventeen children, since it was difficult to be private. Maybe they'd wait till everyone was asleep, including their children. Even now, I find myself speculating.

There used to be a lagoon on the left, past the left barracks, off into the bush . . .

The gravel road slows the jeep, as it edges toward the small wood house where I was born. Set in the centre to observe the two barracks, its back is toward the sea, its legs standing halfway in sand, halfway in dirt. It's the same house, thirty-four years later. The jeep moves even more slowly because of the silence of the place. As it passes the barracks there is no sign or sound of life except the boy on the copra house gone back to his work.

"It's the same house," I say; and to my sister, "Do you remember it?"

"No," she says, "I wasn't born yet."

Two men come out of the house as the jeep pulls to a stop near the front steps. I recognize one of them as the man who took over after my grandfather was fired as overseer of St. Mary's Estate. An emotion like resentfulness rises in me. It is only a memory of my grandfather, in his sixties; after twenty years, he was to be let go and, from what I could pick up at three or four years old, this new man was the cause. The new man, the overseer, is now an old man. His youth had been thrown in my grandfather's face and his ability to husband cocoa. I'm amused that something learned such a long time ago can still call upon the same emotion and have it come, fresh and sharp like this. I put on a smile and walk up the steps, my hand outstretched, saying, "Hi, I was born in this house. I just want to look around." He cracks a smile in his stern face, as recognition passes over his eyes and confirms, "Oh you is a Jordann," saying my last name as it has always sounded—like the name of a tribe, a set of characteristics ranging criminal to saint, axe women to shango priestess, obeah woman. My grandfather's life put the sound into my last name. My grandmother's life put the silence after it. Jordann, like a bearing, like a drum.

My grandfather had children and outside women and outside children. He could read and he could write, which made him valuable. He was the overseer for twenty years at St. Mary's. He had an ornate hand and was such a strict parent that all his children wrote exactly like him. He rode two horses, Noble and Buddha. Noble was white and Buddha was black. Noble for show and

Buddha for faithfulness. He drank rum at the first shop and the second shop, drinking and gambling out the pittance that he made tending St. Mary's for a white man. He wrote letters and took care of everyone else's business. He gave advice freely, he took only advice which could ruin him. He always walked straight up and stiff, the length of his six feet. Until the last years which he spent here, he lived a life of grace, depending on what was not possible, riches, and escaping payment of the debts he incurred dreaming about it. Grace only lasts forever with God, not with white men, so papa was disposed of when age was tired of holding out on his face and when he was unable to create a vision of acres of rich purple cocoa trees for the estate owner. Then everything caught up with him, mostly his debts and we all went to live in town, except he.

He first went to live in a house up a steep cliff which he could not mount because of his sore foot and then settled into a shack near the road where he sold ground provisions, callaloo bush, okra and pepper. Finally he got a job as an agricultural officer, walking miles into the bush to talk to farmers. The last entries in his diary, the ones before he died, only said, optimistically, "can't go to work, sick today."

The dirt around the house is mixed with sand and broken bits of shells. During neep tide, the sea comes in as far as the front yard, lashing against the pillow tree trunks which the house stands atop. We get the okay from the new man and head toward the beach. My sister and our friend follow me as I tell them,

"There used to be a lagoon over there; once it caught on fire. This is where we used to put garbage. See the shells are better here. This is a place for a kid to hunt shells and stones. This is where I used to play."

They follow me, looking at me a little strangely or perhaps trying to see what I see. My childhood—hunting up and down the beach for shells, stones, bits of bottles, snails, things washed up by the sea, lagan; the blue red transparent shine of 'garlent'; seeing how far you could walk; pointing to Point Galeoto; swearing we could see Venezuela; digging into crab holes.

"This is a place for a kid," I say. "Every Good Friday, a tree would appear in the lagoon. Mama said it was a sign of Christ."

We move away toward the lagoon. It is the dry season. The lagoon is still there despite the years of garbage throwing. Then we walk back toward the house, along the beach, and I point toward a river's mouth rippling into the sea, two hundred yards to the right of the wooden house.

"It was hard to cross there, the tide was too strong sometimes."

And then I see it, and I feel something in me hesitate to walk toward that side. It is a huge green house, hidden from the wood house by trees but visible on the sea side. It used to be yellow, it seems to me; but I could be mistaken. Rust, brought on by the spray of the sea, swells on its sides. It is empty and it is closed. I turn to my sister,

"That fucking house. Do you see that fucking house!"

My sister looks at me, understanding. I cannot bring myself to move toward the house or that part of the beach.

"That goddamned house. It's still there."

I feel such anger and yet, still, my feet do not move toward it. So angry, I feel nauseous. "Fuckers!" I yell, but the wind and the sound of the sea lift the word and balloon it into a feeble scream. The uselessness of that sound stops me and I explain to our friend who looks perturbed, "That's where they used to live."

In fact, they didn't live there. They came with their children every July. Then we had to be reverential toward them; we could not walk to that side, especially if they were on the beach. They left at the end of August and then, we kids would rush, with my mama who went to clean the house, to see what they had left. Even what they had left we could not touch, thank God, because mama wouldn't allow us. Mostly, we children envied the real doll's head that lay here or there and the shoes discarded. Their children always wore shoes and socks. We ran about like mad things in bare feet and washed-out clothing.

For two months, this wasn't our place. For two months papa bowed and scraped, visibly. And mama warned us grandchildren not to misbehave or embarrass the family.

And still after this long, the imperative of habit and station causes my legs to stand where they are. Do not go near the house. It is the white people's house. It is their place and we are 'niggers'. Reaching back into me, thirty-four years, a command, visceral, fresh as the first day it was given. It still had the power of starvation, whip and . . . blood. I turn and we walk back toward the wood house and the stern-faced new man.

This is where I was born. This the white people's house. This is the overseer's shack. Those are the estate workers' barracks. This is where I was born. That is the white people's house this is the overseer's shack those are the slave barracks. That is the slave owner's house this is the overseer's shack those are the slave barracks.

This estate has been here for hundreds of years. Papa was the overseer. It is the end of the twentieth century and the slave barracks are still standing; one, with people living in it; the other refusing to drop into the earth, even though it has no walls. Tamasine and Plait Hair used to live in the barracks. Uncle Johnny used to live in the one that's half gone. The walls were thin cardboard and the daily gazette was used as wallpaper.

To sleep beneath the raw stench of copra, night after night, for two hundred years is not easy; to hear tired breathing, breathless fucking, children screaming, for five hundred years is not easy. And the big house was always empty, except for two months of the year. The slave barracks whose layers of gazette paper stretched for hundreds of years, was packed with Black humanity, rolling over and over and over without end, and still. This is where I was born. This is how I know struggle, know it like a landscaper. An artist could not have drawn it better.

"Fuckers. Fuckers. Fuckers." I hear myself muttering, under my breath. "Fu-u-ck, they're still there."

I go up the steps of the wood house, asking the new man,

"Sir, who owns this place?"

"Hackens and them, nah," he replies, leaning his now gray head as if I should know or remember, "They always own it."

"Always?"

"Yes." The new man nods as he speaks, "You know, them is big shot."

I must not have remembered about the house; because now, I can see it from the front of the wood house, too. Twenty of us were born in the two rooms of this wood house, while that one stood empty, locked. I'm looking to where I had instinctively not looked before. The house is still there, green, the windows locked, rust bleeding from its joints.

We climb into the jeep saying good-bye to the new man.

Always.

The jeep hobbles up the gravel road past the quiet barracks. The boy on the roof doesn't stop his work this time to look at us. We get to the sign post. "St. Mary's Estate," it says once again, judiciously. Red-eyed, I have a picture of the green house in my head, ablaze.

TOPICS FOR EXPLORATION

1. What do the "duennes" represent for the narrator? How are they symbolically related to her present situation?

2. What gives the narrator "a sense of coming home"? What part does memory play in enlivening the scenes of her visit? Find concrete sensory images or descriptive details that recapture the past for her. Is there any indication early in the story that her attitude to this place has changed since she was a child?

3. The narrator is a member of the Jordann clan. What is the significance of this identification with family, and how does a sense of belonging affect the narrator?

4. As overseer of St. Mary's Estate for twenty years, the narrator's grandfather lived a "life of grace." What happened to him later?

5. What are the main symbols of colonial exploitation that inflame the narrator's anger? What is the significance of the big house inhabited two months a year and the slave barracks inhabited "for hundreds of years"? What does it mean for "Black humanity"?

6. How is the narrator's rage signalled by different stylistic devices used by Dionne Brand, such as repetitions and parallel structure? Why does she use the pronoun *they* rather than the name of the estate owners?

7. How does this visit to the place where she was born affect the narrator? Has anything changed since her childhood? What is the meaning of the repetition of the word *always* at the end of the story?

SUGGESTIONS FOR FURTHER STUDY

1. Compare Alootook Ipellie's response to the imposition of white culture with the reactions of Basil H. Johnston in Unit Four and Loretta Jobin in Unit Five. How are their responses to their personal experiences different? How does each differ in tone from the others?

2. Compare the French Manitoba village described in Kristjana Gunnars's story with Saint-Boniface in Gabrielle Roy's memoir. What do they have in common? What can account for the difference in perspective between these two pieces?

3. Compare Bharati Mukherjee's privileged childhood in the factory compound with the lifestyle of Jashmed in Rohinton Mistry's story in Unit One. What characteristics do they have in common? How do they view the West? What are their views of modern India?

4. Compare the observations Mukherjee makes during her 1973 trip to India with those made by Ramgoolam in Neil Bissoondath's "Insecurity" in Unit Five. In what ways is the post-colonial political turbulence similar in both places? How it it different?

5. Compare "homecoming" in any two of Minni, Gunnars, and Brand. How has life in Canada altered the perspective of these authors when visiting their homelands? How have the different experiences that emigration has provided changed their characters? What feelings are raised by renewed contact with their places of origin?

6. What is it about the conditions that haven't changed in their homelands that enrages Dionne Brand and Bharati Mukherjee? Mukherjee speaks through a personal narrative; Brand creates a fictional narrator for her story. Whose voice do you find more convincing? Why?

DOUBLE BIND: CANADIAN IDENTITY

INTRODUCTION

The "double bind" of Canadian identity consists of several paradoxes. For many Canadians, especially those with recent experience
as immigrants or a strong ethnic identity, belonging to two cultures
can be either enriching or bewildering. While this double bind
could apply to any author in this collection, in this unit we are
concentrating on some specific problems. First, double-bind identity can mean feeling at home in both cultures, compartmentalizing
life into two discrete, complementary modes which can easily be

reconciled. But the double bind might also mean being more at home in one culture than the other. If their cultural identity is more ethnic than Canadian, people may feel stigmatized and isolated from their community; if it is more Canadian than ethnic, they might be estranged from their roots, unable to understand their cultural origins, and perhaps regretful of the loss. Finally, the double bind could mean alienation from both cultures. If people cannot identify with either culture (or both cultures) strongly—or are rejected by both as "inadequate"—they may feel lost in the ambiguous no man's land between the two cultures.

Tony German examines the double standard of Canada's colonial relationship with the "mother country," Great Britain. He recalls his discovery that English "superiority" is more imaginary than real. German shows how he needed to overcome the ethnocentric British domination in his own life before he could assert his pride of identity as a Canadian.

Pablo Urbanyi, in his humorous letter-essay "Rebirth," satirizes the difficulties of a new Canadian coming to terms with blatant North American materialism. Addressing his Argentinian friend, he has trouble explaining the quandaries of those who have too much to one who has too little.

The double bind for Native populations presents special difficulties. In her essay, Jenine Dumont describes her long struggle with her identity as a Métis. Unaware of her "part-Indian" heritage as a child, she was startled into awareness by discrimination at age eight, but tried to "be white" until she was thirty. Caught between two cultures, Dumont, who is a descendant of Gabriel Dumont of the Northwest Rebellion, could not freely acknowledge her ancestry— to herself and others—until she was a grown woman and could turn a hidden feeling of insecurity into an outward pride in her heritage. Drew Hayden Taylor, however, has turned this ambiguous situation between two worlds to comic effect. As a blue-eyed Ojibway, he is called "pretty like a white boy" and is often mistaken for a white by Native people. He savours, in his essay, the paradox of being a minority in his own minority group. Often he has to argue for his Indian status. Caught between two cultures that judge identity by appearance, Taylor feels suspicious of the reaction he provokes in both cultures. In a final gesture of asserting his identity, he humorously secedes from both Ojibway and Caucasian races to become an "Occasion"—a one-of-a-kind.

Canadian members of visible minorities often have difficulties with their ancestral culture, if they have become "too Canadian." David Suzuki confronts this problem in his visit to Japan, where he observes how the expectations based on his physical similarity to the population are broken by his Western language, tastes, and attitudes. Although there is a "biological connection," he is a *gaijin* (foreigner), who is unfamiliar with traditional Japanese values. Unlike his immigrant grandparents whose motives are a mystery to him, he is caught between two cultures as a Canadian in Japan and a third-generation Japanese in Canada. Sun-Kyung Yi also experiences the "immigrant's split personality" as a Korean Canadian. Unable to sustain a difficult double role—at home, at school, and at work—she finds herself drifting away from the very conservative cultural expectations she encounters in a Korean company in Toronto, from which she is demoted for being "not Korean enough." Although a member of both cultures, she feels that she is "accepted fully by neither."

Austin Clarke, too, is at some distance from both his cultures: Canadian and Barbadian. In "A Stranger in a Strange Land," he describes his alienation in Canada where he has no roots, no childhood landscapes, no deep friendships, and his expatriation from Barbados where he has not lived for 30 years. The double bind of being neither one nor the other affects the "psychical well-being" of immigrants who, Clarke believes, are greeted in Canada by "institutions" rather than human faces.

This "cultural schizophrenia," for some Canadians, persists as long as discrimination and stereotyping force us into definitions we refuse to identify with. On the other hand, feeling at home in both, one, or neither of the cultures seems to be a condition of living in Canada that we cannot—indeed, may not wish to—resolve.

Life is Theatre
or
O to Be Italian in Toronto Drinking Cappuccino on Bloor Street at Bersani & Carlevale's

Back then you couldn't have imagined yourself
openly savouring a cappuccino,
you were too ashamed that your dinners
were in a language you couldn't share
with your friends: their pot roasts,
their turnips, their recipes for Kraft
dinners you glimpsed in TV commercials—
the mysteries of macaroni with marshmallows.
You needed an illustrated dictionary
to translate your meals,
looking to the glossy pages of vegetables
melanzane became eggplant,
African, with the dark sensuality of liver.
But for them even eggplants were exotic or unknown,
their purple skins from outer space.

Through the glass oven door
you would watch it bubbling in pyrex,
layered with tomato sauce and cheese,
melanzane alla parmigiana,
the other-worldliness viewed as if
through a microscope
like photosynthesis in a leaf.

Educated in a largely Jewish highschool
you were Catholic.
Among doctors' daughters,
the child of a fruit vendor.
You became known as Miraculous Mary,
announced with jokes about virgin mothers.

You were as popular as pork on Passover.

You discovered insomnia, migraine headaches,
menstruation, that betrayal of the self
to the species. You discovered despair.
Only children and the middle aged are consolable.
You were afraid of that millionth part difference
in yourself which might just be character.
What you had was rare
and seemed to weigh you down
as if it were made of plutonium.
What you wanted was to be like everybody else.
What you wanted was to be liked.
You were in love with that Polish boy
with yellow hair everybody thought
looked like Paul Newman.
All the girls wanted to marry him.
There was not much hope
for a fat girl with good grades.

But tonight you are sitting in an Italian café
with a man you dated a few times,
fucked, then passed into the less doubtful
relationship of coffee and conversation.

He insists he remembers you as vividly
as Joan Crawford upstaging Garbo in *Grand Hotel*.
You're so melodramatic, he said.
*Marriage to you would be like
living in an Italian opera!*

Being in love with someone who doesn't love you
is like being nominated for an Oscar and losing,
a truly great performance gone to waste.
Still you balanced your espresso expertly
throughout a heated speech,
and then left without drinking it.
For you Italians, after all, he shouted after you,
life is theatre.

—*Mary di Michele*

Mary di Michele was born in Italy. She has written six books of poems. Her most recent volume is Luminous Emergencies *(1990). She is now working on a novel.*

Tony German

Tony German is an established author, a screenwriter, an experienced naval officer, staff officer, and businessman. He writes historical fiction for young adults, including such titles as Tom Penny *(1977),* River Race *(1979),* Tom Penny and the Grand Canal *(1982), and* A Breed Apart *(1985). He is the author of a major history of the Canadian navy,* The Sea Is At Our Gates *(1990). His articles and stories have been published in different Canadian magazines, newspapers, and professional journals; he has also done work for film and radio.*

Bloody Brits

One of those scenes that sticks in the young mind and stays forever happened to me in 1935 when I was eleven years old. My mother, who'd been born English, had taken my sister and me "home" with her for a visit and we were at a Sunday tea-party in a country garden. It was quite lovely I remember, the garden. Bright with sunshine and summer flowers and a table laden with goodies. But I was trapped. Trapped by a tall and stately lady clad in tweeds. She talked at me, looking down from under the brim of her bee's-wing hat, the kind that English ladies wore pulled firmly down with both hands to cover the ears. Her head was tilted somewhat back. Her eyes were hooded and they sighted down her high-bridged nose, lining me up for a broadside.

"Ahhh", she said to me, with that commanding confidence I came to know. "Ahhh," she said, "Tony." Pause. "Tell me. Do you have the whaah-less. Yet. In Canadah."

The Wireless. Yet. In Canada. That's what she said. Actually said. And she'd said it, not asked it. And here we were staying near by with my aunt and uncle in their charming (my mother insisted) cottage in Kent just half an hour by train from Charing Cross, and their whaah-less was run by one of those big glass-jar batteries full of water and electrodes because their charming cottage had no electricity, no heat, and to get to the toilet and the bath you had to go out a side door into the perishing cold. And it wasn't a summer cottage either. They lived there year round. Did we have the bloody wireless. Yet.

I don't really remember what I said back. Perhaps I muttered something about my prized crystal set or listening to Jack Benny en famille on Sunday nights. But I do remember looking up at those flared nostrils and hooded eyes with the eyebrows arched above. And I remember what I felt. Condescension. I was being patronized. I may not have known the actual words but deep down I got the feeling. I was a colonial, jolly good little chap and all, but everything stems from the Mother Country and in due course Canadah would get the wireless and other such wonders as Imperial majesty might bestow. QED.

It was the single jarring event of that whole summer and it cracked the romantic picture of this England I had crossed an ocean to view wide-eyed. It was a fabulous time for wide-eyed viewing. Nineteen thirty-five was the Silver Jubilee of King George V and I saw it all. The gilded coach, the bearded King and bejewelled Queen, the magnificent escort of Household Cavalry, plumes and sabres and helmets and breastplates all agleam. Hooves clattering. Massed bands playing and banners curling and lines of scarlet Guardsmen stretching ad infinitum down the Mall.

Then Spithead, the fabled roadstead where the might of the Royal Navy lay in awesome, ordered ranks. Their guns thundered salutes, sailors raised their caps and hurrahed precisely thrice as the Royal Yacht steamed grandly by. Britannia ruled as she must have done forever. In Portsmouth, to confirm it, mighty *Victory* lay with her hundred guns, soaring masts, and the snowy quarterdeck where Nelson fell to the villainous French in deathless glory. And the gun-decks below, painted entirely red—oh, joy—for when the scuppers ran with blood.

The Tower of London had real Beefeaters and the Crown Jewels, and at night a breath-taking floodlit pageant in the moat. It peaked, I remember well, when a splendidly costumed Sir Walter Raleigh laid his head, unflinching, on the block. With an astonishing piece of stagecraft it was lopped clean off. Madame Tussaud's wax warriors and heroes, kings and queens in splendid cavalcade, surely lived, and lived right here. And where else, as attested by her Chamber of Horrors, could murders be so gorgeously bizarre? Everywhere we went it seemed there were castles, courtyards, battlements, hill forts, and standing stones. At a cousin's ancient country house was a gigantic oak, quite hollow—we climbed inside—which had hidden King Charles from the Roundheads just as sure as local legend said.

I was stirred by all these deep-rooted wonders that were England. Truly excited. But I was not at all surprised. Seeing it all merely confirmed that the world and its story and all things wise and wondrous did indeed spring from this sceptred isle. I knew because I'd been reading about it all my life.

I'd Changed the Guard at Buckingham Palace with Christopher Robin, thrilled to Scrooge's ghosts. I'd braved shot and shell as a powder-monkey under Drake's flag. G.A. Henty sent me off too, *With Clive in India, With Wolfe at Quebec*. I'd even been *In the Thick of the Fray at Zeebrugge* in a Royal Navy motor torpedo-boat kindness of a somewhat lesser talent called Percy F. Westerman. And Stevenson of course. I *was* Jim Hawkins.

Now, this summer, I was face to face with it all. Even the strange Englishisms like Red Indians and ice hockey (as though there were some other kinds) didn't faze me. Nor did the fact that kiddies bathed, not swam, off stony beaches while fathers dozed in rented deck-chairs wearing braces, trousers rolled and handkerchiefs on heads, knotted at the corners. Those were excusable foibles and quite familiar in advance because we got the English comic papers at home. There was *The Tiger* for young fry, which I'd devoured, and, for my advanced age, *The Champion*. It cost a dime I think and it was full of stories similar to those in the luscious fat maroon-coloured annual called *Chums* that was under the Christmas tree each year.

The tales were all of British boys, nigh-fatally encumbered with instincts of decency and fair play, prevailing over all. The enemy might be the bully of the Lower Fifth, an avaricious mine-owning Portugee, a boastful American athlete. There were treacherous Spaniards, inscrutable Chinese, whole armies of Arab fanatics riding the Sahara, and even crafty, sneaking half-breeds in ever-frozen Canada. ('Breeds, they called 'em, and they used knives against our hero's fists.)

Oh, yes. Britain had become my world. This subtle and pervasive and surely calculated Imperial campaign to recapture with the written word each succeeding generation that occupied those red bits on the map had me in thrall. It was not just cricket and the law that cemented the Empire. It was books, books, books. And I was part of it. Until my tweedy lady. It was right then, when I think back, that I knew I wasn't English. That there was a difference that went much further than accent. Canada was mine. This England was theirs. And this happy breed looked at us colonials down its snoot. Tweedy lady's condescension, like the Parsee's cake crumbs under the rhinoceros's hide, has been under mine ever since.

British was not just best, mind. It was only. Viz. another tweedy lady some years after. A different one, gentler this time, dowdy and seemingly quite sweet. She was with her husband, who had "Brigadier General, British Army, Retired" stamped on his forehead, and they were on board the same boat in which my wife and I were enjoying a sightseeing cruise of the Amsterdam canals. Among the points of interest was the waterside view of a fine old house-cum-warehouse with curlicued gables. In it was born, as our young tour-conductor told us fluently in four languages, the great Admiral Maarten Tromp. Tromp did bloody battle with Admiral Robert Blake off Dover and Dungeness, he said, and swept the English Channel with the legendary broom at his masthead. Then, in the last few minutes under way, the young man circulated engagingly for his tips.

He paused at the two elderly Brits.

"Ah, yes," said she, speaking loudly as to any foreigner. "We did enjoy the tour. Your English is really excellent and we were so impressed with your knowledge of English history. Oh. . . ." She stopped. On her face astonishment, revelation. The scales of ages fell away and her last look was of betrayal. "Oh," she said softly, and her shoulders sagged, "I suppose it was Dutch history too."

The droves of Brits who came to Canada post-Second World War from demi-paradise, wracked and riven as it was, brought talents and skills and thwarted energy. And the same old blithe conviction of superiority inherited from generations long past. As one who had been devastated by arch-Brit as a tad, I watched with baleful interest, awaiting, I suppose, some ultimate revenge. But as I watched, these newcomers permeated. I think that's the word. For they did not follow form. They did not come to the immigration sheds, awed and grateful, as entering a promised land. Commonwealth was a palatable synonym for British. Their slice of Canada was only proper due. And they utterly ignored a basic thrust of the new Canada by failing to cluster in an ethnic group.

They eschewed the staunch title "New Canadian". Nowhere did they form tight-knit communities with street signs in Olde English. No restaurants boasting English cooking did they start, thank heaven, though other-ethnic entrepreneurs did hire them for their accents to dish up cock-a-leekie and steak-and-kidney pie and bring their quaint hygienic practices to ersatz pubs. No distinctive dress came with them from across the sea. We'd seen kilts before, though Scots were never really Brits, and the bespoke-tailored set with bowler hat and brolly and county tweeds largely stayed behind.

They brought no new high days with them, no special New Year's to get sozzled on. The Irish had long since staked out St. Patrick's Day and the Glorious Twelfth and booze-worship generally. St. George's Day didn't take. Guy Fawkes could have sparked an annual spectacle had the wretched man succeeded in blowing up the

House of Commons, but failure doesn't wash. Victoria Day stood as a reminder of past glory. Acting smartly, some properly organized Brits could have clinched it for themselves with, say, a maypole in front of each town and city hall. But the-24th-of-May-is-the-Queen's-Birthday was lost to Canadian compromise, adjusted so everyone could have a long week-end in spring. That made it a fair cop for any ethnic group. A pity, because Multiculturalism today would certainly pick up the tab for the maypoles.

Canadian tax money is available from one source or another to any group claiming cohesion by some exotic cultural glue. But while Ukrainian, Greek, and Caribbean groups flourish, I am told the Canada Council has had not a single application for morris-dancing. Gaelic and Celtic chairs abound at universities. Fair enough. But Gaels and Celts are tribes really and not your basic Brit. There are good things galore in the mystic net of Canadian cultural programs. Why don't Brits group up and climb aboard?

Their trouble is they just cannot come to grips with the simple fact that, once outside their blessed plot, they are in fact an ethnic group. Nowhere in the world—much less in a country where one of the languages approximates their own—can they consider themselves to be dubbed, nay, branded thus. Who? Us? Ethnic? No bloody fear. But you are, you know. You bloody are.

By and large Canadians are a welcoming and tolerant lot. There are some ugly exceptions in our history. Mackenzie King's denial of the Jews and forty years of foot-dragging over the West Coast Japanese come to mind. We are rather too easily put upon, a pushover for invasion by pseudo-refugees on the one hand, and on the other too bureaucratically clogged to welcome the genuine with expedience and compassion. Sure, there are red-neck pockets here, and the odd cry that the taxi business is cornered by Haitians, that Italians are railroading nomination meetings, and that the Hong Kong Chinese will own us all. But where else—wisely or not—are people given money to nurture their own ways, to live in the country but stay in their own cultural stream? Strange it is. But in the main, ethnic groups are not resented by Canadians. With the prime exception, dear friends, of you, you bloody Brits.

Because you are the only group that has ever dominated Canadians, first the French, then the English-speaking, on their own turf. Dominance spawns resentment, and Canadians still rest uneasy with the memory of yours. Earlier waves, don't forget, swept the Plains of Abraham and behaved as though they'd settled things. They fashioned the Château Clique and the Family Compact in their own image and brought world-class experience to diddling the Indians. More Brits came as professional soldiers to stop the unspeakable Yankees, to hang about the garrison mess and make off with the richest girls in town. They came as skilled administrators to establish peace, order and maternal government; as trained servants, too, who knew their place and ruled these less cultivated households cunningly from below stairs.

Courtiers even, direct from London, brought vice-regal splendour to Rideau Hall in boozy backwoods Ottawa. They excluded lumber barons and back-benchers and spittoons from their ken. Generations of social aspirants were withered by their savoir-faire. Then came the stream of idly well-bred remittance men to set social levels through dressing for dinner and to establish cultural leadership with what D.H. Lawrence described as "The Oxford Voice". It was, he said,

> so seductively
> self-effacingly
> deprecatingly
> superior.—
> We wouldn't insist on it for a moment
> but we are
> we are
> you admit we are
> superior.—

Now, post-war, it was not only that specific accent, that Voice, that caste. Brit social strata had sprung some leaks and the juices of the old aristocratic self-assurance had seeped throughout its many layers. Accent of course never could overcome the accident of British birth. But from Oxford to the Old Kent Road, whatever nuance they might possess, these new-wave types would cow you with it, seize control of the home and school or union local or whatever with nothing but articulate aplomb. The very sound could plough the diffident native under with subliminal avocations of deeper, richer reservoirs of wisdom and of power in fact long gone. The old arrogance could be called up in a trice, and, if all else failed, that ultimate weapon, calculated condescension. Tweedy lady had come by it with no effort at all. Domination? Let me try to count the ways.

When my eldest child was eight I took him on his first canoe trip. It was not ambitious. In the Gatineau, quite close to home, a couple of portages and you can leave the world behind. Our first night we settled into our sleeping-bags with that special luxuriousness that stems from a day of pack and paddle. The tent flaps were turned back to the embers of the fire, the silhouetted pine, the glassy stillness of the lake. A beaver splashed. A loon called. I lit the candle and pulled from my pack the book I'd selected with such care. This was a great enchantment to open to my son. Reading. In a tent with the wilderness outside, going on forever. His eyes shone. He was captured along with me as I read the wondrous tale.

Then the loon laughed. And laughed. And the sound of it echoed round and round the lake, mocking. He'd heard me, that loon. No wonder he laughed. I was reading *The Wind in the Willows*. Here. By this gem of a lake in the Canadian Shield I was reading to my own son about an English water-rat rowing an English mole up a peaceful English backwater. What was I doing?

But hold, Loon. What had we on our shelves at home for kids in 1958 other than English books? And a few American. Fine books, wonderful books. But, give or take Ernest Thompson Seton and L.M. Montgomery, scarce a Canadian book in a carload. Even the Grey Owl I'd read so avidly had betrayed my whole generation by turning out to be a Brit. And the books I read to all my kids were the ones I'd read myself, or that had been read to me. Bears in a London street. Rabbits in Mr. McGregor's garden. Cheshire cats in thin air. Moles in row-boats . . .

In any loon's language now, that's an ethnic group. And burrowing mole-like, the lot of them. Right into my own offspring's heart. Going on this way, what possible protection would my grandchildren have?

Attack is the best defence. Right at the source. With my confidence puffed by modest success in Canada, I took the first book I'd written for young fry to a London publisher. Right in that panelled sanctum the senior editor, gracious lady, allowed it was good stuff. But, "The setting, you know. The background. The way things are in Canada. So different. Our young readers would just not feel at home. You know."

I knew all right and I snarled at her. I snarled that London publishers had waxed fat for generations selling Billy Bunter to the Sikhs, and they never cared a brass farthing what young Sikhs felt about anything. "Besides." I rose to leave, groping for the most devastating thrust I could muster. "Besides," I said, "we bloody do have the whaah-less. Yet. In Canadah."

She stared, uncomprehending. I stomped down Long Acre to Leicester Square in a fine rage, feeling better every step.

TOPIC FOR EXPLORATION

1. What is significant about the discussion of the wireless (radio) in the cottage in Kent in 1935? What contrast is it designed to reveal? What do "colonial" and "Mother Country" mean to the

British woman? Find other ironic examples of British ethno-centrism.

2. What spectacles does Tony German see as a boy at the jubilee in England in 1935? How do "these deep-rooted wonders that were England" affect German's view of himself as a colonial?

3. What picture of British boy heroism does the author discover in books and magazines? How is he affected by literary exploits of British imperial glory? What role does literature, including literature for children, have in imposing the dominant culture and shaping one's sense of identity? How has the lack of Canadian literature, in the past, contributed to German's view of himself?

4. For what reason did British refugees, after World War II, reject the status of immigrant and "cluster in an ethnic group"? Why did they refuse to see themselves as "ethnics"? Is part of German's purpose in his essay to prove that the British *are* "ethnic"?

5. How does the "Oxford voice" attempt to establish itself as a force of superiority over other Canadians? Does it succeed?

6. How long does it take for German to free himself from the British-centred outlook? How does he turn the tables in his encounter with the British publisher's editor? Does he manage to overcome the expected British ethnocentrism?

Jenine Dumont

Jenine Dumont lives in Edmonton, Alberta. She has a Bachelor of Science degree, and works full-time as a nurse. Her essay reprinted here was first included in the anthology of writing by Native women of Western Canada, Writing the Circle *(1990).*

◆

I Didn't Know I was Different

I was born in 1944 to Gabriel Dumont and Victoria Lafromboise at Duck Lake, Saskatchewan. My father was a grandnephew of the famous or infamous Gabriel Dumont of the Northwest Rebellion. To the Métis, Gabriel Dumont was always considered famous, but as a child I interpreted from history that the accepted adjective was infamous.

I was born in Duck Lake but did not live there. My mother returned to her home town to have two children after moving to the Birch River area in Manitoba. My first home was a ranch in the Old Fort district on the Woody River. My father managed the ranch that was owned by a wealthy Duck Lake resident. We probably lived there until I was two years old. I was the first girl after three boys, so I was given a lot of attention by family and friends alike. I was six years younger than the youngest boy and exactly twelve years younger than the oldest whose birthday was two days before mine in December. My oldest brother and I had a special relationship.

We moved to the town of Birch River after leaving the ranch and rented an old house which first looked like an old store-front finished in grey stucco, sprinkled with coloured glass. I remember enjoying the two years we lived there. My brother and I played with neighbouring children without incident. My father worked at various jobs, one I remember was bull cook for the provincial government road gang who were building roads eight miles north of Birch River in the Pasadena district. This led to a job as manager of the community pasture in the area, owned by the Department of Lands

Branch and Wildlife. In the summer of 1949, the family moved out to the pasture and lived in two railroad shacks. The larger building was used for a kitchen, living-room, and sleeping area for my parents and my sister and me. The boys slept out in the smaller shack. In the fall, we moved back into town and rented a small but comfortable house behind the Royal Cafe. My oldest brother had to quit school to help out financially; this was a sore point with him all of his life. I remember that he bought a brown snowsuit for my sister, who was somewhat of a tomboy; it really made her look like a tough little boy. On 9 April 1950, Easter Sunday, my youngest sister was born. When mom brought her home, I said, "She looks like an Indian." I didn't know I was part Indian, and it was two years before I knew.

The next summer, we went back to the pasture and lived in the two railroad shacks again. We spent the winter there, too. The next year, the government built a two-bedroom house with a big yard landscaped by elm and spruce trees and a caragana hedge in the front. We thought it was heaven. The government officials thought they could use the smaller bedroom for an office; I don't know where they thought we would all sleep. They ended up using the larger railroad shack for an office down by the corrals, where it was more appropriately situated.

I began grade one when I was six and a half years old because of my December birthday. I loved school and knew a lot before I started. My youngest brother, who was in grade six, and I were the only family members attending the school. The school was a one-room school with grades one to nine. The two or three pupils in grade nine took correspondence courses and were supervised by the teacher. My first year passed without incident.

For my second year of school, we had the same teacher, and everyone was pleased because she was superb. My brother was in grade seven, and they happened to be studying social studies one day when Duck Lake and the Rebellion was discussed. The teacher, who knew our family, asked my brother if that was where our father was from. His reply was, "Yes, they're all a bunch of Indians there."

Nothing more was said, but a few days later or perhaps the next day the kids started teasing us, calling us Indians and half-breeds! This went on for some time. I couldn't understand why the teacher did not stop them, although the teasing occurred at lunch time and recess. One lunch hour, all the kids stayed inside the school while my brother and I were outside alone. Then one day, because we were Catholic, my brother and I were let out of school half an hour early when the Anglican missionaries came to the school to give a service. We walked and ran the two miles home as fast as we could to get home before the other kids. Our parents were surprised to see us home in thirty minutes. I had a sore throat that night, was in bed with a chest cold the next day, and missed school for two weeks. We must have told our parents about the teasing then. When I went back to school, the teasing had stopped. I assume my parents had intervened. My brother skipped school a lot that year and eventually dropped out. He was fourteen years old.

That was when I realized I was part Indian. I believe that was also the first time my father talked to me about being proud of my heritage. Over the years, he would often say, "Hold your head up high and be proud; it doesn't matter what they say."

I was particularly close to my father and believed him, so I did as I was told.

I walked that way so much that in high school people thought I was a snob; I really was shy and afraid of being hurt. I had some difficulty being proud of my Indian ancestry, as there were constant reminders that Indians were inferior. My own mother referred to Indians as "les sauvages" (the savages), as if they were inferior. I remember thinking, "Why are you saying that, we're part Indian too?"

I got a lot of mixed messages. We had a group of Métis friends with whom we spent holidays. All the women were the same, trying to be white and rather intolerant of Indians or the mixed bloods who had more Indian ancestry than we did. I remember my father as being very tolerant and being friendly to Indians. I never heard any of the other men make any racial statements.

Other memories stay with me. Once, when we lived in Birch River, I went to the butcher shop for my mother. The owner was always very nice to us. He used to give us wieners when we came into the store. This particular day I went in while a salesman was there, and the butcher gave me a wiener as usual. As I took it and turned to leave, the salesman, addressing the butcher, said with a laugh, "One of your little Native friends?"

I remember seeing that the butcher was somewhat embarrassed. Little things like that would keep reminding me that I was not white.

I spent a lot of years trying to be white. We used to always say that we were French. Shortly after I met my husband, I asked him if he was prejudiced. I think he must have replied negatively. It never seemed important to tell him I was part Indian. I think he figured it out himself. He's of Icelandic ancestry, and they seem to be a rather non-judgemental people.

After we were married, we lived in northern Manitoba for a year in a town that had a large Native population. I remember denying my ancestry once while I was there. That bothered me for a long time. It took me until I was thirty years old to really come to terms with being part Indian. I had two children of my own by then, and you can be sure I told them they were part Indian. When my daughter was in grade two she told a friend about her Indian ancestry and this girl started to tease her and call her Indian. I went to the child's mother who stopped the teasing. I certainly didn't want history repeating itself.

When I was thirty-five and my last child was a precocious two year old, we stopped in a small northern Alberta town to buy something at a drugstore. My son was touching things, etc. When I went to the counter to pay for my purchase, the clerk looked through me with disdain and I got this terribly chilled feeling. It's a feeling that I cannot describe. It comes when you know that someone dislikes you because of your race. I thought I had come to terms with my Native blood. Maybe I have, but other people have not.

I think the prejudice I was exposed to as a child affects the way I interact with people as I am not an open person and do not make friends easily. When I compare myself to my sisters, who did not suffer the same prejudices I did, I find them to be much more open and congenial. I would like to think there is less prejudice in the world, but is there? I have a ten-year-old son writing a story about an Indian Chief who killed a white-man's wife and then this white man relentlessly hunts down the Indian. The story is supposed to take place one hundred years ago. I guess the stereotypes are still there. Where else would this ten year old get his ideas?

TOPICS FOR EXPLORATION

1. Jenine Dumont didn't know she was Métis until she was eight. What were her parents' motives for hiding the family history from her? How did this ignorance of her roots deny her self-image and proud heritage?

2. Dumont grew up surrounded by "mixed messages," such as the truth about the "famous or infamous" Gabriel Dumont, a founder of Manitoba and hero of the Northwest Rebellion. Why did she have difficulty being proud of her Indian ancestry?

3. How did the sudden discrimination of the schoolroom affect Dumont? How did it contribute to her siblings' lack of success in school?

4. What reasons does Dumont give for trying to pass for white? Why did she deny her ancestry until she was 30? How is she caught in the double bind of having Native and white ancestry?

5. How has Dumont been affected by racial stereotypes and prejudice in her own life? How are they still affecting the life of her children? Does she offer any strategy for coping with racism?

David Suzuki

David Suzuki, born in Vancouver in 1936, is a writer, educator, journalist, TV and radio host, and a world-renowned geneticist. He appears regularly in the popular CBC television series "The Nature of Things." He has been an active spokesperson on social and environmental issues. This excerpt comes from his book Metamorphosis: Stages in a Life, *published in 1987.*

Ancestors—The Genetic Source

My genes can be traced in a direct line to Japan. I am a pure-blooded member of the Japanese race. And whenever I go there, I am always astonished to see the power of that biological connection. In subways in Tokyo, I catch familiar glimpses of the eyes, hairline or smile of my Japanese relatives. Yet when those same people open their mouths to communicate, the vast cultural gulf that separates them from me becomes obvious: English is my language, Shakespeare is my literature, British history is what I learned and Beethoven is my music.

For those who believe that in people, just as in animals, genes are the primary determinant of behaviour, a look at second- and third-generation immigrants to Canada gives powerful evidence to the contrary. The overriding influence is environmental. We make a great mistake by associating the inheritance of physical characteristics with far more complex traits of human personality and behaviour.

Each time I visit Japan, I am reminded of how Canadian I am and how little the racial connection matters. I first visited Japan in 1968 to attend the International Congress of Genetics in Tokyo. For the first time in my life, I was surrounded by people who all looked like me. While sitting in a train and looking at the reflections in the window, I found that it was hard to pick out my own image in the crowd. I had grown up in a Caucasian society in which I was a minority member. My whole sense of self had developed with that perspective of looking different. All my life I had wanted large eyes and brown hair so I could be like everyone else. Yet on that train, where I did fit in, I didn't like it.

On this first visit to Japan I had asked my grandparents to contact relatives and let them know I was coming. I was the first in the Suzuki clan in Canada to visit them. The closest relative on my father's side was my grandmother's younger brother, and we arranged to meet in a seaside resort near his home. He came to my hotel room with two of his daughters. None of them spoke any English, while my Japanese was so primitive as to be useless. In typical Japanese fashion, they showered me with gifts, the most important being a package of what looked like wood carved in the shape of bananas! I had no idea what it was. (Later I learned the package contained dried tuna fish from which slivers are shaved off to flavour soup. This is considered a highly prized gift.) We sat in stiff silence and embarrassment, each of us struggling to dredge up a common word or two to break the quiet. It was excruciating! My great uncle later wrote my grandmother to tell her how painful it had been to sit with her grandson and yet be unable to communicate a word.

To people in Japan, all non-Japanese—black, white or yellow—are *gaijin* or foreigners, While *gaijin* is not derogatory, I find that its use is harsh because I sense doors clanging shut on me when I'm called one. The Japanese do have a hell of a time with me because I look like them and can say in perfect Japanese, "I'm a foreigner and I can't speak Japanese." Their reactions are usually complete incomprehension followed by a sputtering, "What do you mean? You're speaking Japanese." And finally a pejorative, "Oh, a *gaijin!*"

Once when my wife, Tara, who is English, and I went to Japan we asked a man at the travel bureau at the airport to book a *ryokan*—a traditional Japanese inn—for us in Tokyo. He found one and booked it for "*Suzuki-san*" and off we went. When we arrived at the inn and I entered the foyer, the owner was confused by my terrible Japanese. When Tara entered, the shock was obvious in his face. Because of my name, they had expected a "real" Japanese. Instead, I was a *gaijin* and the owner told us he wouldn't take us. I was furious and we stomped off to a phone booth where I called the agent at the airport. He was astonished and came all the way into town to plead our case with the innkeeper. But the innkeeper stood firm and denied us a room. Apparently he had accepted *gaijin* in the past with terrible consequences.

As an example of the problem, Japanese always take their shoes off when entering a *ryokan* because the straw mats (*tatami*) are quickly frayed. To a Japanese, clomping into a room with shoes on would be comparable to someone entering our homes and spitting on the floor. Similarly, the *ofuro*, or traditional tub, has hot clean water that all bathers use. So one must first enter the bathroom, wash carefully and rinse off *before* entering the tub. Time in the *ofuro* is for relaxing and soaking. Again, Westerners who lather up in the tub are committing a terrible desecration.

To many Canadians today, the word "Jap" seems like a natural abbreviation for Japanese. Certainly for newspaper headlines it would seem to make sense. So people are often shocked to see me bristle when they have used the word Jap innocently. To Japanese-Canadians, Jap or Nip (from "*Nippon*") were epithets used generously during the pre-war and war years. They conjure up all of the hatred and bigotry of those times. While a person using the term today may be unaware of its past use, every Japanese-Canadian remembers.

The thin thread of Japanese culture that does link me to Japan was spun out of the poverty and desperation of my ancestors. My grandparents came to a Canadian province openly hostile to their strange appearance and different ways. There were severe restrictions on how much and where they could buy property. Their children, who were born and raised in Canada, couldn't vote until 1948 and encountered many barriers to professional training and property ownership. Asians, regardless of birthplace, were third-class citizens. That is the reality of the Japanese-Canadian experience and the historical cultural legacy that came down to the third and fourth generations—to me and my children.

The first Japanese immigrants came to Canada to make their fortunes so they could return to Japan as people of wealth. The vast majority was uneducated and impoverished. But in the century spanning my grandparents' births and the present, Japan has leapt from an agrarian society to a technological and economic giant.

Now, the Japanese I meet in Japan or as recent immigrants to Canada come with far different cultural roots. Present-day Japanese are highly educated, upper-middle class and proud of their heritage. In Canada they encounter respect, envy and curiosity in sharp contrast to the hostility and bigotry met by my grandparents.

Japanese immigrants to North America have names that signify the number of generations in the new land (or just as significantly, that count the generational distance *away* from Japan). My grandparents are *Issei*, meaning the first generation in Canada. Most *Issei* never learned more than a rudimentary knowledge of English, *Nisei*, like my parents, are the second generation here and the first native-born group. While growing up they first spoke Japanese in the home and then learned English from playmates and teachers. Before the Second World War, many *Issei* sent their children to be educated in Japan. When they returned to Canada, they were called *Kika-nisei* (or *Kibei* in the United States). Most have remained bilingual, but many of the younger *Nisei* now speak Japanese with difficulty because English is their native tongue. My sisters and I are *Sansei* (third generation); our children are *Yonsei*. These generations, and especially *Yonsei*, are growing up in homes where English is the only spoken language, so they are far more likely to speak school-taught French as their second language than Japanese.

Most *Sansei*, like me, do not speak Japanese. To us, the *Issei* are mysteries. They came from a cultural tradition that is a hundred years old. Unlike people in present-day Japan, the *Issei* clung tightly to the culture they remembered and froze that culture into a static museum piece like a relic of the past. Not being able to speak each other's language, *Issei* and *Sansei* were cut off from each other. My parents dutifully visited my grandparents and we children would be trotted out to be lectured at or displayed. These visits were excruciating, because we children didn't understand the old culture, and didn't have the slightest interest—we were Canadians.

My father's mother died in 1978 at the age of ninety-one. She was the last of the *Issei* in our family. The final months of her life, after a left-hemisphere stroke, were spent in that terrible twilight—crippled, still aware, but unable to communicate. She lived the terminal months of her life, comprehending but mute, in a ward with Caucasian strangers. For over thirty years I had listened to her psychologically blackmailing my father by warning him of her imminent death. Yet in the end, she hung on long after there was reason to. When she died, I was astonished at my own reaction, a great sense of sadness and regret at the cleavage of my last link with the source of my genes. I had never been able to ask what made her and others of her generation come to Canada, what they felt when they arrived, what their hopes and dreams had been, and whether it was worth it. And I wanted to thank her, to show her that I was grateful that, through them, I was born a Canadian.

TOPICS FOR EXPLORATION

1. Why does David Suzuki question the validity of the "biological connection" in determining individual identity? How does environment override genes?

2. Although Suzuki resembles them physically, he cannot communicate with his relatives in Japan. He is a *gaijin* (a foreigner). How does being a *gaijin* exclude Suzuki? Why is he rejected at a *ryokan* (a traditional Japanese inn)?

3. What are some cultural practices of Japan that Westerners misunderstand? Find examples in this account of mutual incomprehension based on cultural differences.

4. How have the different generations of Japanese Canadians responded to the experience of the new land? How do people of Suzuki's generation (*Sansei*) view their immigrant ancestors (*Issei*)? Why are the hopes and motives of *Issei* still a "mystery" to Suzuki?

5. Why does Suzuki feel caught between two cultures when, as a Canadian, he visits Japan?

6. Suzuki takes a pragmatic stance on the question of immigrants' adaptation to life in their new country. Do you agree that Suzuki's assimilation—which might be called cutting off the "link with the source of one's genes"—is part of his process of becoming "Canadian"? How typical is the model represented by Suzuki's family?

Pablo Urbanyi

Pablo Urbanyi was born in Hungary but grew up in Argentina, where he worked as a journalist and a cultural commentator. He immigrated to Canada in 1977, and now lives in Ottawa. He has published two novels, Un revolver para Mack *and* The Nowhere Idea, *and a collection of short stories,* Noche de Revolucionaires. *The story included in our anthology first appeared in* Canadian Fiction Magazine *in 1988.*

Rebirth

Ottawa, 27 August 198...

Dear Alberto,

I really must apologize for not replying at once to that letter you sent me more than two years ago. There are many, though not countless, reasons for the delay. On the one hand, living in this wonderful world of global communications, I often found myself saying: "Hell, why bother to write? When you've got something to say, you just hop on a plane and fly down there and tell him all about it over a cup of coffee." I realize now that you can say that to yourself for two or three years, maybe even a lifetime, while you sit and wait for the money for the ticket. On the other hand, with all due respect, you must admit that your letter is full of dumb questions about the food, the customs, the clothing and the climate— the kind of things you can find out about in any good tourist guidebook in greater detail than I could ever provide. Then you ask me about the people, and right at the end you ask after me, how I am and how I'm getting on in Canada.

What can I tell you about the people? Society here is organized in such a way that from the time you're born you can fend for yourself. People practically don't matter. But since you ask I could describe the people (today's people, "post-modern people" they should be termed since here what's modern is passé: everything is "post-") by quoting a local poet who knows more about these things than I do. In a long poem depicting a remote past in which man, happily and without prejudice, ate raw meat and never had any cavities, this writer defines his contemporaries in a parody of Kipling's poem "If": "If you get up early in the morning and return home in the evening to get drunk . . . If you watch T.V. for three hours while you get drunk . . . If you have doubts and seek information on the latest sexual techniques, on today's God, on microwave cooking . . . If you pay your bills regularly . . . If you are taken in by special offers and dutifully buy everything they tell you to . . . If you use bathroom tissue correctly . . . If you don't know where you came from or who you are or where you're going . . . You will be a postmodern man, faceless in the crowd."

The final vision of the poem is truly apocalyptic: all humanity plunges into the abyss, each man carrying the brand of the beast on his forehead (which in this case does not symbolize Rome but the United States).

I look at it in the same way that you probably do. What the poet thinks is only one opinion among many. Man today doesn't need lofty truths but rather immediate answers to his daily problems, categoric replies and drastic solutions to the life he drags along the ground behind him. It would never occur to post-modern man to hold a skull in his hand and pose an unanswerable question. He would rather brandish a toilet roll with pride and exclaim: "Eureka! I've found it!" And stuffing it under his arm or dumping it into his supermarket cart, he would continue on his way, brimming with confidence, common sense, positive thinking, optimism, every inch a man of action, repeating at every step "Everything's fine".

From what I've said so far, you should be getting the picture. Speaking about myself and about how I'm getting on, you shouldn't still think in terms of the person I used to be. You've got to think of me as someone who adapted and was born again. So in this letter I'm going to outline briefly the metamorphosis I underwent, and I'll leave for another day the description of the effects of that change on my daily life. I can tell you already, though, that my next letter will be entitled "One Day in the Life of Pavlov Urbanovitch in the Ottawa Gulag". Ottawa is the city I live in at the moment.

When I arrived here I naively thought that having been a Hungarian immigrant in Argentina at the age of eight and having grown up in Buenos Aires, I was an old hand at the game and had seen it all, so that managing a second bout of immigration would be a piece of cake. I thought I would take the world by storm. How wrong can you be! There's been a good deal of progress in the meantime. Just think: the Americans have put a man on the moon.

I was unable to get very far with my great powers of deductive reasoning and theoretical speculation or with my desire to fashion in the air a better, more harmonious, efficient, organized world, with every little thing in its rightful place. It was there in front of me, but I couldn't see it. I had to shelve my elaborate theories worked out in cafés and humbly accept what was there. In other words, I had to experience, to soak up experience. There's a good deal of sense in the Latin saying "*Experientia docet stultus*" (Experience is the teacher of idiots).

There are a lot of things I could tell you—about the doors here and the trouble I had getting them open; or the taps they have, in so many different shapes and sizes, and the times I soaked myself before I figured out how to use them properly; or how, like a fool, I used to say hello to women in the street I'd never met before because they all looked alike to me, with the same hairstyle and make-up, all dolled up in the latest fashions which make them look extremely attractive and totally unique—a far cry from the grey uniformity you see in underdeveloped or communist countries. Yes, my friend, everything is bright and cheerful here. But let me give you a concrete example instead of rambling on like this.

Let's begin with man, man going about his daily business with a roll of toilet tissue in his hand and a question in his mind: "Is it or isn't it?"

This was the situation I found myself in for the first time one day, propping up my cart in the Supermarket, the Cathedral of Consumerism, opposite the High Altar of Bathroom Tissue, attempting, without experience or knowledge, to perform the daily rite: shopping.

Oh ignorance! Life in this world is a good deal richer and more varied than some simple-minded architects of utopias would have us believe. People actually live in Utopia here. I was struck dumb as I surveyed with awe the rolls of bathroom tissue that rose upwards like organ pipes toward heaven. How can I explain it to you or describe the scene? Words fail me. But I know I'm no poet, so I won't try to wax too lyrical. I'll just paint the basic picture, starting with the colours: daffodil yellow, flesh pink and sky blue, from the lightest to the darkest hue of cream, any colour to match your bathroom décor (I only found out about this later), and classical white like the purest driven snow. There were specialized tissues too—tissues for dogs, tissues for cats, tissues for your most intimate needs. Then there were the printed tissues—with pictures of Bambi and the whole Disney menagerie for children; pictures of Hollywood stars (I can't remember if Ronald Reagan was among them) and scenes from recent films for adolescents; pictures of

Japanese (or maybe Chinese) rural scenes and reproductions of Renaissance paintings for people with artistic sensibility; pictures of vintage cars for the casualties of fashion overcome with nostalgia. And all these came in a variety of different qualities: tough or extra-tough, soft or extra-soft (for people with haemorrhoids); one-ply, two-ply, three-ply; smooth or pleated . . . I won't go on because you'll think I'm making it up.

I felt like Dante in the Black Forest searching for his Virgil. The shock was so great on this first encounter that I ended up buying nothing. And that was as much a crime against society as it was against my family sitting at home waiting for me.

But God came to my rescue, and I found some other Argentinean émigrés who acted as my Virgil and pointed me in the right direction. There was a psychoanalyst, a doctor and three university professors, one of literature, one of economics, and the other of philosophy. They all agreed that "Hey, in Argentina there isn't any bathroom tissue at all," and that this was a good reason for continuing to live in this part of the world. They understood my problem perfectly since they'd had it at one time themselves, and generously got together one evening to help me solve it. The psychoanalyst, who's as fat as a barrel and sat there the whole time with a bag of candy in his hand, avoided any uncouth interpretations and was encouraging: "Don't forget that you came here to indulge in certain luxuries and pleasures. Buy whichever one you like best and gives you the greatest satisfaction. Personally, I always buy the cheapest make, except when I get constipated and tied up in a vicious circle full of anxiety. I speak from experience." And with that, he popped a candy into his mouth. I asked the doctor about the different colours and the problem of hygiene and he explained: "Listen, as soon as you step foot in North America you've got to stop thinking like that and start generalizing. It's true that I have come across the odd case of a nasty allergic reaction, but they've been very infrequent and exceptional. Generally speaking, the colours tend not to run and you should have faith in American technology. My advice to you is to test carefully, little by little, and if you notice the slightest reaction, change colour." The economics professor took a different line: "Look, it'll be worth your while. Sit down with your family and work out how much you use per day, per week, per month and per year. That way you'll have a clear idea of your overall budget. Oh yes, and to make allowance for diarrhoea, you just apply the theory of possibilities." The professor of philosophy, as bald as Socrates, sighed: "What can I say? In my opinion, the ideal bathroom tissue hasn't been made yet. Perhaps in another world, in a different social system . . . ." "And what kind of tissue would that be?" I asked. "Well, em, er, the recyclable kind, well . . . of course . . ."

Before I go on and in order not to hurt your patriotic feelings by getting into pointless arguments about whether or not there is bathroom tissue down there and if it's available on the black market like the dollar, I should point out that I only take the opinion as a spontaneous exclamation brought about by the biased division established by developed countries when they communicate with the underdeveloped ones. This division could be rendered into everyday language by "Countries with clean backsides and countries with dirty backsides". So much so that many North American diplomats (who, since they have no bidet in their own homes, cannot conceive that there could be one in someone else's in another part of the world and so find the tissue problem truly alarming; I do too) cram their suitcases with as many rolls as they think they'll need when they visit a third-world country. Now I can go on.

Do you think I was any the happier having received these initial clarifications? Not on your life. I was still overwhelmed with doubts and uncertainties. My hand still trembled when I reached out to tear off a sheet of paper and I couldn't avoid accidents. My helpers—unwittingly, of course—in their eagerness to demonstrate their individuality, their ability to fend for themselves and to affirm their personalities, forgot to advise me on the scientific aspects of the problem. They overlooked the need to establish the kind of solid intellectual foundation and impeccable background, based on research, that would enable a person to make his way through that jungle on the right path. There's no religion on earth that has life *that* carefully worked out and lacks its mindless mysteries!

And as happens with all great discoveries that alter one's destiny, I also discovered, by accident or by chance, the solution to the problem. One day I was passing a newspaper stand and noticed a magazine called *Perfect Consumer*. It was a non-profit publication, pure and uncontaminated (a true rarity in this world), and contained a section entitled "The latest tests on bathroom tissues currently available". Full of expectation, I bought a copy.

I would only bore you if I gave you the names of all the toilet tissues and listed all the data given on the subject. I reckon you would need a lifetime or a course or to have been born here in order to understand it all. So I'll just go straight to the conclusions presented in the main article. These were written in a straightforward intelligible style (you can't complain here because they always take your mental capacity into account so as to guarantee effective communication) and read as follows: "Headed by the world renowned eminent scientist John Haighsmith, 46 and father of three, a team of experts from the prestigious University of Toronto undertook three months of intensive research financed by this magazine (at a total cost of $38,000.00) using a series of specially designed tests (there's no description of the tests or of the methodology used) and came to an indisputable conclusion concerning bathroom tissues currently available on the market: in comparison with Kitten X2-X2, Tiger XX-X1, Romance XX-X2, Intimacy XX-X3, and Passion ZZ-Z1, Swan XZ-Z1, being two-ply and manufactured with original, non-recycled cellulose, is the safest and most reliable tissue available. Despite the high price of Swan XZ-Z1, over an average period of ten years the consumer stands to make the most substantial savings by virtue of the lower rate of tears and related mishaps. It should also be borne in mind that, according to the reports generously submitted by the Ontario Medical Association, the white variety of Swan is the most sterile and hygienic, accounting for the lowest number of recorded cases of allergic reaction. (Unfortunately, the consumer will have to forego pleasure of matching his interior design or of putting that finishing touch to his bathroom décor or whatever other fantasies he might have.) Consequently, this is the only bathroom tissue recommended by the O.M.A., not to invalidate the money-back guarantee, readers are advised to study the instructions concerning the correct use of Swan tissue in the box on the preceding page."

I reckon with this example (that could be applied to any other of a thousand products, from toothpaste to condoms) I've put you in the picture. I can assure you that at last I have found true happiness, I feel that my inner self has been strengthened, my individuality has blossomed and my entire personality moves with greater conviction along the path I'm following.

I know more about the subject than anybody now and can speak about it with confidence. My hand no longer trembles as it reaches out to tear off a sheet. My fears have vanished. And if I sometimes think that there's a little swan swimming down there ready to peck me, or a kitten ready to sink its claws into me, I can't blame society or the commercials on T.V. that use these animals. The problem is in my mind where I tend to make these free associations rather too easily.

At any rate, experience has confirmed the findings of experts, and I can now be proud of fending for myself.

Best wishes
Pablo

P.S. I almost forgot. Are you still thinking about emigrating over here? It's true, as you say, that things are easier to buy here. While you're making up your mind and to make it a bit easier for you, I can send you a pack of Swan with eight rolls in it, which is the most economical way of buying it. The best way of sending it, I think, is by diplomatic bag if I can get hold of an Argentinean diplomat going home or a Canadian who's being posted there. Let me know what you think.

TOPICS FOR EXPLORATION

1. Pablo Urbanyi uses letter format to tell his friend in Argentina how he is getting on in Canada. How do you know his letter is fiction? What are the advantages and disadvantages of this literary convention?

2. Discuss how Urbanyi uses irony and humour so as to make a satirical comment on Western consumerism.

3. What is the meaning of his Kipling parody of the "post-modern man"? Why are "immediate answers" more important to post-modern people than "lofty problems"?

4. What is the "metamorphosis" that Urbanyi has undergone? Why is the "second immigration" difficult? What kind of difficulties does he anticipate for a person coming to Canada from a third-world country? How seriously does he treat the problem of adaptation?

5. What does Urbanyi's experience with the choice of toilet paper reflect about his life in "Utopia"? How does he resolve his confusion about too much choice? Who helps him? Are the proposed solutions valid? How is his anxiety about bathroom tissue an ironic parody of North American culture?

6. How is Urbanyi caught with a foot in each of two worlds?

Drew Hayden Taylor

Drew Hayden Taylor was born in 1962 on the Curve Lake Reserve in Ontario. He has worked as a journalist, author, and director for such media as television, radio, press, and theatre. His one-act plays Toronto at Dreamer's Rock *and* Education Is Our Right, *as well as the full-length play* The Bootlegger Blues, *were published in 1990. In his writing, he tries to incorporate elements of traditional Native storytelling, including humour.*

Pretty Like a White Boy: The Adventures of a Blue Eyed Ojibway

In this big, huge world, with all its billions and billions of people, it's safe to say that everybody will eventually come across personalities and individuals that will touch them in some peculiar yet poignant way. Individuals that in some way represent and help define who you are. I'm no different, mine was Kermit the Frog. Not just because Natives have a long tradition of savouring Frogs' legs, but because of his music. If you all may remember, Kermit is quite famous for his rendition of 'It's Not Easy Being Green'. I can relate. If I could sing, my song would be 'It's Not Easy Having Blue Eyes in a Brown Eyed Village'.

Yes, I'm afraid it's true. The author happens to be a card-carrying Indian. Once you get past the aforementioned eyes, the fair skin, light brown hair, and noticeable lack of cheekbones, there lies the heart and spirit of an Ojibway storyteller. Honest Injun, or as the more politically correct term may be, honest aboriginal.

You see, I'm the product of a white father I never knew, and an Ojibway woman who evidently couldn't run fast enough. As a kid I knew I looked a bit different. But, then again, all kids are paranoid when it comes to their peers. I had a fairly happy childhood, frolicking through the bullrushes. But there were certain things that, even then, made me notice my unusual appearance. Whenever we played cowboys and Indians, guess who had to be the bad guy, the cowboy.

It wasn't until I left the Reserve for the big bad city, that I became more aware of the role people expected me to play, and the fact that physically I didn't fit in. Everybody seemed to have this preconceived idea of how every Indian looked and acted. One guy, on my first day of college, asked me what kind of horse I preferred. I didn't have the heart to tell him 'hobby'.

I've often tried to be philosophical about the whole thing. I have both white and red blood in me, I guess that makes me pink. I am a 'Pink' man. Try to imagine this, I'm walking around on any typical Reserve in Canada, my head held high, proudly announcing to everyone "I am a Pink Man'. It's a good thing I ran track in school.

My pinkness is constantly being pointed out to me over and over and over again. 'You don't look Indian?' 'You're not Indian, are you?' 'Really?!?' I got questions like that from both white and Native people, for a while I debated having my Status card tattooed on my forehead.

And like most insecure people and specially a blue eyed Native writer, I went through a particularly severe identity crisis at one point. In fact, I admit it, one depressing spring evening, I dyed my hair black. Pitch black.

The reason for such a dramatic act, you may ask? Show Business. You see, for the last eight years or so, I've worked in various capacities in the performing arts, and as a result I'd always get calls to be an extra or even try out for an important role in some Native oriented movie. This anonymous voice would phone, having been given my number, and ask if I would be interested in trying out for a movie. Being a naturally ambitious, curious, and greedy young man, I would always readily agree, stardom flashing in my eyes and hunger pains from my wallet.

A few days later I would show up for the audition, and that was always an experience. What kind of experience you may ask? Picture this, the picture calls for the casting of seventeenth-century Mohawk warriors living in a traditional longhouse. The casting director calls the name 'Drew Hayden Taylor' and I enter.

The casting director, the producer, and the film's director look up from the table and see my face, blue eyes flashing in anticipation. I once was described as a slightly chubby beachboy. But even beachboys have tans. Anyway, there would be a quick flush of confusion, a recheck of the papers, and a hesitant 'Mr. Taylor?' Then they would ask if I was at the right audition. It was always the same. By the way, I never got any of the parts I tried for, except for a few anonymous crowd shots. Politics tells me it's because of the way I look, reality tells me it's probably because I can't act. I'm not sure which is better.

It's not just film people either. Recently I've become quite involved in Theatre, Native theatre to be exact. And one cold October day I was happily attending the Toronto leg of a province-wide tour of my first play, *Toronto at Dreamer's Rock*. The place was sold out, the audience very receptive and the performance was wonderful. Ironically one of the actors was also half white.

The director later told me he had been talking with the actor's father, an older Non-Native type chap. Evidently he had asked a few questions about me, and how I did my research. This made the director curious and he asked about his interest. He replied 'He's got an amazing grasp of the Native situation for a white person.'

Not all these incidents are work related either. One time a friend and I were coming out of a rather upscale bar (we were out YUPPIE watching) and managed to catch a cab. We thanked the cab driver for being so comfortably close on such a cold night, he shrugged and nonchalantly talked about knowing what bars to drive around. 'If you're not careful, all you'll get is drunk Indians.' I hiccuped.

Another time this cab driver droned on and on about the government. He started out by criticizing Mulroney, and eventually to his handling of the Oka crisis. This perked up my ears, until he said 'If it were me, I'd have tear-gassed the place by the second day. No more problem.' He got a dime tip. A few incidents like this and I'm convinced I'd make a great undercover agent for one of the Native political organizations.

But then again, even Native people have been known to look at me with a fair amount of suspicion. Many years ago when I was a young man, I was working on a documentary on Native culture up in the wilds of Northern Ontario. We were at an isolated cabin filming a trapper woman and her kids. This one particular nine-year-old girl seemed to take a shine to me. She followed me around for two days both annoying me and endearing herself to me. But she absolutely refused to believe that I was Indian. The whole film crew tried to tell her but to no avail. She was certain I was white.

Then one day as I was loading up the car with film equipment, she asked me if I wanted some tea. Being in a hurry I declined the tea. She immediately smiled with victory crying out 'See, you're not Indian, all Indians drink tea!'

Frustrated and a little hurt I whipped out my Status card and thrust it at her. Now there I was, standing in a Northern Ontario winter, showing my Status card to a nine-year-old non-status Indian girl who had no idea what one was. Looking back, this may not have been one of my brighter moves.

But I must admit, it was a Native woman that boiled everything down in one simple sentence. You may know that woman, Marianne Jones from 'The Beachcombers' television series. We were working on a film together out west and we got to gossiping. Eventually we got around to talking about our respective villages. Hers on the Queen Charlotte Islands, or Haida Gwaii as the Haida call them, and mine in central Ontario.

Eventually childhood on the Reserve was being discussed and I made a comment about the way I look. She studied me for a moment, smiled, and said 'Do you know what the old women in my village would call you?' Hesitant but curious, I shook my head. 'They'd say you were pretty like a white boy.' To this day I'm still not sure if I like that.

Now some may argue that I am simply a Métis with a Status card. I disagree, I failed French in grade 11. And the Métis as everyone knows have their own separate and honourable culture, particularly in western Canada. And of course I am well aware that I am not the only person with my physical characteristics.

I remember once looking at a video tape of a drum group, shot on a Reserve up near Manitoulin Island. I noticed one of the drummers seemed quite fairhaired, almost blond. I mentioned this to my girlfriend of the time and she shrugged saying 'Well, that's to be expected. The highway runs right through the Reserve.'

Perhaps I'm being too critical. There's a lot to be said for both cultures. For example, on the left hand, you have the Native respect for Elders. They understand the concept of wisdom and insight coming with age.

On the white hand, there's Italian food. I mean I really love my mother and family but seriously, does anything really beat good Veal Scallopini? Most of my aboriginal friends share my fondness for this particular brand of food. Wasn't there a warrior at Oka named Lasagna? I found it ironic, though curiously logical, that Columbus was Italian. A connection I wonder?

Also Native people have this wonderful respect and love for the land. They believe they are part of it, a mere chain in the cycle of existence. Now, as many of you know, this conflicts with the accepted Judeo-Christian i.e. western view of land management. I even believe somewhere in the first chapters of the Bible it says something about God giving man dominion over Nature. Check it out, Genesis 4:?, 'Thou shalt clear cut.' So I grew up understanding that everything around me is important and alive. My Native heritage gave me that.

And again, on the white hand, there's breast implants. Darn clever them white people. That's something Indians would never have invented, seriously. We're not ambitious enough. We just take what the Creator decides to give us, but no, not the white man. Just imagine it, some serious looking white man, and let's face it people, we know it was a man who invented them, don't we? So just imagine some serious looking white doctor sitting around in his laboratory muttering to himself, 'Big tits, big tits, hmm, how do I make big tits?' If it was an Indian, it would be 'Big tits, big tits, white women sure got big tits' and leave it at that.

So where does that leave me on the big philosophical score-board, what exactly are my choices again; Indians—respect for elders, love of the land. White people—food and big tits. In order to live in both cultures I guess I'd have to find an Indian woman with big tits who lives with her grandmother in a cabin out in the woods and can make Fettuccini Alfredo on a wood stove.

Now let me make this clear, I'm not writing this for sympathy, or out of anger, or even some need for self-glorification. I am just setting the facts straight. For as you read this, a new Nation is born. This is a declaration of independence, my declaration of independence.

I've spent too many years explaining who and what I am repeatedly, so as of this moment, I officially secede from both races. I plan to start my own separate nation. Because I am half Ojibway, and half Caucasian, we will be called the Occasions. And I of course, since I'm founding the new nation, will be a Special Occasion.

TOPICS FOR EXPLORATION

1. How does humour help to communicate a serious subject in this essay of self-definition? Do you think that this humour masks Drew Hayden Taylor's true feelings about his ambiguous status?

2. How does Taylor feel about being part of a blue-eyed minority in a larger brown-eyed minority? Why does he feel he does not fit in either group?

3. How does Taylor present himself as a victim of the "preconceived idea of how every Indian looked and acted"? Why is he treated with suspicion by other Native people?

4. Taylor relates a number of incidents involving misunderstandings about his identity. How do some of these incidents reveal

racial tensions between white and Native people? What is the role of "show business" in creating and maintaining Native stereotypes?

5. What irony is implied by Taylor's talking about being "pretty like a white boy"? What does it tell us about racial self-image among aboriginals and whites?

6. What are the advantages of Native culture, according to Taylor? How does he satirize some of the pretensions of white culture?

7. What does Taylor think about the possibility of living in both cultures? What absurdist solution to the problem of belonging does he find in the end? What are the serious implications of his humorous decision to "secede from both races"?

Sun-Kyung Yi

Sun-Kyung Yi is a freelance author who has written for The Globe and Mail *and* The Toronto Star. *She has recently published a couple of articles dealing with the problems of the Korean community in Toronto. The article reprinted below is from* The Globe and Mail.

An Immigrant's Split Personality

I am Korean-Canadian. But the hyphen often snaps in two, obliging me to choose to act as either a Korean or a Canadian, depending on where I am and who I'm with. After 16 years of living in Canada, I discovered that it's very difficult to be both at any given time or place.

When I was younger, toying with the idea of entertaining two separate identities was a real treat, like a secret game for which no one knew the rules but me.

I was known as Angela to the outside world, and as Sun-Kyung at home. I ate bologna sandwiches in the school lunch room and rice and kimchee for dinner. I chatted about teen idols and giggled with my girlfriends during my classes, and ambitiously practiced piano and studied in the evenings, planning to become a doctor when I grew up. I waved hellos and goodbyes to my teachers, but bowed to my parents' friends visiting our home.

I could also look straight in the eyes of my teachers and friends and talk frankly with them instead of staring at my feet with my mouth shut when Koreans talked to me.

Going outside the home meant I was able to relax from the constraints of my cultural conditioning, until I walked back in the door and had to return to being an obedient and submissive daughter.

The game soon ended when I realized that it had become a way of life, that I couldn't change the rules without disappointing my parents and questioning all the cultural implications and consequences that came with being a hyphenated Canadian.

Many have tried to convince me that I am a Canadian, like all other immigrants in the country, but those same people also ask me which country I came from with great curiosity, following with questions about the type of food I ate and the language I spoke. It's difficult to feel a sense of belonging and acceptance when you are regarded as "one of them." "Those Koreans, they work hard. . . . You must be fantastic at math and science." (No.) "Do your parents own a corner store" (No.)

Koreans and Canadians just can't seem to merge into "us" and "we."

Some people advised me that I should just take the best of both worlds and disregard the rest. That's ideal, but unrealistic when my old culture demands a complete conformity with very little room to manoeuvre for new and different ideas.

After a lifetime of practice, I thought I could change faces and become Korean on demand with grace and perfection. But working with a small Korean company in Toronto proved me wrong. I quickly became estranged from my own people.

My parents were ecstatic at the thought of their daughter finally finding her roots and having a working opportunity to speak my native tongue and absorb the culture. For me, it was the most painful and frustrating 2 ½ months of my life.

When the president of the company boasted that he "operated little Korea," he meant it literally. A Canadianized Korean was not tolerated. I looked like a Korean, therefore I had to talk, act, and think like one, too. Being accepted meant a total surrender to ancient codes of behaviour rooted in Confucian thought, while leaving the "Canadian" part of me out in the parking lot with my '86 Buick.

In the first few days at work, I was bombarded with inquiries about my marital status. When I told them I was single, they spent the following days trying to match me up with available bachelors in the company and the community.

I was expected to accept my inferior position as a woman and had to behave accordingly. It was not a place to practice my feminist views, or be an individual without being condemned. Little Korea is a place for men (who filled all the senior positions) and women don't dare to speak up or disagree with their male counterparts.

The president (all employees bow to him and call him Mr. President) asked me to act more like a lady and smile. I was openly scorned by a senior employee because I spoke more fluent English than Korean. The cook in the kitchen shook her head in disbelief upon discovering that my cooking skills were limited to boiling a package of instant noodles. "You want a good husband, learn to cook," she advised me.

In less than a week I became an outsider because I refused to conform and blindly nod my head in agreement to what my elders (which happened to be everybody else in the company) said. A month later, I was demoted because "members of the workplace and the Korean community" had complained that I just wasn't "Korean enough," and I had "too much power for a single woman." My father suggested that "when in Rome do as the Romans." But that's exactly what I was doing. I am in Canada so I was freely acting like a Canadian, and it cost me my job.

My father also said, "It doesn't matter how Canadian you think you are, just look in the mirror and it'll tell you who you *really* are." But what he didn't realize is that an immigrant has to embrace the new culture to enjoy and benefit from what it has to offer. Of course, I will always be Korean by virtue of my appearance and early conditioning, but I am also happily Canadian and want to take full advantage of all that such citizenship confers.

But for now I remain slightly distant from both cultures, accepted fully by neither. The hyphenated Canadian personifies the ideal of multiculturalism, but unless the host culture and the immigrant cultures can find ways to merge their distinct identities, sharing the best of both, this cultural schizophrenia will continue.

TOPICS FOR EXPLORATION

1. What does it mean to be a "hyphenated Canadian"? According to the author, what are the ordeals of people straddling two cultures? Can you think of any advantages of the "split personality" that she discusses?

2. Why does the author say that Koreans and Canadians have such difficulty in merging? Why don't some Canadians view Korean Canadians as Canadians? Why doesn't the president of "little Korea" tolerate Canadianized Koreans?

3. Find a few examples of cultural differences mentioned in this article. When talking about cultural differences, what are some ways to avoid cultural stereotyping?

4. Although she takes part in both Korean and Canadian cultures, why is Sun-Kyung Yi "accepted fully by neither"? How does this double bind result in "cultural schizophrenia"?

5. What is the ideal of multi-ethnic interactions postulated by the author? What kind of attitude change would it require in both the host culture and the immigrant cultures?

Austin Clarke

Austin Clarke's story "Doing Right" appears in Unit Two.

A Stranger in a Strange Land

One thing you do not know about me, and which I have been thinking of for the past few days: I have no real, true friends in this country, even after all these years; for those persons I hold dear, are all in Barbados, or are scattered throughout the other West Indian countries.

Those are the persons who grew up with me; went to the same schools, were in the same choir; in the same cadet corps; the same scout troop, the 23rd Barbados; who attended St. Matthias Anglican church, for matins, Sunday school and evensong and service, from the age of 6 until I left Barbados in 1955; who were with me on picnics, outings and excursions; who attended cadet and scout camps up in the country; who were prefects and head boys at Combermere School for Boys, and at Harrison College (also for boys, until recently when it became co-educational); persons with whom I could, and did, discuss the most personal things—joys and sorrows, the insoluble and very important crises of growing up.

I cannot pick one person in this country, my new "home," with whom I am free to share these confidences. And I am not speaking about the trust a man should put in a woman. I am talking about male children, who grow with you into boys, and eventually into men. A significant part of my history and development ended when I set foot in Toronto. This certainly must be the meaning of alienation, if not of rootlessness. It can manifest itself in what the host society rushes to label as delinquent behaviour. No doubt much of the criminal behaviour of immigrant youths, and not only West Indian youths, may be ascribed to this absence of roots and ruins.

The roots I call the mores; and the ruins, the statues and the buildings of glass, steel and concrete, and the sensibility of our new friends of our transplanted "home," which is not always uniformly consistent with the way we see ourselves. This is the only meaning of the statement that, "immigrants behave differently from Canadians."

Individually, it is the difference between acquaintanceship and friendship. Metaphorically, it explains the immigrant's reliance upon materialistic accomplishments: large house, loud behaviour, conspicuous tastes. All this to the detriment, perhaps the inability, of transposing the roots and the ruins of the country of birth and of breeding.

In Barbados, I breathe in the smell of the soil, I taste the scandals of the landscape. The mud through which I trample and the sand that pours through my fingers are the roots and ruins I spoke about. It does tend to make my tentative accomplishment in this country empty, and at the same time, over-important and inflated.

"We are the hollow men. / We are the stuffed men. / Leaning together / Headpiece filled with straw. Alas! / Our dried voices, when / We whisper together / Are quiet and meaningless / As wind in dry grass / or rats' feet over broken glass / In our dry cellar."

It took T.S. Eliot, himself an outsider in England, to grasp this essence of alienation, even though he may have had other personal crises in mind when he wrote this poem. We do know, however, that he was never accorded his wish to be an Englishman, even though he tried to be one, even though he is known as an English author; and this denial came in spite of the posture of snobbish Britishness he himself affected.

By nuance and by innuendo, and in crude sections of English society, he was not permitted to forget that The Dry Salvages (a poem that described his background in the United States) was not London. "I do not know much about gods." I would paraphrase his words to read, "I do not know much about Toronto's gods." In Toronto, I forget that back in Barbados are those ruins, roots and mud essential to my mental health, as "that river is a strong brown god"; and in forgetting of this part of Barbados now that I am here in this developed country, "the brown god is almost forgotten by the dwellers in cities." I forget them to the detriment of my psychical well-being.

So you see my dear, the reason for my silence, my reticence, sometimes my petulant reticence about things that normally summon passion. You see also, why we are the hollow men, and why our "voices when we whisper together are quiet and meaningless."

I stay awake at night, afraid to accept the reward of my toils during the day, because the night is a conspirator for "death's other kingdom" so I remain awake, alone at an hour when I am trembling with the tenderness of nostalgia, for those broken ruins and roots of Barbados. Awake, trying to delay and to postpone the inevitable behaviour of "dwellers in cities": That for the softest desire, I must face an institution, for relief from stress, I must face an institution, for the solution of a problem of passion, I must face an institution, because there are no persons, no friends of childhood.

Good night—this is not my cynicism, nor my vengeance upon you because you were born here, it is simply a benediction, and my recognizing your blessed advantage that you are able to sleep with your ruins and your "river," which are as comforting as they tell me a water bed is.

TOPICS FOR EXPLORATION

1. Why does Austin Clarke feel he can't share his most personal experiences in Canada? Why does "a significant part of [his] history and development" end when he arrives in Toronto?

2. How does the metaphor of "roots and ruins" help us understand the meaning of alienation experienced by immigrants?

3. Why wasn't T.S. Eliot accepted as English even though he behaved with "snobbish Britishness," according to Clarke?

4. What effects upon his "psychical well-being" does the forgetting of roots have for Clarke? Why does he face "institutions" rather than people in Canada?

5. Why can't Clarke be comfortable with the double bind of being Barbadian and Canadian?

6. Clarke sets out to make an argument that is more emotional than rational, and at some points it may be slightly swayed by nostalgia. How does the infusion of personal emotion strengthen the power of his thesis? What other rhetorical devices does he employ to reflect the feelings of an outsider?

SUGGESTIONS FOR FURTHER STUDY

1. Compare the British self-image of Tony German's memoir with that of Catharine Parr Traill (in Unit One) a hundred years earlier.

2. Compare Jenine Dumont's view of school as a breeding ground of discrimination with Carol Geddes's piece about education in Unit Four. What features do they have in common?

3. How does David Suzuki's response to his Japanese-Canadian experience compare with Joy Kogawa's in *Itsuka* (Unit Two)?

4. Both Suzuki and Sun-Kyung Yi have opted for an identity determined by culture rather than genes. How does this alienate them from their "genetic sources"? Compare the difficulties of this double bind experienced by these two authors.

5. Compare the confusion and culture shock experienced by Pablo Urbanyi in "Rebirth" with Austin Clarke's alienation in "A Stranger in a Strange Land" and the alienation of Sun-Kyung Yi from "little Korea." How different are their respective responses to the immigrant predicament?

6. Contrast the identity problems faced by the two authors with Native ancestry represented in this unit, Jenine Dumont and Drew Hayden Taylor. What different ways have they chosen to respond to their dilemmas? What effects have their choices had upon their lives in a predominantly white culture?

7. Compare Austin Clarke's essay in Unit Seven with his short story "Doing Right" in Unit Two. How does the theme of alienation express itself through two different forms, one fiction and the other non-fiction?

SELECTED BIBLIOGRAPHY

Birbalsingh, Frank. *Jahaji Bhai: An Anthology of Indo-Caribbean Literature*. Toronto: Tsar, 1988.

Black, Ayana. *VOICES: 16 Canadian Writers of African Descent*. Toronto: HarperCollins, 1992.

Borobiolo, John. *Breaking Through: A Canadian Literary Mosaic*. Toronto: Prentice-Hall, 1990.

Brand, Dionne. *No Burden to Carry: Narratives of Black Working Women in Ontario, 1920s to 1950s*. Toronto: Women's Press, 1991.

Carter, George Elliot. *Fire on the Water: An Anthology of Black Nova Scotia Writing*. Lawrencetown Beach, N.S.: Pottersfield Press, 1991.

Fanning, Peter, and Maggie Goh. *Home and Homeland*. Oakville, Ontario: Rubicon, 1992.

Goh, Maggie, and Craig Stephenson. *Between Worlds: A Collection of Writings on the Canadian Immigrant Experience*. Oakville, Ontario: Rubicon, 1989.

Grant, Agnes. *Our Bit of Truth: An Anthology of Canadian Native Literature*. Winnipeg, Manitoba: Pemmican, 1990.

Hutcheon, Linda, and Marion Richmond. *Other Solitudes: Canadian Multicultural Fictions*. Toronto: Oxford University Press, 1990.

King, Thomas. *All My Relations: An Anthology of Contemporary Canadian Native Fiction*. Toronto: McClelland & Stewart, 1990.

Lee, Bennet, and Jim Wong-Chu. *Many-Mouthed Birds: Contemporary Writing by Chinese Canadians*. Vancouver: Douglas & McIntyre, 1991.

Leith, Linda. *Telling Differences: New English Fiction from Quebec*. Montreal: Véhicule Press, 1988.

Minni, C.D. *Ricordi: Things Remembered: An Anthology of Short Stories* (ed. C.D. Minni). Montreal: Guernica, 1989.

Moses, Daniel David, and Terry Goldie. *An Anthology of Canadian Native Literature in English*. Toronto: Oxford University Press, 1992.

Oiwa, Keibo. *Stone Voices: Wartime Writings of Japanese Canadian Issei.* Montreal: Véhicule Press, 1992.

Perreault, Jeanne, and Sylvia Vance. *Writing the Circle: Native Women of Western Canada.* Edmonton, Alberta: NeWest, 1990.

Petrone, Penny. *Northern Voices: Inuit Writing in English.* Toronto: University of Toronto Press, 1988.

Scheier, Libby, Sarah Sheard, and Eleanor Wachtel. *Language in Her Eye: Writing and Gender. Views by Canadian Women Writing in English.* Toronto: Coach House Press, 1990.

The Telling Book Collective. *Telling It: Women and Language Across Cultures.* Vancouver: Press Gang, 1990.

Tiessen, Hildi Froese, and Peter Hinchcliffe. *Acts of Concealment: Mennonites Writing in Canada.* Waterloo, Ontario: University of Waterloo Press, 1992.

Waddington, Miriam. *Canadian Jewish Short Stories.* Toronto: Oxford University Press, 1991.

COPYRIGHTS AND ACKNOWLEDGEMENTS

The editors wish to thank the publishers and copyright holders for permission to reprint the selections in this book, which are listed below in order of their appearance.

UNIT ONE

MY ACADIE is a translation of "Mon Acadie" by Ronald Després from *Paysages en contrebande . . . à la frontière du songe* (Éditions d'Acadie, 1974). The English translation is reprinted from *Unfinished Dreams: Contemporary Poetry of Acadie* with the permission of Goose Lane Editions. Copyright © 1990 Fred Cogswell and Jo-Ann Elder.

SASKATCHEWAN'S INDIAN PEOPLE—FIVE GENERATIONS By Pat Deiter-McArthur (Day Woman). Reprinted from *Writing the Circle: Native Women of Western Canada* (Edmonton: NeWest Press, 1990). Reprinted by permission of the author.

THAT LONESOME ROAD From *That Lonesome Road: The Autobiography of Carrie M. Best*, Copyright © 1977 Carrie M. Best, The Clarion Publishing Company Ltd., 1977. Reprinted by permission of Carrie M. Best.

BRITAIN'S CHILDREN WHO CAME TO STAY Adapted from *The Little Immigrants* By Kenneth Bagnell. Reprinted from *The Review* no. 5 (1980). Reprinted by permission of the author.

A HOLOCAUST SURVIVOR'S STORY By Miriam Rosenthal. Transcribed and edited by Allan Gould. Reprinted from *Toronto Life* (November 1981). Reprinted by permission of Allan Gould.

LEND ME YOUR LIGHT From *Tales from Firozsha Baag* by Rohinton Mistry. Used by permission of the Canadian Publishers, McClelland & Stewart, Toronto.

UNIT FIVE

INDEX OF AUTHORS
AND TITLES

To the Owner of this Book:

We are interested in your reaction to *Pens of Many Colours, A Canadian Reader*, by Eva C. Karpinski and Ian Lea. With your comments, we can improve this book in future editions. Please help us by completing this questionnaire.

1. **What was your reason for using this book?**

    _____ university course

    _____ college course

    _____ continuing education course

    _____ personal interest

    _____ other (specify)

2. **If you used this text for a program, what was the name of that program?**

3. **Which school do you attend?**

4. **Approximately how much of the book did you use?**

    _____ 1/4 _____ 1/2 _____ 3/4 _____ all

5. **Which chapters or sections were omitted from your course?**

6. **What is the best aspect of this book?**

7. **Is there anything that should be added?**

8. **Please add any comments or suggestions.**

- -
(fold here)

(fold here and tape shut)

Canada Post Corporation / Société canadienne des postes

MAIL ▶ POSTE

Postage paid | Port payé
If mailed in Canada | si posté au Canada
Business Reply | Réponse d'affaires

0116870399   01

01168703991-M8Z4X6-BR01

Heather McWhinney
Editorial Director, College Division
HARCOURT BRACE JOVANOVICH CANADA INC.
55 HORNER AVENUE
TORONTO, ONTARIO
M8Z 9Z9